Charles M. Alexander
II Timothy 2:15.

Clyde R. Ray

380 Ashton Drive

Athens, Georgia 30606

Finished reading this
wonderful Book July 20, 1996
I've never read a sweeter or
more enjoyable book.

Clyde R. Ray

To anyone else who reads this
book: Be sure to study closely
all of the wonderful pictures.

Charles M. Alexander
II Timothy 2:15.

Charles M. Alexander

A ROMANCE OF SONG
AND SOUL-WINNING

BY

HELEN C. ALEXANDER

AND

J. KENNEDY MACLEAN

SWORD of the LORD
PUBLISHERS
P.O. BOX 1099, MURFREESBORO, TN 37133

Printed 1995 by SWORD OF THE LORD PUBLISHERS
Murfreesboro, TN 37133
ISBN: 0–87398–144–8

CHARLES M. ALEXANDER

Approved of God, a workman not ashamed,
The Word of Truth ever by thee proclaimed,
In joyous song, in loving deed and word,
Sharing the joy and presence of thy Lord.

Sower and reaper over all the earth,
How great thy work, how precious is its worth,
How many greet thee on that heavenly strand,
Whom thou didst lead to Jesus by thy hand.

And thou, dear workman, who didst serve so well
Thy Lord and Master, and His love didst tell,
Art still amongst us, though we fail to see
Thy happy face, we still are near to thee.

Bearing to Heaven thy sheaves of golden grain,
From fields of labour, weariness and pain,
At that fair haven and celestial shore,
Thou'rt safely landed to return no more.

Of seed thou sowedst, others are reapers now,
And we must still on earth the good seed sow,
That we may all in Heaven with thee rejoice,
Hearing the " Well done " in our Saviour's voice.

October 13, 1920.   *BARROW CADBURY.*

CONTENTS

LIST OF ILLUSTRATIONS

CHAPTER ONE

His Master Passion

IN the dawn of human history there lived a man of strangely beautiful character. Little is known of the detailed events of his life beyond its remarkable family setting, the fact referred to by Jude in the New Testament that Enoch was a prophet-author, and the astounding fact that he, alone of the race except for the prophet Elijah, escaped the common lot of all—death.

At Enoch's birth, his father, Jared, was a hundred and sixty-two years old, while his great-grandfather's great-grandfather, Adam, head of the family and of the human race, was still in his prime at the age of six hundred and twenty-two. Enoch was the father of Methusaleh, the longest-lived man of whom there is any record, who reached the age of nine hundred and sixty-nine, dying the very year of the Flood, at which time his grandson Noah was six hundred years old.

Enoch himself spent only the comparatively short span of three hundred and sixty-five years upon earth. Mighty achievements in the fields of civilization and of art are recorded of other men of these early ages, but with Enoch the glory of spiritual attainment outshone all else, and alone is mentioned. Of no other, in the sixteen centuries before the Flood, is it recorded as of Enoch, that " he walked with God." " He pleased God," adds the testimony in the portrait-gallery of the Epistle to the Hebrews. He died—he died—he died, runs the biographical record of the ancient days, but of Enoch it is said, " he was not—for God took him," " by faith he was translated, that he should not see death." There is a beautiful old legend of Enoch, which pictures him taking long walks with God. One day, says the legend, they walked so far that they found themselves nearer heaven than earth, and God said to Enoch, " It is too far for you to go back to earth, you may as well come right into heaven now " ; and in the words of Scripture, " Enoch was not found, for God had translated him."

In this twentieth century after Christ, another life has been lent to the world, which shines out amongst his contemporaries with a clear, steady glow like that of Enoch in the early ages. The short span of fifty-three years rounded out its cycle, and while its activities and achievements were manifold, and its influence world-wide, the outstanding glory of it was the deathless beauty of a character aglow with God and the radiance of an overflowing joy. Charles McCallon Alexander was a Southern American and a Presbyterian Christian, but in an unusual way he seemed to belong to all English-speaking peoples and the whole church

of Christ, beyond any distinctions of nationality or of sectarianism. He set the
Christian communities of many lands singing, teaching the joyous duty of praise,
the meekness of trust, and the glory of service ; he brought back the Word of
God as a reliable authority for faith and practice, and as a daily guide and companion, to thousands of his fellow-beings. But the most impressive work of his
life was that of which he was least conscious—the revelation to men of what God
could make of a human life entirely surrendered to Him, and of the way in which
He could use that surrendered life to reach others. Himself set on fire of God,
the burning glow of Charles Alexander's love for God and for man, and of his
quenchless zeal for service, drew men to him ; and in the warmth and light of his
personality their lives kindled also with the Divine fire. In seeking to discover
the source of his attractiveness men found themselves on holy ground, so real
was the sense of his Master's presence. " He walked with God," may be as truly
said of Charles Alexander as of Enoch. Those who lived nearest to him—his
family, his fellow-workers, his servants—knew best how intimate was that daily
fellowship with God, which caused him to grow in the graces of patience and gentleness, of courtesy and of unselfish thought for others, and in a beautiful simplicity
and humility which made him more and more childlike in spirit as the years passed,
and as his fame increased. It was not " salvation by character," but " character
through salvation." And when Charles Alexander was needed by his Master for
work elsewhere, he was so suddenly and unexpectedly called from his busy
service on earth, without a moment's knowledge of departure, that it may also
be said of him as regards the spirit, if not the body, " by faith he was translated
that he should not see death," and " he was not—for God took him."

Charles Alexander's life on earth was full of romance—from his boyhood
amongst the Southern mountains of Tennessee, under conditions not far removed
from pioneer days and affected by the civil war ; surrounded by the negroes,
with their humour and their innate love of rhythmic music ; in touch with the
Red Indians in their wild mountain reservations ; to the days of young manhood,
spent in the great bustling metropolis of commerce on the shores of Lake Michigan,
and the new, raw, growing towns of the Middle-West. Then came the sudden,
mighty expansion of his opportunities, laid immediately at the feet of Christ
and developed beyond all expectation. As the apostle of sunshine and of song,
he travelled through the Antipodes, through India, Ceylon, the British Isles, Canada,
and the length and breadth of his own land, through China, Korea, Japan, and
the islands of the sea. Finding a wife and founding a home in England, he came
to belong to that land almost as much as to the native land he loved with such
loyal pride ; but the ceaseless call of his apostleship would not let him rest in
luxurious ease, but drew him on, with his wife at his side, until he had circled the
earth four times with the message of hope, joy and salvation. He had only just
returned to his English home when the call came so swiftly, telling him that his
work in the body was finished for a while, until at the day of " the first resurrection " it shall be restored to him, rebuilt and newly-dowered with unimaginable
energies and powers, to serve his spirit as a perfect counterpart. With faith-clear
eyes, Charles Alexander looked forward, as Enoch had done from the far-back

beginnings of history, to the glorious new morning when the Sun of Righteousness shall arise, and the prophetic vision shall become a reality : " Behold, the Lord cometh, with ten thousands of his saints." In the meantime, " he, being dead, yet speaketh," and this story of his life shall, with God's blessing, carry forward the messages that fell from his lips and spoke from his life, and stir into activity a bolder witness for Christ amongst those left behind.

From the time of his real surrender to Christ as a youth of twenty-three, Charles Alexander's gifts of personality, of song, and of leadership, were all devoted to one chief aim—the desire to bring other men to *know* the Son of God, to trust Him first for salvation, according to the revelation of Scripture, and then for everything else. His highest ambition was revealed by his life-motto : " Study to show thyself approved unto God, a workman that needeth not to be ashamed, rightly dividing the Word of Truth." With the Word of God as his sword, and a marvellous prayer-life as his constant source of spiritual energy, this knight-errant of the Cross went forth to his service. It was as natural to Charles Alexander to talk to his Heavenly Father as to any human being. Reverently, and yet with the boldness and intimacy of sonship, he consulted the Lord about every detail of his life, and poured out his heart in grateful thanksgiving. The Lord Jesus Christ was more real and dear to him as Saviour, Friend, and Master, than any earthly person. Not having seen Him, he loved Him, and, believing in Him, he rejoiced with joy unspeakable and full of glory. The obligations of such Divine love were the compelling force of Charles Alexander's life. The love of Christ constrained him to become an ambassador through whom God besought men to be reconciled to Himself. " What is the highest test of friendship ? " Alexander would often say, " Surely, *obedience*—the consuming desire to discover and carry out with joy the will of the one whom you love and trust. ' Ye are My friends,' said the Lord Jesus, ' IF ye do whatsoever I command you ' ; ' IF ye love Me, keep My commandments.' " If Charles Alexander laid this test on others, he first placed it most severely upon himself, both in his human relationships and in his personal attitude towards God. Towards his mother, his wife, his family and intimate friends and co-workers, he was as one who served with unstinted devotion and utter selflessness. He sought to please, to help, to relieve and to comfort, and to lift every burden that could be transferred to his own strong shoulders and willing heart. Towards God he lived as one who should not henceforth live unto himself, but unto Him who died for him, and rose again. Among all the commands of Christ, he regarded as most urgent and decisive His words spoken to Peter and Andrew, when He called them from their boats and their nets to be the chosen witnesses of His life, death and resurrection : " Follow Me, and I will make you fishers of men." And they straightway left their nets and followed Him. Many a time, when speaking on the duty of soul-winning, Alexander would say, " You claim that you are following Jesus. Are you fishing for men ? If you are not fishing, you are not following."

Alexander believed in Christ so sincerely that he believed what He said. The law of his life was the parting injunction of the Lord Jesus to His disciples, " If a man love Me, he will keep My words." When Christ spoke of Satan as a personal

Being as real as Himself, and warned of his ability to destroy both body and soul in hell, Alexander neither scoffed, nor minimized the danger, but devoted his life to the saving of his fellow-men by pointing them to the Saviour, and urged every Christian to do the same.   Speaking to a group of men who had taken their stand for Christ in Dundee, Scotland, in 1903, he said, " Be a soul-winner if you are never anything else.   You will find very few who want to shine in winning souls all the time.   You have a chance here to distinguish yourselves."   Another thing he constantly reiterated was, " The last thing the devil will let you do is to win a soul definitely to Christ.   If you don't believe it, try it.   He will let you never miss a prayer-meeting, or a Sunday morning service ; he will even let you get up and lecture on religious subjects, and do all sorts of religious deeds, if you will just stop short at one thing, and that is to get face to face with individuals, to bring them to a decision for Jesus Christ, and get them to confess Him openly before the world.   I used to get up on the platform and lead the singing without doing personal work, but I knew down in the bottom of my heart that I was using my arms too much, and my tongue too little.   Often, when people are ill, it is only the pressure on some nerve which is ruining the whole body.   You cannot be a sane, healthy Christian unless you are trying to win souls.   It is sanity itself. People who go off on a tangent often do so because they shut themselves up in their studies, and forget to go right down by the side of men and win them to God. When I first went to London I called on W. T. Stead, the great interviewer. ' I have always wondered how in the world you interviewed people,' I said to him. ' Start on me, I want to see how you do it.'   Mr. Stead turned round suddenly, and fixing his searching eyes upon me, asked, ' What are you in London for ? ' It made me shake all over, but I have never forgotten it.   What are *you* living for ?   I will tell you what you *ought* to be living for—to win people definitely to Jesus Christ.   Some of you say, ' Well, I try to do it by my life.'   So far as I have seen, the life of most people is largely made up of talking, isn't that right ? I believe that the last thing you are willing to give to God is your tongue.

" Doing personal work makes you live a clean life.   When you begin to talk about Jesus to a friend, perhaps the first thing he will say to you will be, ' Yes, and you lost your temper yesterday ! '   Then you say to yourself, ' I am not fitted for personal work.'   Don't stop doing the work, but give up the thing that hinders it.   One time in Marshalltown, Iowa, there was a girl who saw other people doing personal work, and she wanted to do it.   So she talked to another young lady. Just about the middle of the meetings a play came to town, and the next night they both went to the theatre.   In front of the young lady who was not a Christian sat the girl who had talked to her about accepting Christ.   She leaned over, and touching her on the shoulder, said, ' Oh, you are here, are you ?   What made you come ? '   She replied, ' I thought it was a nice clean play.'   ' Yes,' said the unsaved girl, ' but don't you ever talk to me again about being a Christian. You had better go down to the front in the Gospel tent yourself, with the rest of them.'   Another young lady, who was engaged to be married, was asked by her brother, ' Nellie, is Will a Christian ? '   She replied, ' I don't believe he is.' Her brother said, ' You belong to the Christian Endeavour, and you ought to find out and have a word with him.' 'I am going to the dance to-night,' she said, 'and I will speak to him about it.' During the evening she asked the young man, 'Will, are you a Christian?' He replied, 'Why, no; of course not, are you?' She said, 'Yes, I am.' 'Then what on earth are you doing here?' And he was quite right. You see there are lots of things you may have to quit if you do personal work, and some people don't want to pay the price.

"The only way to learn *how* to do personal work is by doing it, and the place to begin is the first place you find open. Carry your Bible with you always, and use it to show the Way of Life. There is something about the Word of God which convinces men, even though they claim to be infidels. Don't be drawn into an argument, and don't forget what Paul says, 'Love suffereth *long* and is *kind*,' and 'the servant of the Lord must not strive, but be gentle unto all, . . . and patient.'"

In this simple, forceful way, Charles Alexander has frequently addressed a great congregation at the morning service in some formal, conservative church. At the back of his words was the dynamic of the Holy Spirit's touch upon his own life, and many a time before the service closed, hard-headed, unemotional men and women would leave their seats, walk up the aisles, and in a public act of simple surrender, give themselves to Christ for service. This was the direct aim in all of Alexander's public work, whether as singer, or musical director, as editor of hymn-books, or writer of newspaper and magazine articles. In all of the songs, solos and choruses, his purpose was to persuade people to receive Jesus as Saviour, and yield their lives to Him.

Dr. R. A. Torrey has spoken of the way in which Alexander studied other song-leaders and writers, religious and secular. "He improved upon these, until he had set all sorts of people singing the praises of Jesus—peers and paupers, members of Parliament and members of baseball teams, University students and prisoners in the penitentiaries, grey-haired doctors of divinity and golden-haired children, Jews and Gentiles, Protestants and Roman Catholics, Buddhists and Mahommedans." "What feature of the musical side of the revival gives you the keenest delight?" he was once asked. Much as he loved music in itself, and the joy of producing it, his reply was, "I should soon tire of this side of the work if it were not for the soul-saving part of it."

And his public work upon the platform was fruitful, because in private he was always seeking to win individuals to Christ. He never asked others to do what he was not doing himself, and the impression he left, wherever he went, was that of a man so satisfied with Christ that he wanted to introduce to Him every one within reach. Whether as fellow-travellers on steamship or railway-train, as guests in his home, or hosts who entertained him, as fellow-workers or employees, as those with whom he came into business or professional contact—the boy who shined his shoes, the hotel waiter who brought him his meals the barber who shaved him, the cab-driver who took him to his meetings, the doctor or dentist who attended him, the porter who handled his baggage, the policemen on duty, controlling the great throngs during his evangelistic campaigns—all were to him souls in need of Christ. His first interest was to discover whether they had accepted Christ, and if not, to win them first, and then set them to win others.

His earnest zeal in soul-winning was only equalled by the tact and courtesy with which he went about it. His resourcefulness was extraordinary, and he had no set rules of approach beyond those which governed his behaviour as a Christian and a gentleman.

Conversing with a young lady in her beautiful home, he found that she had come under the influence of a theosophist during her college life. Her sweet Christian mother had been praying that she might accept Christ, but Alexander soon saw, what her family already knew, that to win her was no easy task. " I don't want to be preaching at you all the time," he said to her, " but will you do something for me ? If I write out some questions for you to think over quietly, will you write down an honest answer ? " The young lady consented, and he gave her some hard questions, asking her to pray over them.

If you should die to-day, where would you go ? Give me your reason for thinking so.
Do you believe that those who reject Christ will suffer in hell for ever ?
Are you sure you are a saved person ? What verse of Scripture do you base your salvation on ?
Do you love the Lord with all your heart, and with all your soul, and with all your mind ? Do you love your neighbour as yourself ?
Have you ever absolutely surrendered your will to God, and dedicated your life to Him ? If not, will you do it now, unconditionally, and without any reservation ?
How many minutes do you spend each day in secret prayer ?
Do you get everything from God that you pray for ? If not, what is the reason ? God says in His Word, " When you call, I will answer." There must be something wrong with your call or with you. God is always right.
Have you any unforgiveness in your heart against anyone ? If so, will you put it away now ? Are you having the victory over sin in your life ?
Do you love to read the Bible better than anything else, and have you read every verse in it ? Do you study your Bible every day ?
Do you believe in the reliability of every statement made in the Word of God ?
Did you ever lead a soul definitely to accept Christ ?
Is it your custom to speak to some unsaved or saved person each day about Jesus ?
Will you do so from now on ? Have you been baptized with the Holy Spirit ?
Did any one ever say you reminded them of Christ ?

The young lady said she would give these questions careful thought, little realizing how God was going to use them to rouse her soul from the false peace which would have ended in a sleep of death. Some weeks later she definitely accepted Christ as her Saviour, and confessed Him publicly. She immediately sought to win her friends, and ever since her life has been a power for God.

In spite of the marvellous results of his soul-winning efforts which he was permitted to see, Alexander was not always immediately successful, but that did not discourage him. " Some will say," he told an Australian congregation, " that they have tried hard to get souls for Christ, and have no results to show. That's not your business. You do what you can to win them, and leave the rest to God. What does the Bible say God's servants will hear ? ' Well done ! good and *successful* servant ? ' No, not that. It is the *faithful* servant who will get the reward. In America the word one meets with everywhere is " SUCCESS," but " BE FAITHFUL " is the best motto, and that is what God wants. He is looking for reliable men and women that He can depend on."

A letter from Australia, received four months after Alexander had gone Home, brought news of the conversion of a man with whom he had walked the streets of Melbourne for a whole night, seeking to win him for the Lord. After eighteen years, the arrow of conviction, which had never ceased to rankle, was driven home by another, and a soul was won for Christ. Rev. Frederic C. Spurr, who also met Alexander first in Australia, said of him, " He lived but for one thing—to bring men to Jesus Christ. It was his sole passion, and God put His seal upon it. The outstanding memory of Charles Alexander is that of a man who believed with all his soul in the Saviourhood of our Lord Jesus Christ, and who bent every energy to bring his fellows to the feet of Christ." Introducing Alexander to his congregation at Knox Church one Sunday morning in Dunedin, New Zealand, Rev. R. E. Davies said, " Apart from the fact that Mr. Alexander is one of the greatest leaders of sacred song living, he is, I think, one of the greatest personal workers that I have ever met. He possesses the great gift of leading individuals to Christ. I could find it easier to stand here and speak to you as a congregation, than to speak to you individually on the great question of your spiritual welfare. I have a natural diffidence. It is my temperament, and I know it is the same with the majority of you. But we are feeling that we must conquer this diffidence in the interests of the Kingdom of God. If Mr. Alexander can tell us something of this great gift to-day we shall be grateful."

Mr. S. D. Gordon, whose books Alexander did so much to popularize, wrote : " He was always so whole-heartedly keen in winning men to Jesus. All the power of his lovely, winsome personality was thrown unreservedly into the one service he so loved." Men whose special relationship with Alexander was connected with music speak in the same way of him. " The one object of his life appeared to be the winning of others to the service of his Master," wrote Mr. Fleming H. Revell, his intimate friend as well as publisher, " and I never knew any one more uniformly possessed of this master-passion, in private life as well as in public, as Charles M. Alexander." Mr. Geo. C. Stebbins, with whom he came into frequent, affectionate contact said, " The hour of song he conducted daily in the Auditorium at Northfield during the summer conference, was quite the most attractive feature of the day. These services afforded an opportunity for the display of his remarkable resourcefulness, proving impressive and delightful as he only could make them. With God's help, he never lost an opportunity of making an appeal to the unsaved ; and however much people were drawn to him by his attractiveness and his unique and inspiring leadership, they could not fail to see that his master-passion was to win men to his Lord. This was the mainspring of his activities, and gave him a position of pre-eminence as an evangelist of song and a winner of souls." " Charlie was the most indefatigable personal worker I ever knew," wrote Dr. Torrey, when the news of Alexander's sudden Home-call reached him. " I told the men at the noon meeting to-day how I looked out of the window of our hotel in Dublin, when we were waiting dinner for him once, and saw him pleading with the driver of the jaunting-car to accept Christ." Women as well as men were impressed by his intense earnestness in this matter.   Mrs. C. M. Colville, of Cleland, Scotland, wrote, " He was so young and buoyant, and brought such brightness and blessing wherever he went.   Few, if any, ever lived so wonderfully for God's glory and the winning of souls."   A young girl, who had been a guest in Alexander's English home, wrote to his wife, " He did more for me than any one else ever can, because he brought me to know and to love the Lord Jesus.   I pray that I may be able to love and serve the Master as *he* understood service."

Alexander was always insisting that soul-winning was an essential part of *any* service for Christ.   Every one of his special helpers, who was not already a Christian, he led to Christ, and his pianist, soloists, and secretaries were always urged to win souls, as well as to play, sing, and run the typewriter.   Speaking in Cardiff, Wales, to a company of stewards, whom he had invited to tea, he said to them, " Your duty is only partly done when you have shown people to their seats.   Let every man or woman see that you are interested in their salvation. Sometimes it is not necessary to say a word ; a smile or a look may reveal it.   Pick out certain persons and pray for them during the sermon and the singing.   When the time comes for personal work, don't stand still, but *pitch in* !   Every one of you make a dive for some person and make an earnest effort to win him.   If you can't do anything else, tell him you have been praying for him during the service.   If you don't know what scripture passage to use, repeat John vi. 37, ' Him that cometh to Me I will in no wise cast out.'   That verse fits almost every one. After you have got one man, or failed to get him, don't stand still or get discouraged, but *pitch in again* !   Men, go at this work of soul-winning just like you were going to a fire ; for sinners are in danger of eternal destruction, and you may save them." At the end of a service one of these stewards came to him with radiant face, saying he had spoken to not less than twenty people, and had brought six down to the front to accept Christ as their Saviour.

The last ten years of Alexander's life on earth were increasingly devoted to the work of the Pocket Testament League, which has been so largely used to bring about that " Bible Revival " for which he prayed and worked.   His chief delight in this movement was its efficacy in bringing men to Christ and in placing an unfailing practical instrument in the hand of would-be soul-winners.   " For years," he said continually, " I had tried to get people to do personal work, but now I can say, ' *Here is something to do it with !* ' "

Just before leaving New York City for the last time, in August, 1920, Alexander appointed a committee of Christian business men to look after the Pocket Testament League in his absence, little realizing that he would be in heaven within a few short weeks.   One of these men, Mr. Hugh R. Monro, writing on December 19th, 1920, said, " Beyond all else is the abiding impression which so many have spoken of, that of the constant, inveterate, untiring winner of souls. . . . I believe a multitude of us have had our sluggish hearts stirred as we have thought what this passion meant to Charles Alexander, and I trust we may never sink into the same lethargy again."

MARTHA McCALLON IN HER TEENS

JOHN DARIUS ALEXANDER

CHARLES McCALLON ALEXANDER
IN HIS FIRST SUIT

CHARLES M. ALEXANDER'S BIRTHPLACE AT MEADOW, TENNESSEE

THE CHURCH AT CLOYD'S CREEK

WITH HIS
MOTHER AND SISTER

THE ALEXANDER HOMESTEAD AT CLOYD'S CREEK, TENNESSEE

MARYVILLE COLLEGE BRASS BAND, ORGANIZED BY CHARLES M. ALEXANDER

CHAPTER TWO

On a Tennessee Farm

1867 to 1882

IN April, 1865, the terrible Civil War in America came to an end, resulting happily in freedom for the hosts of Southern negroes, and cementing the North and South in a strong political union, to form one of the greatest nations of the earth.

Some twelve months after war had ceased, a happy re-union took place in Cloyd's Creek, a little village of East Tennessee, some miles from the town of Knoxville. Young Lieutenant John Darius Alexander, who had been fighting to uphold the Union, returned to his home village to claim his bride.

The position of the men of Tennessee, especially of East Tennessee, was one of peculiar difficulty when the Civil War broke out. Geographically, and in all other points, save two, they were Southerners, with all the Southern men's pride and belief in the South. But, on the other hand, these people of Scottish race and Covenanting faith were Federalists, and of anti-slavery sympathies almost to a man. So when it came to the test, a large number of East Tennesseans were obliged to declare themselves, not for the North against the South, but against slavery, and against secession from the Union. Their situation was appalling, for they were surrounded by people as passionate and proud as themselves, a people outraged and insulted beyond measure that any of their own kith and kin could take up such an attitude of seeming disloyalty to the South. In the mountains of the South, therefore, the Civil War partook of the fierce and disastrous character of a family feud. The Confederate Government immediately demanded that all men of fighting age should range themselves under the Southern flag to fight the North, and sent companies of soldiers to enlist them. Those who refused were carried off unceremoniously to prison.

This fate befell John D. Alexander, a young descendant of John McKnitt Alexander, one of the famous family of seven brothers who had fled from the North of Ireland to escape religious persecution. Everywhere they carried their staunch Presbyterian faith, providing many a minister to teach the evangelical truth so dear to their fathers. Young John Darius had been educated in a Quaker school at Friendsville, not far from Cloyd's Creek. He had set his heart upon being a minister, but finding the difficulties in his way too great, he had devoted himself to farming. Comfort came to him in his disappointment through the love of the gentle girl who eventually became his wife.

17   B

Martha McCallon came of a Scottish-Irish farming family, and lived with her mother and grandfather, her father having died early. John D. Alexander was at that time a strikingly handsome fellow, "light-complected," in the Southern phrase, with blue-grey eyes and a tall slender figure, six feet high and "straight as a gun-barrel." Martha was small and dainty, with striking black eyes. Her grief may well be imagined when her lover was carried off to prison in Knoxville.

Later on he regained his liberty, and with many of his comrades made his way northwards through numberless adventures, and enlisted in the Northern Army. What joy filled his heart when, after the cessation of the fighting, he was able once more to return to his home at Cloyd's Creek, where Martha had waited for him with all the love and loyalty of her young heart. John was twenty-seven, and his wife a few years younger, when they were married and set up housekeeping in a new log house at Meadow, Tennessee, not far from Cloyd's Creek. They were poor in worldly goods, for East Tennessee was crippled, indeed almost ruined, by the war, to which the young men had given some of their best years. The farms had been deserted, and it was the work of years to re-establish stock and crops upon them. But while John and Martha had few luxuries, they had youth and health and love, and, above all these things, a sincere and living faith in God. Their joy was complete when, about a year after their marriage, on October 24th, 1867, there was given to them a little black-eyed son, whom they named Charles McCallon. Five months later, John D. Alexander was elected Sheriff of the district.

In the South, where the police system is not under the State, but under municipalities or counties, a Sheriff is Chief-of-police to the county. At any time it is a position of honour and responsibility, but in the late 'sixties, on the heels of the Civil War, and in the rough mountain country of East Tennessee, it presented unusual dangers and difficulties. But "John D.," as he was familiarly called by his old comrades, was not only kind and amiable, but possessed great physical strength and self-control, seeming to be without fear of any kind, in the integrity of his clean young manhood. In order to carry out his duties, he moved, with his wife and five-months-old babe, to a white corner house in the town of Maryville. Here little Charles developed, and here his sister, Ida, and brothers, Homer John, and William Leo, were born, at intervals of about two years apart. Charlie grew into a strong, healthy child, with a love of mischief that kept his mother constantly on the *qui vive*. Yet, with all his fun, no one can remember him doing an unkind deed. When old enough, he attended an Academy for small children, taught by a Mrs. Blackburn, and was soon a familiar little figure in the streets of the town.

When Charlie was six years old, the mother and father, with their four little ones, moved into a new home at Cloyd's Creek, and once again took up farming. The new home was a two-storey log house, with wide verandahs like the house at Meadow, and stood on the slope of a hill overlooking the beautiful farm of 640 acres. It soon became a centre of religious influence, and especially of Gospel singing, for not only did John D. Alexander possess a voice of great sweetness, but he was a born leader. He also played the violin, and often the rooms and verandahs of his home would be crowded with neighbours, who came in to enjoy together such old-time melodies as " Come, Thou fount of every blessing," and " There is a fountain filled with blood." In the intervals between the singing, John D. would move about among his guests, chatting with one and another, but chiefly with the young men, and especially with any who might be showing a tendency to break away from the sweet Christian atmosphere of their homes. For he was a man of strong, though quiet influence, and of rare tact, and many faltering feet learned to walk stead-fastly in the way of life everlasting through his gentle ministry.

Speaking in after-years of those happy, care-free days, Charles Alexander said : " One of the earliest memories I have is of singing Gospel hymns, as we sat around the family fireside in our log home amid the hills of Tennessee. My mother sang sweetly, and my father was famous throughout all the region round about as a musical leader. He purchased the first book of modern Gospel songs that came out when Moody and Sankey were doing their great work. Then we kept getting the Gospel hymns as they were published. Almost as soon as I was able to read anything, my father taught me to read music.

" He would take my hand in his, and we never sang a new song together without beating time with the hand. It was thus, as a child, that I learned how to use my hands in leading Gospel singing. I well recall how on Sunday afternoons people would drive from far and near over the hills, and gather on our verandahs, while my father led them for hours in singing sacred songs. Music always thrilled me.

" My father was an elder in the Presbyterian Church, and a leader in good works. My mother was a consecrated woman, full of deep piety, with a strong practical strain. The only papers we took were religious ones, and at night-time we would gather round the fireside, and mother would read aloud. She loved most to read sermons, and Moody's were our favourites. Sometimes when she had read other sermons she would say, ' Well now, children, these are very good, but I'll read you some more of Moody's. He goes right to our hearts, and he bases what he says upon the Word of God.'

" One of the most powerful influences in moulding my life and sweetening it was the long talks with my mother on rainy days. While the rain was beating upon the roof, and the wind was howling in the trees outside, she would tell me the stories of the chief Bible characters, and point out lessons from them. She was full of sympathy for the poor, and was easily touched with the misery of others. She was a clear-headed thinker, original and poetical. The chief books in our home were religious, for my father loved to purchase portions of ministers' libraries.

" In the Cloyd's Creek church to which our family belonged, they had only a small organ, but to my youthful ears its tones sounded wonderful. Never since have I heard a pipe-organ that sounded so fine as that little organ in our church."

" John D." led the singing in the church on Sunday, and would often be at work from early morning to the evening service, when after dark the little church was lighted by candles, carried and held in the hands of the worshippers. Young Charles would stand near the front, his eyes upon his father, watching his movements, deeply interested in the service of song, which was to become his life-work.

Every year, what was known as a " protracted meeting " was held at Cloyd's Creek, during which no effort was spared to bring the young people to decision for God. In the year 1881, when Charlie was thirteen years old, his decision was made.

There came a night when the boy sat through the meeting with a troubled mind. He longed to take his stand for Christ, but hesitated.   Presently the big form of his Uncle William drew near.   " Charlie," he said, gently laying his great hand on the boy's shoulder, " you love the Lord Jesus Christ, don't you ? "   " Yes, uncle," the boy replied.   " Well then, don't you think it is time you made a confession of Him ? "   The boy nodded assent.   He rose and walked timidly to the front at the side of his big uncle, and made his first public confession of Christ.   With tears of joy, his mother came and kissed him.   Old men laid their hands on his head, and with deep emotion commended him to God.   Friends gathered round and prayed that God would bless him and make him a good and useful man, but few can have realized what great things had been done in their midst that night through the decision of one young boy.   The next Sunday he was received into the church by Dr. Bartlett, who, besides being President of Maryville College, was pastor of the church at Cloyd's Creek.   Such was Alexander's love for the little church, that through all the world-wide journeyings of his later years, he loved to keep his name upon its membership roll.   He never forgot the day of decision, and never tired of seeking to win boys and girls for Christ before sin had stained their young lives.   He always treated the voluntary decision of a child as a serious thing, and would often ask for a test in a crowded meeting, as to the age when decision had been made for Christ.   Practically always it would be found that the majority of decisions had been made before the age of twenty, and more often still, under the age of fifteen.

A year later, revival services were held again in Cloyd's Creek church.   Charlie's interest in this protracted meeting was different from that of any other year, for he was overflowing with joy.   One morning it fell to the lot of a good old elder, Mr. Price Chapman, to take the meeting.   It occurred to him that much good might be done if one of the boys should lead them, and after thinking it over he approached young Alexander, who was present.   " Charlie," he said, " I want you to lead the meeting this morning."   The boy stood aghast !   It was impossible. He was only fourteen years old.   He had never done such a thing in his life.   But the old man insisted, and presently came with the Bible, and would have him at least read a few verses.   After much persuasion, and with fear and trembling, the boy read the passage given him.   Mr. Chapman insisted that he lead the meeting. " Everybody must take part," announced the boy, and he went on from one to another in rotation, until he came to his mother.   Mrs. Alexander was of a particularly modest and retiring nature, and had never spoken in public in her life, and she sat with downcast eyes.   " Mother, won't you speak for Jesus ? " the boy asked, gravely and earnestly.   There was no resisting the appeal, and his mother rose to break the silence of a lifetime.   Although he had often led the singing in the Sunday School this was his first attempt at leading a meeting.   It is remarkable in showing the beginnings of that extraordinary gift, with which God endowed him, of bringing others into service, and into an open expression of praise and of witness to Christ, while keeping himself in the background.

Simultaneously with his spiritual development, the boy was growing both mentally and physically.   Soon after the arrival of the Alexander family at Cloyd's Creek, a Mrs. Vance, widow of a Presbyterian minister, opened a school for the children of the district, amongst them, young Charles. The Bible was her textbook, and from the first, her young pupils received the impression, which never left them, that mere intellectual knowledge must always be subordinate to heavenly wisdom, which can come alone from God through His Word.

Miss Caroline Waite, another teacher of his boyhood days, writes thus of him :— " Charles was one of my ' boys,' the tenderest and most chivalrous man I ever knew. Once in his early days an errand brought him to my desk, and I noticed, beyond the fun and sparkle of his face, a shining, uplifted look. ' Boy, what makes your face so bright ? ' The mischief was gone, and the voice dropped as he quoted softly, ' A little talk with Jesus.' "

Life upon the farm was full of romantic incident. In those days, when the railways were few, and means of intercommunication slow and difficult, people were thrown upon their own resources, with the result that their originality had a much better chance of development than under modern conditions of social inter-dependence. Cotton must be picked from the fields, and the wool shorn from the backs of the sheep, and afterwards go through the processes of carding, spinning, weaving, dyeing, and being made up into garments, all under the same roof. Fats too must be carefully preserved, and mixed with lye to make soap, so constantly in use in a cleanly household. Then, in readiness for the long winter evenings, when something more permanent than the blazing light of pine-knots and fir-cones upon the log fire would be needed, the metal moulds with their funny long tubes, must be filled with hot tallow, into which a piece of wick is let down. They must then be set aside to cool, until the candles are ready to slip out and store away.

Charlie loved the cool dimness of the fragrant spring-house, built over the running water in the depths of a leafy hollow ! There, resting on boards above the gurgling stream, were the great crocks filled with milk, and cream, and butter, kept as freshly, even in the hottest summer, as if ice-cooled.

What a delight it was to watch the fields of corn, growing until the great stalks, with their broad green leaves and spikey cobs, waved their tassels far above his head, or to quench his thirst on a great slice of water-melon, with its black seeds and crisp, pink lusciousness. How the squashes and fat pumpkins dotted the fields with gold and orange, in the sun of the Indian summer, giving promise of the spiced " punkin-pie " that would follow the turkey and cranberry sauce on Thanksgiving Day !

As the vegetables and fruits appeared in their season, busy scenes would take place in the big log kitchen, where supplies of every kind were being put up into bottles for the needs of the winter. What quantities of delicious peach and apple butter, what pickles and spiced relishes would waft their odours out on to the big back verandah ! Sometimes young Charlie would be called to help stir a kettle of tempting fragrance, or to rock the baby in his cradle and keep him amused, while the mother's hands were full elsewhere. Soon he learned to take his part in the work outside, for a Southerner has a nice sense of distinction between the work which should be a woman's and that which belongs to a man. By the time he was nine, he had learned to feed the stock, carry water from the spring, milk the cows, and presently to drive a yoke of oxen, and to plough a straight furrow. He spoke as from personal experience when he told the following story :—

"A boy, learning to plough, and finding that his furrows were crooked, appealed to his father for some instruction. ' Well, my son,' said the father, ' I'll tell you how to make a straight furrow. When you start off with the plough, fix your eyes on some object at the other end of the field, look neither to the right nor to the left, but plough straight for it.' This seemed reasonable advice, and the boy did his best to follow it out, but, on looking back over his work, he found his furrows more crooked than before. What was the matter ? The instructions seemed all right, but one important point was lacking. The father had simply directed the boy to fix his eyes on ' some object ' at the end of the field. The boy had done this, but it was an old cow, and she was moving ! Don't follow some man, but fix your eyes on the Rock, Christ Jesus, and you'll plough a straight furrow right into Heaven."

Homer Alexander tells that one moonlight night, when he was about seven, and Charles eleven, he was trying to get a calf into the orchard. " Repeatedly," he says, " it would run by the gate. After many trials I gave up in hot despair, and cursed the calf to the fullest extent of my vocabulary. Soon I saw Charles running across the orchard, and was appalled lest he should tell, but he gave me the kindest little sermon and said, ' God might make you die, Home.' From that day he has always been a kind of father and guide to me. He was full of mischief, but I do not remember to have ever heard him utter an oath in all his life—a very rare thing in the South."

When Charles was thirteen years old, trouble and anxiety fell upon the home. His father, with impulsive generosity, had become surety for a friend. The promissory notes fell due, and just as John D. Alexander was beginning to reap prosperity from his strenuous labours, not only was all his available ready money swept away, but more must be found to meet the debt. Rather than sell his land or disturb the farm in any way, he made arrangements with his right-hand man, Isaac Tuck, to " carry on " in his absence from the farm, and accepted the important position of Postmaster on the Atlanta to Chattanooga railway, which necessitated making his headquarters in Atlanta. The separation that must be faced was a terrible wrench, both to himself and the children he so deeply loved, but most of all to the wife and mother, who could only leave the home at rare intervals, to be with her beloved husband. Upon young Charles there fell thus, in his early days, a heavy responsibility, which he bore with manly courage.

For nine years John D. Alexander served the railway, not living to accomplish his heart's desire of being re-united to his family on the Cloyd's Creek farm, for, as the result of injuries sustained in a railway accident, he died in Atlanta at the age of fifty. A successor to his position, in writing years later to Charles of his father, speaks thus of him, " Your father was a saintly Southern gentleman of the old school, nearly all of whom have passed over to the Great Beyond."

CHAPTER THREE

College Life and a Changed Outlook

1882 to 1891

ONE of the critical periods in the life of every boy and girl, is when the necessity comes to leave home for the first time. Fortunately for young Charles, his first break with the home ties did not take him far away from the sweet influences that had surrounded him through his early years.

Twelve miles from Maryville, on an upland of the Shenandoah Valley, stand the buildings of Maryville College, scattered over a beautiful campus of two hundred and thirty acres, one thousand feet above sea-level. Close by is a peaceful road that was once the great war-trail of the Cherokee Indians, and from the campus there are glorious views, in every direction, of the tumbled ranges of the Smoky Mountains, or of the Alleghenies.

As far back as 1819, Maryville College, then known as the Southern and Western Theological Seminary, had been founded by Isaac Anderson, and had done much to preserve and develop the religious atmosphere brought to the South by Scottish Covenanters, who had settled these regions of East Tennessee in the pioneer days. Maryville Theological Seminary was a strictly Presbyterian institution, and gained such a reputation as a centre of learning, that many men of other denominations entered as students. Repeated revivals throughout the surrounding country fostered its growth, especially as the life was extremely simple and the expenses low. Many preachers of culture went out from it, who were dead in earnest and sure of their message. In 1842, the State conferred upon it a Charter, giving power to confer Degrees, and from that time onwards the institution was known as " Maryville University," its character being changed from that of a theological seminary to a college on general lines of education. From among its graduates, since the change took place, have come many famous doctors, lawyers, statesmen, and ministers. The outbreak of civil war in 1861 brought its days of activity to a sudden close, for Maryville was in the very heart of the war zone. The College campus was used as the camp of Sherman's army. Professors and students scattered to the varying calls of duty, for that part of East Tennessee was bitterly torn asunder in rival sympathies with the North and with the South. Almost immediately, the College closed its doors and ceased to exist. Its funds disappeared, its buildings fell into disrepair and ruin during the four years of devastating war. Through the heroic efforts of Professor Thomas J. Lamar it was opened again in September, 1866, two-and-a-half years after the war had ceased, with thirteen

23

students, whose number, by the end of the year, had increased to forty-seven. It was only by the splendid sacrifices of professors and donors who had its interests at heart, that the College survived and grew through the following years of struggle. Professor Lamar himself took the position of Acting President, until, in March, 1869, through his earnest recommendation, Dr. Peter Mason Bartlett was established as the third President of the College. During the next few years, new college buildings were erected and the campus extended. When Charles reached the age of twelve in his farm home at Cloyd's Creek, there were more than two hundred students at Maryville, and a substantial Endowment Fund had been established.

From the first, John D. Alexander and his wife had cherished a holy ambition that their eldest son might be called to the work of the ministry, and planned for him a college education. Into the Preparatory Department at Maryville, young Charles entered as a student in 1882. It was a wrench for the boy, now almost fifteen years old, to tear himself away from the home he loved so dearly—and in which he had been trying to fill his absent father's place—from his sister and two sturdy young brothers, and especially from the little mother whose tender care had enwrapped him from babyhood. But his parents were insistent. So the day came when old Deacon Hudgins, who had volunteered to take the boy from Cloyd's Creek into Maryville, drove up to the Alexander homestead with his team and wagon. The good-byes over, and the little trunk lifted in, Charlie climbed up into his seat beside the old Deacon. So long as they were in sight, his mother stood waving farewell, and the boy, through a mist of tears, waved in return. Then they cleared the hill-crest, and for a while drove on in silence. Charles Alexander often told of that experience: " I well remember the day when, as a youth, I started out from my country home for the University. Good old Deacon Hudgins said, ' Charlie, you are going to a good college, but you will not be free from temptation there, and it will be easy for you to find bad companions. You will not have the influence of your good home, and your father and mother, to keep you straight. Just you remember you belong to God, and to our little Church in Cloyd's Creek. We believe in you, and we'll be watching to see how you turn out. Don't do anything to disgrace God, or our Church, or your friends.' I have never forgotten those words. In my most mischievous hours, I always remembered that the people at the little Church would be thinking of the disgrace I should bring them if I went wrong. It was a great factor in keeping me true and pure."

For the next seven years, Maryville was the scene of young Alexander's activities, and of his intellectual growth and development. For a while it was not easy for the boy, fresh from his life on the farm, and with the love of " all out-doors " filling his soul, to fall into settled habits of study.

The originality which marked him out from other men made it impossible to force his irrepressible nature into any common mould, but from the first he won the affections of all about him, and when he passed from the Preparatory to the College Department, he had become so popular with both Faculty and students, that he was an acknowledged leader in all that went on.

Maryville, like other colleges, had its athletic side, and Charlie Alexander was always to the fore on the base-ball field, and in boxing and wrestling, in both of which he excelled. On the edge of the College campus were a number of cabins inhabited by negroes, amongst whom Alexander was well known, and with whom he was as friendly as with his white college companions. The negroes were often a source of fun to the college boys. Old Zeb Lane, who lived with his ample wife and numerous children in one of the neighbouring cabins, had a great many pigs, which, to the annoyance of the students, constantly strayed over the College campus, rooting up the lawns. One morning, when most of the class-rooms were thronged, a hog of unusual size and strength was seen by a few of the boys who were not in class. Producing several lengths of rope, they quickly made a kind of harness, with long trails of tin cans attached, and in a few minutes a terrible din broke forth, as the pig, thus decorated, and uttering blood-curdling squeals, rushed past the class-room windows. Students and teachers saw a funny comedy. Thinking to free her favourite, fat old Mammy Lane sprang on to the trailing rope, turned a somersault, and found herself sitting on the road, face to face with the astonished young minister who happened to be passing at the time !

Another incident that Charles Alexander often told was of a young coloured man named Sam Lee, who was occasionally employed on the college grounds. Towards the end of term, Sam was often on hand, and bowing with a sweep of his ragged old hat, would offer, in the most ingratiating and obliging tones, to give his help. One day, as he was assisting young Alexander to pack, Sam said, in the most pathetic of voices, " I s'pose, Mistah Cha'lie, you ain't got no clo'es you ain't a-gwine to wear no mo' ? Ef you should be th'owin' anything like that away, I sho' could make good use of it." " Well, Sam," said Alexander, " how about shoes ? What size do you wear ? " " Well, Mistah Cha'lie, that mos'ly 'pen's on circumstances. Sometimes I wear sixes, an' sometimes I wear 'levens ! "

Even then, Alexander was more interested in the study of human nature than in the routine work of the class-room. As he said one day, years later, on one of his visits to Glasgow :—" A little ragged boy, selling papers on the street, is always more interesting to me than the finest picture of a boy that was ever painted."

When Charles had been at the college for a couple of years, Professor Samuel Tyndale Wilson, who became its fifth President seventeen years later, joined the Faculty of Maryville University. He was at once attracted by this boy, so full of mischief and exuberant life, yet whose nature seemed overflowing with generous, kindly thought for others. From that time onwards, Dr. Wilson watched his development with keen interest, and a life-long friendship sprang up between them. In 1920, Dr. Wilson wrote from Maryville : " The memories of Charles M. Alexander will linger around this College Hill as long as time shall last."

In 1884, when young Alexander was sixteen years old, the whole of East Tennessee was stirred by a visit of Moody and Sankey to Knoxville, where they held a series of meetings in Staub's Opera House. Although sixteen miles away from Maryville, the interest was so intense that the college authorities arranged for the students to attend some of the meetings. Seated high up with his friends in the gallery of the Opera House, Charlie watched eagerly for the first appearance of the men of whom he had heard so much. When Sankey seated himself at the little organ, and lifted his voice in his favourite hymn, " The Ninety and Nine," the boy's heart beat fast with emotion.   The faces crowding the Opera House faded from his sight, and all that he saw, almost as in reality, was the Good Shepherd searching the bleak mountain-side for the poor lost sheep, finding it at last, and bearing it back in triumph to the safety of the fold.

On that night, the boy's mind received the indelible impression, that in singing Gospel hymns, the accompaniment, while as beautiful as can be obtained, must always be subordinate to the singing.   The singer, too, must keep himself in the background, so that the message of the song might present its appeal unhindered to the minds of the hearers.   This is, of course, an entirely different purpose and ideal from that of the ordinary concert platform, where the main object is the exhibition of the beauty of vocal tone, and the flexibility of the voice as an instrument, and in which the words are chiefly useful as a medium for this purpose, rather than because of the message they contain.

Mr. Moody preached that night on Abraham.   In his final appeal, those willing to accept Christ were invited to rise to their feet.   There was a general movement.   Men and women rose here and there throughout the building.   A dim yearning awoke in the boy's soul, that he, too, might be thus used of God to bring people to decision for Him.

About this time, in the library of the University, Charles came across a book called *The Autobiography of Charles G. Finney*.   He took it out and read it, and it opened a new world to him.   So strongly did it grip him, that he read it through a second time, and then a third.   Determined to know more of this wonderful man, he bought his other books, as far as he could find them, and carefully read and studied them.   About the same time, he read Major Whittle's memoir of P. P. Bliss, one of the sweetest writers of American sacred song, the author of " I am so glad that our Father in Heaven," and other well-known hymns.   This book showed him that the aim of a Gospel singer should be, from first to last, the winning of souls ; and in training other singers, he constantly induced them to read it.

Another book that influenced him greatly was the *Life of James Gilmore*, and an ambition to become the greatest musical conductor in the world gradually took possession of him.   He began to study music seriously, theory and harmony, and learned to play one brass instrument after another.   But he was busy with his books as well, and by the time he was seventeen, had earned a First Grade Teacher's Certificate, authorizing him to teach nine subjects in any of the public schools in the local counties of his native State.   In 1885, he was appointed teacher, for the summer months, of the school which the State had opened at Cloyd's Creek.   This school he continued to direct in the two following summers. Having a free hand, he ran it upon original lines.   Music and singing soon occupied chief place.   Adult singing classes were formed, and public speaking had a prominent position, giving a constant outlet for the natural eloquence of the Southerner.

There was no limit to young Alexander's schemes for waking up the community, and when, at the close of his third summer, he arranged an exhibition of his school's accomplishments, the whole countryside took half-a-day off.

The boys and girls of the school frankly adored him, and his discipline seemed to be perfect. At the end of his last term, the County Superintendent reported: " Of all the schools visited, I have never seen one under such control."

In the autumn of 1887, Alexander went to Washington College for a year, as this college made a specialty of the study of music. The next summer he set out with two musical companions across the mountains towards North Carolina. At the end of the first day's tramp, they were welcomed with that simple hospitality for which the Southern mountaineers are famous, and the music that rang beneath the rafters was enjoyed by others brought in from some of the surrounding farms. At last they reached the village of Marshall, North Carolina, where a singing school was arranged for several weeks, which lengthened out into three months.

From Marshall, Alexander returned to Maryville University, no longer as a student, but as the first Professor of the Faculty of Music, which the authorities had just established there. Immediately he set to work to organize a brass band in the college, undertaking to raise the whole of the money needed for purchasing the instruments, and for other expenses. For this purpose he arranged a series of concerts, and soon sufficient money was raised. The band speedily became famous in all the district round, and was in constant demand. At this time Alexander had just reached his majority, and was proud and happy over the success that had come to him. His sister and two brothers were now students in the college, and were as proud of Charles as were his parents.

Alexander's love of teaching, and of the glory of his native mountains, led him back across the ranges to North Carolina when the summer came round again. This time he was at Bryson City for a while, and then was called to a piece of work that, in all his varied life, was, in some ways, the most unique. High up in the North Carolina mountains, upon a large State Reservation, was a tribe of Cherokee Indians. Charles Alexander, who was known to Mr. Spray, the District Superintendent, was invited to form a brass band among the young Indians, and for a while lived among surroundings which, save for the lack of danger, were those which had greeted the coming of the earliest pioneers of western civilization. The Indian boys who were to form the band were freely decorated with feathers, and bore weird names, such as " Mark Wolf," " Josiah Baredevil," " Isaiah Bigmeat," and so on, indicating both their natural origin, and the new Christian influences which were changing their lives. The bandstand was built in the branches of a large oak-tree by the river side, and Alexander and his extraordinary pupils were often surrounded by a curious crowd of Indian men, women and children. By his patience, good humour, and the strange power of his loving influence, Alexander soon succeeded in teaching these youths, who were quick to respond, so that in a marvellously short time they were able to play together as a band. From this experience he gained a new knowledge of how to adapt himself to unaccustomed surroundings and people, and to enter into their lives and interests.

The lure and fascination of the mountains of Tennessee and North Carolina still continued to draw the feet of young Alexander through his summer vacations, even after he had become fully established as Professor of Music in his home University at Maryville. His heart went out to the lonely yet proud-spirited mountaineers, living amid the solitary splendours of Nature in their scattered log-cabins, or gathered in small, rugged communities almost entirely cut off from touch with the rest of the world.   He knew that, in spite of their serious natures, they loved to sing, and that in the right kind of music could be found the most direct and re- lieving outlet for their pent-up emotions.   Mere music might become an in- sidious danger to these very natures, opening the floodgates of the soul to an emotionalism which might sweep away the solid foundations of character, but music dedicated to the service of Christ could only soften the heart and lift the soul.

The summer of 1890 found Alexander back again among the Cherokee Indians on their valley Reservation high up on the Smoky Mountains.   His fame as a leader had spread to many of the mountain communities, and in the following autumn he responded to an urgent invitation from a little North Carolina town named Waynesville.   He established his singing school there with about one hun- dred students, and the session was in full swing, when, late one Saturday after- noon, a telegram was handed to him.   It was from his mother in Atlanta, and brought the sorrowful news that his father was dying, and if he wished to see him alive once more, he must come at once.   For a while the young man was over- whelmed with grief by the sudden shock, for the father, whom he was losing, was not only the strong man upon whom they had all leaned, but a loving parent whose friendship was their life, and to whom they were devoted with all the ardour of their warm, Southern hearts.   To his sorrow was added an embarrassment, for he could not pay for the return journey across the mountains, until the money that would be his at the close of his Waynesville work had been received.   He went at once to call upon a Bank president in the town, whom he knew, telling him of his difficulty.   " I have no security, Mr. Howell," he said, " but if you will advance the money I need, to get home, I will pay you back without fail."   " Certainly I will," said his friend at once.   " How much do you want ? "

Even now the difficulties were not solved : the last passenger train by which he could make connexions to Atlanta had already gone ;   there was no other till Monday, and he failed in his effort to persuade the conductor of a freight train, which was about to start, to allow him to travel upon it.   Thirty-five miles over the mountains at Asheville, a train left for Atlanta early on Sunday morning, but how could he get there in time ?   At last, he managed to hire a horse and buggy with a negro driver, and as the evening shadows were stealing through the valleys they set out on their long, lonely drive.   The road was only a rough mountain track, and the night was dark, and as they pushed on through the over-arching trees they lost all sense of direction.   Sometimes a mountain torrent thundered beside them. Again, the horse's hoofs, without warning, would ring with hollow sound on a wooden bridge.   They knew there were no hand-rails, and caught their breath until they were safely across the ravine that yawned below them.   All through the night they plodded on, until at last the crimson streaks of dawn began to glow behind the mountains.   At five o'clock they drove safely into Asheville.   The train was caught, and to his unspeakable relief Alexander reached Atlanta in time.

All through the hours of that anxious night, great emotions had swept the young man's soul.   Though he had truly given his heart to God years before, the last few years of growth in knowledge, of increasing popularity, and of success in his musical work, had led him into a worldly ambition for a brilliant musical career, which had dimmed his vision of spiritual things, and had tended to cool the ardour of a desire to live for others, and not for himself. The sudden shock, however, of an impending loss that he had never anticipated, for his father was but fifty years old, brought him face to face with the realities of life and death, of heaven and hell. He knew his father's fervent, steadfast faith in Christ, and longed intensely to hear some expression of it once again from his dying lips.

His sister, Ida, and two brothers, Homer and Leo, were all at Maryville College, and in telegraphing them of his arrival in Atlanta, he also sent a message over the wires to Dr. Samuel W. Boardman, President of the College, earnestly asking that prayers might be offered on his father's behalf. On November 21st, 1890, Dr. Boardman wrote the following letter to the three who were under his care: " I was deeply moved at the reception of the telegram from your brother Charles this morning, and was not willing to lose a moment in securing those prayers of all the members of the senior class which I knew would be immediately and most earnestly offered for your father's recovery. Please let me know daily of the intelligence you receive. Whether we live or die we are the Lord's. Jesus will never leave us comfortless. With tenderest sympathy, your friend, Samuel Boardman." The prayers that went up from Maryville did not fail to reach the Father's ear. In His wisdom, He said " No " to the request for recovery. But the prayer was not unheeded, for God used the sorrow He saw fit to send, as an instrument which resulted ultimately in the bringing of thousands of souls, the world over, from sin to Himself.

The few days spent together on the threshold of eternity wrought a revolution in Alexander's life. " Father, are you trusting in Jesus ? " he asked, on the evening that proved to be the last. The answer came with a smile, and at midnight of November 23rd, 1890, the faithful servant passed into his Master's presence. Years later, in telling of this experience, Alexander said : " While I was teaching in North Carolina, I had a telegram from my mother, saying my father was not expected to live ; and I hurried to Atlanta, Georgia. On my journey I had time to think, and the world changed in a very few hours. Father lived for a week, and during that time my outlook upon the world was changing all the time. I was looking at things in the light of eternity. The night my father died there came to me, as never before, the worth of a human soul. He could not take any of us with him ; he must go alone. And I saw how the thing that mattered, more than everything else, was to be sure that the soul was safe in God's keeping.

" I did not even feel certain about my own conversion. When, following my father's death, I had to go across the city for an undertaker, late at night, it seemed to me as if my heart would break. I was not absolutely sure whether my father was in heaven, for I had not studied the Bible closely enough to know. I knew he was an elder in a church, and all that ; but as I went along the street I cried to God : ' If there is any way that Thou revealest Thyself to people, whether by vision or voice or impression, give me the certainty that my father is with Thee, and safe ' ; and I promised Him that I would serve Him all my life if He would give me the assurance. As clearly as anything I ever experienced, the impression came to me, ' Your father is up here safe with Me.' There and then I promised to serve Him all my life, looking up at the stars, and the load lifted right off me.

" Filled as I was with thoughts of eternity, the buildings on each side of me looked like mere rubbish, though I remember that before, when I went down those streets, I used often to say, ' I should like to own one of those splendid blocks.' But now, every time I saw a man coming out of a saloon, I wanted to go up to him and throw my arms about him and tell him : ' You are going to hell, man. Why don't you accept Jesus Christ ? ' A great longing to save souls came to me that night, and has been with me ever since."

Charles and his mother took the precious form of John D. Alexander to his old home at Cloyd's Creek, and on that journey, so full of sorrow, they were drawn together in a love that was more than the ordinary love between mother and son, as the sense of matured and protecting friendship grew in the young man's soul.

There was widespread grief throughout the whole country-side when John D. Alexander died. Maryville College, though twelve miles away from the Alexander homestead, was closed on the day of his funeral, as a mark of respect, and hundreds of the students drove over the hills to Cloyd's Creek—for no railway connected the two in those days.

The funeral service was conducted by Professor Samuel T. Wilson. Led by the students, the crowd surrounding the grave sang two of the hymns in which John D. Alexander had often led them : " We shall sleep, but not for ever," and " Beyond the smiling and the weeping."

Immediately afterwards, young Alexander, now the head of the little family, set to work to organize things upon the farm in the best way possible. Land there was in plenty, and beauty without stint, but the ground was poor, and there was no money for artificial enrichment of it. Nor could enough labour be obtained. It was a constant struggle to keep sufficient crops to maintain the stock. Ike Tuck, sturdy and faithful, was Charles' right hand on the farm, assisted by several negroes whose cabins lay on its outskirts. Within doors, the mother toiled incessantly, bearing her loneliness with a brave heart. In spite of the loss of the beloved father, and of the constant struggle to keep things going, the home was full of heaven's sunshine, and when the three from Maryville College returned for the Christmas vacation, songs of praise often rose to the heavenly courts.

Charles made no secret of the fact that his ambitions had changed. His mind was firmly settled upon Gospel work, and not long after his father's death an opportunity came to join forces with Mr. John Kittrell, a Quaker evangelist.

A letter from Homer Alexander, written when the tidings of his brother's death reached him in 1920, says : " When father died in Atlanta, Charles conse-crated his life, body and soul, to God. If ever a man let his light shine, he did for these thirty years. Is it not wonderful how he testified, in hotels, in homes, everywhere, his light always shining ? How many years he crowded into those thirty ! burnt out, as has been said, for God ! When they brought father home, it was that precious boy who kept a brave heart and smiling face. Immediately almost, he hunted up Kittrell and began to work for God.   Everybody knew where he stood."

John Kittrell was a remarkable character.   In his earlier days he had been a drunkard and a notable fighter, refusing to have anything to do with religion, but a serious illness brought him face to face with death, and in his distress he called upon God.   A sudden change took place.   He began to love the Bible, and, as his strength slowly returned, he would carry it out under the shade of a tree and read it hour after hour.   One day he astonished his friends by announcing that he was going to preach.   A marvellous change had taken place in his character : he had been noted for his implacable hatred and ungovernable ferocity.   Now he was remarked everywhere for his gentleness and love.   A small, spare, angular man, with steady brown eyes and a soft musical voice, he would talk to his audiences in the tender tone of a father advising his children.   But his eyes could still blaze, and his voice rise in denunciation of sin, when he came face to face with the fierce feuds and the lawlessness that still existed in many of the mountain villages of Kentucky and Tennessee.   There was a great contrast between him and the slender, cultured, college youth, who became his partner for six months in evangelistic work, and who enthusiastically admired the older man's utter fearlessness and consistent piety.   Together they visited a number of towns in Tennessee, North Carolina, and Alabama, and many a time in after-life Charles Alexander spoke of what he had learned from the zeal and rugged earnestness of John Kittrell.   Until the end of Alexander's life a tender friendship existed between the two.

This first test of evangelistic work made it clear to the young singer that it was the calling of God for him.   But he felt the need of deeper training, especially along the lines of Bible study, and of Gospel singing and conducting.   Making inquiries, he learned that the very course he was seeking was to be found in the curriculum of the great Bible Institute founded by D. L. Moody at Chicago.   Forthwith he set to work to get everything on the farm into running order, so that it would be possible for him to leave for a few months, as he expected, for the northern State of Illinois, which seemed so far away to them all.

Dr. Samuel T. Wilson, of Maryville University, writing twenty-eight years later, said : " I remember the Faculty meeting in which we agreed to suggest to him that he give his life to Gospel song.   I myself wrote him a letter of introduction and recommendation to present at the Moody School."   Alexander's application to be admitted to the Institute as a student was accepted, and early in 1892 all was ready for him to bid farewell for the first time to his beloved South.

CHAPTER FOUR

Student Days in Chicago

1892 to 1894

IT was characteristic of Charles M. Alexander, and prophetic of his future influence with men, that when he left home for the Moody Bible Institute in Chicago he did not go alone. That missionary zeal, which in later years was to burn with such intensity, had already begun to glow. Almost as soon as he resolved to go into training for Christian service, he induced eight of his friends in the University of Maryville to go with him. Many a time, in after-years, did he persuade young men and women to enter his beloved Moody Institute, often cheerfully helping them with the expenses of their training.

One of these, an English girl, wrote from California after his Home-call :— "I praise God for what your dear husband meant to me, and for his generosity in making it possible for me to take the Bible Course at the Moody Institute in Chicago nearly twenty years ago. God will remember his part in whatever He has been able to accomplish through me."

After a night and a day in the train, the nine young fellows from Tennessee reached Chicago in the evening. The great city, full of noise and clatter and confusion, on the edge of the vast expanse of Lake Michigan, was as great a contrast as could be from the quiet Southern town and glorious mountains from which they had come. Glad they were, indeed, to escape from the busy streets, and pass through the doors of the Institute, where they were warmly greeted, and made to feel at home immediately. One of the students came forward, smiling his welcome, and grasped the hands of the strangers. "I see that you are new students," he said, "I hope you will have a good time." Others came and helped them to carry their baggage up to their rooms. "You are on the shady side of the building," said one, "so you will have to make up by having sunshine in your soul."

The Dean of the Moody Bible Institute, at that time, was the Rev. Reuben Archer Torrey, who was also pastor of the adjoining Chicago Avenue Church, the work of which provided a splendid outlet for the activities of the students.

Little did the eager-hearted lad from the South realize the close and intimate association that lay before them when he looked into the strong, masterful face and keen, grey eyes of the head of the Institute. From Dr. Torrey's clear and definite teaching he began from the first to gain a deeper and more intelligent knowledge of the great Book which he had learned to love at his mother's knee.

WITH HIS "SUNBEAM" CHOIR IN CHICAGO DURING STUDENT DAYS AT THE MOODY BIBLE INSTITUTE

JOHN KITTRELL,
THE QUAKER EVANGELIST

CHARLES M. ALEXANDER IN HIS MARYVILLE COLLEGE DAYS

THE WILLIAMS-ALEXANDER TENT AT FORT DODGE, IOWA, AUGUST, 1895

THE WILLIAMS-ALEXANDER TABERNACLE AT SANDWICH,
ILLINOIS, NOVEMBER, 1897

M. B. WILLIAMS
WITH HIS DAUGHTER, CAROLYN

MILAN B. WILLIAMS AND
CHARLES M. ALEXANDER

CHARLES M. ALEXANDER IN 1897

All through his days at the Institute, young Alexander was also in more or less close touch with its great founder, Dwight L. Moody. From the early days of his boyhood, Moody had been one of his heroes, and through life he regarded Moody and Abraham Lincoln as two of the strongest forces for righteousness in the history of the modern world. From Moody, more than from any other man, he learned the power and far-reaching influence of simplicity, both of speech and of life. From him also he learned how to use the melting, welding power of united song in breaking down the barrier of reserve that often separates speaker and audience, and in bringing a crowd into a receptive mood.

While entering with all the enthusiasm of his Southern nature into the new work and opportunities opening before him, the many miles that lay between him and his Tennessee home did not make Charles forget those he loved so well. Indeed, for all his four-and-twenty years, he was as home-sick as a schoolboy. He tells of the comfort brought by the message of a choir of little girls, whose adored leader he afterwards became. " When I left my home in Tennessee and went to Chicago, I thought the people were very cold. I was home-sick, away from family and friends. On my first Sunday in the city I stepped into Moody's church. I had heard so much about the work there, and I wondered if I would get anything out of the singing that would satisfy the cravings of a home-sick heart. I was surrounded by hundreds of strange people. The great choir behind the pastor sang several hymns. They did it well, but when they had finished my heart was untouched. The pastor rose and looked at the gallery in the back of the church and said, ' The girls' choir will now sing.' I heard a little harmonium start up a simple melody, and a choir that I had not noticed, composed of little girls from the very poor class, rose, and these words floated down from their sweet little voices : ' God will take care of you.' The message dropped into my heart like honey, as I thought, ' Of course He will,' and I handed my home-sickness over to Him."

During the first months at the school, he began to find that the double strain of his new work, and the effort of continuing to lift the home burdens, was telling upon him, and, fearing a serious breakdown, he consulted a doctor. After a thorough examination he was told to return next day. Depressed by the doctor's gravity and hesitance, he dreaded lest he should be given his death-sentence. Heavy-hearted, he presented himself on the following day. " When did you last laugh ? " asked the doctor. Young Alexander had to confess that for fully a month he had not felt light-hearted enough to laugh. A few straight questions brought out the story of his anxieties, added to by overwork undertaken to help his fellow-students from Tennessee with their finances, and he was solemnly warned by the doctor of the injury he was doing both to himself and others, by incurring liabilities beyond the power of any man to carry. The doctor's advice bore fruit, and it is certain that never again did a month pass by without his indulging in that infectious laughter which all who knew him so loved to hear. Indeed, there came a time, later on, when he thought he was laughing too much, and wondered whether it was right for an earnest Christian to be so gay. He tells of the way in which Moody would gather the students round him for a confidential talk. " He once noticed that many of us were wearing long faces. I am quite sure I was one of

C

them, for I had been studying that sentence in the New Testament where it says that every idle word shall be accounted for.   I had usually been of a lively disposition, trying to cheer the fellow who was downhearted, but when I began to study that verse I thought I was wrong.   I had been trying to get my face so that no smile would ever come upon it.   In one of his sane morning talks, Mr. Moody spoke about that verse.   Looking up with such a bright, happy look, he said, ' Young men, do not think that the teaching of this verse means that you shall go round with a long face, and never have a happy word for anyone.   A cheerful word is not an idle one.' "   From that time onwards, Alexander enjoyed the perfect freedom which makes an unrestrained delight of service.

The Moody Institute is a beehive of activity, and every one who enters it must study and work with a will.   The Bible is the principal textbook, and the study of it is conducted on a thorough basis, so that in addition to any other knowledge gained in the school, the students are all intimate with the Word of God, and know where to turn in it for the messages needed by hungry souls.   In addition to their studies, the students have specific duties assigned to them, and do practical work from the start.   Theory and practice thus go hand in hand.

Alexander had not been long in the Institute before he was appointed to lead the singing in a big tent pitched in one of the very worst districts of Chicago, known as " Little Hell."   He and his fellow-worker were patronized from the beginning by a gang of young " toughs," thirty-nine in number, and known as the " Huron Street Gang," led by a notorious outlaw called " Louis the Iceman." Evening after evening the gang would file in and fill a line of seats near the front. The two youthful evangelists feared the worst, but to their surprise the gang sat for the most part quiet and attentive.   Alexander determined to learn the reason of their unusual conduct.   To his relief and amusement, he learned from Louis that the leader of another gang, Ferd Schiverea, had, by a freak of fancy, decided to patronize and protect a tent mission in a near-by district.   "And we're goin' to stick to you and this tent, and beat Ferd Schiverea's to a frazzle," said Louis. He was true to his promise, and all through the season Alexander's tent enjoyed the powerful protection of " Louis the Iceman " and the Huron Street Gang.

These experiences in the Chicago slums taught Alexander many a valuable lesson.   He learned not to mind interruptions, and even to take advantage of them.   He came to understand the poor and wretched of the great cities, and to have a sympathy for them which never left him.

In addition to intensive textual Bible study, an outstanding feature of the Moody Bible Institute has always been its Chair of Music.   In this department, students were enabled to study Gospel music and singing in all its branches, with a view to becoming singing evangelists and choir-leaders.   Through this side of the work, Alexander became intimately acquainted with H. H. McGranahan, at that time head of the Musical Section ; also with Daniel B. Towner, George C. Stebbins, J. H. Burke, and other famous composers.   Amongst those who profoundly influenced him in this formative period were Major D. W. Whittle and Major Cole ; also Harry Munroe, the leader of the famous Pacific Garden Mission.

At first, Alexander, already an experienced conductor of bands and of singing in his Southern University and the surrounding district, was given unimportant assignments. His ability was soon recognized, however, and he was appointed choir-master in the large Sunday school connected with the Moody Church. It was no light undertaking, for the school numbered eighteen hundred children, drawn chiefly from the slums, and full of life and mischief. Some of the boys tried to upset their new leader with varied interruptions, and Alexander saw that he must get the mastery. One day, after a hymn had been announced, a boy shouted something funny, and the whole school burst out laughing. Waiting until quiet had been restored, the conductor said sympathetically, "Don't laugh at that poor little boy, he may be just from the country, and doesn't know any better. You shouldn't laugh at him." That put an end to interruptions, and in a little while he had won the hearts, as well as the respect, of his youthful congregation.

One of the deep things that Alexander put to the test of experience in those Institute days was the reality of prayer. "The beauty of the Institute," he once said to a friend, "is its atmosphere. The teaching you receive touches every point of your life. I remember the first time I learned definitely that the Lord hears and answers prayer. I had come up from my Southern home, expecting only to stay for a few months, and my clothes began to get rather worn.

"I had long questioned the students, when they would speak about having prayers answered for temporal things, wondering whether the seeming answers to prayer wouldn't have happened anyway. Now *I* had come to the place where I must have help. I had no money, and no means of getting any at the time, to spend on clothes. Dr. Torrey had told me that if I would like to stay, he could arrange my work so that I could pay for my room and board. I went into my room and opened my Bible at Philippians iv. 19: ' But my God shall supply all your need according to His riches in glory by Christ Jesus.' And I looked up to my Father in Heaven and spoke just as I would to my earthly father, asking Him for a suit of clothes, and telling Him that I needed it in order to do my work in His service. I said that I was giving my life to His work, and that I would trust Him to send me a new suit of clothes, and promised Him that when it came I would never be ashamed to tell where it had come from. I rose from my knees as confident that I would get a suit of clothes as that I was in that room.

" The next day I was sitting in my room, with the door open, when a friend of mine, who was passing, came in and said, ' Alec, wouldn't you like to have a suit of clothes ? ' I said, ' I certainly would.' ' Well,' he said, ' I have received a cheque for forty dollars from a wealthy friend of mine. I don't need all the money, and if you will accept a suit of clothes from me, I will take you down to my tailor.'

"I immediately thanked God for the answer to my prayer. The next day, on my way down to the tailor's shop, there was a joy in my heart, not so much because I was going to get a suit of clothes, as because of the certainty that I was in communion with God, and had learned to trust Him fully. My friend was going to spend half his cheque on me, but as you know, even in those days, twenty dollars wouldn't buy much of a tailor-made suit in America.

" I asked God before I went out to help me select the very suit of clothes I should have, one that would wear well. Looking over the cloth in the shop, I was naturally shown the best piece, and asked its price.   The tailor said it would cost forty dollars.   I said, ' There is no use looking at that.'   We passed on to other cloths, but nothing seemed suitable.   At last the tailor said, ' You liked the first piece best, didn't you ? '   I said I did.   ' Well,' said the tailor, ' a man came in the other day and had a suit made from that piece of cloth.   It didn't fit him, and he wouldn't have it.   The suit has never been worn.   If you want it, and it will fit you, you may have it for eighteen dollars.'   I tried it on, and it fitted me exactly, except the trousers, which had to be shortened a little at the bottom.   It was a fine suit, and it did me good service.   I had not only a good suit of clothes, but two dollars left over for collars and ties ! ''

Years later, when Alexander had become world-famous, he told, in a great gathering, of this answer to prayer.   Some friends of his in Iowa read the story.   The husband turned to his godly little wife, saying, " I should think Alexander would be ashamed to tell that story nowadays.   Besides, don't you know that if the Lord had really given him that suit of clothes, He would have seen to it that it fitted him exactly ? ''   " Well, anyway," said his wife, " the Lord saw to it that the trousers were not too short ! ''

While eagerly enjoying his studies, and the opportunities for practical Gospel work in Chicago, the urge upon his soul to carry the news of salvation to any place from which a call of hungry hearts might come, led him, with Dr. Torrey's consent, to accept the invitation of Dr. Francis E. Smiley, who thus describes their first meeting : " During the summer of 1892, I first met Charlie Alexander, a tall, thin, pale, black-eyed youth from the sunny South.   I needed a musical director for my evangelistic campaign beginning in the Fall.   His personality attracted me, and Professor Towner suggested that I come into the class and hear some of the students.   He arranged that Alexander should sing a solo, and we soon settled our business arrangements.

'' Our first meetings were at East Liverpool, Ohio.   Arriving early, he had time to size up the town and learn something about the revival meeting.   It was a united effort of all the churches.   The committee had secured the Skating Rink, comfortably heated it and seated it, so that, with the galleries, it accommodated about three thousand people.   Mr. Alexander met me upon the arrival of my train. He had scarcely greeted me before he began his protest : ' Say, doctor, I can't lead this singing.   Why, they have three thousand chairs in that big building ! ' ' Pick up that grip,' I replied, but he was not to be so easily turned aside.   He was dead in earnest.   Had he had the fare, or had I consented to advance it, he would have taken the first train back to Chicago.   At seven-thirty we were at the Rink. ' Old man,' said I, as I slapped him on the shoulder, ' I'll stand by you.   Pitch in !   I know you have it in you.'   Before him was a sea of faces.   He soon had the audience singing heartily and gave swift evidence of that genius which, under the guidance of the Holy Spirit, has blessed the souls of multitudes.''

Twenty-three years later, when Charles Alexander and Dr. J. Wilbur Chapman were holding meetings in Washington, Pa., the newspapers revived memories of another campaign with Dr. Smiley.   The *Washington Daily News* of February 28th, 1916, says : " Washington people, especially the older residents, who remember the meetings of nearly a quarter of a century ago, will welcome Mr. Alexander as an old friend who is coming back amongst them after many years. His voice has lost none of its power during the years that have passed since last he was here." For two weeks from February 23rd, 1893, Dr. Smiley held evangelistic services in the First Presbyterian Church closing in the Washington Jefferson College Gymnasium, then newly erected, on March 9th. "From the first," says the *Daily News* of 1916, " the meetings met with success—in fact they were the most successful evangelistic meetings ever held in Washington before or since, and every night it was necessary to hold overflow meetings in the churches. The song services conducted by Mr. Alexander were a great feature, and the old papers say that this alone drew great crowds of people. At the beginning of each meeting he conducted a song service of half-an-hour, and the newspapers of that time say that he was a vocalist of exceptional ability, possessing a full, rich voice, which added very materially to the success of the meetings."

The tremendous popularity of the singing, and of the young song-leader himself, who was at this time twenty-five years old, might well have turned his head, and have aroused some of the personal ambitions of earlier years, but the consecration of his life to God was deep and sincere, and one of the remarkable things of his whole career was, that in spite of constantly increasing fame in Christian service, and of world-wide affection from the hearts of Christian people, the sweet humility and genuine unselfishness of his nature deepened with the years. His mind and heart were filled to overflowing with Christ, and the needs of perishing souls, so that there was no room for self-consciousness of any kind.

Some of the letters written to his mother, during this period, are wonderfully illuminating, while all of them breathe that devoted affection which he always felt for the dear ones at home, and was never ashamed to express. " Dear Mother and folks," he wrote on November 16th, 1892, " your good letter deserves better attention than I have paid it. I have asked our blessed Jesus to watch over and guide you all every day. I have had a great deal to do since I received your letter. I am an editor of the *Institute Tie* and have charge of the children's choir in the big church, and also lead the big Sabbath school there. We have a grand concert piano and organ to play for us. I am so thankful for all this, but I have found that the sweetest rest is gained by keeping close to the Master's side, and I want you all to pray earnestly each day for me that I may grow more in faith, and that God will give me health. John iii. 36 is a good foundation to build upon. The quartet that I organized last summer was re-united and went on to Boston to sing with the Rev. Mr. Torrey. I hope and pray that Homer is in college, and if not, that he will go as soon as possible, no matter what may be in the way. May God's richest blessing rest upon you every one."

Later on, Alexander sent for his beloved only sister to join him at the Institute for a course of study, and his brotherly pride in her was unbounded. On November 16th, 1893, he wrote :—" Dear little Mother, My ! how long it has been since I wrote to the dearest little woman on earth to me. Forgive once more, won't you ? When I think of how many things you have to worry you, I wonder how you stand them all, and then I pray for you, and sometimes think I should do more—go to you and help you.   But it seems to me that if you can go through the winter half-way and not worry, we should sell out everything there, put the money in the bank, and have our headquarters in Maryville.   I want to get you where you can be perfectly free from the worry.   I can't bear to think of the stock going hungry.   I know how discouraging it is for Homer, but if he will only see to things until I can get there, we will make out some way.   You see, if I were to come home now, Ida would have to come too, and lose her advantages, which she is taking in so much to her benefit.   I wish you could just see her, looking so much prettier and so much sweeter than any other girl, when they have a social, and when I know she has scarcely had a cent to do it on, and always looks nice.   It has been a pleasure to me to work for her ; although it seemed I could scarcely pull through, God has helped me and all has come out right.   She sang very well, they told me, in the solo class this morning.   Now, I don't want you to worry about us ; I think I can keep her up.   So you and Homer keep your money, keep good and warm so that when we come home we'll find you good and well.   If you knew how I pray for you and dear old Homer, you would never once think I had forgotten you.   I feel safe about dear Leo.   That farm is a hard place, but at the beginning of each day, if you will lay your care upon Him, He'll take it ; don't you take it back.   I want you and Homer every day to ask God to cure me sound and well, for my health has been my great drawback.   Read Matthew xviii. 19.   If things worry you too much, little woman, and you get sick, you must write.   If Homer gets discouraged, let me know, and we'll come home as soon as we can.''

His loving thoughtfulness for his family is seen in all his letters, and he was always planning to make their burdens lighter.   The way in which he asks for particulars concerning affairs on the homestead, reveals his practical knowledge.

The delay in writing at this time had been caused by an illness which he had sought to conceal from his dear ones at home.   As will be seen, the summer of 1893 had been more than ever strenuous in connexion with the World's Fair, when extra work in the summer heat took the place of a needed vacation.   An anxious letter from his mother called forth a second one from him immediately.   On November 17th he wrote :—'' Dear Mother, you have received my letter, no doubt, by this time, but I will write you again to allay your fears.   I was very sick for a while, but had all the attention anyone could wish, and flowers came bunch after bunch.   As far as money is concerned, I did not need much, for my scholarship pays my board, room-rent and washing—no doctor's bill.   I am not well by quite a good deal, but the Lord will cure me when it is time.   You and Homer pray that He will soon make me sound and well, and that I may give my whole time to work for Him.   Yes, I will pray that Cloyd's Creek will have a great revival.   May God bless you and the dear white head in leading souls to Jesus.   There is no place that I could wish for a mighty outpouring of the Holy Spirit more than there. I have often thought I should like to stay a year or two just to work and build up a school and a church.   I have a girls' choir in Moody's church every Sunday. You should hear them sing !   I also have a boys' choir with about forty-five in it. Don't you ever lose a chance of talking kindly to those girls about giving their hearts to Jesus ; get them alone and tell them over again how He died for them and wants to save every one of them now. Do that quietly, and pray with them, and insist that they read the Gospel of John. Write soon, for my heart is wrapped up in you two, the one at Maryville " (his youngest brother Leo) " and the one here. I pray times without number for you all. Let us all go to work for Jesus. What else is there worth working for ? I read of a woman in Pennsylvania—just a simple woman—who went around at her work praying day after day that God would send a great revival in the village. Soon after, such a revival as they had never heard of broke out, and no one could account for it until they heard how the woman had been praying. God loves you as much as He did her. You pray for Cloyd's Creek. I hope we shall all be together soon and can talk it over."

One of the greatest experiences of those Chicago years of training was the share assigned to him, as one of the army of Christian workers organized by Moody, to help in his campaign during the great World's Fair held in Chicago in 1893.

Alexander found time to attend sessions of the great " Parliament of Religions," where the most eloquent and impressive speakers and lecturers, representing every great religion of the earth, addressed thronging audiences. He never lost the impression received then of the utterly selfish outlook of every other religion but that of the Bible, and came through the intellectual exercise with a faith more firmly fixed in Christ, and in the saving power of His precious blood.

During part of this strenuous time, he was assigned to lead the singing in the meetings addressed by the famous Scottish preacher, John McNeill, and a warm friendship resulted between the two from that date. He also became acquainted with such men as Fleming H. Revell, the well-known publisher, brother-in-law to Mr. Moody ; Henry Varley, the great evangelist ; A. T. Pierson, and Ira D. Sankey ; also with Lord Kinnaird, J. E. K. Studd, of the London Polytechnic, and Mr. J. Louis Fenn, of Liverpool, with whom he was afterwards closely associated.

During the summer of the same year, Mr. Milan B. Williams, a man already known for his fearless evangelism, was invited by Dr. Torrey to lead some of the tent missions in Chicago for a period of four months. During one of the months, Mr. Williams supplied the pulpit of the Chicago Avenue Church, and later lectured at the Institute. Here he met Charles Alexander, who was assigned to lead the music in his tent meetings. A friendship sprang up between the two men which was destined to be lifelong.

About a year later, as the days of preparation drew to a close, Alexander's thoughts turned constantly to the wider work awaiting him in the evangelistic field. He was now almost twenty-seven. Who should be his colleague in the work ? He could not decide. Finally one day, about the first of September, he fell upon his knees asking God to direct him, and making a complete surrender of his own will in the matter. The answer came suddenly. Six days afterwards, Dr. Torrey received a telegram from Mr. Williams asking for a singer to be sent to him for about two weeks. Dr. Torrey chose Charles Alexander, who joined Mr. Williams in Waverley, Iowa. But the partnership was longer than had been anticipated, for the brief period lengthened into eight years, during which the two men conducted numerous campaigns in many parts of the Middle West.

CHAPTER FIVE

Ardent Evangelism with M. B. Williams

1894 to 1902

THE man with whom Charles M. Alexander was to be so closely linked for the next eight years, was already well known in the Southern States, and in parts of the Middle West, as a successful, energetic evangelist. Born in the State of New York, the son of an infidel father and a faithful Christian mother, he had been truly converted in his boyhood. Immediately after his conversion he began to work for his Master, and, to his great joy, his father became a Christian. M. B. Williams entered Y.M.C.A. work, becoming State Secretary for Georgia. It was here that he became acquainted with that unique evangelistic orator of the South, Sam Jones, from whom he learned many of his methods. He developed great platform gifts as a speaker at conventions, and wherever he went, thousands flocked to hear him. As his work grew, he was constantly looking for some one who would share it, and felt that Alexander was the man. Their first work together as partners, at Waverley, in the autumn of 1894, was a time of tempest, and to men less strong might have proved discouraging. Williams at first did not give the impression of unusual strength, and had a quiet, reserved manner. Yet this man of thirty-four and his twenty-seven-year-old associate went as fire-brands through the cities of the Middle West. In his bold preaching, Williams searched out sin wherever he found it, exposing it mercilessly, before sowing the Gospel seed. The singing, under Alexander's inspiring leadership, drew the crowds, softening the surface of the soil for the work of the harrow.

Iowa was even then making efforts to become a Prohibition State, but in each individual town a 65 per cent. vote was needed to settle the question of whether it should be " wet " or " dry." In many places the parties were so evenly balanced, through the slackness of professing Christians, that the liquor interests triumphed.

In Waverley, religious life was at a low ebb, and although both men worked with a will, preaching, pleading, singing, and dealing with individuals, the results were disheartening, and too few took their stand for Christ. Finally, feeling that the time had come to cease their pleadings, Williams closed the campaign with a philippic, and a prophecy concerning the town, that almost paralysed his hearers.

However, the opposition which they had met only served to rouse both men to further efforts. A local Methodist minister named Pye, who had stood by them all through the struggle, was so impressed with their methods and ability that he went to the committee then arranging the programme for the State Methodist

Conference, and what he told them of Williams and Alexander led to an invitation being immediately sent to attend the Conference and speak to the ministers.

Williams made so logical and eloquent an appeal for the suppression of the liquor trade, and Alexander so charmed them by his singing and winsome personality, that soon a perfect deluge of invitations poured in upon them.

During the next six years, they conducted meetings in thirty-four towns in Iowa alone, twelve thousand people joining the Protestant churches as a result.

It was during the Waverley meetings, that Charles Alexander came into contact with the original personality of Fred Siebert, to whom he always gave the credit of awakening him, as no one else had ever done, to a sense of the urgent need of winning people everywhere to Christ by individual effort.

" Fred " was an Iowa plough-boy of German extraction, who had made his way West, and there learned to drink and gamble, and had won a name as a " broncho-buster." He was wonderfully converted, and attended the Williams-Alexander meetings in his native town of Waverley. Finding that he was out of work, and assured of his sincerity, Williams engaged him as caretaker of the big tent in which the meetings were being held. But Fred did more than look after the tent. His soul was on fire for God, and in his desire to win souls he knew no timidity, and was as ready to tackle a university student as the lowest drunkard. Alexander says of Fred, " He had one of the greatest passions for souls I have ever seen in anyone. Personal dealing was his talk, morning, noon, and night. I loved and admired him, and found that the chief thing keeping me back from doing personal work was an unsurrendered will. Fred's life was a constant rebuke to me. One day, Williams sent me to take charge of a meeting, and Fred came along to help. It was a rainy morning, and few people were out, but there was not one person in the building, saved or unsaved, who did not have to speak at that service. It was one of the best meetings I was ever in. From that time I began to do personal work, and I am more convinced every day that this is the work for every believer in Christ.

" Fred had studied his Bible every spare moment, in order to fit himself to meet the difficulties that came up in his personal dealing. In those five years he was with us he led twelve hundred people definitely to Christ, and he did it in such a way that they were glad to be talked with about their soul's salvation."

The first city visited in 1895 was Manchester, Iowa. The Opera House was taken for the meetings, and was crowded night after night, until at last even standing room was at a premium, and people had to be turned away. Pastors from other towns, within a radius of one hundred miles, came into Manchester to attend the meetings. Between six and seven hundred people accepted and publicly confessed Christ as their Saviour, amongst them many men who had boasted of their infidelity. Every member of the brass band which led the singing under Alexander's direction was soundly converted. The Opera House cancelled all its theatre engagements, scores of quarrels were settled, old feuds buried, and, as the local paper states, "The town has virtually been born again." One of the pianos which accompanied the orchestra was played by a talented young musician named Edith Fox, a girl in her early teens. This young life was one of the many whose whole course was changed by the blessed instrumentality of Charles Alexander's influence. He persuaded her to enter the Moody Bible Institute as a student. Here she met and became engaged to a fellow-student named Ralph C. Norton, and, after their marriage, entered with him into a life of devoted Christian service. One day, years later, speaking to Charles Alexander's wife of her early experiences, Mrs. Norton said, " I can never tell you what his influence has meant to my life. Of all the men I knew at that time, he was the only one who was interested in me for my own sake, with no underlying motive. I always call him my Sir Galahad."

Ralph C. Norton, writing to the Philadelphia *Sunday School Times* after Alexander's Home-call in 1920, calls him " the greatest leader of song of this generation —but beyond that, a leader of men. For Charles M. Alexander used his gift of leadership in song for one end, and there we have the passion of his life—to lead men to the personal acceptance of Christ as Saviour. Linked to this passion of his was a complementary one, that of inspiring others to undertake the same ministry. Untold numbers are in Christian work to-day because of his influence—among the number my own wife, who, through his efforts, turned from the concert stage to the Moody Bible Institute and to a lifetime of Christian service."

In March of 1895 Williams and Alexander were in Belle Plaine, Iowa. Here the closing report read, " Hundreds have been saved; all kinds of men, of all classes and conditions. The Tabernacle meetings of the evangelists, and the singing, are the all-absorbing topics on street, in home, in round-house, depôts, yard, car, and engine. Every department has been touched. No undue excitement has been found, and some of the conversions have occurred in the homes or places of labour, in the quietness and blessedness of the hour. Such work will last, such work is genuine. Belle Plaine stands to-day a Prohibition town. The singing of Mr. Alexander and his large chorus choir added greatly to the power of the meetings."

Casey, Illinois; and Independence, Cedar Falls, Fort Dodge, Webster City, Delhi, and Estherville, Iowa, were among other places visited in 1895.

During November, Charles Alexander spent a short time with Williams at his home in Atlanta, Georgia. D. L. Moody was holding some of his great meetings in the city at the time. One night, Alexander was invited to sing to the four thousand people gathered to hear Mr. Moody. The *Atlanta Constitution*, says of his singing :—" His clear, musical voice completely filled the auditorium, and every member of the congregation listened with breathless attention to the song, which seemed to be endowed with a melody almost divine."

The year 1896 was filled with a continuous stream of evangelistic work, almost entirely in Iowa. Among the notable campaigns were those in Waterloo, Sioux City, Marshalltown, and Carroll. This year also saw the beginning of three strong friendships in the life of Charles Alexander. One of the remarkable things in his ever-widening experiences, was not only the constant accession of new friendships that came to him, but the extraordinary depth and permanence of them.

Early in the year, the Williams-Alexander party was increased by the addition of William A. Sunday, known among all his friends as " Billy." An Iowa man by birth, of Scottish and German parentage, his father a victim of the Civil War, Billy Sunday had become a noted baseball player. Strolling one evening along a Chicago street with five baseball companions, he paused to listen to the singing of a band of workers from the Pacific Garden Mission, under the leadership of Harry Munroe, the famous Rescue Mission leader. This eventually led to his conversion, and to his leaving the baseball field, with his fame in the world of sport and the money it was bringing him, to become an obscure Christian worker in the Y.M.C.A.

He boldly gave his testimony for Christ, and was often invited to do so by Dr. J. Wilbur Chapman in his evangelistic services. Dr. Chapman was impressed with the thought that Billy Sunday should preach. " But I have no sermons," said he. " I will give you seven of mine," said Dr. Chapman, "and that will last you for a week in one place, and then you can move on and preach them in another." Sunday stayed some time in association with Dr. Chapman, who then gave him a note of introduction to Williams and Alexander, with whom he worked for a number of years.

Sunday and Alexander quickly came to love each other, and in after-years were always happy when their work brought them occasionally together. Sunday wrote of him in 1920 :—" To have known Charlie Alexander was an invitation to sing. His personality was as infectious as the laughter of little children. He was the pioneer in inspiring great audiences to sing Gospel hymns, and his name is imperishably connected with evangelistic music."

Another friendship that meant a great deal to the lonely spirit of Charles Alexander, in his homeless wanderings in Christ's service, was that formed with the Leavitt family in Waterloo, Iowa. In spite of tremendous opposition on the part of the liquor element, this town was swept with a revival. More than a thousand people—men, women, and children—took their stand for Christ, about eight hundred of whom were added to the churches. Amongst these was a young man named Leavitt, whom Alexander led to Christ. His father was a prominent banker in the town, and his mother, a sister of Mr. Marshall Field, of Chicago.

Alexander was invited to their beautiful Christian home, and Mrs. Leavitt, a lady of culture and refinement and wide experience, became deeply interested in him and his work. As she watched him at the meetings from day to day, she saw the extraordinary power he already possessed over an audience, and also the great possibilities that were yet latent in him.

One day she took him aside to talk about his future. " There is nothing you cannot do," she said, " if only you will work for it. I have seen some of the greatest conductors in the world, but you have it in you to be the equal of any of them." This encouragement meant much to the young Southerner, whose modest nature made him at times inclined to hold himself in check.

The friendship with the Leavitt family continued to deepen, and a room was placed permanently at his disposal. " Make this your home," Mrs. Leavitt said, " this shall be your room. Come whenever you can." What this generous offer meant to the young man of twenty-eight, separated by six hundred miles from his home and loved ones in Tennessee, and moving constantly from place to place, can well be imagined. For the next six years the Leavitt home in Waterloo became his. The friendship of the level-headed banker, of Mrs. Leavitt, and their daughter Lucy and her brothers, steadied and stimulated him, besides helping to satisfy the hunger of his home-loving heart. The blessing was mutual, and through the opportunity of spending his vacations here, Alexander was led to originate that great system of Bible Classes which opened the Word of God to so many, especially young men and women, and brought them into aggressive Christian service.   Miss Grace Saxe and Miss Frances Miller, both famous afterwards as Bible teachers and workers amongst young people, were started in their career through the impelling force of Charles Alexander's consecrated zeal in Waterloo.   Writing from California to Alexander's bereaved wife, in October, 1920, Mr. Joseph Leavitt said : " Our tears surely mingle with yours in this great sorrow.   He was a brother and a close friend to me.   When I think of his constant cheerful manner, his affection, his consideration, his thoughtfulness, his consistent Christian character, his continual desire to help others, his true humility, how poor the rest of us are in comparison.   I am so glad we saw you both here last year.   My mind goes back twenty-four years, when he brought so much sunshine into our home."

But of all these friendships, one was destined to be particularly intimate and lasting.   In his work in Sioux City, Iowa, Alexander came into touch with French Oliver, a young piano salesman, with a wonderful voice, which he had, for a while, used upon the stage.   As a boy of ten he had been converted, but had drifted away from Christ.   Alexander was attracted to him, and did not rest until he had brought him back to his Lord.   He himself tells of what happened : " I had led a big Tennessean to Christ ; he was six feet four inches tall, and I took him to train.   I bought a Bible, *Pilgrim's Progress*, and a book of Moody's sermons. He had been used to reading novels, so I got him a story called *Titus, the Comrade of the Cross*.   I just baited him with that the first thing.   He got interested in the story and in the Bible itself, and promised me that what time he did not have to have for recreation, and sleeping, and eating, the next few weeks, he would either spend in reading one of those three books or on his knees.   You should have seen that man grow !   He developed wonderfully in the knowledge of the Lord and in doing personal work, and finally he got so that he could lead music.   He is now an evangelist and preacher."   Writing in 1921, French Oliver says : " I soon read the small books which Mr. Alexander had given me, and began a systematic study of the Bible.   Many were the hours I spent on my knees, with the open Bible before me.   The deepest insight I have into the Word of God I attribute to the love for it, which came to me alone in my room at Waterloo, when I settled the matter of my life being wholly given up to the Word of God and soul-winning."

Charles Alexander tells the story of how they came to adopt their famous text. " Oliver and I agreed to spend our next Christmas vacation together.   We went to a little boarding-house, and those were two of the most profitable weeks I have ever spent.   I was training him, but found that while I was helping him I was helping myself.   We sang and composed music, read the Bible, and talked over Christian work.   On New Year's Eve we decided that for the coming year we would take a year-text, and the year-text was Second-Timothy-two-fifteen.   Instead of saying ' Good night ' to each other, one would call out ' Second-Timothy-two-fifteen,' and the other would answer, ' Second-Timothy-two-fifteen.'   The first man awake in the morning would call out ' Second-Timothy-two-fifteen,' and the other the same.

" Finally the time came for us to part.   I went down to the depôt to see him off. A great many people were on the platform.   My friend was standing on the open platform at the back end of the train, and instead of saying ' Good-bye ' I called out ' Second-Timothy-two-fifteen.' ' Second-Timothy-two-fifteen,' he replied. The train drew out. ' Second-Timothy-two-fifteen,' I shouted ; and the same words came back.

" The train was getting clear of the depôt. ' Second-Timothy-two-fifteen,' I shouted for all I was worth ; and ' Second-Timothy-two-fifteen ' came back to me very faintly. ' Second-Timothy-two-fifteen ' I let go once more, but I didn't hear any answer. I could see nothing but the white of his handkerchief fluttering in the wind, but I knew that he was shouting ' Second-Timothy-two-fifteen.' Listen to the rest of my story. For the whole of the year we stuck to that text. Every letter I sent to anyone had across it ' Second-Timothy-two-fifteen,' and a lot of my friends did the same. Twelve months later I was back there again, conducting some young people's services, and was speaking of the great advantage of having a year-text. I had been asking them to adopt this text that I had started out on, when a young fellow got up. ' I am glad,' said he, ' Mr. Alexander ever took " Second-Timothy-two-fifteen " for his year-text.' ' Twelve months ago I was down at the depôt seeing some people, when I heard a fellow shouting for all he was worth, " Second-Timothy-two-fifteen ! " to a man on the end of the outgoing train, who was shouting back, " Second-Timothy-two-fifteen ! " ' Well,' I thought. ' What is this " Second-Timothy-two-fifteen " anyway ? ' So I made a bee-line for home, and looked it up in my Bible. I wasn't a Christian then, but the first words of that text just hit me fairly between the eyes : " Study to show thyself approved unto God." Then I went on and read the rest : " A workman that needeth not to be ashamed, rightly dividing the word of truth." I asked God to forgive my sins and help me to show myself " approved," and, thank God, He has done it.' Another man then got up and said : ' I have never seen Mr. Alexander before to-night, but, the first Sunday I spent in this town, that man who has just spoken came to me and pointed me to Christ. He was saved through hearing Mr. Alexander calling out " Second-Timothy-two-fifteen," and I was saved through his having heard it.' "

In February, 1897, Mrs. M. B. Williams passed away. The tender sympathy that characterized Charles Alexander's whole life was deeply stirred for his friend, and for the three motherless girls, Faith, Carolyn, and Grace, to whom he was as a loved elder brother. The girls were at school, but, during the following years, were occasionally with their father in the meetings. With chivalrous tenderness, Alexander helped the lonely father to watch over and protect them.

Carolyn afterwards became the wife of French Oliver. When Alexander and his wife were in California early in 1919, they met Dr. and Mrs. French Oliver constantly. Carolyn Oliver often spoke to Charles Alexander's wife of all that the loving influence of " big brother Charlie " had meant to her early girlhood.

Faith Williams, writing on October 16th, 1920, said : " Charles held a very large place in my heart. He came into my life at a time when I was greatly overwhelmed with grief, because of the death of my mother, and he graciously and tenderly comforted the three of us during the following years. How conscientious he was in seeking to develop us into the kind of women he was anxious to have us be. How anxious we, too, were to please him, and to rise to what he expected of us. Every memory of those days of fellowship with him is a delight."

Time and space do not allow the thrilling experiences of the next few years to be told in detail. In some of the college towns, remarkable revivals were experienced. At Monmouth, Illinois, in 1908, as at Shurtleff College, near Upper Alton, in the same State, two years later, practically every student in the College took a stand for Christ. One evening, just before they left Upper Alton, an elderly lady, listening to the flood of kind words being poured upon Alexander said, half playfully : " I hope you will not be spoiled by all these compliments." He replied, " I know myself too well for that. I know it is not me, but what I have, that these good people admire." The pastor of the Baptist Church, writing of this incident adds : " This was both characteristic and true. Although naturally gifted to a high degree, it was the happy homage of Christ in his life, that, over all, attracted everybody—the brilliant flashing of his sunny piety."

A letter from Charles Alexander to his sister, written from Chicago in May, 1897, shows how tenderly he kept in touch with his own loved family, during the stress and strain of his work. " Dear Ida, I have been in the hospital, and had an operation performed, but am now well. So you see why I did not get to be with you. Of course I did not want you to know about it, to cause you uneasiness. Now that it is all over, we can laugh about it. I am going to say something I dislike to say, that is, I can't come home after all. The money I expected us all to enjoy together went to doctors, nurses, and druggist, but I hope to be stronger now than ever. I am mailing you and mamma a picture and a gold pen. I am mailing Homer a Bible I had bound and fixed for him, strong, and splendid print, good helps in the back. Let him give his old one to Matt for me. I leave Chicago for Vinton, Iowa, to sing in the big tent again this summer. I wish you would all learn to lead meetings, and know your old Bibles from beginning to end. Homer and Matt might speak in school-houses and little churches, and make a great team for God. You are all dearer to me than anything on earth, and my future plans always include you all."

Perhaps of all the campaigns of these years, none was more extraordinary than that which swept Shenandoah, Iowa, in November and December, 1899. Here again, the liquor element was completely routed, and a dramatic scene took place in one of the streets of the city, where a " jug-breaking " was publicly celebrated and much alcoholic liquor was emptied into the gutters.

In Hiawatha, Kansas, where Williams and Alexander held a campaign in January of 1901, the *Brown County World* states that " Hiawatha saw a sight in Main Street the like of which was never seen before." There were no saloons in Kansas, but the difficulty was amply made up for by the drug-stores, which were allowed to keep liquor for dispensing, upon a doctor's prescription. The result was, that the drug-stores became, for practical purposes, very much like saloons. Williams had vigorously denounced the state of affairs, until the worst offender, a druggist named A. J. Eicholtz, came under the power of God, and boldly led the way to the town's reform. One morning, although the weather was bitterly cold, and the ground covered with snow, the streets were thronged by a crowd gathered around a roughly-erected platform, on which stood Williams and Alexander and Eicholtz. After a hymn had been sung, and Williams had spoken a few earnest words, Mr. Eicholtz made a brave speech, saying that this was the happiest day of his life, that he was now a Christian, and, God helping him, he would never again sell a drop of liquor. Mr. M. B. Williams then, assisted by Eicholtz, smashed one bottle after another, until three hundred dollars' worth of liquor had been poured out upon the snow, amid ringing cheers from the crowd. After this, six hundred and fourteen decisions for Christ followed, and the indifference all over the town to the things of God was changed into enthusiasm and loyalty to Christ.

Just a year later, Alexander had the enjoyment of a rare holiday with Williams in Punta Gorda, Florida. He wrote to his mother on January 7th, 1902 :—" My dear Mother, your letters all gave me great joy. You will be surprised to know I am here with Mr. Williams for a few weeks' hunting. I was so weary the last weeks, I did not answer any letters at all, and am sure you will love me as much when you know why. I am sending you some money to-day. Tell dear old Homer to go on to Ann Arbor, if he feels sure that is where God wants him. It takes as consecrated a man to be a doctor as a preacher, for God never receives anything but the whole heart. Homer must have big thick soles to his shoes, as Leo has, and never stir out without his overcoat. I can only pray that God will lead us all."

The youngest brother, Leo, was in Chicago, at this time, at the Moody Bible Institute, and Charles, away down in the tropical heat of Florida, did not forget the needs of his brothers in the chilly northern climate. Homer wrote to him from Ann Arbor in March :—" I am studying physics, anatomy, histology, and electro-therapeutics. These branches of science are all useful, and will be accredited either on a degree of medicine or Bachelor of Arts. The 'medics' are worked extremely hard here." Later on, Homer Alexander felt drawn to give his life to definite religious work, and subsequently became a Presbyterian minister.

In the early spring of 1902, M. B. Williams decided to avail himself of a long-looked-for opportunity of spending a few months on a trip to the Holy Land. Neither he nor Alexander had the least thought in their minds that this was to mean the parting of the ways in their association as co-workers, for they purposed to take up their campaigns together again, as soon as Williams should return to the United States. But God had other plans for them both, and while their friendship remained unbroken and warm as ever, their feet were led into separate paths.

A letter from Mr. Williams, written on June 23rd, 1904, to Mrs. Richard Cadbury, of Birmingham, England, shows how strong the bond of affection remained between the two men :—" I know you will pardon my informal letter of regret at not being able to accept your kind invitation to your daughter's wedding to my dear old chum. There is only one Charles Alexander, others may imitate, but he remains unique and alone. It was like taking my heart out to lose him, my work can never be the same again. While as a companion the loss is irreparable, you and yours have gained what I have lost, but no one can rob me of the heritage of all those precious memories."

CHAPTER SIX

Circling the Globe with Dr. Torrey

1902

THE impending departure of M. B. Williams for Europe and Palestine left Charles Alexander at liberty to make his own arrangements for the Spring of 1902. There were several invitations to be considered, and he was wondering how best to make use of his time for the Lord, when, suddenly and unexpectedly, a new vista opened before him.

He and Williams were in the midst of a campaign in Kansas, when a long-distance telephone call gave a clear indication of what his Lord would have him do. The call that thus came to him, across six hundred miles, was fraught with a deeper meaning than he could have dreamed, and launched him upon a sea of world-wide influence, for which the hand of God had been training him through his years with Williams. A strange sequence of events had led to the sending of this message. In 1899, D. L. Moody had received an urgent invitation to visit Australia with Mr. Sankey. He had been unable to accept it, and his death soon afterwards drove Christians all over the world, who were depending upon his leadership, to their knees in prayer. The death of John MacNeil, of Australia, author of *The Spirit-filled Life,* had aroused the Christian people of that island-continent to a sense of responsibility and the need for spiritual activity. In 1901, Mr. G. P. Barber and Dr. Wm. Warren, of the Evangelization Society of Australasia, were deputed to visit Great Britain and Ireland, in the hope of securing a visit from some Spirit-filled evangelist. They failed to find one whom they cared to invite, and started on their homeward journey by way of the United States. A son of Mr. Barber's was studying at the Moody Bible Institute in Chicago, where a weekly prayer-meeting had been organized to pray for world-wide revival. Mr. Barber and Dr. Warren found that it had been continuing for two years without a break, under Dr. Torrey's leadership. They were at once impressed that this was the man they were looking for, and laid their concern before him. Arrangements were made for him to leave Chicago on December 23rd, 1901, travelling to Australia by way of Japan and China. Dr. Torrey had been asked to take a singer, and he longed for the help and companionship of such a man as his old student, Charles Alexander, whom he had loved since he first came to Chicago. Hence the long-distance telephone call. The invitation was accepted by Alexander, and the plan formed that was to mean much to both men and to the Kingdom of God.

In the dawn of this new and surprising opportunity, Alexander's first thoughts

PUBLIC DESTRUCTION OF
ALCOHOLIC LIQUORS AT
HIAWATHA, KANSAS,
JANUARY, 1901

"BILLY" SUNDAY. MILAN B. WILLIAMS. CHARLES M. ALEXANDER.

CHARLES ALEXANDER WITH HIS HELPERS:
FRENCH E. OLIVER, HARRY TOOGOOD, FRED SIEBERT, AND BILLY BECK

CHARLES M. ALEXANDER WITH
DR. AND MRS. TORREY, IN 1902

DR. TORREY AND C. M. ALEXANDER AT ADDINGTON,
AUGUST, 1902

AT THE ADDINGTON RAILWAY WORKSHOPS,
NEAR CHRISTCHURCH, NEW ZEALAND

were of his mother and home.   As soon as the last campaign with Williams in
Newton, Kansas, was over, he hurried to the loved circle in Tennessee.   A hallowed
time was passed together, and then, strengthened by the love and prayers of those
nearest and dearest to him, he went forth on his new mission.

As the train bore him away across the two thousand five hundred miles which
stretched between his home and Vancouver, he wrote to his mother on February
28th, 1902 : " Your sweet face is treasured in my mind, and I believe I have indelibly
stamped upon the tablets of my heart every little kind act you have performed for
me through the past few days.   The fond remembrance I shall carry away, as
a fragrant perfume that shall sweeten every hour until I see your dear face again.
I know I shall be a great deal better man than ever before.   I never wanted just
to drop everything, and never leave your presence, so much as now.   I think I
could sit by the day and the month and be happy with you.   You see I have
an old-fashioned case of love !   Your letters will be more than gold to me.   I sang
to a crowd in a Chicago hotel, and they cheered me, but the sweet smile of my
mother and the kind words of my sister and brothers were more to me than that."

Two weeks later, when, for the first time in his life, Alexander was sailing over
the ocean, his thoughts still centred round the home from which he was being borne
further away with every hour.   The pain of parting was heavy upon him.   " My
dear Mammy," he wrote on March 15th, " your dear face and everything you did
stays by me, and I dream of you often.   How I thank the Lord that He let me go
home this time.   The remembrance is so sweet and uplifting, I want to be better
every time I think of our little seasons of prayer.   Ida has so improved, and
seems to know God in such a way, that my admiration moved away up for her,
and the love deepens.   Pray for me, honey.   I will try to write you so much
that you will *know* I love every one of you.   We are just steaming into the lovely
harbour at Honolulu.   In eight days we shall reach the Fiji Islands, then seven
or eight days more to Australia.   My heart is with you all more than ever."

On March 30th, the S.S. *Miowera* docked at Brisbane, and two days later,
by Alexander's thoughtful arrangement with the Chicago agent of the C.P.R.,
his mother heard of his safe arrival.   He left the boat at Sydney, and a railway
journey of five hundred miles brought him to Melbourne.   Dr. Torrey had not yet
arrived from the Orient, and Alexander found himself a stranger in a strange land,
unknown and unexpected, with only a few shillings in his pocket.   His first hours
in Melbourne were a severe test, and only the assurance in his soul that his call
had been of God, could have helped him to overcome the obstacles that barred his
path.   The final arrangements for his going to Australia had been so hurriedly
made, that Dr. Torrey, who expected to reach Melbourne first, had not mentioned
his coming, and all the plans had been made without taking him into account.

Mr. J. J. Virgo, General Secretary of the Australasian Y.M.C.A., and one of
the four secretaries of the Melbourne Mission, had been appointed to train and
to lead the huge united choir for the final meetings in the Exhibition Building.
Already he had been hard at work rehearsing the choir in some of the Sankey hymns,
and, being possessed of a splendid voice, was prepared to do most of the solo work.

On entering his office one day, during the busy time of preliminary organization, Mr. Virgo found a young man apparently waiting for him. " Are you being attended to ? " asked Mr. Virgo, after a swift glance at the eager, alert face. " Say, are you Virgo ? " inquired the stranger, with a distinct American accent, answering one question by asking another. Mr. Virgo admitted his identity. " I'm Alexander," was the next remark. But that meant nothing to Mr. Virgo, for he had never heard of him. When Alexander had explained his presence in Australia, and Mr. Virgo had told of the arrangements already completed by the committee, two bewildered men looked into each other's eyes. For a moment there was a tense silence, then Alexander spoke. " I guess I'm not wanted here," he said quietly, " I had better get back to America." In that moment a divine purpose might have been wrecked, if the two men thus flung across each other's way had been thinking only of personal interests. Fortunately, they were made of finer stuff. Virgo's heart went out to the lonely singer from America in a noble act of self-surrender and self-sacrifice, and he asked him not to come to a hasty decision. For himself, he knew what he would do. He met the committee at once, told them of Alexander's arrival, explained that his secretarial responsibilities were so heavy that he must be relieved from his duties as choir conductor, and proposed that Alexander should be made leader of the music. It was a big act, and it marked the beginning of a lasting friendship between the two. Eighteen years afterwards, Mr. Virgo wrote : " He was my dearest man friend. Wasn't he just a lovable fellow ? I have been going back over the years to that happy day when I discovered him waiting in my office in Melbourne. No event that I recall serves otherwise than to make me thank God for the privilege of knowing and loving him."

It did not take many days for Alexander to win the affection of others besides Mr. Virgo. Rev. S. Pearce Carey, M.A., the chairman of the Melbourne Mission, tells how he first met the young American singer in committee. Full of prejudice, and fearful of innovations, Mr. Carey remarked rather curtly that they wanted " no fooling ! " Alexander made no answer, except by offering his hand across the table ! " And now that the mission is over," said Mr. Carey, about five weeks later, " one of its happiest memories is the Alexander choirs. What an unspeakable mercy it would be if our churches should determine to make their choirs and their singing throb with power after the fashion of the ' beloved Alexander.' In a long talk we had last night, he bade me ask all the converts of the mission to underline the first four words of Genesis, and to make them their life-motto. The more I have been privileged to know Alexander, the surer I have become that the secret of all his winsome power lies in this—that in all his beginnings there is God."

The first home in which Alexander was entertained was that of Mr. G. P. Barber, at Essendon, a beautiful suburb of Melbourne. He never forgot this first experience of warm-hearted Australian hospitality. Another who showed Alexander unfailing kindness was the Hon. James Balfour, M.L.C., the " grand old man " of Australia, whose fatherly friendship became deeper and stronger as the years went by. When Dr. Torrey arrived, he was greeted by a Charles Alexander quite at home in Melbourne, without a trace of his first loneliness.

Dr. Torrey was just the man needed at this period of religious history in Australasia, when destructive criticism was first beginning to make its entrance among the rank and file of church members. Born in New Jersey, the son of a New York banker, he had enjoyed the best possible educational advantages of the United States. He matriculated at Yale University when only fifteen years of age, and took his A.B. degree with honours at nineteen, his B.D. following in due course. While studying in the theological seminary, and afterwards in the German universities of Leipzig and Erlangen, he passed through a bitter spiritual experience, becoming a thorough sceptic, but found his way gradually out of the barrenness of doubt into a more definite and exultant faith than he had known before.

Before going to Germany, Dr. Torrey had spent four years in the pastorate, having been ordained at the early age of twenty-two. Returning to America, he organized a Congregational church in Minneapolis, then for six years became superintendent of the City Missionary Society of that city. It was in this work that he attracted the attention of D. L. Moody, who invited him to become the head of the Chicago Bible Institute at its foundation in 1889. Five years later, the Chicago Avenue Church asked him to become its pastor, and in these combined positions, and at conventions, he had a wide sphere for evangelistic teaching and preaching.

He was only forty-six when the call of God brought him to Australia, although the white hair, close-cropped, grey beard and moustache made him look older. But the erect figure, broad shoulders, and manly face, gave evidence of great strength, while the bright complexion and clear eyes showed the freshness of youth.

The first meeting of the campaign was held in the Melbourne Town Hall, which was crowded with ministers and church workers, and was presided over by Rev. S. Pearce Carey. The meeting began with a song service, entirely in the hands of Charles Alexander. He literally took the crowded meeting by storm, for leadership such as his had never been seen in Melbourne before. A local paper thus describes him : " Mr. Alexander, tall and slender, is a great singer, not merely by virtue of voice and temperament, or natural genius. His religion, with its glow, its tenderness, its gladness, runs to music as naturally as a bird to song. His face is spirit-fine, when he sings. ' Shine up your face,' is one of his favourite sayings, and with him it is no artificial expression, but the light of the heart shining through. As a leader, his sway over a chorus is phenomenal, and his enthusiasm so contagious that people who can't sing, and *know* they can't, *do* sing, when his ' Wake up there, folks ! ' rouses them from their lethargy."

Rev. W. H. Fitchett, LL.D. editor of *The Southern Cross*, and well known throughout the British empire as an author, described a midday meeting in the Town Hall. " Nothing is more striking in the great mission now in progress than the charm and effectiveness of the singing. Mr. Alexander is a conductor of the first order, and he exercises a curious spell over an audience. He drills a thousand people with the decision and authority of, say, a first-class drill-sergeant. He scolds, exhorts, rebukes, and jests, with almost more than ordinary American versatility and readiness. And the amusing feature is that the great audience enjoys being scolded and drilled. The singing, with its ease, its fire and exultation, and the note of triumphant faith which runs through it all, melts the audience as fire would melt wax. The floor of the Town Hall is one great mosaic of men's faces, the majority of them middle-aged, many of them old. Time and care have ploughed deep furrows on most of them. They seem at first an audience for whom music has ceased to have any office. But as the singing goes on, the tired faces relax, the eyes brighten, the lips begin to move. A wave of sunshine seems to run over the human landscape before one. Music, as the servant and vehicle of religion, has fulfilled its true and highest office. It has set a thousand human souls vibrating in gladness. No one need doubt that the Gospel can be sung as effectively as it can be spoken. And what other creed can be set to music in this fashion ? ''

On the very first night, the " Glory Song " had floated out over the audience, touching all hearts with its tender pathos, and holding their attention by the swing of its melody. Almost immediately, the first Australian Alexander hymn-book appeared, with messages of Gospel song that were quite new to Australia. It was everywhere hailed as a potent agent in the cause of aggressive evangelism. Alexander's publisher was Mr. T. Shaw Fitchett, a son of the author. Any permanent business relations with Alexander meant the formation of a sincere friendship ; in this instance, the very difference of temperament was an added attraction.

" My memories of Charles," wrote Mr. Fitchett long afterwards, " are a quiet and constant happiness. The night he wandered into my office twenty years ago and asked, ' Are you T. Shaw Fitchett ? ' he electrified me with his sunny smile and charm, and his voice of the South. I remember well, how he drew what he called a ' cut ' from his pocket, and asked if we could print a few thousand leaflets from it. It was a block of the ' Glory Song.' In half-an-hour we were more than half-way to loving each other ; in another ten minutes we were off to the Coffee Palace for dinner and a yarn. Before I left that night, I had made him disgorge all the ' cuts ' from his trunk, and all the hymn-prints of which he had the rights, and persuaded him to let me rush up a complete hymn-book. Within a week or ten days, his first hymn-book was on the market, supplying him with the means to set ten thousand people singing. From that time, loving and uninterrupted friendship was ours—a golden thread running through twenty years. The joy of it all ! The midnight bursts of work and planning in Sydney ; the motor rides ; the unexpected visits at my home and office ; the happy days across two oceans and a continent with you both ; the days at ' Tennessee ' ; I could go on indefinitely—but you know it all, and have memories dearer, deeper, fuller."

At the close of the Melbourne Mission, a hymn-book, beautifully bound in red leather, was presented to Alexander, bearing the inscription in gold lettering : " To the ' Radiant Personality ' from his Perspiring Publisher. A token of affectionate regard." Early in the third week, the evening meetings were transferred to the huge Exhibition Building, of which Melbourne is justly proud. Surrounded by beautiful gardens, the illuminated palace, with its electric lights shimmering on top of the dome, makes an impressive night-picture. The crowds, that had thronged it when the Australian nation was being launched inside, were less significant than the spontaneous rush of thousands of people who were drawn to it by the Word of God, on the first night of the Torrey-Alexander meetings.

Once again Dr. Fitchett speaks to us from *The Southern Cross* : " Climb up by stairway and ladder to the top of the organ and look down. You see a tiny frock-coated figure standing on a little red island in the midst of a sea of faces. To his right and left are grand pianos, and between them a cabinet organ. Mr. Virgo sits at one of the pianos. The figure on the red island has apparently done something, for the sea all around him breaks up into waves, that surge up till they reach his feet. A few silver notes float up from the pianos. They are faint but unmistakable—the preliminary bars of the 'Glory Song,' and there is a thrill of recognition. The chorus is sung by the choir, then by one gallery after another, and finally by the people on the floor of the building.

> Oh, that will be glory for me,
> Glory for me, glory for me,
> When, by His grace, I shall look on His face,
> That will be glory, be glory for me.

" Then the man on the island, who has been responsible for these bursts of song, goes off into a series of Indian-club exercises, and one word, ' *Ev*'rybody,' comes floating up, to be chased by such a volume of melody that the roof rings to the shout :—

> Oh, that will be glory for me!

" The music stops, and, beginning at the little island, the wave subsides. Its crest runs back, and back, and back, under the dome, till it reaches the barricade. One half expects a splash of people to be thrown up over the great screens which form the barrier! Then there arises a mighty, humming melody. The words are indistinguishable, but the air is one that every one knows. Seven thousand people are singing, just above their breath, ' Nearer my God to Thee,' and up in the organ loft the effect is even greater than when the ' Glory Song ' rang out.

" Another pause, and then, ' There is Power in the Blood ' declare seven thousand voices. No wonder that one of the missioners shouts, ' Well done ! I never heard such singing, even in Philadelphia.' This conductor is used to doing things on a big scale, and here is a mighty musical instrument, worthy of a master-hand. That slender man with the silver voice, the ready wit, the charming smile, knows how to use his instrument. He draws out its full value, and who shall say how many souls are won before ever the Word is read or the text announced ? "

The choir for these services in the Exhibition Building was composed of twelve hundred and fifty singers. Alexander did not care to use the great organ, which he preferred as a solo instrument, but substituted two pianos, finding that the quick, incisive notes of a piano held the singing of a large crowd together far better, and did not detract from the value of vocal harmonies like an organ. Alexander's average day's work during the Mission included at least three or four services, besides committee meetings and other business. There was often barely time for meals, and about six o'clock he would be back in the Exhibition Building. Here he would find an eager crowd, two hours before time. Without any delay, Alexander would start the congregation singing.

Between the hymns, he would give short talks about matters of practical Christian living. " I should like to know," he would sometimes say, " how many here have family prayers in their homes? All who do, hold up their hands." When the response failed to satisfy him he would add, " That is far too few ! How many of you will start it now ?   Hands up ! " and he would encourage and persuade until he had gained the largest possible result.   Upon Bible study and soul-winning he laid a similar emphasis.   " Who in this hall has read the Bible through from beginning to end ? " he called out suddenly one day.   Only about fifty hands were held up out of the crowd.   " Ah," exclaimed Alexander, " I've caught some of you preachers now ! "   Then he asked, " Who will undertake to read it through within the next twelve months ?   It can be done in that time, can't it, Dr. Torrey ? "   " It can," replied the latter, " three chapters a day, and five on Sundays will do it."

News of the great work in Melbourne was constantly wafted across the ocean to the home in Tennessee, which was never forgotten. A letter from Mr. William Howat, a Melbourne lawyer, brought glad tidings to Alexander's mother.   " I have been delighted with your son's singing," he wrote on May 9th, 1902, " and with his leadership of the great choir.   His face beams with the glow of Christ's indwelling.   He has gladdened thousands of the Melbourne folk.   How his eyes have brightened, as he spoke to me of you !   Again I thank you for having given to the world so rich a treasure as your son. . . . He is materially influencing the future of the people inhabiting the towns and cities of Australia."

On May 10th, the great Melbourne Mission ended.   From May 11th until June 27th, without a day's break except for travelling, Dr. Torrey and Alexander held missions in six other towns in the State of Victoria.   The first to be visited was Warrnambool, hitherto known for its connexion with horse-racing, but mightily stirred by the ten days of evangelistic upheaval.   This was followed by a week in Geelong, where again Alexander formed some specially strong and lasting friendships.   He was entertained at the home of Mr. and Mrs. George Hitchcock, who showered loving hospitality upon him.   Staying in their home at the time was their nephew, Rupert Lowe, a fine young Australian who had done recent service through the war in South Africa, and was just recovering from the effects of his experiences.   His gentle, poetic nature attracted Alexander, and when the mission party left Australia, Rupert Lowe accompanied him as his secretary. During the four years that followed, Lowe was almost like a younger brother, helping Alexander in ways of which nobody knew that he needed help.   For he had told no one of an accident during a yachting trip in Florida with Williams, when a heavy trunk, slipping from the top of a pile, had caught him on the back, hurting his spine.   As a result, walking, or the lifting of a heavy bag, caused him constant pain and weariness.   No sign of this was ever shown, when he stood, full of fire and activity, before an audience.   Only Rupert Lowe knew, and loyally guarded his knowledge, while doing all he could to save Alexander's strength.

The Ballarat Mission, which followed, was notable for introducing to the people of Australia the little white card, with its arresting message, " GET RIGHT WITH GOD."   " One day in Ballarat," said Alexander afterwards, " things were not going very well.   I went to my room, wondering how the city could be aroused. There was a printing-office just across the street from my window, and suddenly it occurred to me to have a large number of cards printed, for distribution throughout the city, bearing simply the four words : ' Get right with God.'   We had used them in America with splendid results.   I went across and ordered fourteen thousand. It seemed a large number, but I took the risk. They were given out in the streets, in houses, everywhere. The city was greatly stirred, and many were won to Christ through those little white cards. One was handed to a young business man. He glanced at it, thrust it into his pocket, and continued his work of calling on different firms. Every time he put his hand into his pocket to get his business card, he felt this other one, because it was longer. He knew well what was on it, and, without looking at it, the words seemed to stand out like letters of fire. The result was that he gave his heart to God and became an earnest worker for others."

From June 14th to 18th, Dr. Torrey and his associate were in Bendigo, and here, for the first time, Alexander met the young musician, Robert Harkness, who was to become his pianist for the next twelve years, and whose songs were to reach all over the world. Mr. Harkness had been appointed accompanist for the mission. His father, of good old English stock, had been Mayor of Bendigo more than once, and was famous in the locality as a man who had not feared to stand squarely on his Christian principles while in office. Alexander was drawn to the young musician from the first. They had no opportunity for private conversation on spiritual matters until the last day of the mission. Then they had a serious talk, which Mr. Harkness somewhat resented, refusing to come to an immediate decision. But Alexander's kindly manner, as they descended the stairs together, touched him. They parted at the door, and Mr. Harkness took his bicycle to start for home. Suddenly Alexander called out from the cab he was entering, " Come down to the train at three o'clock this afternoon, and go up to Maryborough with me for a week." Mr. Harkness agreed, and on his way home decided to accept the Saviour. When he joined Alexander at the railway station he was a new man in Christ Jesus.

From that day onwards, he became Alexander's second self in the music. He learned to know every piece in the red song-book, and as soon as a number was given out, he would strike the first chord on the piano. So closely did leader and pianist work together, that they often seemed fused into one, without any need of spoken directions. This fusion was not reached immediately, but was the result of constant work together, day after day, through the years.

The mission party now consisted of Dr. and Mrs. Torrey, Charles Alexander, Rupert Lowe, and Robert Harkness. After a short mission of three days in Terang, they sailed from the Port of Melbourne for Tasmania. Two weeks were set aside for Launceston, where Mrs. Henry Reed entertained the mission party. Grief over her husband's death had so overshadowed Mrs. Reed, that she had almost forgotten how to smile. The sunny, encouraging manner of Charles Alexander, combined with that tender sympathy of heart that always kept his merry ways from jarring on those in sorrow, drew her out, restoring to her some of the sunshine that had seemed gone for ever with her loved one's presence. On July 16th, Mrs. Reed wrote him: " In reading the Revelation, the thought came into my mind, that perhaps the dear Lord will be so gracious as to appoint leaders of His praises even in Heaven. If you are faithful down here, He may honour you with such a position up there. What do you think of ' Ten thousand times ten thousand, and thousands of thousands ' ! "

Numbers turned to Christ, and one of the conversions that greatly stirred Launceston was that of Jim Burke, the champion pugilist of Tasmania, a man of desperate character and evil reputation. One night, to the surprise of everyone, he was seen in the meeting, and was one of the first to take an open stand for Christ. Dr. Torrey had received a post card from Jim Burke saying, " Please call at my house, my wife is sick." On calling, Dr. Torrey found that he had been mistaken for a doctor of medicine ! He invited the pugilist to the meetings, and the reckless fighting-man was completely changed. " I testified for Jesus last night, at the Christian Union, and several came out for the Lord," wrote Jim Burke a few days after his conversion. " The people, in the street where I live, sing, ' It's good enough for the pugilist, and it's good enough for me.' "

From Launceston the mission party went to Hobart, Tasmania's capital, one of the beauty spots of the world, lying on the shores of its lovely harbour, with Mount Wellington in the background. The Mayor, Alderman Kerr, a fearless, sincere Christian, extended a public reception to the evangelists. Accompanied by the Salvation Army band, and followed by a large torchlight procession, the new arrivals were taken straight from the station to the Town Hall, which was packed with an enthusiastic audience. Rev. Henry Worrall describes his first impression of Charles Alexander : " He has risen and thrown off his great overcoat. In repose, we thought his face bore signs of weariness, but he looks down from the platform on the crowd, and smiles. That smile transfigures the man ! Now there is sunshine in his face, and laughter in his eyes. He knows nothing of the stereotyped forms of public address. He spoke to us as if he were a big brother of ours, who had returned after a long absence and needed no introduction. The platform disappeared by some strange magic, and there, upon the hearthstone of our home, stood our brother Charlie, talking with mother, father, brothers and sisters. Hobart fell in love with Charles Alexander the first moment it saw him, and heard him say, ' Well, people, how *are* you ? ' Mr. Alexander told them that they might not like all that Dr. Torrey said, for he hit hard. ' If you sprinkle pepper on your hand, it wouldn't hurt in the least unless you had a sore there, and Dr. Torrey's pepper might touch some sore places.' He urged them to join heartily in personal work for Christ ; to pray, and not to criticize. ' When a horse stops to kick he is not pulling. Did you ever think of that ? ' said Mr. Alexander."

Some of the meetings were held in the Theatre Royal, and once more Mr. Worrall describes Charles Alexander at work : " The man was created for music as a canary was made to sing. He baffles description. Every chord in his soul is a harp-string, tuned to a noble key. There were great and impassioned moments yesterday, when he seemed to be not a singer, but an instrument, swept by the touch of an invisible hand. The performance is all so easy, so wonderful, so magnificent, that it casts a spell upon all. Fourteen hundred men and women, packed in pit and stalls and galleries, sit thrilled by melody. He woos the most incongruous audiences till they sing, simply because they cannot help it."

After the first few days in Hobart, it was found best to concentrate the meetings in the Methodist Church, which was larger than the Town Hall or the theatre, and could accommodate two thousand three hundred people. One night, Alexander's quick eyes caught sight of four little lads in the west gallery of the church.   Not one of them was more than nine years old, and they were gazing in wonder at the singing crowd.   " Say, boys, I'll give you a hymn-book each if you will sing that chorus ! "   By the magic of his persuasion they did it !   Never was a prettier scene enacted.   Four unknown little fellows began to sing so sweetly, that the vast audience broke out into a storm of applause.

On July 24th, the last night of the meetings, the crowds were so great that it was necessary to divide into two services.   At seven o'clock the church was packed with women ;   at 8.15 the throng of women passed out at one end, and a mass of men re-filled the church.   The hymn, " God be with you till we meet again," was sung by the men as if they never wished to stop.   Voicing the grateful farewell of the city, Mr. Worrall said :   " The historian of the next century, if he were wise, would not ignore the influence that has been exerted on the national life and character of the people by these wondrous evangelistic services . . . . Mr. Alexander, by his radiant personality, has deeply impressed himself on the religious life of Hobart, and leaves our city to-day, bearing with him the purest affection of thousands whose hearts have been thrilled by the glory of his sweet songs."

From Hobart, the Torrey-Alexander party sailed again to Australia, returning to Ballarat for a second short mission.   They then travelled northwards to Sydney, where a three-weeks' campaign opened, on August 5th, in the Town Hall.   Long before the hour announced, the hall was filled in every part by some four thousand people.   When Charles Alexander began his work with a carefully-trained choir of two hundred and fifty voices, a look of surprise passed over their faces. " Surely," said some, " there is a mistake !   They've sent the wrong man.   That can't be the Melbourne Alexander ! "   This was because there was an electric sharpness in the voice of the leader as he drilled his choir again and again.   " But," says *The Southern Cross*, " when he swung round on the audience, and his genial, kindly face lit up with emotion, as he sang ' The Old-time Religion,' a very different feeling swept through the crowd, and when his silvery voice rang out, ' Makes me love everybody,' the revulsion was complete.   Audience and choir at once fell in love with Mr. Alexander, and took him to their hearts.   In half-an-hour's time he had taught them 'The Glory Song,' 'The Old-time Religion,' and 'Oh, Wonderful Story.'   Mr. Alexander had captivated Sydney."

Throughout the three weeks, midday meetings for business men were held in the Centenary Hall.   It was amusing to see several hundred men struggling with a song entitled, " A Little Talk with Jesus," and trying to sing in fast time :

> In trials of every kind, praise God I always find,
> A little talk with Jesus makes it right, all right.

But, as a description of the meeting tells :   " Mr. Alexander had them in hand, and was determined that they should learn it.   ' Now this is a song with a hook in it, it will get hold of you and do you good !   It will stick to you like a burr ! That's good ! This is the livest meeting I've seen in Sydney. Let's make this the brightest spot in the city for the next two weeks.' "

At the morning service on a day of prayer, Alexander took the first hour. Between the outbursts of song he called for Scripture selections, and bright,

sparkling testimonies. " Now tell us, folks, have you had any home prayer
meetings ? If you have, how did you get on ? " In a moment the people were
on their feet. An Anglican clergyman, a sweet old lady, a Salvation Army major,
and many others, followed in quick succession with their joyous record. All the
time Alexander stood smiling, punctuating the reports with " That's fine," or
with a word of prayer, or a verse of " Count your blessings." " But I must quit,"
he cried at last, " and let Dr. Torrey preach." " No, no," called out Dr. Torrey,
" you are preaching the sermon this morning," and the testimonies continued for
a while. Then Dr. Torrey got the people on their knees, and they wrestled in prayer
for an outpouring of the Holy Spirit on the city. At noon, when a halt was called,
many refused to leave. To numbers present, it was a day of Pentecost.

On August 23rd, the evangelists set sail for New Zealand. Steaming through
the beautiful Sydney harbour and out through the Heads, four days of stormy
ocean voyage brought them to Wellington, the capital of the colony. A most
interesting echo of those days came, eighteen years later, in a letter from Mr.
Harry N. Holmes, then holding an important position in the London Y.M.C.A. :
" As the result of the great campaign held in Wellington, N.Z., in 1902, a Young
Men's Christian Association was formed in that city. I became its secretary in 1904,
remaining there for eight years. All the other Associations in New Zealand, and
the strong work existing to-day in every town in that country, largely received
their inspiration from Wellington, and from the great mission conducted there by
your husband and Dr. Torrey. Strangely enough, a young medical man called
in to see me to-day, who made the decision for Christ during that series of meetings.
This is only one among thousands of results of their visit to New Zealand."

A month's campaign in Christchurch, a town so English, as it lies upon its
River Avon, that you might imagine yourself in Shakespeare's Stratford, was filled
with the same wonderful evidences of God's power to save. Here, as at
Wellington, efforts were made to reach the men employed in the railway workshops,
at Addington, a few miles out of the city. Ministers and choir members from
Christchurch accompanied the mission party. A railway truck, with a small organ
hoisted upon it, formed a rough platform for speakers and choir, and an incident
that occurred during the song service, snapped by a friendly camera, has given
one of the most characteristic pictures of Charles Alexander at work. He had
provided himself with bundles of hymn-books, and when the men crowded round
for the singing to begin, he called out, " How many of you fellows will accept a
book of songs with my love ? " Hands went up all over the crowd. In a moment,
one packet after another was torn open, and Alexander was flinging the books out
to the men. The well-known picture shows him laughing in delight, as the men
scrambled for their treasures.

On all the long railway journeys from one part of New Zealand to another,
the train rarely stopped for a quarter of an hour or longer at any station, without
finding a crowd gathered for even a short service, led by the two men whose fame
had spread abroad through the colony. At one of these, close by the lorry which
made an impromptu platform, a little crippled boy, in an invalid's chair, lifted
his pale face to watch every movement of the evangelists with keen interest.

Alexander, as he stood to sing a solo, holding in his hand a copy of his *Revival Songs*, caught sight of the boy. Instantly bending over the edge of the lorry, with a kindly word or two, and pulling his fountain-pen from his pocket, he wrote in the book : " With my love, Charles M. Alexander." " Write and tell me if you like it," he said. Not long afterwards, he received a beautiful letter from the boy, telling of the joy and blessing the unexpected gift had been to him.

Timaru, Oamaru, and Palmerston all received short visits from the mission party. When they reached Dunedin, Charles Alexander had a real foretaste of Scotland. The hilly streets, with their mountainous background, and the burr of the Scottish accent everywhere, made it hard to realize that the mother country lay on the other side of the globe. Here, in the Garrison Hall, a crowd of two thousand five hundred gathered day after day. Though their voices swelled, perhaps, most triumphantly on the familiar psalms and paraphrases, they caught up the new songs eagerly, and soon Dunedin, like other cities, was ringing with the revival melodies. A special gathering for clergymen and ministers, presided over by the Professor of the Theological Hall of the University, was the means of spreading the influence and spiritual activity of the mission throughout southern New Zealand.

On Monday, September 29th, about two thousand people gathered at the railway station to bid farewell to their new friends. A hurried journey, with a stop at Invercargill for two days of large meetings in the Drill Hall, and the party arrived at the Bluff, whence they sailed, on October 1st, for Melbourne. Here a great farewell meeting was held in the Town Hall on October 6th, and soon the party were on their way by rail to Adelaide, where they joined their ship, S.S. *Rome*. After touching at Fremantle, Western Australia, their first port of call on the other side of the ocean was Colombo, Ceylon. Except for a trip to Kandy, the native capital of the island, which gave them some glimpses of the glorious scenery, they did not break their journey until reaching Madura, in India. Here for a few days they held meetings with the missionaries and others, and one night, through an interpreter, Dr. Torrey addressed a large congregation of Hindus.

In Madras, which they reached after a railway journey of seventeen hours, they were welcomed by Miss Mary Hill, an old student of the Moody Bible Institute, who was secretary of the Young Women's Christian Association. For about a week they held constant meetings, which a terrific monsoon did not succeed in hindering. A great work was done among the non-Christian student population, and about a hundred men and women from various ranks of life took their stand for Christ during the meetings. A great many Hindu church-members rose in a Sunday morning service to say that, though professedly Christian, they had never known till then the full assurance of being " *in* Christ." About thirty prayer circles were established in the city of Madras, and for some time afterwards news reached the evangelists of the wave of blessing that followed their visit.

The journey to Calcutta was made under difficulties, for, owing to the heavy monsoon rains, portions of the railway line had been washed away, and it was necessary to take a circuitous route. The change of plan gave an unexpected opportunity for preaching the Gospel at a railway junction, where they had to wait for several hours, to the delight of the missionaries and Indian Christians.

On reaching Calcutta, they were greeted by Mr. Campbell White, then the energetic secretary of the Young Men's Christian Association, and for two weeks meetings were held in the large Y.M.C.A. Hall.

The singing, both in Calcutta, and in Bombay, took a great hold of the people. Robert Harkness's playing, Charles Alexander's solos, and the way in which they themselves learned to sing many of the new hymns, brought a breath of rejoicing and freshness to the workers for Christ in those Indian cities. The spiritual life of the missionaries was revived, and many souls were brought to Christ.

It was in Calcutta that the story of Second-Timothy-two-fifteen made history again. Some of the soldiers, who attended the meetings in large numbers, were converted. One of them, who took a bold stand for Christ, told an interesting story of what had led to his decision. His mother was in England, and one day, as she picked up a London journal, she read in it a report of some of the meetings of the Torrey-Alexander mission in Australia. The account she read told the story of Second-Timothy-two-fifteen, taken down by a reporter as Alexander told it in Melbourne. The soldier's mother, as she read the story in England, was so interested, that she sent it out to her godless son, who was in the Indian Army in Calcutta. As he read it, the wonderful text laid hold of him. " I am not studying to be approved of God," he thought, and decided then and there to accept Christ and take an open stand in the meetings. It was remarkable how the famous text made an introduction for the evangelists wherever they went. Charles Alexander told of their arrival at Hobart, in Tasmania, when a great crowd, whose faces were all strange to them, were gathered on the dock. " But one big fellow," he said, " put his hand to his mouth and shouted, ' Second-Timothy-two-fifteen,' and we felt at home right away."

In Bombay, the last Indian city visited by the mission party, a series of meetings was held for a week. Again great blessing followed, and at these meetings, as well as at some held in Dr. and Mrs. Hume's wonderful schools for famine children, many people, old and young, were led into a clear knowledge of Christ as their Saviour.

At last the day came, when, leaving India behind, they took ship for the shores of England.

CHAPTER SEVEN

Gospel Songs and their Ministry

NO one ever asks why the birds sing, because we know that they act in obedience to Nature's law, and burst into song as naturally and as easily as they breathe or fly. And no one who ever heard Charles Alexander sing, or who watched him as he lifted a great crowd, on the wings of music, into the heavenlies, needed to be told that he, like the birds, sang because there was within him a holy impulse which he could not resist. It was not his profession to sing ; it was his very life.

Long before the dawn of those great opportunities which drew him round and round the globe, inspiring Christians everywhere to the joyful service of praise and of zeal for souls, Charles Alexander had learned the power and the value of sacred song. In the home of his boyhood in Tennessee he had seen the influence of it upon the lives of the community in which he lived. He had seen it at work in the scattered villages of the beautiful Tennessee and North Carolina mountains. In his first evangelistic work with John Kittrell, he had seen its power to melt sin-hardened hearts. Through his days of training at the Moody Bible Institute he had been a keen student of religious movements. In an article on Gospel hymns, he says : " I do not recall any religious awakening without Gospel singing. Music was a vital part of the revival under the Wesleys. The revival of 1859 was a time of hymn-singing. Gospel songs were fully half the power of the Moody and Sankey meetings, and we all know what a prominent part music played in the Welsh Revival. I have yet to see the first church that remained empty for long, where each person entered heartily into the singing of hymns. When singing is delegated to the few, with no responsibility upon the rest of the audience, the interest dies, the numbers dwindle, and all kinds of expedients must be resorted to in order to draw the people. This method crowds out music from its proper place, which should be co-ordinate with preaching. In order to maintain this equality, every individual must be made to feel his responsibility in the singing part of the worship. This is as true in a church service, as in an evangelistic meeting."

More, perhaps, than any man of this or any other generation, Charles Alexander revealed and demonstrated the great resources and possibilities of sacred song. From the time when he first realized that this was to be his God-given calling, he set himself to make people sing and to give them something worth singing. To the end, he was never satisfied with past achievements, and would constantly test one theory after another, working out his results with scientific care and exactness. On first acquaintance, his methods seemed to be full of spontaneous simplicity, but, behind the seeming ease of his work, lay the careful preparation into which the calculating brain and glowing heart had poured their best efforts.

He realized, to an unusual degree, the rivalry of Satan in the matter of music, which God has ordained for praise of Himself, and which, when perverted to other uses, may ruin, rather than upbuild, human character. Because of this strange fact, earnest Christians have at times refrained from music altogether, lest it lead them away from God. But Charles Alexander loved to trace the holy use of joyful music through all God's dealings with those who have trusted Him in every age of the world's history. He loved to read and tell how David appointed " singers with instruments of music " under the leadership of Chenaniah, who " instructed about the song because he was skilful " ; of how they " lifted up the voice with joy," as they, with all Israel, accompanied the Ark of God homewards from the house of Obed-edom. He loved to picture the dedication of the new Temple by Solomon, when " the trumpeters and singers were as one, to make one sound to be heard in praising and thanking the Lord " ; the re-dedication under Josiah, when " the singers, the sons of Asaph, were in their place " ; " the dedication of the wall of Jerusalem," rebuilt by the faithful efforts of Nehemiah and Ezra, which was celebrated " with gladness, both with thanksgivings and with singing," when the singers sang so, loudly, and the rejoicing of men, women and children was so exuberant, that " the joy of Jerusalem was heard even afar off."

In the New Testament, he read with delight of the songs of the angels at Bethlehem, announcing the arrival of the Son of God on the earth ; of the " psalms and hymns and spiritual songs " which rose from the gatherings of the first believers, from the time they knew that their Lord was risen from the dead ; of the songs of unconquerable faith which echoed through the old prison at Philippi in the darkness of midnight ; of the revelation of that " new song " which will make the vaults of Heaven ring throughout eternity. But, most of all, he loved to read of the close of that long, tender conversation between our Lord and His disciples on the eve of the crucifixion, when, before descending the stairs from the upper room in Jerusalem, and making their way in the moonlight to the garden of Gethsemane on the slopes of Olivet, they sang a hymn together ! " How I would have loved to hear His voice singing a hymn ! " Alexander would often say.

Whenever he met with any objection to his fondness for interesting people in freshly-written songs and hymns, his rejoinder was, " Well, I love the good old standard hymns as much as you do, but don't forget that we are told in the Psalms to ' sing unto the Lord a *new* song.' " Praise and prayer were parts of a whole to him. He rarely began even a preliminary practice with a choir, without saying, " Let us have a word of prayer first, and then the singing will go better." He never for a moment permitted his choir to think that the beauty of a song was an end in itself. Always, the purpose for which it was sung was held up before them. This is why he insisted constantly upon clear enunciation of the words, and upon the intelligent interest of every member of the choir. He would often pray, " Help them to sing with the heart, and with the understanding also."

At the beginning of the mission in Bangor, Ireland, in the Spring of 1911, an incident occurred, illustrating his concern for the spiritual responsibility of the singers. Charles Alexander met the choir the day before Dr. Chapman arrived. Eager and expectant, the singers gathered. The first thing he asked them to sing was the chorus, " O Lord, send a revival, and let it begin in me ! " As soon as they had learned the melody, he told them the story of the young Welsh girl who had first uttered the words in a small meeting, and had started the blaze of revival which spread all over Wales in 1905. Over and over again the Bangor choir sang, until the hall rang with the melody. Lifting his hand, Alexander suddenly hushed them into silence. " Now you know the tune," he said, " but what do the words mean to you ? Have you thought that, before Dr. Chapman ever preaches a word, you have a chance to sing the message ? We want a revival here. Why should it not begin in the choir ? Let us sing it softly now, and make it a prayer." The earnest appeal that followed brought great results, for the Holy Spirit was working, and nine members of the choir who had never before taken a stand for Christ, rose to acknowledge Him openly as their Saviour.

The wonderful effects gained by Charles Alexander through his skilful use of song aroused curiosity everywhere. Over and over again, people tried to explain his power as personal magnetism, and spoke of him as hypnotizing the crowds into singing. But these things were generally said by those who had little experience of the power of the Holy Spirit, when the instrument of an entirely consecrated life is placed at His service.

To explain how it was that some of the simple songs he used could produce such wonderful spiritual results, Charles Alexander was constantly asked to write articles for newspapers and magazines. In one of these, he told the people of Boston : " There is a wonderful influence in song, and that influence spreads with great rapidity when once it gets started. To become quickly popular, songs must be easy to learn ; there must be a simple, easy, flowing melody, and a small range, not much over an octave, and a picture in every line of every verse. The words must be simple, but full of faith, hope and promise. I never make up any final list of songs before I go to a meeting. As soon as I come on the platform I begin to study my audience, and then select my first song in accordance with my impression of what the people desire, or of what may reach them. If the first verse does not go well, I go no further with it, and sing something else. It is not my method to sing new songs exclusively ; I frequently have a new one first, in order to get the people interested, and then follow with an old one which has appropriate relation to the other. For instance, what can be more effective than to begin with ' He will hold me fast,' and follow with ' Safe in the arms of Jesus ' ; or, after the solo, ' Is He yours ? ' ' Blessed assurance, Jesus is mine ' ? "

An incident which occurred in a men's meeting in the Sydney Town Hall one night in August, 1912, illustrates the influence of this way of using the hymns. Choir and congregation had been singing " Where is my wandering boy to-night ? " The second verse was sung by the men of the congregation, standing. A wave of the hand brought the whole of the vast company to its feet, as if in earnest entreaty, when they began the last verse. The voicing of the line " Bring him to me

with all his blight " spoke of a yearning desire to make the words tell. Without
a break, the chorus, " Lord, I'm coming Home," followed on, making the answer
very personal to those who sang it.

> Coming Home, coming Home,
> Never more to roam ;
> By Thy grace I will be Thine,
> Lord, I'm coming Home.

It welled up from the floor, and floated down from the galleries time and again,
bringing to mind how many wanderers are always to be met with in any such
gathering.   These need a word of invitation, and it was given by Dr. Chapman in
his tenderest tones.   His appeal for decision made, Dr. Chapman was about to
ask those who desired it to rise for prayer, when from the centre of the hall, a dozen
seats back, there rose an old man, bent with age, grasping his hat and stick to make
his way, as it seemed, out of the building.   It was a palpable interruption to the
appeal, but the old man, instead of turning to leave, went straight up to the
reporters' table, near the platform, and knelt there for prayer.   " God bless you,"
was the fervent prayer uttered by the preacher, echoed in hushed tones through
all the audience, as the aged wanderer " came Home," to the Lord.

It was a great discovery for Charles Alexander, when he realized that busy
men who thought they could not sing, or take time for singing, were like a crowd
of boys, when they came together in a meeting, and sang just as heartily.   He
found that down in every man's heart there is a love of song, and that even the
men who had no sympathy with Christianity as they knew it, liked the Gospel
hymns, and would come to hear them.   Many and many a time these songs clung
to a man day and night, and eventually led him to Jesus.   Alexander never sang,
or set others singing, without feeling sure that some one would be laid hold of, and
be transformed into a new being.   This expectancy, and its constant fulfilment,
so revived him, that he could go to a crowded song service, and after three or four
hours' work, feel fresher than at the start.   In London, during the never-to-be-
forgotten Albert Hall Mission, it was an almost everyday experience, throughout
the two months, for people to stay from two o'clock till six.   " Dr. Torrey," to
quote Alexander's account of those marvellous days, " would take up three-
quarters-of-an-hour preaching, and all the rest of the time, before and after the
sermon, men and women in the galleries and boxes would be calling for some simple
Gospel song.   After a hasty meal, we would go back and sing again till nearly eleven
I have never seen any other kind of music that would get hold of people like this."

The contrast between the effect of an ordinary song and that of a Gospel hymn
was always pressed home by the great leader.   " Long ago," he said, " I found
that when I got people worked up by a concert or something of that kind, it stopped
there.   I would be all exhausted, and to no purpose.   I would ask myself :
' Where did I take those people ?   Where did I land them, anyway ?   There must
be something more in the world than this.'   Now, when I am at work from ten
o'clock in the morning until nearly midnight, I go home feeling satisfied that I
have been doing the *best* work in the world.   But I believe in taking pains to use
hymns that really help and save people, and not wasting time on others."

AN
AFTERNOON
MEETING
IN
BINGLEY
HALL,
BIRMINGHAM,
ENGLAND,
JANUARY,
1904

ST.
GEORGE'S
MARKET,
BELFAST,
IRELAND,
1903
Meeting timed
to begin
at 8 p.m.
See the clock--
6:30 p.m.!

BUSINESS MEN'S NOONDAY MEETING IN MELBOURNE TOWN HALL, MAY, 1902.
Dr. Torrey preaching. C. M. Alexander and J. J. Virgo by piano.

SOME MAKERS OF GOSPEL HYMNS

WITH GEORGE C. STEBBINS

WITH PROFESSOR DANIEL B. TOWNER

MISS ADA R. HABERSHON

HENRY BARRACLOUGH

ROBERT HARKNESS

" You fellows know," he said once to a business men's club in Toronto, at which he was the principal guest, " that if you try a thing and it doesn't do the business, you quit it.   I get the songs that *do the business*, and if I find one that won't, I cut it right out.   I hesitated a long time before I would use the song, ' Tell mother I'll be there.'   I have been criticized all over the world for using it, but you would not criticize if you knew what it has done, and what letters and testimonies I have received about it.   The song had an interesting origin.   When President McKinley was in office, his mother lay dying in Canton, Ohio, several hundred miles away.   She sent word that she wanted to see her boy once more before she died.   President McKinley chartered a special train, and telegraphed ' Tell mother I'll be there.'   A Gospel-song writer caught up the idea and wrote the song.   A friend of mine cut it out of a magazine, and sent it to me with a suggestion that I try it in my work.   I pasted it in my scrap-book, more for my friend's sake than because I saw any merit in it, and carried it around for a year before I ever used it.   One night in Newton, Kansas, my last campaign with Williams, I was called on to sing a solo.   I saw in the audience a great crowd of railway men, and said to myself : ' I wonder what would reach those men.'   With some doubt, I finally decided to try this touching song, and was surprised at the extraordinary result.   Many of the men confessed Christ immediately.   When the meeting was over, one big, burly engineer came up to me and said, ' Mr. Alexander, I promised my mother on her death-bed that I would become a Christian ; but, instead of that, I have been going to the devil faster than ever.   Preaching never touched me, but this song did.   If you will sing it to-morrow night, I will bring the men.'   He did bring them for many nights, and he used to call out : ' Sing " Tell mother I'll be there." '   I used the song every night, and I have been using it ever since.   I have seen as many as one hundred and fifty men at a single meeting rise and confess Christ, during the singing of that hymn, before the sermon was begun.   Everywhere it has been the same.   It reaches all classes, because everybody has a mother.   It has been criticized from a musical, and from a literary, standpoint, but no song has ever been written that can take the place of it.   Those who criticize are unable to replace it with a better."

Of all the songs with which the name of Charles M. Alexander is linked, perhaps the " Glory Song " stands first.   Both the words and music of it were written in Chicago by Charles H. Gabriel, one of the most popular Gospel-hymn writers of America.   " I remember quite well," Alexander once wrote, " the first time I ever saw this song.   In looking over a new song-book, I just glanced at it, and said, ' That man has wasted a page, for I do not believe that song will be sung much.'   Some months later, however, I stepped into a large Sunday-school convention, and heard an audience singing it.   It took such a hold of me that I could think of nothing else for days thereafter.   I got all my friends to sing it.   I dreamed about it, and awoke to the rhythm of it.   Then I began to teach it to large audiences, and soon whole towns were ringing with the haunting refrain.

The " Glory Song " captured Melbourne in a single night, and from there swept through the whole of Australia.   " At the close of our first revival campaign in Melbourne," wrote Charles Alexander, " it seemed to me that everybody in the

E

city was singing the ' Glory Song.'   People going away on the suburban trains were singing it.   Brass bands played it, and it was sung and played in all sorts of out-of-the-way places.   The last day I was in Melbourne, I had to rise early to catch a train for Warrnambool.   As I came out of my room the maid was scrubbing the floor of the hall outside my door, and softly crooning :

> When by His grace, I shall look on His face,
> That will be glory for me.

I went down to the hotel office, and took the receiver off the telephone, wishing to ring up to a friend across the city.   As I placed the receiver to my ear, I heard the girl at the telephone exchange singing, as she clicked the pegs into their places :

> Oh, that will be glory for me.

As the train passed through Terang, a couple whom Alexander had met in Melbourne came down to the station to meet him, and they had a few words together.   The lady said, " Mr. Alexander, I am sure you will be interested to know anything about the ' Glory Song.'   I learned it at the meetings in Melbourne.   I have been over to-day to see a friend on her death-bed.   I sang one verse of the ' Glory Song,' and she said, ' Oh, that is glorious ; please sing another.'   I sang another, and while I was singing the chorus, ' When by His grace I shall look on His face,' she passed to see the King in His beauty."

" I suppose few songs have spread all over the world as the ' Glory Song ' has done," Charles Alexander was frequently heard to say.   " I have received translations in Chinese, Dutch, German, Italian, Danish, Welsh, Zulu, and other languages, and have received letters from places all over the globe, where it has become a favourite.   Some people try to analyse it, and say that it has no power, but people keep right on calling for it, and singing it."

A touching story is told by Charles Alexander of the influence of this song. " When Dr. Torrey and I were conducting our campaign in the great Town Hall, Sydney, Australia, we distributed leaflets with the ' Glory Song,' words and music, and an invitation to the meetings printed at the bottom.   We would ask the people, if they already possessed a copy of the song-book, to post the leaflets to friends in the country who never get new songs, or to put them in parcels as they sent them away.   One day, after I had asked them to do this, a lady, when she reached home, was sending some shoes to be mended.   She happened to think about her ' Glory Song ' leaflet, and put it into the bundle with the shoes.   The next day she went down to the shoemaker's to get them, and found the old fellow pegging away, with the tears rolling down his cheeks.   She asked, ' What is the matter ? ' and he answered, ' Do you remember the " Glory Song " that you put into the bundle ?   Last night I got my little family round the organ and we sang it.   I noticed the invitation to come to the Town Hall and hear Torrey and Alexander, so I went last night.   I heard that man preach, and I gave my heart to God.   I have sent my wife and children up to this afternoon's meeting, and I am just here praying that God will save them.'   And God did save them.   The next night the whole family publicly confessed their acceptance of Jesus Christ."

Many books could be written about the songs used by Charles M. Alexander.

A number of them were composed under the direct inspiration of his influence. Robert Harkness tells how he was led to write the music to one of his early hymns— "Never lose sight of Jesus": "Mr. Alexander came upon the words in Glasgow, and said to me: 'I want you to put a new tune to them.' I looked at the words for a long time, and began to write settings. I suppose I wrote a dozen, submitting them to him, but somehow or other he could not be pleased. In desperation I put the hymn aside. At last, in Aberdeen, a month later, he said: 'You really must write a tune for that hymn.' I sat down in the drawing-room at the piano, and he went up to pray that I might get the right tune. At once I struck upon the chorus, and began to play softly. He rushed out of his room, with his coat off, and said, 'That's the tune! Hold on to that!' So the tune came quite naturally at last, and has since become popular everywhere."

Occasionally the hymns came to Charles Alexander from unexpected sources, and would never have been known, but for that intuition of his, which made him so keenly sensitive to the true value of a hymn. He tells how, on opening his letters one morning in Philadelphia, he came upon the manuscript of a short hymn. The writer of the accompanying letter said, that, in reading the reports of the meetings, she had been impressed by the confidence with which prayer was spoken of, and ventured, because of this, to send a hymn she had just written, entitled "Pray Through." It had been refused by several publishers, and she said that if Mr. Alexander thought it would be useful, he might have it. He soon began to use it, and found it most helpful wherever it was sung. Later on, he met the composer, and asked her what had suggested the thought of the song to her. She told him she had had a great deal of trouble, and was so overwhelmed by it, she felt that no human power could bring relief. At breakfast one morning, after days of prayer, she opened a letter which completely removed her trouble. As she finished reading the good news, the thought, which is the title of the hymn, "Pray Through," came to her, and before she had left the table she had written the song, both words and music.

An experience of his own was always printed below this song in Alexander's hymn-books:—" I was standing at a bank counter in Liverpool, waiting for a clerk to come. I picked up a pen and began to print on a blotter, in large letters, two words which had gripped me like a vice: PRAY THROUGH. I kept talking to a friend, and printing, until I had the big blotter filled from top to bottom with a column. I transacted my business and went away. The next day my friend came to see me, and said he had a striking story to tell me. A man had gone into the bank soon after we had left. He had grown discouraged with business troubles. He started to transact some business with that same clerk over that blotter, when his eye caught the long column of PRAY THROUGH. He asked who wrote those words, and when he was told, exclaimed, 'That is the very message I needed. I *will* pray through. I have tried to worry through in my own strength, and have merely mentioned my troubles to God; now I am going to pray the situation through until I get light.'"

"Looking this way"; "He will hold me fast"; "He lifted me"; "I surrender all"; and numberless other hymns from Alexander's wonderful collection, are surrounded by an ever-growing romance of blessing and uplifting influence upon the lives of people. How many quarrels have been made up, and how much coldness melted, by the haunting repetition of the old negro melody—

> Makes me love ev'rybody, . . .
> And it's good enough for me.

This brings to mind the way in which Charles Alexander always traced the music of Gospel songs, which was wafted over the British Empire from America, to the influence of the negro melodies. In contrast to the regular rhythm of the older standard hymns, a Gospel song has a lilting swing and flow that is essentially American, and owes its origin to the pathetic strains of the days of slavery. Yet there must have been some other influence behind those negro melodies, for they are nowhere found amongst the Africans in their own continent. Charles Alexander's theory was that they were built up by the Southern negroes, in the pathos of their helpless condition, upon the foundation of those minor strains of the old Scottish psalms and songs, brought over by the pioneer settlers from the land of their birth to the Southern mountains of their adopted country. Whenever he wanted to train a writer of Gospel hymns, Alexander would always try to get him saturated with the rhythm and bubbling freshness of the music of the coloured people. Another thing he learned from this source was the constant reiteration, in the words of a hymn or chorus, of some one main thought that he wished to lay hold of the mind. This may be seen in his choice of the hymns he made use of, and in those which he helped to inspire.

A reference must also be made to his constant use of short, gripping choruses, which he so largely used among the children, but found were just as useful to the " children of larger growth." " This is portable—you can carry it round without a morocco-covered book," he would often say, in teaching such choruses as, " I am included " ; " When God forgives He forgets " ; " Travelling Home " ; or " Shine." With regard to the children, he always insisted that, to a very large extent, children get their theology from the hymns which they sing. As this again is true of grown-up people as well, Alexander felt that no pains should be spared to ensure that the teaching of the hymns in his collections was strictly in accordance with that of the Word of God ; and he preferred, wherever possible, the actual words of Scripture. This was the reason why he loved so dearly the hymns written by his old friend Major D. W. Whittle (El Nathan), so often set to music by his co-worker James McGranahan.

Never did Charles Alexander tire of the ministry of song, which to him was an ever-fresh delight. When asked to account for this, he was once heard to reply, " It is the work the Lord has given me to do, and I guess He will tell me when it is time to stop." Without doubt, many a soul greets him to-day in heaven because of the Gospel songs he taught the people of many lands to sing.

CHAPTER EIGHT

Opening of the British Campaign
1903

FROM early boyhood, Charles Alexander had heard and read of those islands across the ocean from which his forefathers had come to the Southern mountains of Tennessee. Many a time, in fancy, he had ranged over the wild Scottish mountains, swathed in their grey mists, or had wandered through the green fields and cathedral cities of old England. As he left behind him the glare and glitter of the Orient, and the ancient cities of India, his heart beat fast with expectancy at the thought of seeing the country of which he had so long dreamed.

He reached London in December, 1902, a week or two in advance of Dr. and Mrs. Torrey, who had broken their journey by a short stay on the Continent. He was accompanied only by his secretary, Rupert Lowe, and Robert Harkness, the pianist. Tidings of the marvellous outpouring of spiritual blessing in Australia had been reaching England during the past months, by private letter and public report, from the Antipodes, and also from India. As a result, an earnest invitation had been sent, asking the evangelists to break their journey to America by a stay in the British Isles. When Dr. Torrey arrived in London, a public welcome meeting was held in Exeter Hall on January 9th, 1903, when the large hall was filled to overflowing. The meeting was presided over by Mr. T. A. Denny, and a hearty welcome extended by Lord Kinnaird, Rev. F. B. Meyer, and Rev. Thos. Spurgeon. Prebendary Webb-Peploe, Mr. Henry Varley, and Dr. J. Monro Gibson also took part in the service, which followed a reception. Hundreds who had been workers in the Moody and Sankey meetings had the joy of coming into personal touch with the two men, who were, by the leading of God, to be so closely bound up with the cause of evangelism in Great Britain for the next three years. Before the evening ended, Charles Alexander sang a solo, with the refrain :

> Come in, come in, Holy Spirit,
>   Thy work of great blessing begin ;
> By faith I lay hold of Thy promise,
>   And claim complete vict'ry o'er sin.

So deep was the impression, that, after a few moments of hushed silence, the audience was only restrained with difficulty from breaking out into a round of applause.

A three weeks' mission began at Mildmay Park the following day. The great Conference Hall was chilly and gloomy, and was only half-filled, and the people who had gathered there were not easily stirred into enthusiasm. But when the

evening came all sombreness had vanished, and the singing, followed by the earnest
addresses of Dr. Torrey, soon made the atmosphere radiant with anticipation of a
great work of God.   Alexander succeeded in making the new messages in Gospel
song take hold of the hearts of the people who filled the Conference Hall night
after night, and he also began at once, in his own inimitable way, to draw the people
out into taking part themselves.   Many of the afternoon meetings were turned
into times of praise and testimony.   Very soon, lips that had been tightly closed
became accustomed to frequent and natural expression, which made them ready,
as nothing else could have done, for the work of soul-winning.   Many of the old-
time hymns came with freshness and power, and Alexander's manipulation of the
forces at his disposal was a revelation in musical leadership, while the brilliant
playing of Robert Harkness aroused keen interest.   Night after night, following
Dr. Torrey's appeal, Alexander's voice would plead in song.   The question—

> Would you believe, and Jesus receive,
> If He were standing here ?

came as a direct and arresting challenge.   Sometimes he would repeat the last
phrase, making a long pause before the final word, until, in the solemn hush
that fell upon the crowd, the singer seemed to fade from sight, and a vision of
Christ came to the listening congregation.   When Dr. Torrey repeated the call
for decision, men and women rose to signify their allegiance to the Lord Jesus.

At the close of the Mildmay Mission in London, the Torrey-Alexander party
went northwards without delay, to be welcomed in Edinburgh on the evening of
February 1st, for the opening of their Scottish Campaign.   The weather had been
stormy for some time, and on that first Sunday morning in the northern metropolis
snow was falling heavily.   In spite of this, a large company of Christian workers
gathered at Carrubbers Close Mission from all parts of the city, to extend a warm
greeting to Dr. Torrey and Mr. Alexander.   Prof. (afterwards Sir) A. R. Simpson presided.   The sweet, childlike trust of his earnest prayer, and the vim and enthusiasm
with which Alexander led the people in song, augured well for the work of the
coming weeks.   That evening Synod Hall was filled to overflowing, as well as St.
Cuthbert's Church, where Dr. Torrey was preaching.   There had been some doubt
beforehand as to how the unconventional methods of Charles Alexander would
appeal to the cautious reserve of the Scottish people, but he was well acquainted
with the ultra-Scottish temperament of the dwellers in his native mountains, and
knew what to expect, so was not disappointed to be on probation for a while.

Mr. J. Kennedy Maclean, who was present in this first gathering at Edinburgh,
and in many another that followed, writes :—" No zone could long remain frozen
in his sunny presence, and all doubts, and fears, and hesitations, melted away as
soon as his gracious personality began to diffuse its warmth and radiance.   The
glow of those wonderful days comes to me across the years, as I look back upon
scenes and experiences that did for me, and for others, much more than we realized
at the time.   It was a new thing that was being done through the medium of Mr.
Alexander's superb leadership.   He not only sang himself, but by the force of his
genius compelled every one who heard him to sing too.   Taken captive by the

" Glory Song " just as Australasia had been, Edinburgh awoke to the rare possibilities of these new songs, which swept the city like one great emancipating and redeeming chorus. In his solo work, it was not only the rich quality of Mr. Alexander's voice that carried home the message with such powerful effect. His serious, earnest manner gave a sense of reality to his words, forcing a conviction upon the hearers that he really meant what he was singing."

At the public welcome to Scotland that was given to the evangelists, Dr. James C. Russell, as Moderator of the Church of Scotland ; Principal Rainy, representing the United Free Church of Scotland ; Principal Hodgson, speaking for the Congregational Churches ; and ex-Bailie W. S. Brown, representing the civic authorities, voiced the welcome of thousands of Scottish Christians. In the theatre, in which some of the meetings were held, the great gallery was reserved for University students. Throughout the month, daily scenes were witnessed of numbers turning to Christ. " One night," says Dr. Torrey, " in scholarly, classic, conservative Edinburgh, two hundred men walked down the aisle and confessed their acceptance of Jesus." From Edinburgh the mission party went to Glasgow, where they laboured through March. The first meeting in St. Andrew's Hall was held on Sunday afternoon, March 1st. One who was there that day says : " In a small hall, entering from Kent Road, we met Mr. Alexander, who said, ' Is there no place where we can have prayer before we go up to the big hall ? ' Three of us turned in behind a curtain, where we knelt down and prayed earnestly. At the close of the afternoon service he called the choir together and got them to run over the ' Glory Song.' In the hall at night, which was densely packed with a great throng, he led the choir in his best style, and as the ' Glory Song ' was sung, a wonderful impression was made. That great crowd saw the man at work, and admired and were impressed by his musical gifts, but they had not heard the earnest prayer behind the curtain in the early afternoon."

The month of April was spent in the granite city of Aberdeen. A letter from Charles Alexander, dated April 17th, from the Central Hotel, Bridge Street, was received by Miss E. W. MacGill, who, years later, came into close touch with him through the work of the Pocket Testament League. As secretary of the Grove Street Institute, Glasgow, founded by her father, she had been among the foremost workers in the Glasgow campaign, and had been sending reports of the follow-up work in that great city. " It is uplifting," wrote Charles Alexander, " to hear your report, and I am going to read part of it at the meeting to-night, for it is too good to keep to myself. It has been snowing steadily here for four days, but we are having packed houses, and last night there were fifty-nine conversions. This afternoon we had a children's meeting. At the big services we have an additional choir, made up of girls between the ages of ten and sixteen, and they make quite a bright feature in the meetings. Our eyes are looking homeward now, for it will only be about two months until we land in America." A week later he wrote again to Miss MacGill :—" The crowds keep up and many are being converted. I want you to be taking notes of the most interesting incidents in connexion with our mission in Glasgow, and also to study the far-reaching influence of the work, so that you may be able to tell it in compact and striking form when you come to us in Belfast. Now don't disappoint us in this. So often people come, and are not prepared to speak. Afterwards they say, ' I knew so many interesting things, but could not think of them.' So you can prepare before-hand." This letter shows one of the things that had laid hold of Alexander's soul. He always felt that too much effort was made in the usual work of the churches to produce upon people a deep and powerful *im*pression, without giving sufficient opportunity for *ex*pression. Wherever he went he was always trying to rouse people who professed to be Christians into definite effort for the salvation of others, and he knew that nothing would stir them so readily as constant, fresh testimony about recent and genuine signs of God's working.

It would make a long list, to tell of all the deep and wonderful friendships formed by Charles Alexander among his new acquaintances in Scotland. Lord and Lady Overtoun took a prominent part in the missions, and extended their warm hospitality to the mission party. Sir Samuel Chisholm, Councillor (now Sir) Joseph P. Maclay, Mr. John W. Arthur, Mr. William M. Oatts, and Pastor D. J. Findlay were amongst those who were bound to him in friendship from that time onwards. He renewed acquaintance also with Lord Kinnaird, Rev. John McNeill, and others whom he had met in his student days at the Chicago Bible Institute.

From Scotland, the mission party crossed to Ireland, and during the month of May a series of meetings was held in Belfast which stirred the whole city. The halls and churches used at first were found quite inadequate, and finally St. George's Market was taken, and seated to accommodate seven thousand people.

Dr. Henry Montgomery—an old friend of Mr. Moody's—and Dr. Harry Guinness, were among the principal leaders in this wonderful revival. A Belfast banker writing to Charles Alexander's mother on June 2nd, 1903, said :—" Your son captivated every one. He was a great favourite on account of his winning, Christ-like spirit."

In June, the five months' campaign in England, Scotland, and Ireland came to an end. It had been a wonderful crown to all the marvellous experiences of Charles Alexander's first journey round the world in the service of Christ. And now, after an absence of fourteen months from his native land, his face was turned homewards at last. With the party to America went two of the daughters of Dr. Henry Montgomery, who were bound on a visit to the Moody Institute, also a London journalist, Mr. David Williamson.

Belfast's farewell to the mission party was a memorable one. An immense crowd had gathered on the dock, and were singing, led by the Salvation Army band, when the evangelists appeared. " Is there a man here who will accept the Lord Jesus Christ ? " appealed Dr. Torrey, after a few earnest words. Right there, on the crowded dock, there were nine responses to his invitation. As the ship began to move out into the water, Alexander leaned over the rail of the upper deck, leading the throng on shore with a waving handkerchief. Out across the ever-widening distance floated the message from thousands of throats, " God be with you till we meet again." When the sound of voices died away on the breeze, the fluttering of handkerchiefs from the mile-long crescent of the dock could still be seen. A voice at his elbow caused Alexander to turn. " The captain sends his compliments, sir, and shall he blow the whistle ? " And to the waiting people on shore came a last, long-distance message of farewell from the vanishing ship.

" It was my happy fortune," writes Mr. David Williamson, " to travel with Dr. Torrey and Mr. Alexander on their return to America. At first, some of the passengers held aloof from the evangelists, but very soon the irresistible sociability and kindliness of Mr. Alexander thawed the ice. Before long we had the usual ship's concert, and Dr. Torrey was asked to preside, and Mr. Alexander to sing. Both men took part in deck-games, and were the most popular of passengers when we neared New York. Mr. Alexander realized the interest which the long tour of Dr. Torrey and himself had awakened, and I recollect his intense anxiety that he might be saved from any indiscreet or vainglorious remarks to the journalists who, he knew, would seek interviews. Very soon we had proof of the fame of the evangelists, for reporters came on board before the ship docked. How clearly that first evening in America comes back to my memory ! We stayed at the Murray Hill Hotel, where D. L. Moody used to stay, and Mr. Alexander was delighted to be once more in his native land. Characteristically, he insisted on going that night to the Water Street Mission, to grasp Sam Hadley by the hand, and teach a song to some of the poor wastrels in the hall."

Only the man who returns to his own country for the first time after so long an absence could enter into the exuberance of Charles Alexander's feelings. Yet he knew what it meant to be a stranger in a strange land, and he did not forget that while he was at home once more, the two Irish girls who were travelling with the party were experiencing that strange sense of loneliness. The sisters Montgomery had just retired to their room after returning from Water Street, when a knock brought them to the door. There stood Alexander, holding in each hand a magnificent rose with a sturdy, yard-long stem. " I wanted you to have an ' American Beauty ' rose to make you feel at home ! " And with a radiant smile he was gone. Alexander could hardly restrain his eager impatience to reach Chicago, for not only would that complete the last link in the long chain of journeyings that had circled the globe, but there at the Moody Institute were his sister, Ida, and his brother, Homer ; and soon, ah, soon, a train from Tennessee would be bearing northwards his younger brother, Leo, and the beloved little mother who had been enshrined in his loving heart through all the days of their separation. On Chicago station they were met by D. L. Moody's son-in-law, Mr. A. P. Fitt, and others from the Bible Institute. " Hardly had they arrived," to quote Mr. Williamson again, " than the journalists and photographers also arrived. Next day, and indeed for four or five days, columns upon columns of letterpress, illustrated with photographs, appeared in all the Chicago papers. It was curious to observe how Australian and British recognition of Dr. Torrey and his colleague had made their own countrymen realize their worth. A welcome meeting was held in the Auditorium, and a wonderful affair it was. Two hours before it began thousands assembled, and it was said that only Theodore Roosevelt had previously drawn such a crowd. In that hall was one who had never before witnessed Charles Alexander's consecrated genius in moving so vast an audience. It was his mother, and she was overcome with the sight, as well she might be. In later years she was destined to be present on several memorable occasions, but this was her first and unforgettable experience of hearing her son sing to thousands, and making them sing also." A Chicago lawyer, the Hon. Luther Laflin Mills, presided at the meeting in the Auditorium. On the platform, besides the choir of six hundred under Prof. D. B. Towner, were many well-known Christian leaders, amongst them Dr. C. I. Scofield, Dr. James M. Gray, Major Cole, and Dr. J. Wilbur Chapman.

Charles Alexander captivated the great American audience quickly, as in Australia, India, and Great Britain, and soon they were singing his revival melodies as only Americans can sing when aroused to the highest pitch of enthusiasm.

The welcome meeting in the Auditorium was followed by a busy week of conference in the Moody Church and Bible Institute. Major Cole led the daily prayer meeting. Besides the addresses of Dr. Torrey, there were many other speakers, including Dr. Chapman. Alexander also took part, and directed the music. His informal talk on prayer, based on the hymn " Pray Through," made the power of prayer of more definite value to many. He also gave interesting addresses on the missions in Australia and " The Place of Music in Christian work."
" When we were students at Moody," wrote Mrs. Betts, of Chicago, in 1920, " Mr. Alexander was used of God, on his return from his world-trip with Dr. Torrey, to show us the immeasurable difference between service led of the Spirit, and that which was self-planned, and self-directed. He made my heart hungry to know the Lord better. I shall never forget a prayer service he conducted for a few students, so freighted with the Spirit's presence that we were melted before God."

Miss MacGill received another letter from Charles Alexander, dated June 24th, 1903. " I thought I should have oceans of time when I reached here and got the first welcome meeting off our hands, but I have not had any time to speak of. It has been business, business, speaking, and singing, all the time. Miss Lucy Montgomery and her sister are enjoying their stay splendidly. The people here want to keep Miss Lucy, but she feels she must go back home to help her father. I delivered the beautiful handkerchief to my mother, and she sends you her love. Thank you for the good you did when you came over to visit us at Belfast. I heard a great many people speak of the blessing you brought in your messages. Mr. David Williamson, who came over here with us, has returned home. He made a valuable addition to our party, both in the work he did with the newspapers and as a speaker. Next Tuesday I am going to my Southern home for a week or two. About the middle of August we sail again for Liverpool, then Dundee in October, and Manchester in November."

Before leaving America, Charles Alexander spent a few days at Northfield, Massachusetts, where the great schools stand as a lasting monument to Dwight L. Moody. " Mr. Alexander revelled in his visit to Mr. and Mrs. Will. R. Moody," wrote a friend, " and in telling them of the many traces he had found of the Moody and Sankey missions in Great Britain and Ireland ; also of the work of Mrs. Will Moody's father, Major Whittle. He made a pilgrimage to D. L. Moody's grave on Round Top, and thought nothing of singing as early as eight o'clock in the morning to the girl students, following it up with other public engagements. When last at Northfield, he was an unknown student from Chicago. He had returned a renowned evangelist, but there was not a trace of self-satisfaction about him. He only rejoiced at the opportunities for service, and seized them every hour."

The beginning of September, 1903, found Dr. Torrey and Charles Alexander once more in England. Dr. (now Bishop) J. Louis Fenn, who was the organizer of the great Liverpool missions, and was a loyal friend to Charles Alexander, describes a wonderful scene at the beginning of this new period of work in Great Britain. " Dr. Torrey and Mr. Alexander arrived in Liverpool from America on Sunday morning, September 5th. On the Monday afternoon, the committee on arrangements met the evangelists in the Y.M.C.A. The Rev. Musgrave Brown, Vicar of St. Clement's Church, and chairman of the executive, cordially welcomed them, calling on Dr. Torrey to give an outline of the work he hoped to do. When Mr. Alexander was asked to speak, he smiled and said, ' I don't talk.' But he taught them the chorus, ' O Lord, send the power just now, and baptize every one.' Over and over again this was sung by the company, largely composed of clergy and ministers, and the sense of God's presence was so great that spontaneously they fell upon their knees." From that hour no one doubted the success of the mission.

Writing to his mother from Dundee a month later, Charles Alexander himself told some of the incidents of the Liverpool meetings. *October 8th.*—" My darling mother," he wrote, " your beautiful letters have reached me, and have done me good. They contain so many things I want to hear, that I prize them highly and read them over and over, especially the little sweet spot that you always put at the close. It does warm my heart to know my little mammy cares to say such beautiful things to me. I think you would be interested in a short sketch of my trip over, and what I have done since arriving in Liverpool. We had twelve in our party ; Mrs. D. B. Towner and Miss Marguerite Towner, the two sisters Montgomery, of Belfast, Mr. Harkness and myself, came from Chicago through Montreal, where we met Dr. Torrey, his wife and family. There are three daughters, Edith, Blanche, and Margaret, and one boy, Reuben, who is a fine fellow. Dr. Torrey has secured rooms for his family on the seashore at Southport, north of Liverpool. Blanche is here, at Dundee, with us now. Prof. Towner is coming before we leave here. Miss Grace Saxe came over the last week of the Liverpool meetings to take up Bible-class work in connexion with our missions. Besides Rupert Lowe and two lady stenographers, I have a man helping me specially with the hymn-books —a Mr. Solaini. He is a fine Christian man of ability, only converted two years ago, and most interested in the work. He is the only man in our crowd who wears a silk hat, and we are very proud of him ! Mr. Lowe has developed splendidly. During the summer months he was away at the Keswick Convention, and then did some work among children at the seaside.

" It will be hard to give you an idea of the great Liverpool Mission, but I must tell you some things about it. We were in the Philharmonic Hall, which seats three thousand five hundred people. We had thirteen hundred and ninety choir members ; of course only about four hundred each time could be packed on to the platform, but they were beautifully arranged, and the hall was so adapted to singing that the effects were marvellous. Two hours before time the people would begin to gather, and the police would have to line them up four deep all around the building, so that there would not be such a rush when the doors were opened.   In five or six minutes the hall would be full, including galleries.   It was inspiring to stand on my special raised platform and see the thousands of upturned faces. I wish you could have heard the men sing the ' Glory Song.'

" You will want to know the result of the meetings.   When I tell you that four thousand eight hundred people confessed Christ in three weeks, you will know that the Lord worked wonderfully in the city.   Some of the nights, men would be lined up hours before time, standing in the rain and singing the songs.   There were about four thousand children packed into the building one afternoon—the best-behaved audience of children I think I have ever seen ; quiet, clean, well-dressed, gentle boys and girls.   While I was conducting the music, someone handed me a little note saying that on the platform back of me were about thirty blind children, and suggested that it would be nice to have them sing alone.   We were singing, ' Never lose sight of Jesus,' written by Mr. Harkness.   I told the children that we had some little blind friends on the platform who would sing it for us.   You can see that the title of the song would be very suggestive when sung by any-one who was blind.   They rose promptly, and in their sweet, soft voices sang :

> Day and night, He will lead you right,
> Never lose sight of Jesus.

A hush fell upon the audience, and many were melted to tears.   I am sure it will touch your heart when you read about it now.

" The greatest day that I have ever seen in evangelistic work was on the last Sunday we were in Liverpool.   We had our workers' meeting in the morning at eight o'clock.   There were about two thousand five hundred people out at that time of day.   I gave a hundred thousand ' Get right with God ' cards to the workers, and they went out and distributed them everywhere.   In the afternoon we had a women's meeting.   Before I went, I had asked the Lord to give me a song that would melt the people and win many to Christ.   I had an impression that I should use, ' Tell mother I'll be there.'   Two hundred and ten women came forward at the close of Dr. Torrey's sermon, and thirty-three said they had decided while the hymn was being sung.   I told the men about it at the evening meeting, and we sang it again.   One hundred and fifty men rose to say they would accept Christ before Dr. Torrey began to preach, and three hundred more came forward with them to confess Christ afterwards, making six hundred and sixty decisions for Christ in one day.   I am sure you will rejoice with me in all this.   It has been raining almost every day since we came to Dundee.   No doubt you have heard of the ' grey days ' which they have in Scotland ; everything looks grey, but the people are very kind.   You should see them open their Bibles in the meeting whenever a reference is given."

In the missions held by Torrey and Alexander, a beautiful feature was the voluntary help given in soul-winning by friends from other cities.   During the summer of 1903, Charles Alexander's Australian secretary, Rupert Lowe, had become acquainted, in one of the schoolboy camps, with young Dr. Neville Bradley of Liverpool.   Dr. Bradley came to Dundee to help in the mission, and night after night would bring a string of raggedly-dressed men whom he had found on the streets and invited to the meetings.   His zeal in leading these poor fellows to

Christ attracted the attention of Charles Alexander, and a warm friendship sprang up between the two men, whose lives were afterwards closely interwoven. The Dundee Mission was followed by a fruitful month in the city of Manchester, where, day after day, St. James's Hall was crowded to overflowing, thousands being turned away, unable to gain admittance. Almost five thousand people gave their hearts to Christ, to the joy of many of the veteran Christian workers of the city.

The year was now drawing to its close, but in spite of frost, and snow, and rain, and the difficulties of winter travel, three weeks of December were devoted to a tour of the smaller towns in Scotland, where, in every place visited, the songs and the preaching resulted in the salvation of souls.

At Christmas-time, Dr. Torrey joined his family at Southport, Charles Alexander going alone to London. This lonely Christmas was a time of spiritual crisis in his life. He had now reached the age of thirty-six, a time when most men are experiencing the joy of their own homes and family circles. Many a time in his years of ceaseless wandering and incessant labour for Christ, his lonely heart, so richly endowed with the power of affection, had cried out for its hunger to be satisfied. He was universally beloved both by men and women, and had friends everywhere. But though he always valued true affection, the popularity and earthly fame, which might easily have hurt a character less firmly rooted in God, only seemed to deepen his humility and his dependence upon his Master. Perhaps it even added to the acuteness of his heart-hunger, because of the scrupulous care which governed all his friendships with women. His innate sense of chivalry, and his sensitive jealousy for the reputation of the Lord's work, taught him to hold in check that warm heart of his till he was sure of the Lord's leading.

But this Christmas Day, confined to his room in a London hotel by a chill, far from his family and friends in America, a lonely longing for one on whom he could rightly lavish the wealth of his great love threatened well-nigh to overwhelm him. He fought the matter out upon his knees, yielding his will to the will of God ; ready to face, if need be, a life of loneliness, if that should be the Heavenly Father's plan for him. For the first time in his life perhaps, he told the Lord that his own search for a wife was over, and that he would leave to God the choice of His own time and way of revealing any such joy, if it should ever be his. Then, with a mind at rest from thoughts of self, he picked up a book he had just received from America, entitled *Down in Water Street*. It told of miracles of conversion among the poor, wrecked lives that drifted into the Rescue Mission in New York under the direction of his old friend, Sam Hadley. One chapter so laid hold of him that he wrote at once for permission to have it printed separately, for free distribution, under the title, *The Old Colonel : A Love Story*. Below the title he printed the following words :—" Last Christmas night I was alone in the big city of London, and, memories of happy Christmas nights at home crowding for place, I could not sleep. I had read a few of the first pages of a new book before retiring, so rather than occupy my time with old thoughts, I turned on the light and began to read the chapter which composes this booklet. My heart melted as I read. I had always thought love had a boundary line, but now I feel there is none. I believe I have been a better man since the moment I finished this story."

CHAPTER NINE

An End to Loneliness

1904

ON Sunday, January 17th, 1904, the great mission began in Bingley Hall Birmingham. For some days beforehand, Charles Alexander had been in the city, rehearsing his choir of sixteen hundred voices, and meeting committees of stewards and personal workers, to ensure that all preparations were complete.

The first Sunday's meetings were full of encouragement, and on the Monday night a gathering was held before the evening service to give a public welcome to the evangelists. The Lord Mayor, Mr. John Henry Lloyd, who was prevented from being present, was represented by his predecessor, Alderman Samuel Edwards, who expressed the Lord Mayor's hearty sympathy, and gave the introductory address. Others who took part in the public welcome were the Rev. Dr. J. H. Jowett, chairman of the Committee ; the Rev. J. J. Hunt, vice-chairman ; Rev. T. E. Titmuss, secretary ; and Mr. George Cadbury, the Christian philanthropist.

For the next four weeks, a human tide surged twice daily in and out of the doors of Bingley Hall, and the city began to ring, as Melbourne had done, with the strains of the " Glory Song " and of other revival melodies. Each Sunday morning a service was held at eight, culminating in a great rally of men's Adult Schools, when eight thousand men thronged the Hall at that early hour, and hundreds of decisions for Christ were made. In addition to the Bingley Hall services, a daily noonday gathering of business and professional men crowded out the large lecture theatre at the Midland Institute. A few important gatherings, for ministers only, were also held in the mornings, bringing a new fire and glow of the Holy Spirit into many a pulpit, not only in Birmingham, but in the whole of the Midlands.

The weather, which seemed at its worst, had little or no effect on the attendance of the throngs which grew denser as the weeks passed, and although both Dr. Torrey and Charles Alexander caught heavy colds, which would have laid most men low, the work was not checked.

Special prayer meetings were held, and God marvellously gave to their voices power to carry on, in spite of all. Just as Alexander began to find the strain of the solo work well-nigh impossible, unexpected help was supplied by the arrival of Mr. J. Raymond Hemminger, who had been sent over from America to study the directing of Gospel music, and solo work, under Alexander. The song " God is now willing, are you ? " will always be remembered in Birmingham as his most telling appeal. The marvellous playing of Robert Harkness, as he accompanied the immense volume of congregational singing under the magical skill of the song-leader, aroused much interest among many lovers of music in Birmingham. Often-times it seemed as though the solitary grand piano was turned into a whole orchestra, as every part of its keyboard seemed to speak at once, from the deep rhythmic bass, which boomed like drums, to the flute-like tones of the upper notes, which floated in counter melodies above the swelling waves of eight thousand or more voices. Such old familiar hymns as " Shall we gather at the river ? " seemed re-born, while the newer ones, such as " Never lose sight of Jesus," " It's just like Him," or "Loyalty to Christ," were echoed in streets, factories, and homes.

A letter from Charles Alexander to his mother, written early in February, reveals his never-failing thoughtfulness for his loved ones in Tennessee, and especially for the little mother on whose comfort he had lavished the additional means with which God had blessed him through the sale of his hymn-books. All such money was to him a gift from God and a sacred trust, of which not *one*-tenth but *ten*-tenths was to be used for His glory and under His direction. " Your sweet letter came to-day," he wrote, " but I am sorry you were uneasy about my health. We did have to work very hard before Christmas, and I was tired, but it was only a bad cold. I wish you knew what I think of your merit, honey. I am what I am, because I had you for a mother. If I have accomplished good, I know your good blood runs in my veins. These are the largest meetings we have ever had, day after day, for so long in succession. There have been over five thousand conversions in the first three weeks."

A true spiritual revival, resulting perhaps from prayerful organization, but coming direct from Heaven itself, swept through the city of Birmingham. " What has impressed me above all things," wrote Dr. J. H. Jowett, after the great Bingley Hall Mission, " has been the missioners' quiet and immovable assurance of the fellowship of God. Their communion with the Divine has not been ostentatiously declared—it has been most powerfully assumed. Dr. Torrey and Mr. Alexander have come to their meetings with the fragrance of the Presence Chamber round about them, and, as though it were the most natural thing in the world, they have confidently assumed the companionship of the King. It may appear to be a very ordinary matter when thus recorded in cold print, but to stand in the presence of men over whose spirits there is no shadow of uncertainty, and who rejoice in the sun-clear fellowship of the Eternal, is to be confronted with an experience which subdues one in most fruitful awe. When these men speak of God's presence, they speak as those who know.

" Closely allied to this, and indeed part and parcel of it, is their clear and calm confidence in the marvellous ministry of prayer. Mr. Alexander's estimate of prayer is that of a child ; not that it lacks intelligence, but because it is so filled with sunny and unshaken trust. He speaks of the ministry of prayer as one speaks of the sunshine or fresh air. God has privileged us to commune with Him in matters directly affecting the body as well as in the higher interests of the soul. These men have a great treasure in God ; it is their inheritance, and they draw upon it with unclouded assurance and serenity. The missioners have but one object in their work—the conversion of souls. . . . They work for converts and they get them."

At the close of the last Sunday-night meeting in Bingley Hall, on February 14th, it seemed as if the crowds could never be persuaded to break up and go home. Dr. Torrey unostentatiously slipped away from the platform while the Benediction was pronounced. Hundreds then left their seats and surged around the platform, while the old parting message, " God be with you till we meet again," was sung time after time, followed by a few more words of prayer uttered by the Rev. Luke F. Wiseman. A scene then occurred which wonderfully revealed the genuine aim of Charles Alexander's work. Prevented by the surrounding crowd from quietly slipping away, as he had intended, he was marooned on the pedestal of his crimson-covered dais, and became the centre of hundreds of upstretched hands, and of cries of affectionate farewell. With quick intuition, signing to Mr. Harkness to strike up the melody, his appeal rang out over the throng, which threatened to become a noisy mob : " Friends, we must not close such a mission as we have had together, like this. I appreciate your love, but I want our last vision to be of Jesus." As if touched by a magic wand, the excitement of the crowd was hushed, and their voices rang out, singing—

> See from His head, His hands, His feet,
> Sorrow and love flow mingled down.

Again and again it was sung, each time more softly, and finally in a whisper, with bowed heads. On lifting their eyes, the crowd, now reverent and subdued, saw that the place on the high red dais was empty, and quietly dispersed to their homes.

This scene was being closely observed, from a far distant corner of the great Hall, by a young woman, who had been pleading and praying till the last moment with some factory girls whom she sought to lead to Christ. It was perhaps one of the things that impressed her most deeply with the pure aims, and earnest sincerity of the young song-leader, who with a party of his friends had been visiting her mother's home a few days earlier. She had sought to hide, even from herself, the deep heart-stirrings which had been awakened by the man whose characteristics reminded her strangely of her own loved father, and little did she realize that in his heart also had sprung up a deep conviction that God was about to give him that for which his lonely spirit had yearned.

How their acquaintance had first been formed was once told by Charles Alexander himself in the *Sunday Strand*. When asked about the romance of his life, he had hesitated, feeling that it was too sacred a thing to be made public. But, moved by the plea that to know how this deepest of earthly joys had come in answer to prayer might lead others to put their trust in God, he reluctantly consented. " It is true," he wrote, " that for years I had longed for a wife who could go with me into all kinds of society, and who would love the poor, the drunkard, and those who were away down in sin ; a soul-winner and a real help-meet. I had reserved the right in my mind to choose my own wife, and had decided that she must have this and the other qualities of mind and heart, but had never been able to find one who combined all the desired qualifications. During the Christmas season of 1903, which I was spending alone in London, I surrendered the whole matter to God, never dreaming that His answer would come so quickly, or that Birmingham would be the place where I should find my wife. During an after-noon meeting in Bingley Hall a week or two later, I noticed a young lady upon one of the platform seats. Immediately a feeling came over me that there was the answer to my prayer. I did not know who she was, but observed her closely, and grew to love her, for I saw that she was after the salvation of souls. I noticed that in the after-meetings she usually went down to the back of the Hall, and was not afraid to stay late, and work long and earnestly, sometimes with the most wretched-looking and poorly-clad women and girls. The more I saw of her the more thoroughly I was convinced that, as far as I was concerned, she was my choice, though I was still asking the Lord constantly to take everything into His hands.

" I had noticed a silver-haired lady with her, evidently her mother. One day early in the mission, this lady gave me an invitation to spend my rest-day at her home. I accepted, and after she had gone, I turned to some one and asked who the lady was. ' Why, that is Mrs. Richard Cadbury,' I was told. This was a surprise, as I had already visited the home of some of her relatives. It was not until the last rest-day of the mission that I, with several others of the mission staff, was entertained at Uffculme. Strangely enough, and quite unknown to each other until afterwards, my future wife and I were praying earnestly on that same Friday night for the Lord's guidance in this matter. Each of us had a hard battle to fight with our own self-will, but each finally surrendered to the Lord, to have, or not to have, as He should will.

" It was not until two days after the mission had closed that I spoke a word to Miss Cadbury about it, and then—why, it was all settled in a few minutes. We were on our knees almost as soon as I had spoken to her, thanking the Lord for bringing us together, and for the wonderful joy, which we took as a gift direct from Him."

To both Alexander and his future wife, when love was first confessed and accepted, the unmistakable leading of God was as clear as noonday. To them both, the revelation had come with a bewildering ecstasy of holy joy. Never before had either opened the sacred deeps of the heart, and when love came in floods of overwhelming force, they gratefully accepted it as from the hand of God.

Brought up amid the refinements of a beautiful home, Helen Cadbury had seen existing between her father and mother a love so wonderful as to border on the heavenly. As she grew up, it had seemed to her that upon her parents, in their love for each other, had been bestowed a blessing as rare as it was rich and over-flowing. That became her ideal. Married life, if it ever came to her, must mean a union just as sweet and as perfect, or she would tread a single path. She had reached her twenty-seventh birthday without meeting anyone to whom she felt she could give her heart. Then suddenly, as the world might have regarded it, but at the moment of God's own appointing, the currents of two lives, that had hitherto been widely separated, were united and flowed as one.

Apart from the two chief figures in this divinely-guided romance, the one who entered most fully into their happiness was Helen Cadbury's mother. From the very first she had felt drawn to Charles Alexander. Something about him

F

reminded her of her own beloved husband. The unswerving loyalty to Christ and the Bible, the largeness of heart, the sympathy and quick intuition, the graciousness of manner, and the warmth of love, that had characterized his life, were also reflected in that of the man who was so soon to become her son-in-law. Because of these radiant qualities, he brought something back to her lonely heart that she thought had gone from it for ever. His gentleness towards her was a thing beautiful to behold. Without many words on either side, they understood each other almost from the first time of meeting ; and their tender affection deepened with their fellowship in Christ.

Richard Cadbury had been one of Birmingham's most distinguished captains of industry ; a philanthropist, who in his business and his public life had consistently lived the Christianity which he professed and preached. Above all else he was a soul-winner, and his children had been trained to put thought for others, especially for the poor and the outcast, first in their lives. Many a night had Helen Cadbury accompanied her father into the dark streets and alleys of the slums, seeking to lead poor drunkards to the Saviour. She and her mother had been bound together in a special way through the five years that had passed since her father's sudden death, while on a visit to Jerusalem with his family in 1899. Her three brothers, and two of her sisters, all older than herself, were married. Two younger sisters, Margaret and Beatrice, had been away from home during most of this period, and at the time of the engagement, Margaret was in Italy, and Beatrice at college in London. Only Helen had been left to share her mother's loneliness in the big family home that had once been filled to overflowing. It was still a family centre, and on Saturdays it was Mrs. Cadbury's joy to welcome as many of the children and grandchildren as could gather round her. Hitherto love for her parents had been the controlling passion of Helen's life. The protection of, and fellowship with, her beloved mother had been a sacred trust and a constant joy, and nothing but the gift which God had now bestowed upon her would have ever drawn her from her mother's side.

Tidings of the event were soon wafted across the Atlantic Ocean to Alexander's home in Tennessee. " At last I am engaged," he wrote to his mother, " to the sweetest girl you ever saw. I am as sure that you and all of the family will love her as that I am writing here. . . . It would take many sheets of paper to tell you all, as we shall tell you when we see you next summer. We hope to be married in July, and shall probably sail immediately for America, where we shall see your sweet face. It seems to me that I love everybody more than ever, especially you at home."

Before the next campaign began in Ireland, Wynd's Point, the Cadburys' beautiful home in the Malvern Hills, was offered to the mission party for a rest. They were, in all, a company of twelve, including singer, pianist, and secretaries, besides Miss Grace Saxe, who had recently arrived in England to follow up the work of the Torrey-Alexander missions with great Bible-classes. When they met upon the station, Charles Alexander, to the surprise of all, was nowhere to be seen. Just before the train started, a message was brought by Mr. J. Kennedy Maclean, assisting in secretarial work, that Alexander was staying a day or two longer in Birmingham to organize Miss Saxe's Bible-classes, one of which was to be held in the great Institute founded by Richard Cadbury.

Two days afterwards Mr. Maclean was on his way to Malvern with unexpected tidings. He wrote back to Alexander:—"Solitary and alone, but with a letter which almost burned a hole in my pocket, I was driving up a snow-covered mountain road, when the carriage came to a sudden stop, and I saw Dr. and Mrs. Torrey gazing in at me. 'Where's Mr. Alexander?' was the first question. I handed over the letter which had kept me so warm. After reading a few lines the Doctor looked up at me and asked: 'Is this serious, are you sure it's no joke?' I assured him that it was serious. I drove on and soon came upon a merry crowd putting the finishing touches to a snow-man. 'Where's Mr. Alexander?' was the shout. I gave evasive replies to the eager questions. Just before luncheon the Doctor announced that he had some good news to impart, and soon read your letter at the dining-table. There was electricity in the air! When the first shock was over, all expressed their joy and delight."

The only passing regret was in the hearts of Dr. Torrey's children, who had known and loved Alexander since his first days at the Moody Institute. "All my friends are going one by one," wrote Blanche. "You will still be my 'Uncle Charles,' won't you? You see I have known you ever since I was nine years old. Your sunny, Christ-like character has had a great influence over me since we have been in England, and has made me long to be more like Christ too. I have learned that no matter what happens to ruffle my temper, I can and should be sweet, for you have been an example to me." Reuben's letter ran: "I think it is Miss Cadbury who ought to be congratulated on getting you. If I knew her, as I doubtless shall some day, I should most certainly write and tell her so. I can understand perfectly how your heart and mind will be wrapped up in this new affection, but I beseech you to reserve a little corner for your old 'Pal.'"

"I am glad of the news," wrote Dr. Torrey. "I am sure you can do better work married, but I have never before met anyone whom I would have been glad to see you marry. Miss Cadbury will become more to you every year. You think you are in love now, but you won't know what love means until you have been married for years, as Mrs. Torrey and I have."

Soon letters of congratulation began to pour in upon the happy couple from friends in all parts of the British Isles; then eagerly-awaited letters from the United States; and, later still, expressions of genuine gladness from the many friends in Australia, New Zealand, India, and elsewhere.

Many of those who had taken a leading part in the Torrey-Alexander missions in Great Britain rejoiced in the link formed by this engagement with Christian enterprise across the Atlantic. A letter from Lady Kinnaird to Charles Alexander said:—"Lord Kinnaird and myself send you our best wishes for your happiness. Hers is a well-known and honoured name, and we pray God to bless you both. I am glad that this country, which owes you so much, gives you one of the best gifts, by God's guidance."

Letters from Lord Overtoun, Mr. Albert Head, and others, expressed the same pleasure in the news that had reached them. Mr. Wm. Oatts, of Glasgow, wrote to Miss Cadbury :—" A truer or more loving friend I do not know. He is so like his Master, and that smile upon his face has won many to the Saviour."

Mr. David Williamson, whose friendship and counsel had so often helped Charles Alexander in learning to understand the English mind and point of view, greatly rejoiced with him, and in his letter to Miss Cadbury said :—" Mr. Alexander's friendship with me has been most intimate and happy. When I look at him, the phrase of Henry Drummond—' one of Heaven's favourites '—comes to my mind. In all the days and in all the varied experiences I have shared with him, there has been just the same crystal character exemplified. The life of an evangelist has its special trials, and yet it has been the noble task of many a wife to make her husband's work doubly effective. It means, for some, a perpetual giving-up, a yielding of home claims in order that God may be glorified in the sphere beyond the home. God gives His own letters of introduction, and I believe He has guided you two souls in this matter. Mr. Alexander has had exhausting demands on his sympathies, and now he will have at least some return of the sympathy he has so freely given to the multitude."

The same thought is expressed in a letter from Dr. Horace B. Wilson, whose life has been devoted to medical missionary work among the poorest inhabitants of the Birmingham slums :—" Although we do not like to lose you from this city, you are taking up a sphere of work whose circumference is ever extending and knows no limit. Probably you cannot conceive what a restful satisfaction it will be to him to have your sympathy and counsel. Such a man must inevitably at times have intense loneliness—our Saviour knew it ever on the human side—and your intimate companionship in Christ will be of unutterable value to him, and through him to the world."

Of the hundreds of letters that poured in from over the seas, only a sentence or two can be given here. The Leavitt home in Waterloo, Iowa, which had been Charles Alexander's for six years, was filled with rejoicing for him. " It seems quite too good to be true," said Miss Lucy Leavitt, " but no better than you deserve. You have succeeded in making so many people happy that it is only fair that you now should have your full share. Father was so interested he wanted to start for England at once to see the bride-elect." Mr. William A. Sunday wrote :— " You already have thousands of friends over here, for every one who is a friend of Charles is also a friend of yours. I know you must be a sensible, kind-hearted, and most estimable young lady, or Charles would never have asked you to become Mrs. Alexander, and I congratulate you on having exercised such admirable judgment, for you have secured one of our very best. Charles and I are old friends and have fought many a battle for Christ and truth." Mr. Fleming H. Revell, of New York, wrote to Alexander :—" We rejoice with you in your happiness. As you know, we have learned to love you ourselves. Our only criticism was in the seeming indifference you felt to your own best and truest interests, but now you have redeemed yourself by entering upon the one thing needful to make you the all-round man you ought to be."

Before his departure for Dublin must bring the first parting, Alexander found time to send for his friend the photographer, Reginald Haines, of London.

He could not tear himself away from Uffculme without as many reminders as possible to greet his eyes of the two already so dear to him, and the sweet home in which his treasure was enshrined. Nearly seventeen years later, when a harder parting had taken place, and Charles Alexander's wife was left behind again for a little while, she received a letter from Mr. Haines, in which he said :—" I have met and talked with men in all walks of life, but I have only met one Charles Alexander ! Perhaps you may remember me coming to Uffculme just after you were engaged. In all my life I have never seen a man so full of happiness before, or since. He was brimming over with spiritual and physical pleasure, that I venture to say comes to few men. I have spent hours with him when I should have been working, but I did not think one wasted. Although we were on such different planes we had much in common. We usually started on photography, but were soon on other themes. So interesting and original in everything, I fell in love with him when first he arrived in England, and happily have never fallen out."

Bound up with these days of romance were the flowers of spring. Some bunches of violets had been purchased by Alexander. He presented these to his friends in the party, during their stay at Uffculme, Miss Cadbury amongst the others. The following day while walking round the grounds at Uffculme, some early snowdrops were seen pushing up through the light covering of snow, and were gathered by Miss Cadbury. Some days after their engagement, in turning over the leaves of her fiancé's Bible, she came upon some pressed snowdrops. Hurrying upstairs, she was soon back with a withered bunch of violets in her hand. These tokens, with the exception of a copy of *Down in Water Street*, were the only gifts that had ever passed between them before God gave them to each other, and became the symbols of their affection, appearing in many of the wedding gifts that brought the loving wishes of their friends. In a small silver frame, within a wreath of snowdrops and violets painted on ivory, stands the motto, which was also engraved in the bride's wedding-ring, " Each for the other, and both for God."

The public activities of such a man as Charles Alexander must naturally bulk largely in the story of his life. And yet, the telling of these things may not necessarily be the greatest help to others walking the path of life.

Fiction takes note of personal happenings, and these form its special appeal to youthful minds, which seek, as they read, to experience in imagination the thoughts and feelings of the characters in which they are interested. All too often, this natural tendency is made use of to enthrall with neurotic sentimentality. Why should it not be the serious mission of the life-story of a good man, to lift before a generation, where true marriage is too often desecrated, an ideal so loftily pure and yet so warmly human, that others may be inspired to consecrate their affections to the same Divine control that moulded the heart and mind of Charles Alexander ?

Such deep affection as his, so loyal, so constant, so tenderly patient—is too rarely beautiful an example of genuine Christianity to be hidden from view as " a treasure hid in the ground." The favoured life upon which its riches were in fullest measure bestowed, may have but a short earthly span to run, and must not shrink from revealing at least a part of those holy emotions which stirred his loving heart. Instead, therefore, of giving descriptions of his missions with Dr.

Torrey in Dublin, Bristol, Bradford, and Brighton, during the interval before the wedding-day, extracts will be given from his letters to Miss Cadbury.

February 26th. On the train to Liverpool.—" My dear ' Answer to Prayer,' You seem to almost have a halo about you, as I think of you as an answer from on high to my call. Canaan is a fair country. God will keep this new union of ours, and I feel sure His Spirit led you to quote the verse : ' Perfect love casteth out fear.' It seems almost too much to believe that you can really love one whom you have known so short a time. Thy *gentle* mother gave me the very verse I needed, on top of the other, ' Be stedfast, unmoveable, always abounding in the work of the Lord.' I have a number of hard questions to settle in the next few days. Pray for me that they may be settled for the best interests of our King. The nearer we get to Christ, the nearer we shall be to each other. I have just been thinking that the best way to prepare to make you happy is to be helpful and kind to those who need me where I am. We shall soon be on the ship." *February 27th. Dublin, Ireland.*—" I slept all the way across to Dublin and felt ready for a rapid ride to Metropolitan Hall, where they gave me a real Irish welcome. One speaker made a beautiful allusion to your lovely self, and *everybody knew.*"

March 1st.—" Last night I posted you a package of books. In it you will find a Bible for B—— and a *Daily Light* for each of the maids and the men who work about the house, garden, and stables. I also promised the coachman's wife an Australian Souvenir. It has been snowing and blowing furiously here to-day. Just as I jumped from a jaunting-car, a girl with a pinched, cold face and blue fingers confronted me with a bunch of violets ; and, honey, cold as I was, I melted, and paid the little maid a sixpence, for I felt the flowers too sacred to pay only a penny a bunch. Sweet thoughts of *you* come and fill all the chambers of my soul, and I bless God for the day I met you. . . . My choir here is superb. I wish you could come over and hear them. An old gentleman said to-night that he had been in missions all of his life, but he had never seen the Spirit of God working as He is here now."

March 4th.—"I enclose two letters from my good friend Mrs. Leavitt, of Waterloo, Iowa. She is sixty-eight years of age. I lived in their house for six years. She knows me as probably no one else knows me. I was looking through my papers and found this, the most beautifully-written analysis that was ever penned to me. I hesitated a little at sending it to you, for fear you might think it egotistic. You have not known me long. A prominent lawyer has invited our party to drive several miles through some beautiful scenery, but I am afraid I shall not feel able to go, with my cold. I sit here and recall your sweet face, as you chatted on hour after hour in your sane, wholesome, honest, sweet way. You are so pervasive, you seemed to quite fill the room when you entered. I have locked you up in a room I had despaired of ever having filled—the banquet-room of my heart. . . . One letter I enclose is from the man who sent Mr. Hemminger over here for me to train. I trained him for his work before he started out. The other is from a good woman, who, like your little mother, is working and waiting until she goes to be with the husband she lost. . . . every moment is full of *you*, honey."

March 9th.—" My lovely one, you have opened every door of my soul, and as you have moved through its halls and chambers you have purified and whitened its walls, as they have touched your own pure soul in solemn communion. As you sit now in its throne-room—my Queen—from your royal position there radiates a life-giving brightness that floods the darkest corners of this eternity building, and up from your presence floats a rare perfume like a holy incense, pervading every fold of this mysterious structure—my soul." *March 13th.*—"My ' Loved and Longed-for,' My heart seems as if it would melt sometimes whenever a suggestion of you comes to my mind. Only a few short weeks, and yet I feel as if I had always known you, and you were made for me. . . . It is a joy to me to know that you are so interested in Miss Saxe's method of Bible study. I wonder if you will absorb enough to use the same method sometime, with others. You may have to explain it many times, so it would be well to watch Miss Saxe's way of presenting her subject. I love to hear of your victories in soul-winning." *March 15th.*—"It grows worse every day—this old-fashioned love affair ! I never would allow free rein to my heart before. I feel like a man out of prison since I may love you, and call you *mine*. Two snowdrops, and two sweet violets shook their modest petals at me when I opened your letter. . . . Your mother's letter was a gem, and such a comfort."

March 16th.—"My Constant Comfort, When I tell you, honey, that I *trust your trust*, your heart can rest. You can always rest assured that I trust you absolutely, and have from the first. If I had loved you ever so much and lacked that, I would have been frightened to speak a word of love to you. I must have that for a foundation-stone. The older I grow, the more solemnly do I sit down to a sheet of white paper, to write words upon it. Since you began to write to me, I feel it more keenly than ever—the cast of the sentences, the appearance of the page, even the date and signature seem to speak volumes. There was a dignity and warmth about your letter this morning that left such a steady glow upon my soul, that the whole day has been sweetened, and a number of people have received kind words because of it. I consider letter-writing a God-given method of doing good. Give my love to our gentle mother, and tell her she is making a better man of me every time I think of her." *March 17th.*—"How eagerly I watch the post, and how generously I am rewarded—*you do not fail me at any point*, bless your heart. I follow you round on your missions, from day to day, with all the eagerness of a little boy under the spell of his first Indian story." *March 18th.*—" You will have to prepare yourself for the limelight these coming months—you have been so carefully shielded and tenderly cared for, that I almost pity you, sweet child, when I know what is ahead of you. But I *never* doubt your ability to pass through it *all, like a queen.*" *March 19th.*—" This morning my maid had no letter for me from you, but later she brought one up, and—if anybody should ask you if I ever dance, tell them, ' yes ! ' My cold is not well, but I could sing better to-day than at any time during the mission. I am thankful to God for it."

March 21st.—" I have just come from getting a young actress off to Belfast. She professed conversion in our Mission, but afterwards began to drink again. She is on her way to an inebriates' home. Pray for her. She has been married, and is parted from her husband, and is only just twenty-five ! Last night was one of victory. Scores of men came out for God—four soldiers among them."

March 24th.—" I try to hold my heart quiet until Monday, but it breaks away

from me. . . . I only posted a letter to you a few short hours ago, but here is such
a brilliant little letter from your pen, I can't resist telling you how it sat you down
in front of me.   I could close my eyes once again and see the lovelight in your
dear eyes—how it lifts me as I think of it !   You quite won my heart with the
darkey poem.   I have not analysed to the very bottom of my heart and intellect
on the point of poetry, but I fear that all other poetry must be second to the sweetness and abandon of the darkey jingle.   Honey, you have me ! "

March 25th.—" Your letters came like a breeze from Canaan.   I read them
over and over.   Those verses were like new wine.   I feel you are a part of me."

March 26th.—" I am sending you some work done by a sunny-faced Irish
soldier, who has been at every meeting.   He made this especially for me, to be
used in *our* home. . . .   He came to call, and I asked him down to dinner with me.
At first he refused, saying that he would disgrace me, if I was seen in the hotel
dining-room with him.   At that I picked him up bodily, and started for the door.
On our way down the stairs he pulled me over and hugged me.   Honey, this old
world is hungry-hearted, but you have filled my heart, and I thank God."

April 20th.—" Your sweet presence is always near.   I can hold your face in
my mind now, and remember all of the changes I have watched come and go. . . .
I enclose a letter from a sweet little cousin whom I have helped to educate."

Dr. Henry Montgomery, of Belfast, also assisting in the Dublin campaign,
wrote to Mrs. Alexander after her husband's Home-call :—" How beautiful it was
for you, to live with such a man as your husband.   He was one of the saintliest and
sunniest children of the King I ever knew.   His musical gifts were, to me, unequalled ;
it was indeed a delight to know him, and an inspiration to be with him.   When I
first knew about your engagement, we were in Dublin together.   I was taking
overflow meetings for Dr. Torrey, and helping in other ways.   Your beloved was
then living in Russell's Hotel, Stephen's Green, and I used to run in and see him
to have a chat and prayer together.   He told me about your engagement, and then
looked up into my face with one of the brightest and purest smiles of unalloyed
happiness I ever saw in a human countenance.   The joy of the Lord was in his soul,
bubbling out in unselfish desire to serve everybody around him."

Only a few short hours were the lovers able to share together at the close of
the Dublin Mission, but Mrs. Cadbury, with her daughters, Helen, and Beatrice, who
was at home for the Easter vacation, spent a few days in Bristol, greatly enjoying
the wonderful meetings in progress at Colston Hall.   A few days later, Mrs. Cadbury
and Helen were speeding across the Continent, to spend a week in Rome with
Margaret, before bringing her back with them.   Charles Alexander revelled in the
descriptions that came to him of their journeyings, and the scenes they were
enjoying.

April 24th.   Bristol.—" My Far-away Love, I have enjoyed, and have preserved,
every post-card or scrap you have written to me.   Your descriptions were so clear
that I have travelled all the way to Rome with you.   I am enclosing the poem I
love so much.   Will you memorize it ?   The work is crowding harder and harder.
We are having two meetings each night, one for women from 6.45 to 8.15, then
men fill the hall.   I had four meetings yesterday.   A love strong as life goes with this."

A characteristic telegram, containing merely a quotation from the Southern poet, Frank Stanton, greeted Helen Cadbury on her arrival at Rome :—

> Seems like a tear stays in my eye
> Since you went away !

April 27th.—" We have had the largest midday meeting to-day we have yet had. Nearly every seat in the hall was filled, and it was a splendid sight. Last night we had about nine thousand in the two meetings, and hundreds professed Christ. Honey, I had a blessed time this morning. Mrs. J. Q. A. Henry came in, and I told her about the sweetest love-story that I have ever read or heard about. I am going to Cardiff to-morrow, to talk on the Missions. Please pray for me, dear."

May 1st.—" We begin in Bradford on Thursday. The Colston Hall was full this, Sunday, morning before 8 o'clock. People began coming before half-past six ! . . . I am glad you are accumulating valuable knowledge. You are to be my own private teacher, and I think I can appreciate a good one. Remember what I said to you about the word ' dainty.' I love that in a woman."

May 7th. Bradford.—" Your sweet faithfulness in writing has helped me more than I can tell you. I believe that trait in your character will strengthen me for better work. I have been watching closely since I first knew you to see if you had it, and if it would last through any strain. How greatly I value dependableness ! I would have loved you, m'honey, if you had not had it, but I thank God you have, and my love has more territory to cover than I thought was mine. I have had to keep occupied deeply with other things, or I believe I should have been ill from the loss of you during this month. Now it is difficult to tie myself down to steady work since I know you are coming this way. The trip to Cardiff was a victory for the Committee. I took Mr. Lowe along, and Mr. Shanklin to play. I gave them ' Second-Timothy-two-fifteen ', and ' Pray through.' Hundreds were turned away from the afternoon meeting, and at night the crush was so great, the crowd rushed the windows and broke them. Best of all was, we. had conversions. The last night in Bristol, four hundred men and boys confessed Christ ; three thousand eight hundred decisions in the four weeks. Our party all love you with a little touch of reverence, for which I am thankful. I do not care whether people have awe in my presence, but I do covet it for you . . . I envy those who have known you so long. I must make up for lost time when we meet."

May 11th.—" I can hardly sleep to-night when I think that to-morrow you will be moving about the rooms of lovely Uffculme ; I long to be there too. I shall come for our rest-day on Friday, but must return by the early train on Saturday. I am anxious to see my new sister. I am quite sure I shall be proud of her, and I know I shall love her, if she is the least bit like you. I am afraid she will be disappointed when she sees a very tired, worn-looking Tennessean creeping out of a cab to greet you all. The preparation here was poor, and it is uphill work—I keep three typists busy, and am engaging another to-morrow. Please, honey, let us have as quiet a time as possible on Friday. I want *you.*" *May 12th.*—" I have just finished my fourth meeting to-day—a stewards' meeting. I believe these informal talks with the stewards are some of the most far-reaching of any I have to do with. I seem to feel your sweet presence beside me while I sing or speak."

For some years previously, dating back to the new intellectual experience of her college days, Charles Alexander's future wife had been passing through a period of spiritual struggle and difficulty. Brought up in the sunlight of sincere, happy trust in the Living, and the written, Word of God, she had made a definite and public decision for Christ at the age of twelve, in one of the meetings at the Mission Hall built by her father, who personally directed the work. Her father himself had tenderly prayed with her during the after-meeting in the inquiry-room, to which she had timidly made her way, voluntarily and alone, amongst a number of other seekers for Christ, who had left their seats in the Mission Hall at the evangelist's invitation. For six happy years, strengthened and built up by the attractively beautiful example of her father's and mother's Christian living, she had sought to win her school-friends and others to Christ. Open attacks on the Bible, and the opposition of worldliness and of rationalism, she had met during her High School days with her beloved and never-failing weapon—" the sword of the Spirit, which is the Word of God." But until she reached the age of eighteen she had never been away from the parents who were her ideal in everything, and did not dream that anyone professing real faith in Christ, could yet be capable of " handling the Word of God deceitfully " ; or that there were " unstable " as well as " unlearned " minds, who might " wrest things hard to be understood, as also the other Scriptures, unto their own destruction," and to the detriment of others who followed their leading.

For this reason, she was perhaps doubly susceptible to the subtle influence of those whom she reverently regarded, not only as intellectual superiors and guides, but as examples, whose spiritual teaching she expected to be as dependable as their high moral standards were, in many instances, noble and inspiring. In fact, without realizing it, she unconsciously began to put morality into the place of that spirituality, which is the only safe and lasting foundation for morality itself. By such gradual degrees that she was hardly aware of it, she drifted from her old moorings, and was at last, with eager forward gaze, enjoying the pleasurable sensation of adventurous risk and daring, as she sailed out into the sea of destructive criticism of the Bible. But in His watchful love, the Heavenly Pilot, from whose hand she had snatched the helm, permitted her to feel her need and helplessness in the storm of sorrow that suddenly overclouded her sky, when the father whom she adored was suddenly taken from her. His clear, child-like faith had constantly disturbed her new sense of exhilarating freedom from the old bondage of ignorance, as she called it. There had been something unsettling in her inability to move him, whose life was so radiantly full of love and tender thought for others, from his firm and steady loyalty of trust in the sternest statements of God's Word about sin and its punishment, and of the lack of any other means of salvation but " the precious blood of Christ," reference to which she had begun to regard as crude and primitive. A few months spent in Germany, after leaving college, for the study of music and language, had opened up another side of life to her. Through her schoolgirl days, she had earnestly sought to draw her friends away from the lure of worldly amusements to the joy of real Christian living and of soul-winning, but in Germany, with her faith unsettled, and her mind more set on self-culture than of living for others, she was tempted for the first time in her life by the attrac- tions of the world. To the grief of her parents, who, while not forbidding her, were yet praying in deep anxiety, she began to attend the Opera, though her old principles against wine-drinking, cards and dancing, and of using Sunday like any other day, still held firm. Her parents' prayers were not in vain. Circumstances caused her return to England earlier than had been expected, and to please her parents, and out of respect for their work, she had no thought of attending the Opera in England ; but music became her idol, and more and more of her time was absorbed in it. Then came the shock of her father's death, and the sense of deep need of those holy truths on which his heart had been stayed. The loneliness and grief of her mother appealed to her deepest and most chivalrous instincts, and for her sake she began to give much of her time again to the work of her father's Mission.

Little by little, her old faith was returning, but at the time of her engagement to Charles Alexander she had not reached the point of entire surrender to Christ, or of submitting her mind to the absolute authority of the Word of God. It was the only shadow on the devotion that had bound mother and daughter together, and Mrs. Cadbury had earnestly prayed that the strong, forceful teaching of Dr. Torrey might bring her daughter back to the child-like trust from which she had departed. Without a doubt, this anxiety for her daughter's spiritual welfare was an added reason for Mrs. Cadbury's joy over Helen's engagement to Charles Alexander. At first, he did not dream of the spiritual struggle through which the one he loved had been passing, but quickly sensing it, he laid bare the wound, determined that it must be thoroughly healed. Dr. Torrey's preaching, especially his noonday addresses on " Why I believe the Bible to be the Word of God " ; " Evidences for the Resurrection " ; and on " Infidelity, its consequences and its cure," had done much to settle her intellectual difficulties, and to bring her back to the realization that the authority of the Scriptures was more to be trusted about things unseen, than the conclusions of philosophy. Now love had come to her, and again she was confronted, as she had been in her father's case, with a man who was the personification of loving tenderness, and yet who never wavered in accept- ing God's estimate of sin and its frightful consequences, while trusting His love. So credulous had she been of the untested statements of those who had influenced her to doubt the Bible, that it actually surprised her to find that there were people of education and of culture who dared to believe in Satan as a personality, as real and actual as that of Christ, or in the possibility of eternal punishment.

From the time of his own father's death, the motive of Charles Alexander's whole life had been the winning of souls. Not all his happiness in the joy of his new love could blind him to the spiritual need of the one he loved so dearly. Patiently and tenderly through the past months, by letter as well as in their rare, sweet days of fellowship, he had sought to make things plain to her, and had prayed that the Holy Spirit Himself might be her teacher, and lead her into all truth. Among the books which he had painstakingly marked in the few leisure moments when he needed rest, was a copy of Dr. A. T. Pierson's *Many Infallible Proofs*. Now, in his letter of *May 12th*, from Bradford, he refers again to these matters :— " I sent you some more books, and do pray that they may help you, but I am depending upon Someone higher than the author of these books. It means so much to me. You are to be my victory or defeat. I am satisfied, if you are on absolute surrender ground, that all will become clear."

May 17th.—"What beautiful thoughts your letter contained. I do not deserve them, but God helping me, I am reaching for the deserving point. You make me very careful what I write to you when I know that you study each sentence so carefully. I don't write as much as I probably would were you careless with my letters. God will use your literary qualities, and the beauty of this is, that in the quiet of home you can reach and move thousands without passing over the threshold. When I think that these words that I write to you day after day will probably be read by you for years to come, I want them to stand the test and strain that years are sure to bring. Almost every sentence I send you bears a thought that has been carefully weighed. I want to tell you the truth in these letters."

May 19th.—"Your letters and corrections of the manuscript have given me a mental treat, as well as the feast that is so satisfying to my heart. I am a great lover of heart, but I am also appreciative of head. I have hunted out some books. Please do not try and read all, but begin with the parts I have indicated. Please read with your fountain-pen at hand, mark with it freely, and let me see when you are through. The distribution of thousands of ' Get right with God ' cards has stirred Bradford. Thank you for all your sympathetic interest in my work. I treasure every sentence you say or write."

Another short visit to Uffculme revealed to Charles Alexander that Margaret Cadbury had also been passing through a time of spiritual difficulty. She had never taken a public stand for Christ, nor had she ever definitely accepted Him as her Saviour. Coming under the influence of theosophy and of one of the many cults of mental healing, during a course of study in a physical training college, she had also drifted from the teaching which had surrounded her in her childhood. Strangely guided, as he always seemed to be in ways of tact, Charles Alexander had gained the confidence of his future sister, and had had some serious conversations with her, finally leaving her with a number of written questions which he begged her to pray over and answer honestly. Speaking of this afterwards to her sister, Margaret Cadbury said, " I could not sleep for nights after Charles had given me those questions. They seemed to be facing me everywhere, and it made me quite vexed that I could not forget them." " What a joy it would be for us all," Alexander wrote on *May 21st*, " if dear Margaret should get a complete victory at this time. Remember me most lovingly to her and your mother. Study the enclosed. Anything that lauds the Bible I love to read, and have you read."

May 23rd.—" Our hearts are full of thankfulness. The two meetings to-day are by far the best in spirit and attendance that we have had in Bradford. You have read *The Life of Bishop Hannington*, I think. It was my great privilege to help young Mr. Hannington, who is here on a visit, through a long talk last night. I have been re-reading some of the letters your mother wrote to me. I think we should have them framed for our private room. They seem to me to have brought a perfume from a higher world."

May 29th.—" We had a splendid morning meeting for the last Sunday, and at half-past two I went across to a packed women's meeting, where a large number confessed Christ. Reuben Torrey and Mr. Hannington are taking a service for young people to-night, and Mr. Lowe is speaking in one of the large Congregational churches. The preparations for the Liverpool meetings have put new life into all of us. A lady who met us in London was here, and told me she had never seen a face so radiant and full of joy as yours the morning we met after the Dublin meetings. She looked at me searchingly, and said, ' It lies with you to keep that face always so.' I have thought it over and over. I don't want ever to do a single thing that will take the shine away from your heart or from your face."

During the Brighton Mission, which was held from June 4th to 30th, Mrs. Cadbury, with her daughters Helen and Margaret, were able to spend a few days attending the meetings at The Dome. A great struggle was taking place in Margaret Cadbury's soul, as the Holy Spirit was leading her into the light. So sharp was the conflict, that for a day or two she refused to go to a single meeting, and would scarcely speak to anyone. One evening, to her mother's surprise, though she was wise enough to say nothing, Margaret accompanied them to the meeting. After the sermon was finished, and the solo of invitation had been sung, an opportunity for making a confession of Christ as their personal Saviour was given to those who had responded. Dr. Torrey then invited any one else present, wishing to give a testimony, to do so. To the astonishment and joy of those who loved her and had been praying for her, Margaret Cadbury rose to her feet, and in a few steady, quiet words, said that up to that time she had never made any public profession of Christianity, but she wished that night to say that she had taken the Lord Jesus Christ as her personal Saviour, and desired to surrender her life to Him in service. It may be imagined what a love-feast took place in a private sitting-room of the hotel soon afterwards! One of the first things Margaret Cadbury said to her brother-to-be was, " Charles, I want to be a missionary." Little did any of them dream that the very next year she would be accompanying the husband, whom she had never seen as yet, to a Medical Mission in South China !

CHAPTER TEN

A Busy Honeymoon

1904

THE day that was to bring so much joy to Charles Alexander, and the one whom he loved, dawned bright and fair. The house and gardens of Uffculme were ablaze with flowers of every hue and fragrance. By one o'clock on Thursday, July 14th, 1904, the old Friends' Meeting House in Bull Street, Birmingham, was crowded with a throng of visitors, many of whom had come from various parts of Great Britain and Ireland. America, too, was well represented in the gathering, although circumstances had prevented members of Alexander's immediate family from being present. According to Quaker custom, there were no decorations of flowers and palms, but the happy faces and the atmosphere of joyous anticipation filled the somewhat sombre building with sunshine. A crescent of empty seats, backed by well-filled rows of "ministers and elders," faced the crowded meeting. In the centre stood the tall, slender figure of Charles Alexander—waiting; beside him a still taller, broad-shouldered figure, that of Arthur Bradley, his best man.

Soon there is a little stir of expectancy. Up the aisle walk Dr. and Mrs. Torrey, who take their places in the semicircle of seats, next to the seat which will presently be occupied by the bridegroom. Another stir, the sounds of a crowd cheering on the outside of the building, and after a few moments, Mr. Barrow Cadbury, the bride's eldest brother, leads her mother up the aisle to take her seat next to the bride's. Again a hush of expectancy, and then the bride, on her eldest brother's arm, passes into the aisle. Her eyes, behind the soft bridal veil already worn by her mother and two elder sisters, are fixed upon one figure, towards whom she walks as if on air. Following her come eight dainty bridesmaids clad in shimmering white, carrying graceful, simple bouquets of yellow marguerites. The first pair are Margaret Cadbury and Blanche Torrey; Beatrice Cadbury, nieces, and cousins following behind them. A beautiful meeting, after the simple Quaker usage, begins after the bridal party have filled the empty crescent.

So many are present who do not belong to the Society of Friends, and might be puzzled by the absence of any pre-arranged order of service, that a few words, explaining the object and conduct of the meeting, are given. A hush of silent prayer that follows is broken by the voice of the bride's uncle, Mr. George Cadbury, as he prays for God's blessing on the pair. Then another period of quiet prayer, and, with a soft rustling of silk, the bridesmaids and the two central figures rise like a foam-crested wave. Taking the bride's right hand with his own right, the clear voice of Charles Alexander, more tremulous than usual, rings out over the assembly :

> " Friends, in the fear of the Lord, and in the presence of this assembly, I take this my friend, Helen Cadbury, to be my wife, promising through divine assistance to be unto her a loving and faithful husband, until it shall please the Lord by death to separate us."

A breathless silence, and then the tones of the bride's voice are heard, repeating a similar declaration of plighted troth. They take their seats again, and the bridegroom slips upon her finger the golden token. Between intervals of silent prayer, a number of short addresses are given, first by Dr. Torrey, and then by others in various parts of the Meeting House. Dr. Neville Bradley reads some beautiful selections of Scripture, and after a while, some one kneels to lead in prayer, for which the whole company rise to their feet. The marriage certificate is then read by the Quaker registrar and brought forward for the signatures of the bridal pair, and of four witnesses—the bride's mother and brother, and Dr. and Mrs. Torrey, who are acting in the place of Charles Alexander's parents. Soon the bridal party have passed joyfully down the aisle, and are being driven through the densely crowded street, and out through the town to the bride's home, three miles away.

A reception was held at Uffculme, the bridal pair standing in the shade of a large marquee to greet the hundreds of friends who had gathered upon the sunlit lawns to share in their happiness. At eight o'clock that evening, Charles Alexander and his wife reached Great Malvern, and, in the quiet of the lovely scenery, enjoyed the long drive together round the range of hills to Wynd's Point, which lies in the Pass between the Worcestershire and Herefordshire Beacon-hills. One glorious day they spent together, walking over the springy turf, and strolling through the leafy woods towards Eastnor. On the Saturday morning, at nine o'clock, they were once more in the train, on the way to Liverpool.

The voyage on S.S. *Lucania* was a wonderful experience for them both. On the morning of July 23rd, they were on deck at six o'clock, and as they steamed up New York harbour, past the Statue of Liberty, and threaded their way through the busy traffic of hurrying ferry-boats and shipping of all kinds, Charles Alexander eagerly introduced his English bride to her new homeland. They were welcomed at the wharf by Mr. A. P. Fitt, who drove out with them to the Netherland Hotel on Fifth Avenue, at the corner of Central Park. All day they were busy sightseeing and calling upon some of Charles Alexander's friends. At six o'clock, Mr. Samuel H. Hadley joined them for dinner at the Netherland, afterwards taking them to the Hadley Hall Rescue Mission on the Bowery. Here, for the first time, Helen Alexander entered among those scenes so familiar to her through the pages of *Down in Water Street*, and was thrilled as she heard the marvellous testimonies, given one after another in quick succession, of God's redeeming grace. At the close of the meeting, a number of dishevelled figures made their way to the penitent form, and Sam Hadley, limping a little from his lame leg, but with the love of his heart shining in his eyes, went from one to the other, laying his arm over their shoulders, and pleading with them to put their trust in Jesus. Alexander and his wife left their seats upon the platform to join in giving words of encouragement and help to those who were deciding for Christ. By ten-thirty the last stragglers had left the hall, and Sam Hadley offered to take his friends into Chinatown to help in a Midnight Mission. It was surprising, at that late hour, to find the Mission Hall crowded with poor derelicts and the Christian workers who had come to bring them a message of hope and deliverance. The singing, as in all Rescue Missions, was vigorous, and again decisions were made for Christ. It was after midnight when the Alexanders made their way, piloted by Sam Hadley, to a little Chinese restaurant in the heart of Chinatown, and one o'clock had struck before they reached their hotel. Charles Alexander had succeeded in giving his bride a taste of characteristic American activity on her first happy day ashore in his native land !

In Philadelphia, where two days were spent, Mrs. Alexander was proud to introduce her husband to a circle of Cadbury relatives, many of whom she already knew through their visits to England. They welcomed him with open hearts and were captivated by his happy manner and courteous ways. A cousin, at whose home they stayed, wrote to Mrs. Alexander years afterwards :—" Charles was a dear fellow. We always liked him since you paid us a visit as bride and groom just after you were married. What particularly impressed us was, that whenever Charles went to your room, he knocked on the door before entering. It is a very slight incident, but it is the one I shall most remember him by."

A long, hot summer day was enjoyed on board a river-boat, steaming up the mighty Hudson from New York City, past the towering wall of the Palisades, and on through glorious scenery till Albany was reached. Alexander spent an hour or two of pure delight, having a coloured quartet who were on board sing one after another of their inimitable Southern songs to his wife. After supper at Ten Eyck Hotel in Albany, a light two-wheeled vehicle with a spirited horse was brought to the door, and under the red glow of sunset, Charles Alexander took his wife for her first buggy-ride, through the clean quiet streets, paved with small red bricks in Dutch fashion, and out through the Park to the peace of the open country beyond. Here they stopped awhile and drank in the loveliness, as the red glow faded from the sky and the glorious full moon rose, flooding the world with silver.

The next day, Alexander planned a new pleasure for his English bride. A ride of forty miles was taken on an open trolley-car through lovely New England country, past little towns with neat, white-painted, frame houses lining the roads, and no fences or hedges to mark the division of properties, giving the appearance of a park rather than of a town. A break was made in the middle of the day to ascend Mount Tom, from the summit of which glorious views were obtained. By evening they had reached Northfield, in the beautiful Connecticut valley, where they received a hearty welcome from the Moody family, including Mr. and Mrs. A. P. Fitt, in whose home they were entertained. Here a week was spent at the Christian Workers' Conference, Charles Alexander leading the music in the great Auditorium on the Seminary campus. Mr. George C. Stebbins, who had been musical director at many of the conferences, welcomed the younger song-leader with charming Christian courtesy, and the friendship already formed between the two grew deeper. August 5th was spent at Niagara, and a day later the happy pair had reached the bustling city of Chicago. A great reception had been arranged at the Moody Bible

"UFFCULME,"
BIRMINGHAM,
ENGLAND.
THE HOME
OF
HELEN CADBURY

THE HALL
AT
"UFFCULME"

THE WEDDING GROUP, JULY 14, 1904

THE ALEXANDER HOME IN KNOXVILLE, TENNESSEE, 1904

WITH SAM JONES IN CARTERSVILLE, GEORGIA

"STRIKE UP A TUNE, OLD MAN."

A COLORED TRIO

THE THREE BROTHERS TAKE A TURN.

Institute, and Charles Alexander was proudly joyous in presenting his wife to many of his old friends.

After five days in Chicago, they were speeding southwards to St. Louis, Missouri. Here the World's Fair was in progress, and the Alexanders stayed for the week-end at the huge Inside Inn, a temporary wooden hotel built on the Fair Grounds, containing seven thousand rooms. Saturday was given up to seeing the Fair. In the Palestine section, Chalil Gandour, who had twice been dragoman to the Cadbury family in the Holy Land, served them delightedly with Turkish coffee and showed them over that part of the exhibition of which he was in charge.

Dr. J. Wilbur Chapman was also staying at the Inside Inn, as he and Alexander were to conduct some Sunday services—the first they had ever held together. A good-sized crowd had gathered in the grounds on Sunday afternoon, when quite suddenly the bright sky was overcast with hurrying clouds, and without warning a terrific thunderstorm broke loose upon them. The crash of thunder and the flashes of lightning were quickly followed by a torrential downpour, which drove hundreds into the spacious hall of the Inn, where the meeting was held with a far larger attendance than would have gathered outside. Dr. Chapman gave a wonderful message on " The New Song," and Charles Alexander led the people in hymn after hymn, till the wooden rafters rang. That night another crowded meeting was held in a great concert auditorium in the city of St. Louis. Alexander was happy in leading back to Christ an old schoolmate, once a prominent Christian worker, who had wandered into the meeting on seeing the name of his old friend advertised.

On August 16th, the goal of the long journey was reached at the family home in Knoxville, Tennessee, where a royal welcome was given to Charles and his wife by the beloved mother, sister and brothers. What never-to-be-forgotten days were those, visiting the old haunts, meeting numerous relatives and friends, and driving out through the country roads to various points of interest ! One moonlight night they drove to a lovely spot overlooking the mighty horseshoe curve of the great Tennessee river. A long day was spent in Maryville, visiting the College and home after home in the little town, where " Charlie Alexander " was everywhere welcomed like a long-lost brother, and where everyone was curious to see the English bride, whom they took straight to their hearts for his sake. He took her to the old candy-store, and bought her, before other purchases, five cents' worth of cinnamon drops, for " auld lang syne," from the very man who had sold him many a five cents' worth in his college days ! It was hard work, when the time came, to tear themselves away from Knoxville, and Charlie's one comfort was the hope that his dear ones would soon be able to visit his new English home. He could not bear to leave them all behind, and arrangements were made for Homer to travel back with them to England ; the others promising to come later. A few days were spent at the Bible Conference, Winona Lake, Indiana, convened by Dr. Chapman, who entertained them to luncheon in his beautiful home. Mr. and Mrs. William A. Sunday were their hospitable host and hostess, and Alexander had the joy of meeting the Leavitts, and many friends of his earlier days. Soon they were speeding back to New York, and then, accompanied by their brother Homer, across the

G

Atlantic on board the S.S. *Oceanic*, after six weeks of as busy a honeymoon as could well be spent in the heat of a tropical summer.

On reaching England, the Alexanders went straight home to Uffculme, where the three received a warm welcome from Mrs. Cadbury and her daughters. They could only tarry for two days, during which one of their delights was in making further plans for the building of the new home on a piece of land adjoining some fields belonging to the Uffculme estate, with only a road and a stretch of green-sward between. On September 3rd, they met Dr. Torrey, Harkness, Lowe, and others of the party, at Bolton, in Lancashire. Mr. W. S. Jacoby—Dr. Torrey's assistant in Chicago—had come to England for a few weeks as Alexander's guest. Saved from the awful curse of drink himself, Mr. Jacoby's marvellous testimony of God's grace, and his beautiful Christ-like spirit in dealing with sin-stricken souls, proved a valuable asset in the work of the mission. Another man, whose life was to be closely bound up with that of the Alexanders, had also crossed the Atlantic with them. This was Mr. George T. B. Davis, of Chicago, who had had experience as a religious editor and writer. He had been sent over to England by a syndicate of religious newspapers, who desired articles, full of incident, describing the Torrey-Alexander missions in Great Britain. The Bolton meetings were held in a large Drill Hall, and were largely attended by workers from the cotton mills, whose innate ability for singing made the music of this mission memorable. The choir, composed almost entirely of working-people, seemed like a single instrument in the hands of an artist, as Charles Alexander drew out the volume of song, shading the expression of the tones, cutting off the voices with staccato effect, or holding a long tender note that died to an almost imperceptible whisper.

Colonel R. A. H. Ainsworth, J.P., a man of wealth and influence, was chairman of the local committee, and also an ardent personal worker. Night after night, he and his wife could be seen going about the audience during the after-meetings, pleading with people to turn to Christ. One night, as the after-meeting was proceeding, Mr. George Davis stood upon the platform, eagerly looking out over the crowd, on the watch for striking incidents. Alexander was leading the choir in songs of invitation, which should form a suggestive background to the entreaty of the personal workers. His quick eye caught sight of Mr. Davis, and at the first chance between the hymns he was down beside him. Several people below the platform had come forward to take their stand for Christ, amongst them some boys. All the personal workers seemed busy, and no one was at hand to talk and pray with these waiting seekers for Christ. Alexander made a call for more workers at the front, and then said to Mr. Davis, " What are you doing here, Davis, while people are down there waiting to be led to Christ ? " " I'm watching for incidents for my articles," was the reply. " Get off the platform and lead some of those people to Christ," said Alexander, " and you'll have some first-hand incidents to tell." A firm, though gentle, push accompanied the words, and almost before he knew it, Davis had descended the steps, and with Bible in hand stood ready for business. But it was a new thing to him to go up to a complete stranger and plead with him about his soul, although he had led many of his Sunday-school boys to Christ. On this first night he could not summon enough courage to speak to a man, but approaching a group of boys who were waiting, soon gathered them around his open Bible, and made the way clear to them. As one boy after another said he would take Christ as his Saviour, the heart of Mr. Davis thrilled with the joy of soul-winning in a way never experienced before. From that day onward he grew and developed in the exercise of that marvellous gift which has been the distinguishing characteristic of his life ever since.

A meeting specially memorable at Bolton, though similar to those held in most of the other cities, was a midnight sweep for drunkards and outcasts, beginning at the close of the Saturday evening service in the Drill Hall. More than a thousand workers formed into two brigades—each accompanied by a brass band—and marched through the streets of the city, singing revival hymns. At eleven o'clock the public-houses closed, the workers entered into some of them, or caught hold of the poor creatures who were thrust outside, and invited and urged them to come to the Drill Hall meeting. What a terrible foretaste of Hell met the view of those upon the platform, as they gazed out over the crowd of more than a thousand besotted, blear-eyed, uncouth men and women, all more or less under the influence of drink! The singing, under Charles Alexander's wonderful leading, quieted and helped to sober them, and then Mr. Jacoby told them of his own marvellous conversion. Hundreds were melted to tears, and many took their stand for Christ.

The month of October was spent in Cardiff, South Wales, where the great Tabernacle used earlier in the year by the Salvation Army in London, was re-erected. It was crowded from the first, and a thing to be remembered was to hear the Welsh people sing " Jesus, lover of my soul," to their famous tune of " Aberystwyth." But they were not slow in catching up the new revival melodies taught them by Alexander. Soon, not only the streets of Cardiff but the towns and villages through the whole of South Wales were ringing with the " Glory Song," " Tell mother I'll be there," " Looking this way," and many others. These songs, the powerful preaching of Dr. Torrey, and the earnest services of the personal workers, were used of the Holy Spirit to bring about a spiritual upheaval in the Welsh metropolis and the surrounding districts. At a great gathering of ministers drawn from all parts of South Wales, the revival flame was caught up, and spread abroad over the land. Doubtless the great campaign in Cardiff was one of the instruments used of God to bring about the wonderful awakening which spread through Wales almost immediately afterwards, attracting world-wide attention.

On November 4th, the second great Liverpool mission began, lasting, with a short break for the Christmas week, until January 23rd, 1905. More than a year had gone by since the first mission in the Philharmonic Hall. In the meantime, the Tournament Hall, a colossal glass and iron building, seated to accommodate twelve thousand five hundred people, had been erected near Edge Lane, one of the suburbs of Liverpool. Although the hall was ten minutes' walk from the nearest street-car, and in spite of heavy snowfalls, the people came in throngs. The choir for this great mission numbered three thousand six hundred and fifty-eight members, the largest evangelistic choir ever brought together up to that time. It had been organized by Mr. F. J. Foxley, who with Dr. J. Louis Fenn, the secretary of the Mission, was responsible for the splendid preliminary preparations which contributed so largely to the success of the meetings.

The old members of the Philharmonic Choir had taken a deep interest in the romance of their beloved leader, Charles Alexander ; and when they gathered, with many others, in the new choir for the Tournament Hall meetings, a plan was quickly set on foot to subscribe for a wedding present for the happy couple. Difficulty was found in settling upon the right gift. Poverty and distress were rife that winter, and it was suggested by Mr. Foxley that the gift which would bring the greatest pleasure to Mr. and Mrs. Alexander would be a great " Wedding Feast " for the poor and outcast of the city. Two thousand three hundred invitations were sent out, and on January 7th, one of the evangelists' rest-nights, the Tournament Hall was crowded with guests. The central area of the hall was set with long trestle tables, gaily decorated with vases of flowers, and loaded with good things to eat. About half of the choir took their places upon the platform to sing, while the other half were ready to wait upon their guests. The front of the platform was gaily festooned with garlands, while flowers and plants surged to a crest around the high, crimson-covered dais. The double galleries that lined each side and the far end of the hall were thrown open, and were soon filled with some thousands of sympathetic onlookers. The faces of many of the guests, as they entered, were haggard, downcast, and forlorn. But as the meal progressed to their enjoyment and satisfaction, a change began to be visible even on their countenances. A crowning touch came at the close of the feast, when, before the tables were cleared, the vases were emptied of their fragrant contents, which were placed in worn button-holes or pinned on to faded shawls. Soon the bustle was over, the moving to and fro ceased, and the meeting began.

After a solo by Mr. Paul J. Gilbert, Dr. Fenn spoke a few words, telling of the first mission, and of Mr. Alexander's marriage to the daughter of that great, good man whose time and money had been so lavishly given to those in need. He then explained that this was a great " Wedding Feast," provided by the choir in honour of Mr. and Mrs. Alexander, whose joy would be full if some wanderers should come home to God that night. Charles Alexander then climbed the red dais, and with shining face smiled back his thanks for the great reception that greeted him. After telling of God's marvellous leading in bringing his wife and himself together, he beckoned to her, and led her up the dais steps to stand by him.

In a moment the great choir-platform, and the rest of the hall, seemed turned into fluttering clouds of white butterflies, as thousands of handkerchiefs waved amidst thunders of applause and affectionate greeting. A few grateful words from Mrs. Alexander were followed by more singing, and after an earnest address from Dr. Torrey, two hundred and seventeen persons yielded themselves to Christ. Once more the jubilant singing burst forth, and it would have been hard to say which was the more radiant—the great choir whose loving generosity had provided so bountiful a gift, or the happy pair who rejoiced that their marriage had been the cause of comfort and blessing to those in need. Of all the tokens of love received from their friends, none was remembered more gratefully than the " Wedding Feast " which took place in Liverpool that cold January night.

THE LIVERPOOL CHOIR WAVES A WELCOME.

DR. TORREY, DR. J. LOUIS FENN, AND CHARLES ALEXANDER
ON THE PLATFORM AT TOURNAMENT HALL

THE WEDDING FEAST AT TOURNAMENT HALL, LIVERPOOL, JANUARY, 1905

CHILDREN'S MEETING AT BOLTON, LANCASHIRE, SEPTEMBER, 1904

AN OPEN-AIR MEETING OUTSIDE VICKERS' WORKS, SHEFFIELD, SEPTEMBER, 1905
(Inset--Sheffield)

CHAPTER ELEVEN

London Sings the "Glory Song"

1905

AT the close of the work in Liverpool, Dr. Torrey and Charles Alexander had a few days of breathing-space before entering upon the great London campaign, which was to cover five months, from February 4th until the beginning of July. But even those few days were to be put to good use. Among the University students and others who had helped in the personal work of the Scottish Missions in 1903, was Mr. W. Talbot Hindley, who had specially interested himself in the telegraph boys. Mr. Hindley's first personal acquaintance with Alexander was formed during one of the Dundee meetings, when he sat among a crowd of seventy or eighty telegraph lads whom he had taken to the service. Alexander's quick eyes soon caught sight of the boys, and, calling a steward, he sent him with a message to present a music hymn-book to every boy as a gift from himself. Afterwards, Alexander spoke to the boys and to Mr. Hindley, and invited them all to meet him for tea. In various ways he gave a tremendous impetus to the work among these lads.

From the time of the Dundee Mission, Mr. Hindley often met his new friend and worked with him, and during the rest-week before the London Mission, prevailed upon him to give a few days to some of the students at Cambridge University.

On a Saturday afternoon, Alexander, accompanied by George T. B. Davis, Robert Harkness, and Paul Gilbert, the singer, met a little group of about twenty-five Christian men in the Henry Martyn Hall at Cambridge. For most of these, it meant a crisis in their lives and revolutionized their service for the Master. Alexander had a heart-to-heart talk with them on the question of soul-winning, and did not shrink from affirming that if any one of them were not trying to win individuals to Christ, it was a sure sign of sin of some kind in his life. A solemn and heart-searching time followed, none too easy for some of the men to go through, but the Holy Spirit had His way that day, and before they separated, every man in the room had dedicated his life to God for personal soul-winning in whatever way He should lead. Throughout Sunday, small private gatherings were held in students' rooms in the colleges, and everywhere the consecrated zeal of the young American set fire to sluggish and indifferent Christian lives. On Sunday evening, a packed meeting of students was held in the Victoria Assembly Rooms, about five hundred being present. The pleading tones of Gilbert's sweet tenor touched all hearts while he sang " Tell mother I'll be there." As Alexander appealed to the men to yield themselves to the Lord Jesus without any reserve, and to make Him King of their hearts and lives, the power of God came upon the gathering. A few timid spirits had begged him beforehand not to ask for any open expression of decision, but Alexander fearlessly proposed that those of them who wished to stand for Christ before the world in after-life, should begin, by humbly, and yet boldly, confessing Him right there and then. In the solemn hush, man after man, casting aside university prejudice and precedent, rose to his feet.

One of these students, Mr. Oswin B. Bull, now engaged in Christian work among the young men of South Africa, wrote to Mrs. Alexander in 1920 :— " It is quite impossible to tell you how much Mr. Alexander's rich and generous friendship meant to me personally. It was one of God's biggest gifts to me, just at the critical time of my life, and I owe him more than I can ever express. His picture has always been before me in my study, and in a thousand ways the thought and memory of him has been a constant inspiration." A striking and most helpful feature of the campaign in London was the assistance given by groups of these Cambridge men in the after-meetings, as they watched for opportunities to speak to other men and plead with them to make their decision for Christ.

Although Dr. Torrey and Charles Alexander had visited London in the beginning of 1903, and had held meetings for three weeks at Mildmay, there had been, up till now, no organized attempt to reach the whole city. But, encouraged by the spiritual results of the missions in Scotland, and in other parts of England, the London Evangelistic Council, with the Right Hon. Lord Kinnaird as its president, and Mr. John H. Putterill as hon. secretary, had made bold plans to stir the great metropolis of the British Empire with a breath of divine things. A five months' campaign was to be spread over the city. The Royal Albert Hall was engaged for February and March. A large temporary wooden building was erected in Brixton to reach the southern part of London through April and May, and for the month of June the huge corrugated-iron building, erected a year before for the International Congress of the Salvation Army, and already used for the Torrey-Alexander meetings in Cardiff, was re-erected upon the Aldwych site in the Strand. Thus every part of the city, and every type of inhabitant in the metropolis, had an opportunity of hearing the Gospel of Christ preached and sung.

Charles Alexander and his wife rented a small furnished house in Gloucester Road, about twenty minutes' walk from the Albert Hall, and here, in their first home—for the building of their own house in Birmingham was not as yet completed —they sought to use their home-life as an instrument to further their public work in leading men and women to God. Day by day, for two months, the Albert Hall was filled in the afternoons and crowded out at night, while noonday meetings for business and professional men were held daily, for part of the time, in Cannon Street Hotel, and in addition, various private gatherings were held in the forenoon. Numbers of individuals and families came from distant parts of the British Isles, from the Continent, and even from America, to share the privilege of a few days or weeks of the great meetings.

The Alexanders received an interesting letter from a young Danish minister whose heart was on fire for God and who thirsted for the inspiration of the London

Mission. They had much joy in making the way easy for him to spend a little while in London, and were happy in the privilege of meeting him. In the years that followed, they heard no more of him, but in November, 1920, a touching letter from Bishop Anton Bast, of the Danish Methodist Church in Copenhagen, reached Mrs. Alexander from New York. " Do you remember," wrote Bishop Bast, " the poor Danish Methodist preacher whom you and your beloved husband helped over to the great London Mission in 1905 ? Well, he is writing to you here. My heart was broken, when here in New York, I read about Mr. Alexander's death. I have followed you both, and your noble work, in all these years, and have many times sent up prayers and thanks for you to the Throne of Grace. Last summer, while I was attending several conferences in America, my dear wife died in Copenhagen. A week from now I shall go back there. Please remember me in my work."

In order to give those who came from such distances the fullest benefit of their stay in London, Charles Alexander spared neither time nor strength. The afternoon meeting in the Royal Albert Hall was advertised from three to four, but he was always on the platform at 2.30, having snatched a hurried lunch after the noonday meeting. When the sermon was over, Alexander would stay and lead the people in song and testimony till five o'clock or after. Soon after 6.30 he would be back again, and often, when the great hall had emptied, and the lights were being lowered at about eleven o'clock, the last to leave the building would be Charles Alexander and his wife.

The interest awakened in the meetings by united prayer, and effort, and publicity, was so great, that over forty thousand applications were received for tickets to the opening meeting on February 4th, and thousands who gathered in the streets for hours beforehand were unable to gain admission. Membership in the choir had been closed when the numbers reached four thousand, and on that first Saturday night about three thousand men and women filled the orchestra and overflowed into the balconies facing the immense throng that covered the sloping floor and crowded every gallery to the roof. It was perhaps the first time, even in the history of London, that so many had come together for a simple Gospel meeting.

A Scottish journalist, seated with a hundred or more other reporters at the Press tables, watched the scene with eager interest. He had been in the Torrey-Alexander meetings in other cities, and as the tall, slender figure of the song-leader, who had just risen from a sick-bed, mounted the crimson-covered rostrum on the platform, he wondered whether this mighty crowd could be subdued and impressed, as others had been on lesser occasions. For a brief moment Alexander stood impassive, gazing out on the great ocean of faces, and inwardly lifting his heart to God for wisdom and guidance. The silence was broken, as if spontaneously, by the strains of the grand old hymn, " Abide with me," as the magic touch of Robert Harkness swept over the piano. Alexander's first word was a request for more light, and, as it came, the sound of many voices swelled like some great organ through the building. Then the clear Southern voice was lifted in a short prayer, asking God's blessing upon the work of the coming months, and pleading that the songs might go out all over London, so that thousands might be sung into the

Kingdom of God.   Soon the hymn " Oh, it is wonderful " was rolling like great
waves of sound through the hall, hushing to a tender note as the words came :—

> Oh, it is wonderful,
> That He should care for me
> Enough to die for me !
> Oh, it is wonderful, wonderful to me !

The response from audience as well as choir was so true and full that the leader's
face lit up with a smile which seemed to radiate over the great crowd.   The
thousands of critics, who had been mere onlookers at the outset, were now thousands
of friends, ready to co-operate in the service of song, and to listen to the plea of Dr.
Torrey for a spiritual effort in the great metropolis, which should bring thousands
to the knowledge of salvation through the Lord Jesus Christ.

From that first night, the inspiration grew and deepened, touching lives from
so many parts of the earth that, through the after-years, Charles Alexander
frequently met once more, in various lands, and under unexpected circumstances,
those who had shared in the great meetings of the London Mission, and many who
had found Christ there.   One day, Charles Alexander and his wife received an
invitation from the well-known artist, Mr. Mortimer Menpes, to take tea with himself and his daughter, authoress of the text describing his pictures.   On arrival
at his home, after the close of the afternoon meeting in the Albert Hall, the
Alexanders were somewhat surprised to find themselves surrounded by a crowd
of actors and actresses, who had just come in from a performance at His Majesty's
Theatre.   At first it was difficult to find points of contact for conversation with
those whose whole lives and interests ran in such different channels, for Alexander
was not content to let such an opportunity slip by with small-talk.   His ready tact
and the charm of his manner soon bridged any sense of distance that followed the
introduction of himself and his wife by Mr. Menpes, and the alert brain was watching
for any possible opening for bringing a message from his Lord.   In one thing he
knew he could interest these people along a line in which they could not compete
with him.   He began to tell some of his darkey stories, with that marvellous
imitation of dialect and facial expression that was sufficient proof of latent histrionic
powers, had he ever chosen to develop them.   The group around him grew, until
in a little while, from all the rooms, the guests had gathered into a circle about him,
and peal after peal of laughter rang out.   Quick as a flash, when he had fully gained
their attention, he saw his opportunity.   " I see you like my darkey stories," he
said, " but there is one darkey poem that my wife can recite to you better than I
can."   His wife, sitting beside him, gave an imperceptible start, for though she
anticipated what was coming, she had never definitely committed to memory the
poem he loved, and feared lest she might fail him.   " I suppose you all know that
song of Sankey's, ' The Ninety and Nine ' ? " said Alexander, looking round at
the group.   But the blank expression of their faces showed that they were
strangers to the sweet old hymn.   Not one had heard of it.   " Well, it is the story
of the lost sheep," he told them, " and this is the way the coloured people have it.
Now, honey, recite it to them."   With a swift prayer for help, his wife's voice

sounded through the hush that fell and deepened in that luxurious room, with its costly Japanese decorations, and its crowd of fashionable men and women :—

> Po' lil' brack sheep, dat strayed away
>   Done los' in de win' and de rain—
> An' de Shepherd, He say : " O hirelin',
>   Go, fin' my sheep again."
> But de hirelin' say : " O Shepherd,
>   Dat sheep am brack an' bad."
> But de Shepherd, He smile, like dat lil' brack sheep
>   Wuz de onliest lamb He had.
>
> An' He say : " O hirelin', hasten,
>   For de win' an' de rain am col'—
> An' dat' lil' brack sheep am lonesome,
>   Out da, so far f'om de fol'."
> But de hirelin' frown : " O Shepherd,
>   Dat sheep am ol' an' grey ! "
> But de Shepherd, He smile, like dat lil' brack sheep
>   Wuz fair as de break ob day.
>
> An' He say : " O hirelin', hasten,
>   Lo ! here am de ninety an' nine,
> But da, *way* off f'om de sheep-fol'
>   Is dat lil' brack sheep o' Mine ! "
> An' de hirelin' frown : " O, Shepherd,
>   De res' ob de sheep am here ! "
> But de Shepherd, He smile, like dat lil' brack sheep
>   He hol' it de mostes' dear !
>
> An' de Shepherd go out in de darkness,
>   Where de night was col' an' bleak ;
> An' dat lil' brack sheep—He fin' it,
>   An' lay it agains' His cheek.
> An' de hirelin' frown : " O, Shepherd,
>   Don' bring dat sheep to me ! "
> But de Shepherd, He smile, an' He hol' it close,
>   An'—dat lil' brack sheep—wuz—me !

The Spirit of God moved through the room, and careless and indifferent hearts were stirred by a breath from Heaven. A big actress, whose eyes were filled with tears, broke the silence. " That makes a person feel pretty solemn," she said. " Could you not give me some kind of a platform pass to the Albert Hall for Sundays, for we have not time to wait out in the crowd for admittance, and I hear it is difficult to get in through the crush." During the next few minutes every card that Alexander had in his pocket was requisitioned, as he wrote an order for admittance to the platform door. Other cards were brought, for every one present desired a pass, and Alexander lifted a silent prayer that some lives might be turned to God.

The following afternoon a number of soldiers, and two hundred Chelsea Pensioners, were in the Albert Hall. Clad in their long red overcoats with brass buttons, these veterans of the Crimean and other wars were conspicuous in the throng. They seemed to enjoy the singing, and listened attentively to the address, but did not appear to be deeply moved, nor did any of them respond to Dr. Torrey's invitation for decision or surrender to Christ. During the hour of singing that followed Dr. Torrey's address, Charles Alexander suddenly turned to his wife upon the platform, beckoning her to mount the steps of the crimson-covered dais upon which he stood. Turning to the old soldiers, he said, " My wife has never spoken to such a big crowd before, but I want her to recite to you the coloured people's version of ' The Ninety and Nine '." Remembering how it had been blessed the day before, his wife tremblingly took her place beside him, and, re-assured by the pressure of the strong hand which held hers as she faced the great sea of faces, her voice steadied itself, and to the listening throng came the quaintly-worded, tender story of the Saviour's love for sinners.

It was evident that the message was touching the hearts of the listeners, for tears stood in many eyes, and when Paul Gilbert, with thrilling pathos, followed with the song, " Tell mother I'll be there," some of the old veterans who had sat stolidly through the service broke down completely. Many of them rose to accept Christ when Charles Alexander made his appeal, and there were numberless responses from other parts of the hall as well. It was with true joy that the audience burst into the song, " Praise God from Whom all blessings flow."

One day, while singing " Blest be the tie that binds," Alexander challenged the audience to make known how many nationalities were represented. People rose in all parts of the hall, and it was found that besides English, Scottish, Irish, and Welsh, there were visitors from Australia and America ; from France, Germany, Russia, Switzerland, Scandinavia, and even from far-away Japan.

At the close of an evening meeting, Alexander noticed twenty-one telegraph boys sitting at the front of the audience. Tired though he was, he made his way to them and shook hands with each boy. In five minutes he had explained the Way of Life to them, and called for a brave, open confession of Christ, if they would accept Him. Eighteen of the boys responded boldly. Alexander had been tired before, but this put new life into him. " When I was a boy," he told them, " a lady said to me one day, ' My boy, keep that shining face of yours for Jesus.' That thought has helped me hundreds of times " ; and he urged the boys to keep their faces sweet and pure for Christ.

A striking feature of the London Mission was the great attention paid to it by the secular Press, and the interest aroused by the music among secular musicians. H. Hamilton Fyfe, the eminent critic, in describing the opening meeting at the Royal Albert Hall, wrote in the *Daily Mirror* of February 6th, 1905 :—" The voice belongs to the most remarkable conductor I have ever seen. I have watched the methods and the triumphs of the most famous baton-wielders of the time—Colonne, Nikisch, Mottl, Weingartner, and Henry J. Wood. Never have I been so much impressed as I was by this bright-faced, energetic young evangelist. As the leader of a choir he has an amazing and almost magical influence, not only over the trained choir ; he simply makes everybody sing, and sing as he wants them to. ' Watch my hand ! ' he calls, and the men's unaccompanied voices rise and fall in crooning cadences with an effect any conductor might be proud of. Watch his hands ? Why we are watching every part of him ; we cannot take our eyes off him ; we are fascinated, hypnotized, bewitched. Never for a moment is he still. Now we see

him ' fine down ' a passage from *fortissimo* to *piano*. All done by a turn of the
wrist ! That marvellous magic hand of his thrills with the feeling he wants to put
into the music. ' Sing it as if you meant it ! ' he cries to the choir. But they *do*
mean it. This is no pretence ; no artistic make-believe. That is why the singing
is unlike anything I have ever heard before. That—and the wonderful conducting
of this astonishing young man." Mr. David Williamson, writing later, said :—" An
interesting thing to remember was a visit from Sir Henry J. Wood, the famous
conductor, who came to the Royal Albert Hall to watch Alexander's methods with
the great choir. Sir Henry was practically won to the system employed by Mr.
Alexander of using both hands rather than a baton."

James Douglas, another famous journalist, wrote in the *Morning Leader*
of February 6th, 1905 :—" Alexander is more than a Choir conductor. He is a
Crowd conductor. In ten minutes he turns this huge multitude into a choir. He
teaches them to obey him. He gives them singing lessons. That superb hymn,
' Abide with me,' serves as an example of his method. He first makes his choir
whisper it, sigh it, croon it, murmur it. Then he calls on the Crowd. ' Don't look
at your books ; look at me ! ' and the Crowd follows his flowing gestures. . . .
The climax is the ' Glory Song,' the battle hymn of the Revival. ' I want you to
sing it all the rest of your life. It will do you good ! ' The choir sings it. The
tune is catching, and the Crowd swiftly snatches it. ' You've been practising it ! '
The Crowd laughs like a happy child.

Friends will be there I have loved long ago.

" This is the first line of the last stanza. He calls upon those who have lost
' loved ones ' to sing it. As the Crowd sings there is a tragic wail in the music.
But the master-stroke is a hymn with the heart-rending refrain, ' Tell mother I'll
be there,' based upon President McKinley's telegram to his dying mother. As
Alexander sings the chorus in clear, poignant, staccato tones, the hall is hushed
with emotion. . . . The dynamite of the Revival is Alexander the Great—he
will make London hum, for he will make London sing."

Alexander welcomed this attention from the secular Press, as he welcomed
all legitimate publicity, for the sake of gaining the ear of " the man in the street "
with the good news of salvation. He was, indeed, an expert in the art of skilful
advertising, of which he was a serious student. But all that was said about his
personal magnetism and hypnotic power over an audience did not puff him up, for
he knew that the power his critics could not fathom was that of the Holy Spirit of
God, flowing through a channel which he sought to keep clean and unclogged, and
using talents which had been unreservedly yielded to Christ.

On the other hand, adverse criticism, while he was always eager to learn from
it, never wounded him, for he was working for results, not necessarily to please
people, and met difficult situations with disarming grace. He loved to quote St.
Paul's motto : " I am become all things to all men, that I may by *all* means save
some " He often showed how people tried to reverse it, and " by *some* means to
save *all*," which is quite a different matter. An extract from a letter received by
Mrs. Alexander from one of her brothers during these busy days, shows how his

character impressed thoughtful observers. " The other day a friend told me of having heard from a total stranger in London a most glowing account of Charles's quiet power of overcoming difficulty, and wise reserve in speech."

When the two months in the Royal Albert Hall came to a close, the interest in the West End of London had grown so tremendously that it was almost heart-breaking to move to another part of the city, but the plans could not be changed.

Through April and May, the centre of activity was in Brixton, and touched the whole of South London.   The last month of June, in which all the threads of the London work were drawn together and concentrated in the big temporary building on the Strand, set the seal to the entire Mission.   A final great gathering was held in the Royal Albert Hall on July 3rd, where testimonies were given, and praise to God was lifted, that must have been wafted as sweet incense to Heaven.

The summer which followed this strenuous campaign was filled with family interests, and with work in America.   The first event was the wedding of Mrs. Alexander's sister Margaret, to Dr. Neville Bradley, of Liverpool, whom she had first met at the Alexander wedding a year before.

Just at this time, the new home, which was named " Tennessee " in honour of Charles Alexander's native State across the ocean, was completed.   Connected closely also with Uffculme, " Tennessee " bound husband and wife together from the beginning with golden chains of memory and tender association.   The furniture was barely in, and there was only an opportunity to spend a single night beneath their own roof, before Alexander and his wife, accompanied by Mrs. Cadbury and her daughter Beatrice, sailed from Liverpool by the S.S. *Carpathia*. It was the first visit of the two latter to America, and Alexander was proud and happy to introduce them to his friends.   Sam Hadley's Mission in Water Street, New York, was of course visited, and Mrs. Cadbury, whose own husband had given so much of his love and strength to the poor drunkards of Birmingham, rejoiced to be in an atmosphere of such love and devotion to those outcast through drink and other forms of sin.   A short visit among the Cadbury relatives in Phila-delphia, and a wonderful journey up the Hudson River, through Albany and the Connecticut Valley, brought them to Northfield, Massachusetts, in time for the Christian Workers' Conference under the direction of Mr. W. R. Moody.   Here, though Mrs. Alexander was laid aside by illness, her mother and sister shared with her husband not only the inspiration of the great conference gatherings, but the glories of that beauty-spot of Nature.   Often in the early mornings, Alexander would take his sister Beatrice on horse-back through the leafy woods, along the banks of gurgling streams on the Ridge above the Northfield campus, where they enjoyed the exhilarating fragrance of the balsam pines and the shade of the great maple trees.

In spite of the terrific heat, to which they were unaccustomed, the English ladies rarely missed being present, hour after hour through the day, in the great Auditorium, where fans fluttered like the leaves of a tree in a breeze.   Especially did they enjoy the hour from ten to eleven, when Charles Alexander had his own special service, between the somewhat heavier lectures and addresses.   How the songs floated out through the open doors on to the sunny lawns that sloped

TWELVE THOUSAND CHILDREN IN
THE ROYAL ALBERT HALL, LONDON

CAMBRIDGE UNIVERSITY STUDENTS WHO CAME TO DO PERSONAL WORK IN THE ROYAL ALBERT HALL MEETINGS
(Inset--Starting for an Afternoon Meeting)   (Inset--Resting Between Meetings)

IN CENTRAL PARK, NEW YORK,
WITH MRS. ALEXANDER'S MOTHER
AND SISTER, AUGUST, 1905

THE ALEXANDER FAMILY AT "TENNESSEE,"
BIRMINGHAM, ENGLAND, SEPTEMBER, 1905

A CADBURY-ALEXANDER GROUP AT "UFFCULME," BIRMINGHAM, SEPTEMBER, 1905

away on all sides from the building ! Between the singing, Alexander would call
on such old friends as W. S. Jacoby, Sam Hadley, or Harry Munroe for a testimony.
However hot the day, no one went to sleep during these services of song !

Plans had been made for Alexander's mother, his sister Ida, and brother
Leo, to visit England during that August. His wife, therefore, with her own mother
and sister, sailed by an earlier boat to England, in order to prepare " Tennessee "
for its welcome guests. For the first time, husband and wife were separated, though
only for a few weeks, by the rolling waters of the great Atlantic, and the parting
was a genuine trial. A little note slipped into his wife's hand just before the boat
sailed, while not failing to arouse in her a sense of deep unworthiness, showed the
depth of his tender love. " I am more convinced than ever," he wrote, " that
you are the greatest woman I have ever known, or will know ; and that I love you
more deeply, I need not say, for you have seen it in my eyes. Good-bye, honey,
my soul is filled with singing. We have reason to thank God that we have had a
safe journey thus far. Anything you do for my mother, Ida, and Leo, will draw
the golden cords tighter." A week or two afterwards, the three from Knoxville,
Tennessee, were warmly greeted at the English " Tennessee," and at Uffculme,
and about ten days later Charles Alexander himself enjoyed one of the sweetest
welcomes home that a man could have. Only for two days, however, could he tarry,
for on September 2nd, the Torrey-Alexander Mission began in Sheffield, whither his
loved ones went also for some of the meetings. In October came a time of good-byes,
for the Alexander trio sailed for the United States again, and the following day
Dr. and Mrs. Bradley started on the way to their new work in South China, where
Dr. Bradley was to have charge of a large Church Missionary Society hospital, as
well as the care of the great compounds for leper men and women.

To the Plymouth Mission, which began on November 6th, Charles Alexander
had to go alone, leaving his wife ill at home. His letters to her reflect the busy
days, and a few extracts are taken from them.

October 12th.—" Dear little home, how precious it is to us ! I almost fancied I
could smell the garden. You have improved, or else I have grown in discernment,
for your descriptions of a day are gems. Honey, you have no idea how refreshing
those little nature touches of yours are. I think you will soon rival the *Daily Mail*
Nature-man ! I addressed two thousand five hundred men at Devonport in the
open air to-day, and there were fourteen conversions. To-night I am to address a
crowd of naval students. My brain is stretched to the limit on business affairs.
Ask God to give me wisdom not to make a mistake and hinder His work."

October 16th.—" I am about three minutes' walk from the water-front. The
old Eddystone Lighthouse is on the hill just round the corner, and the beautiful
harbour is an inspiration. We walk along the edge of it to the Drill Hall where
the meetings are held, and which has been doubled in length since Mr. Moody was
here. It is the longest building we have had except the Tournament Hall at
Liverpool. There are no posts at all in the centre, and it looks like a big tunnel.
We had a number of Cornishmen last night at the men's service. I got them
started in testimony, and they put fire into the meeting immediately. A large
number of soldiers and sailors attend the services, and many of them are coming

out for Christ. Professor Towner and his daughter arrived here to-day from
America, and the Gaylords from the Moody Bible Institute are coming on Thursday
to stay a few days."

October 21st—" I am glad you are to have the experience of writing your
father's life. I have sent for the best American and English biographies, written
by a son or a daughter, for you to study. The best of any I know is that of
Dr. A. J. Gordon by his son; I believe this would be a model for your work. Another
is the life of Dr. Charles Deems, of New York, by his son. The ' daily newspaper '
from ' Tennessee ' is a great source of comfort, and I trust the editor is not weary
of her duty."

October 23rd.—" Professor Towner and I will be busy in all spare moments
for the next ten days, getting our hymn-book for the Moody Institute in shape.
Pray for me while the selecting goes on." *October 26th.*—" To-day we had three
meetings—one at the soldiers' barracks four miles out. We are working hard on
the book. Professor Towner and I want another verse for the hymn that begins :

> Oh hearts that ache, and bleed and break,
>   God knows the depths of all thy woes ;
> He will Himself thy burdens take,
>   And shield thee from the heaviest blows.

My hymn-doctor can do it ! As soon as you can send it, we will mail it to America."

November 3rd.—" We are working all day on our rest-day this week, for the
book is pressing. I went to a small hospital to-day to sing and talk. All of the
nurses are converted now. The matron invited me into a small room where they
had gathered, and each nurse spoke beautifully of her surrender and joy."

During the two weeks' work in Oxford that followed the Plymouth Mission,
Charles Alexander was again alone, for his wife's health necessitated a slight
operation. " I am sure," he wrote to her, " I have never loved you as I do now,
you brave, sweet, lonely girl. I am sure the Lord will reward you for allowing me
to stay here and work for Him when you need me so much. I went to breakfast
with a " higher critic " this morning, and we prayed for you together. Dr. Torrey
has been most tender to me, and said he was led out in prayer for you. I feel
confident that God is answering our prayers, and is revealing Himself clearly and
giving you peace."

The Oxford Mission was not to students exclusively, but to " town and gown,"
always difficult elements to mingle. Some of the students were aggressively
antagonistic. They went up to the meetings for amusement, and took pains to find
it in various ways. For the first few days they had the best of it, and a successful
prospect of breaking up the meetings encouraged them to persevere. But Alexander
was never a man to sit quietly under opposition. He arranged for invitations to
be sent out to some of the leading spirits to meet him in friendly conference. About
twenty gathered round him at the time appointed, and the proceedings had barely
opened when they were taken off their guard. Apparently, they had expected the
song-leader to defend himself ; instead of that he smiled his sweetest, and invited
criticism ! It came in floods. With his arms folded, Alexander stood listening
—and smiling. If he was receiving wounds, he gave no sign of pain. The smile

continued to play round his countenance even when his own and his colleague's methods were being torn to shreds with an outspokenness that showed no mercy, but seemed to delight in its severity. Professedly Christian men were amongst the critics, and were just as merciless as the others. At last the torrent of invective exhausted itself, and the students, satisfied with the way they had presented their case, awaited Alexander's reply with an air of triumph, as though there were nothing further to be said. Smiling yet, calm and unperturbed, he quietly remarked, " Well now, gentlemen, I have been very interested in listening to your criticisms of Dr. Torrey and myself. You don't like our methods ; perhaps you will let me know what methods *you* adopt to bring men to Christ." It was a staggering question. They had not anticipated anything like this, and the bewildered faces showed that the critics had not expected the tables to be turned on them in this disconcerting way. They would have avoided the question if they could, but the evangelist pressed for a reply, receiving the answer he had anticipated —they were not doing it at all. " Well then," he continued, after obtaining this reluctant confession, " until you can show us a better way, we will stick to our own methods." And then he let himself go, his words falling with sledge-hammer force on that little company of men, now more than half-ashamed of the part they had played ; and as he insisted on the duty of every man who called himself a Christian to win others to the Saviour, he urged that sin should be put out of the life and everything yielded wholly to the Lord. 'Very soon he had the gathering turned into a prayer-meeting, with every one down on his knees, and the meeting which had begun with criticism melted into a season of confession and prayer. What that hour meant to that little company it would not be easy to say, for it is in such solemn and heart-searching moments that vital and far-reaching transactions are made with God. While the mission lasted, no further opposition was encountered from the Christian students. The general opposition, too, died down, and before the meetings were over, many were rejoicing in sins forgiven and in lives dedicated to God.

The Oxford Mission ended on November 27th, and on the 28th a great farewell meeting was held at Liverpool in the Tournament Hall, bringing to a close the three years' campaign which Dr. Torrey and Charles Alexander had carried on throughout the British Isles. On November 29th, Dr. and Mrs. Torrey and their family sailed for America, leaving Alexander and his wife to join them on the other side of the Atlantic a few weeks later.

CHAPTER TWELVE

In Canada and His Homeland

1906

JUST as Great Britain had been moved by news of the spiritual revivals in Australia and New Zealand, so now the Christian public in Canada and the United States in their turn were being stirred to expectancy by reports of the great campaign which had been moving Great Britain and Ireland. For the first six months of 1906, Torrey-Alexander campaigns had been planned in Toronto and in Ottawa ; also in Philadelphia, and in the Southern city of Atlanta, Georgia. The meetings in Toronto were to begin on December 30th.

Charles Alexander had now to face a new trial. His wife had not recovered sufficiently to go with him, and the hardest separation they had yet faced now lay before them. It was to prove even longer than they anticipated, for the hope given by the doctors that Mrs. Alexander would be able to join her husband in America during the Spring did not materialize. She grew worse instead of better, and the torture of anxiety through which Charles Alexander passed during this period would have surely hindered his work but for his unshaken trust in God. The greatest human comfort to them both was the close proximity and tender care of Mrs. Alexander's sweet mother and sister at Uffculme.

As the train bore him to Liverpool, to begin his journey to America, he wrote :—
December 16th, 1905.—" My heart and my thoughts are with you. Thank our Beatrice for her intelligent, loving sympathy. I am sure mother is doing all she can to make it easier for you. Most of all, I know where permanent help and peace is to come from. I am depending on Him. Nothing rested me more to-day than when you said He was giving you peace more than you had thought possible."
Midnight, on board R.M.S. " Caronia."—" A tremendous crowd was at the ship's side to see me off. I had a British flag, which I used to conduct the crowd on the dock from the ship as we drew out. People on board seemed touched by the singing. A Toronto business man has been in my cabin talking enthusiastically about the prospects in Canada. We read the evening selection from *Daily Light* and prayed together."

December 23rd.—" I am so glad we kept our Christmas together before I left —the memory of it is sweet each time I think about it. The Editor of *The New York Evening Telegram* sits at my table in the dining-room, and I have been round and round the long decks with him, getting all the information I can. To-night at the concert I am going to sing the ' Glory Song.' *Later*. They joined

NOON
STREET-MEETING,
DEVONPORT,
NEAR
PLYMOUTH

"SUNBEAM"
CHOIR,
OTTAWA,
CANADA,
APRIL,
1905

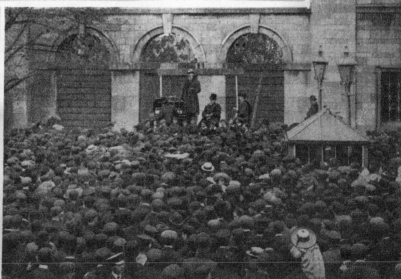

CHILDREN'S MEETING IN
THE DRILL HALL, SHEFFIELD,
SEPTEMBER 16, 1905

OPEN-AIR MEETING AT KEYHAM DOCK, DEVONPORT, ENGLAND, OCTOBER, 1905

NEW
TESTAMENTS
PRINTED
BY
PAKHOI
LEPERS,
DESTROYED
BY
WHITE
ANTS

CHURCH AT PAKHOL, SOUTH CHINA, FEB., 1907

SONG SERVICE AT MELBOURNE EXHIBITION BUILDING, APRIL, 1907, WHERE THE TORREY-ALEXANDER
MEETINGS HAD BEEN HELD FIVE YEARS EARLIER

heartily in the chorus of the 'Glory Song' to-night, and God gave me a chance to speak to a gentleman who needed Christ. I have felt a consciousness of God's presence on the voyage, as if some one was praying and getting answers for me. I hope that same sweet peace has filled your heart ever since I left your dear presence."

On *January 16th*, Alexander wrote from the China Inland Mission Home in Toronto :—" It was nine o'clock on Sunday morning when we reached the dock. Mr. Revell was there to meet me, and took me home with him. After leaving New York, I went on to Chicago, and had a delightful time with Homer and his wife. The baby is a sweet little thing, but when I found that it was named 'Helen' it grew even prettier and sweeter to me. Homer and French Oliver are holding meetings together in Iowa, and are having good results. We held a two days' convention at the Moody Bible Institute, which proved to be a rising tide of blessing. The singing went with great spirit, and we made it a soul-winning convention without any pre-arranged programme. We are well into the Mission here by now. The meetings are being splendidly reported. Last week the reporter on *The Star* led the reporter on *The World* to Christ. He said this was the hardest assignment he had ever had, but when the other man publicly confessed Christ, he said he got more out of it than any press work he had ever done. Crowds of excursionists come in from day to day from all the places round, and I am afraid this beautiful Massey Hall will spoil us for the Armory we are to have in Philadelphia. I hardly dare to say how much I want you, for fear of unsettling you, but I long for you more than ever." Alexander had at this time also to face illness in his own family, thus adding to his anxieties.

February 12th, 1906.—" I have had trouble upon trouble since I left you. I found that Leo had been seriously ill, and took my good Chicago doctor, who is a fine Christian man, all the way home to Knoxville with me. After examining Leo, the doctor took him back to Chicago for an operation, and we hope all will be well. I travelled the whole week and reached Philadelphia about done, but with God's peace in my heart. How I long for you, honey, and am still hoping you may be well enough to come over to me. Dear Sam Hadley died the other day. This morning I went up to New York for his funeral in the Mission Room, where you and I sat together and heard him speak in his wonderful way. They asked me to sing the 'Glory Song,' but it was too much for me, so I had Charlie Butler sing it. We all wept together, but Mrs. Hadley had a look of triumph on her face. Come to me, honey, if you can. Being away from you gets worse every day. This door of opportunity, open just now, only comes to one or two men in a generation, and I am afraid to miss it. My heart is wholly thine for ever."

February 16th.—" Leo is safely through his operation, and Homer is looking after him. Dr. Weirick went all the way to Tennessee, spent about three days' hard work, performed the operation, and will not let me pay a cent. I want you to meet him when you come. He is about as white a man as a person ever meets."

About the middle of February the Torrey-Alexander party began a three weeks' meeting in the great Armory at North Broad Street, Philadelphia, but although it could accommodate about five thousand five hundred people, it proved too small for the crowds that thronged the streets, eager to get in.

H

Instead of the usual noon meetings for business and professional men, several meetings were held in the medical colleges and dental schools, many students taking a stand for Christ. Other interesting and unique features of the Philadelphia campaign are referred to in the following letter from Alexander to his wife :

February 24th.—" I expect to be home in July, but how can I wait to see you until summer ? I have had some uneasy nights thinking about you, but I have to leave you in our good Father's loving hands. We are just starting to Princeton University, where we hope to have a time of blessing such as we had at Cambridge. Mr. Jacoby has come from Chicago, and will probably be with us during the next weeks in Philadelphia. He made a great impression the first afternoon he told of his conversion. We have now taken the Academy of Music, right in the centre of the town, for the noonday and afternoon meetings. The Academy of Music is to Philadelphia something like the Royal Albert Hall is to London. Mr. Wanamaker invited me to lunch with him one day. He handed me the keys to his front door, and told me to come and go when I wanted, but I have not been able to get there. At our luncheon meeting the other day five business men took Christ, and publicly confessed Him on the spot, and the work is still going on. A committee has been arranged to secure an office down town, and we shall probably send Mr. Jacoby to do personal work for all the men that want to come and find help. Two Sundays ago I conducted the service in Dr. J. R. Miller's church, and had a delightful time with him and his wife, going home with them for dinner." We have been to four of the Philadelphia colleges now, three medical schools, and to the college connected with the Baptist Temple."

The meetings referred to, which came to be known as " Revival Luncheons," grew from a visit paid by Alexander, on one of his rest-nights, to a church in West Philadelphia. Barely two hundred persons were present in the basement of the church, but Alexander's message burned with living fire and the people were greatly stirred, until it seemed as if a baptism of the Holy Spirit had fallen upon the little group. A few of the business-men arranged for a hotel luncheon and invited other business and professional men to meet Charles Alexander, with the desire that they, too, might become active in soul-winning. Forty-three were present, and before the luncheon was over the power of God fell upon them. One after another arose, confessing that their lives had not been right. They went out determined to win other men to Christ, and in a short time fifty decisions were reported. These Revival Luncheons were held weekly, Alexander presiding. Almost as soon as the meal began he would ask for testimonies, and the luncheon would be transformed into a revival meeting, which lasted about two hours.

The opening of an Inquiry Office, in the heart of the business section of the city, where men might come for help in spiritual doubts and difficulties, was another plan of Alexander's, which was taken up with enthusiasm by his Philadelphia friends.

The man chosen to undertake the delicate task of dealing with problems of the human soul, was Alexander's friend, William S. Jacoby, whom he had first met in his final year as a student at the Moody Bible Institute. Mr. Jacoby's history had been a remarkable one. Drifting away in young manhood from the influence of a Christian home, he had plunged into a life of sin in which he sought to find pleasure that constantly turned to ashes. Forbidden to go back home by his father, he only paid surreptitious visits, hidden from sight of others by the mother, whose love reached beyond the sin and ingratitude of her son. Finally outlawed from his home town, and discharged both from the Army and Navy on account of drink, he drifted beyond all help but that of the Good Shepherd, Who never fails to follow the wandering sheep. In Jacoby's case, as in many others, He found that which was lost, and brought him home upon His shoulders, rejoicing. So great was the change that took place, that those who have known William S. Jacoby since his conversion, many of whom regard him as one of the saintliest, most Christ-like characters they have ever met, find it hard to believe that the story of his early life is anything but fiction. At the time of the Philadelphia Mission, W. S. Jacoby was Assistant-Pastor of the Chicago Avenue Church, affectionately looked up to by all the students at the Institute, respected by the whole Christian community of Chicago, and reverently loved by many a man whom he had lifted out of drunkenness and sin. Such a man knew well how to comfort and counsel men facing temptation, or who were bowed down with trouble and perplexity. Three days after the office in Philadelphia had been opened, four men had been converted, five backsliders restored, and twelve had received spiritual help through Mr. Jacoby's ministry. One man, who took counsel of him, was troubled about his Christian experience, and his inability to help one of his employees who was drifting into habitual drunkenness. One day, he had been surprised to see his employee in one of the meetings in the Academy of Music, singing " Grace enough for me " with an entirely new expression on his face. As soon as the meeting was over he hurried to shake hands with him, and inquire what had caused the change. " Now," said his employer to Mr. Jacoby, " he has something that I haven't got yet, and I want it." He was soon convinced that his trouble had been unbelief in the Word of God, and left the Inquiry Office with the determination to trust the blessed message and live wholly for God.

It was during this campaign in Philadelphia that Alexander, with his experiences at Oxford and Cambridge fresh in his mind and heart, resolved to make an effort to win the students at Princeton University for Christ. He always felt that in seeking to reach men of intellect and education, the appeal to mere intellect did not come with half the force of the arresting exhibition of God's power in a life that had been marvellously changed from sin to righteousness. He therefore chose to take with him to Princeton a man whose experiences had been somewhat similar to those of Jacoby ; a man who had been brought to the depths by drink, and who had risen so high in Christ since his conversion under Harry Munroe at the Pacific Garden Mission, that to look at him lifted one's eyes past him to Christ. Melvin E. Trotter was now at the head of a Rescue Mission in Grand Rapids, Michigan, where miracles of the grace of God were constantly to be seen in transformed lives. At Princeton, Alexander followed the methods that had proved so fruitful in the English universities, and with Mel. Trotter, he met group after group of the students in their own rooms, answering questions and talking over their difficulties, urging them to yield themselves wholly to Christ.

Then in the larger meetings he would put their decision to the test, and encourage them to take the first step in open confession.

From Philadelphia, the Torrey-Alexander Mission party went south to Atlanta, Georgia, where they held meetings through the month of May.

May 9th, Majestic Hotel, Atlanta.—" The Atlanta people are disappointed not to see you. Your letters have been such a comfort to me. I can scarcely think of the meeting in July without neglecting my work. My heart jumps hard when the vision comes. The fire burns brighter every day, honey."

May 17th.—" Leo is much better. He is here with us now, looking well and hearty. I heard from my mother that she had received a beautiful letter from you. Thank you, honey, for writing so often to her. I think if you were here I could hardly bear you out of my sight. Each day, as my work is finished, I feel that I have worked for God, and my lovely Helen. How I had looked forward to show you the people and places of the South. . . . You are still my Gibraltar. If I did not have such confidence in the unshakableness of your love, there would be nothing strong enough to keep me here."

During the meetings in Atlanta, two outside events are worthy of note. One was a visit to that warm-hearted, original Southern preacher, Sam Jones, in his own home at Cartersville, Georgia. The other was the conferring upon Charles Alexander of the honorary degree of Master of Arts by his old University of Maryville, Tennessee.

At the end of May, the mission party sped northwards again, and for the next few weeks were holding meetings in Ottawa, Canada. Here, perhaps the most notable of many converts was Alf Allen, the champion middle-weight pugilist of Canada. He was drunk when he professed to take Christ for his Saviour, having been drinking heavily for months before, but the genuineness of the change was soon manifest, and was proved by his renunciation of his former calling, and by his entering the Moody Bible Institute in Chicago to train in Christian work.

During six months of strenuous labour in the four great cities—Toronto, Philadelphia, Atlanta, and Ottawa—no fewer than fifteen thousand persons had made a public acknowledgment of their acceptance of Christ.

Unknown at the time, either to Dr. Torrey or Charles Alexander, the end of the mission in Ottawa not only brought to a close the season's work, but also concluded the partnership in which they had worked together since the early part of 1902. The parting of the ways was as yet hidden from their view, but the Divine hand was planning for both of them. More and more serious tidings had been reaching Charles Alexander about the condition of his wife's health, and it was with sorrowful forebodings that he was able to turn at last to the re-union for which he had been longing so earnestly. " Oh, honey," he wrote from Ottawa on *June 24th,* " you don't know how hungry I am to feel the touch of your dear hand, and to look into your wonderful eyes. I need not say how my heart aches for my darling, with all of her suffering. Mr. Jacoby is praying earnestly with me for you. My heart leaps when I think of seeing you." Hearing of the necessity of a difficult operation, he cabled, " Grieve that my violet must be crushed, but its perfume will be rarer." A few days later he set sail from Montreal, and early in July had reached the English home, which to him was an earthly Paradise.

The months that lay between the summer of 1906 and that of 1907 were full of strange experiences, of anxieties, and of new lessons in walking humbly with God. Three times in this period did Charles Alexander stand face to face with death ; once for his wife, once for himself, and finally in the sudden Home-going of the gentle English mother who had grown so dear to him. On reaching England in July, after the strenuous six-and-a-half months' work with Dr. Torrey in his own land and in Canada, he found that the outlook for his wife's health was even more serious than she had allowed him to know. But for them both the joy of meeting, after the long, weary separation, put all other thoughts aside. The serious operation, which gave the only chance for life, had already been deferred longer than was wise, but, as its hope of success was uncertain, it was planned for husband and wife to have at least two weeks of joyful fellowship together before leaving " Tennessee " for a London nursing home. However, only five days had passed after his arrival, when his wife's illness took a sudden turn for the worse, the London surgeon had to be sent for, and the operation performed under great difficulty at " Tennessee." There seemed no hope, but the stricken husband cabled immediately to some groups of praying friends in America.

One cable was sent to a town in Iowa, where there was a prayer circle to whom he had written before leaving the country. One of the most godly members of this group was travelling in another part of the State when the cable arrived, and though the others met for prayer they could not send her the message. Next day they received a letter from her, saying that at a certain hour in the day she had had a strong impression that her friend's wife was in special need, and that for hours she had wrestled with God on her behalf. In Knoxville, and at the English " Tennessee," the two mothers, and other loved ones, were praying.

For two weeks, life hung in the balance, but the crisis passed and gradual recovery began. As this would in any case be slow, and would be more fully ensured by many months upon the ocean, the doctors talked seriously with Charles Alexander about his future plans, especially as they told him that the grief of another long parting might militate against recovery. His position was a difficult one, for not only his own plans but those of Dr. Torrey were involved, further missions together having already been arranged. But Charles Alexander did not hesitate for a moment. The life that God had given him and had now spared, as by a miracle, was to him the highest responsibility of service, and he wrote at once to Dr. Torrey, laying the matter before him.

To add to his perplexities another strange test of faith arose. From some unknown source a cruel slander had begun to circulate, while he was across the ocean, that he was already a married man with a family in America, to whom he had gone, leaving his wife, heart-broken, in her English home. The story did not reach the ears of those concerned in it till just as Charles Alexander landed in England. Both he, and his wife, and others of the family circle, laughed at it as too ridiculous to be noticed, but when it was gradually discovered that the slander had spread far and wide, and was actually gaining credence among reputable people, and that many of the converts of the Birmingham Mission were being persecuted on account of it,

Alexander's friends insisted that something must be done to deny it publicly. In the integrity of his own heart, and the joy of his wife's recovery, the utterly foolish slander had failed to wound either himself or his wife, but when he heard that those who had taken their stand for Christ in Bingley Hall were suffering, he consented to arrangements for a great welcome meeting and Song Service to be held in the Central Hall.

Letters were written by his friends in England to some of those who had known him in his own land since boyhood. At first the news of the slander almost aroused amusement, for his life everywhere had been open and clear, and known and loved for its radiant purity. But soon indignant protests were being hurried back to England in the mail-sacks. One or two quotations only can be given here.

Dr. Torrey wrote on Sept. 4th, 1906 :—" I greatly regret my inability to be present at the welcome meeting to be held in Birmingham for Mr. Alexander. I have such bright recollections of the meetings we held there together in Bingley Hall. Since we left England in December, God has wonderfully blessed us in our work in this country, and has drawn us closer together than ever before. Mr. Alexander has won the affection of every one wherever he has gone here, just as he did in the mother country. We met here many who have known him from boyhood. He was loved before, but is loved more now. I deeply regret that we are to be separated from one another for some months, but I see the necessity of his being with his wife in this time of her physical weakness. It was a wonderful sacrifice on his part to leave her all these months, to follow the call of God and sing the Gospel in this country, but I could not consent to his being away from her now. Alexander is more to me than merely a companion in my work : he is one of my children. I have known him since he was a boy and I have watched him. I first met him in the college town where he grew up and was studying, and I found everybody loved and trusted him there. Then he came to study with us at the Bible Institute and was with us three years. I often wondered as he grew up into mature manhood whether he would ever marry, and when God led him and Miss Cadbury to love one another, Mrs. Torrey and myself were delighted. We are hoping that our separation may be short, and that we may soon be re-united in our work."

Another quotation is from a letter sent by Dr. Samuel Tyndale Wilson, Alexander's beloved Professor at Maryville University, and since 1901 its President. He wrote on August 10th :—" Allow me to perform a work of supererogation in sending you a note of commendation of the life and work of my old pupil, Charles M. Alexander. I have known him since his boyhood, for his old home is only a few miles from Maryville, and he was for seven years a student in our preparatory and college departments. Ever since those days I have kept in close touch with him during his wonderful career as a singing evangelist. I am an intimate friend of his mother's family and of many of his friends scattered over the entire country. I have been familiar with all the events of his life, and have greatly rejoiced in his marvellous growth in usefulness and devotion.

" From his boyhood days to the present he has lived a cheerful, sunny, pure, and exemplary Christian life. His college and Moody Institute record was absolutely clean. His fruitful years in the ministry of sacred song have endeared him to the great evangelical church in America, and his magnetic and happy personality has bound to him even the hearts of hosts that have had no special interest in his religious zeal and mission. While some enemies of the old Gospel, and some very conservative Christians have, of course, sometimes criticized his message or methods, it is noteworthy that never has a charge been made against his personal character. He has that priceless blessing, a flawless record, to look back upon."

On September 19th, shortly before six o'clock, the crowds began to gather outside the Central Hall. "They were the first comers," says a Birmingham paper of that date, "of what afterwards proved to be one of the most extraordinary assemblages ever seen in the city. The Central Hall is a large building that will hold from two to three thousand people, but five times that number were wishful to get in, and a large body of police turned them away in thousands."

In addition to members of the Committee which had arranged the Bingley Hall Mission, and other local friends, the platform was filled with members of the old choir. The Chair was taken by the Rev. F. S. Webster, formerly of Birmingham, afterwards a Prebendary of St. Paul's Cathedral, London, and rector of a large West End church. Dr. Len G. Broughton, of Atlanta, Georgia, U.S.A., had also come, without invitation, to speak his mind.

In a little while the great hall was ringing with the music of hymns which stirred sacred memories in many a heart, and the face of the leader glowed, as all other thought for the purpose of the meeting vanished from his mind, in the joy of hearing his Master praised. Mr. Webster read extracts from the letters of Dr. Torrey and of Mr. W. R. Moody of Northfield, Mass. He was followed by the Rev. T. E. Titmuss, who read other extracts from the pen of Dr. Wilson of Maryville, Dr. J. R. Miller of Philadelphia, and others. Dr. Broughton, who was at the time occupying the pulpit of a well-known church in London, made the great audience break out into laughter and applause as he indignantly refuted the slanderous rumour concerning his friend. When Charles Alexander arose to lead another hymn, it was many minutes before the ovation which broke out could be stilled. "I would never have said a word about this rumour," he remarked, "if my friends had not said I might help some of the converts who are being persecuted. They told me there are some people who will never be satisfied till they hear me say I never married any one until I married Miss Cadbury. It is beneath my contempt, but I want to let you know right now that I never was," (Applause) "and I'm going to tell you another thing—I'm glad I was not." (Laughter and prolonged applause.)

The crowds outside the Central Hall refused to disperse till they had seen and heard Charles Alexander, and when the service inside was over, he was obliged to hurry into the street. From the vantage ground of a lorry, which had been brought, he spoke a few words, and led the waiting people in a song of praise and a short prayer of thankfulness for their love and sympathy in his wife's serious illness. The whole occasion was a remarkable tribute of affection, and a wonderful vindication of a character so nobly pure, that the blackest efforts to stain it fell to the ground.

Years afterwards a testimony was given, which, though it had no connexion with the events of 1906, corroborates the beautiful testimonies called forth by the silly slander. An Australian author, Rev. Donald MacLean, who had become acquainted with Charles Alexander during the Australian missions, was travelling through America in 1913 in search of literary material. His quest took him through the Southern States of Tennessee and Kentucky. In 1914 he wrote to a friend :—

" I went to Cloyd's Creek, in the State of Tennessee, where Mr. Alexander was born. There I mingled with his relatives and met with old identities who knew his father and grandfather. They took me to his birthplace, and I saw the little day-school where he taught in his vacation times. I talked with one of his old pupils. I preached in the little church which he joined as a child, and where his name is still on the roll. I came to the conclusion that whatever Charles Alexander may be to people in other parts of the world, he is the unchallenged hero of Cloyd's Creek. In the great Maryville College, with its seven hundred students, I stayed several weeks as the guest of Dr. Samuel Wilson. Of the many who have passed through the College, none is remembered more affectionately, and of none are they more proud than Mr. Alexander. In Chicago there is the same tradition. Men like Mr. Fleming H. Revell, the publisher, Dr. R. A. Torrey, Mr. Harry Munroe of the Pacific Garden Mission, and other well-known people whom I met, remember with pride that they had been intimate with him. Men who worked with him in the Middle West are as clear in their testimony to the wholesomeness of his life as is his own mother—a life free from reproach of any kind ; one made beautiful by self-sacrifice, and running clear as a stream in his native hills, from its beginning forty-seven years ago until the present day."

Unjust accusations of another kind were constantly hurled at Alexander and the men with whom he was associated, when rumours were spread by enemies of the Gospel that large fortunes were being made out of their evangelistic work. They rarely troubled to answer these, for their lives and private circumstances were well known, and readily open to investigation at any time. On one occasion, at a business men's meeting in Sydney, Australia, in 1909, Dr. Chapman made a public statement regarding the exact conditions under which he and Mr. Alexander accepted invitations. The Australian Committee had paid the travelling expenses of Mr. Alexander, Mr. Harkness, and himself from America. He and Mr. Alexander had undertaken the expenses of the others. Not a penny had been asked for himself or Mr. Alexander, for they did not want people to say that they had come to Australia for money. There was no call for people to contribute a single penny for their special personal fund unless the impulse was upon them to do so.

This was the policy followed throughout the whole of Charles Alexander's evangelistic experience with his various associates, and it was his greatest joy to devote all the money that came to him from the sales of his hymn-books to the carrying on of his work for Christ. Every penny as it came to him went out in gifts of Testaments and hymn-books ; or in loving, carefully-chosen temporal gifts to relieve suffering, and bring cheer and comfort ; or into salaries and other expenses needed for his soul-winning enterprises. When he passed away at the early age of fifty-two, his wife and his mother were proud to know, that instead of bank accounts, he left behind him thousands of grateful hearts and transformed lives. He had learned the secret of laying up " treasures in heaven, where neither moth nor rust doth corrupt, and where thieves do not break through nor steal."

CHAPTER THIRTEEN

A Second World-Tour

1906 to 1907

THE need of planning a long sea-voyage for Mrs. Alexander after her illness turned the thoughts of husband and wife towards the Orient. Dr. and Mrs. Bradley had been in Pakhoi, South China, for about a year, and as soon as Mrs. Alexander's recovery was assured, her mother and her sister Beatrice had set out to visit the Bradleys and rejoice with them over the little daughter that had been given to them. The attraction of a family reunion so far from home quickly decided the Alexanders to make Pakhoi their first objective, and on November 23rd they sailed from Tilbury Docks, London, by the P. & O. S.S. *India*. Unexpectedly severed, by divine leading, from his work with Dr. Torrey, Charles Alexander and his wife not only prayed themselves, but asked their friends to pray, that wherever they went, on land or sea, they might be good witnesses for the Lord Jesus Christ. Travelling with them to China was a young doctor, Hubert Gordon Thompson, of Liverpool, who was going to assist Dr. Bradley in the Medical Mission at Pakhoi connected with the Church Missionary Society.

Every evening during the voyage the three met together to read a chapter from the Bible, and to report any opportunities for speaking of Christ to those on board. As frequently occurs on such voyages, money for sweepstakes on the ship's daily run soon began to be collected, culminating in the excitement of what was called "Calcutta sweepstakes." The Alexanders were astonished to see the number of passengers taking part in this form of gambling. They became acquainted with several young men on their way to business appointments in the Orient. Some gambled so heavily that they had to borrow money before they could land at their destinations. One lonely young fellow, the son of a Scottish minister, became quite intimate with Charles Alexander and his wife, who found that he was beginning to indulge in things he had never done before. His dearly-loved mother had recently gone to heaven, and in a quiet corner of the deck, the boy's heart found relief in talking of her to his new friends. Before he left the ship at Penang he had definitely drawn out of the gambling practices into which he had been enticed, and left the ship with a determination to stand for God amid the difficult surroundings of his new business position.

At Port Said, and at Colombo, as well as at Penang and Singapore, opportunities came for short visits among the missionaries while the ship was in port. Christmas Day was spent on the China Sea. Early in the morning the Alexanders heard sounds of singing just outside their cabin, and found that the stewards had gathered to sing the "Glory Song," followed by several Christmas carols. Hong-Kong was reached on December 29th, and here they were welcomed by Archdeacon Bannister and the Y.M.C.A. Secretary. A day or two later Dr. Bradley arrived in Hong-Kong to take the Alexanders and Dr. Thompson back with him to Pakhoi.

Arrangements were made to organize a Song Service in the Hong-Kong Opera House on their return a few weeks later. Before sailing, a day or two was spent by the Alexanders with Dr. Bradley and Dr. Thompson at the Peak Hotel. From this height they were enraptured with the glorious views across the beautiful harbour, crowded with shipping of all kinds, to the ancient town of Kowloon, on the mainland, with its range of mountains behind.

On New Year's Eve, the little party gathered to watch the old year out upon their knees, and chose as a year-text, John xiv. 1: "Let not your hearts be troubled." Little did they realize how much they would shortly need that precious message! Within a few days, the little Chinese steamer, with its Norwegian captain, and very primitive accommodation, bore them round the coast, through the Straits of Hainan and into the Gulf of Tonquin. It seemed like a dream when, in that distant corner of the earth, the family was re-united. Here they were far from the beaten track of Western travellers, and enjoyed entering into the work of the mission, especially of the hospital and of the great leper compounds for men and for women. They were amazed at the wonderful examples of Christian faith and courage found among many of these sufferers from so loathsome a disease, and cut off, because of it, from intimate association with their fellows.

But it was not until they had accompanied Dr. and Mrs. Bradley on a visit to a leper village out on the plains, that the Alexanders realized what the missionary compound, with all its beneficent and spiritual influences, meant to these poor out-casts from human society. If they were willing, it was possible in the compounds, by strict attention to cleanliness and by skilful surgical and medical treatment, to at least arrest the cruel disease. Employment, too, was found in maintaining their own gardens and doing their own cooking; also in making twine and baskets and other articles which could be disinfected and sold; the women in their compound finding interest in lace-making and embroidery. Most wonderful of all was the daily school, and especially the Bible classes, taught by some of the lepers themselves, whose faces shone with a heavenly light that made people forget the disfigure-ment caused by the disease. One day an incident occurred that was a triumph of Christian patience. Some of the lepers had been taught to run a printing-press. It was not a large one, and they could only print a sixteen-page sheet on one side, owing to the Chinese custom of double-folded pages. As soon as one thousand copies of each sheet had been printed, the type had to be distributed and set up again. For the past eight years they had been at work printing a thousand copies of the Bible. The New Testament had been completed first, and stored away in cases. At last the day had come when the last pages of the Old Testament were completed. When the thousandth sheet was taken from the press, a praise service was held, during which Charles Alexander sang to them and led in a prayer of thankfulness. The leper printers then produced some wooden boxes containing the printed sheets of the New Testament, to show to their friends. But on opening the cases it was found that white ants had worked their way, like a fretwork saw, through the paper. Almost all the cases of the New Testament were the same, and the labour of years had been ruined. But the courageous faith of these leper Christians was undaunted, and, without a murmur, they began setting up the type to print the New Testament over again!

One day Dr. Bradley and Dr. Thompson resolved to take a rare holiday, and a picnic was planned. Early in the morning the party set out across the plain for some hills four miles away, Dr. and Mrs. Bradley, Miss Cadbury, and Charles Alexander riding on horseback, the others taking a different route, borne in Chinese carrying-chairs upon the shoulders of some of the coolies. Half-way to the hills, Mrs. Alexander turned, to look back from her chair, at the sound of horse's hoofs galloping up to them. Her sister Beatrice, with white face, called out: "There has been an accident—I am afraid Charles is badly hurt. You must all come back." Without waiting to be questioned she was gone, and those in the carrying-chairs turned and made their way back across the plain as quickly as might be. On reaching the compound they found the others had arrived before them, and heard that in the middle of a canter Charles Alexander's horse, treading into a deep rut, had fallen headlong, hurling its rider out of the saddle, fortunately beyond reach of its flying hoofs. He had lain motionless on the ground, and, not daring to wait to learn the truth, Miss Cadbury had galloped off to tell the rest of the party. Meanwhile the unconscious form had been carried back in a chair which had followed the riders in case of the ladies needing a rest. Two days went by of which he remembered nothing, but the tender care and skill, by which he was surrounded, was blessed of God in the restoration of his precious life. The terrible blow upon his right temple, which had so nearly been fatal, caused temporary paralysis of the eyeball muscles, and for some months thereafter he was unable to turn his right eye, and the pupil remained shocked open, causing that of the other eye to shrink to a pin-point. Through the Lord's goodness this difficulty gradually disappeared, and neither the appearance of his expressive brown eyes was injured nor his eyesight more than temporarily affected.

The spectacles he was obliged to wear for some months were an amusing mystery to I-shuk, the Bradleys' Chinese cook, for one side of the spectacles had no glass in it, while the other side was completely covered with black sticking-plaster!

The sixteenth of February saw Charles Alexander and his wife, with her mother and sister Beatrice, in Hong-Kong once more. They found that splendid preparations had been made for the service for Europeans in the Theatre Royal. It was advertised, according to the Hong-Kong custom, for nine o'clock at night. About eight-thirty, the Alexander party reached the building and were astonished to find officials on the outside turning crowds of people away with the statement that the building was packed inside. As they entered the platform from behind, they were greeted with the familiar strains of the "Glory Song" and "Tell Mother I'll be there," started up by some British sailors in the waiting audience. The chair was taken by Bishop Lander, and other ministers and missionaries surrounded Alexander on the platform, as for two hours he led the throng in singing, punctuated by

his short, pithy talks and stories.   It was an unusual experience for him, unsup-
ported by preacher or soloist, with only his wife doing her poor best at the piano, and
decorated as he was by his queer pair of spectacles !   But the Holy Spirit can work
independently of circumstances, when there is a willing spirit of consecration, and
His power came upon the gathering in a wonderful way.   Many were present
who had never before been known to attend any religious service, but there were
also unexpected friends who had been in the Torrey-Alexander mission meetings in
the English towns of Bradford, Liverpool, and Plymouth, also two or three from
Australia and New Zealand.   A red-haired young porter from the Matilda hospital
on the Peak was the first to respond to the request for personal workers in the
meeting, and before the after-meeting closed had brought a godless young fellow
down from the gallery, who, after a talk and time of prayer, yielded himself to Christ.
The young porter proved to have been a member of the Tournament Hall Choir
in Liverpool, and had decided for Christ during those meetings a year earlier.

Five days later, the Alexanders were starting off on board the Japanese steamer
Nikko Maru for a further voyage to Australia, Mrs. Alexander's health being marvellously restored, though not yet free from the effects of severe blood-poisoning that
had followed her operation.   Her mother and sister were returning to Pakhoi, and
as their tender drew away from the *Nikko Maru* in the Hong-Kong harbour, they
sang their farewell across the widening stretch of water.

> We'll never say good-bye in Heaven,
>   We'll never say good-bye,

rang out from the voices of Alexander and his wife.   Back over the waves came
the sweet tones of Mrs. Cadbury and her daughter :

> For in that Land of joy and song,
>   We'll never say good-bye.

The voyage to Australia was full of interest, a Sunday night ashore at Manila
giving an opportunity to see something of the work of the missionaries among the
Filipinos.   On landing, Alexander was surprised to hear a voice call out, " Hullo,
Alexander ! " and to find his hand warmly grasped by a missionary who had been
a member of his Bible class in Waterloo, Iowa, eleven years before.

Once more, upon the voyage, wonderful opportunities occurred of witnessing
for the Lord Jesus Christ among their fellow-travellers.   On March 13th, the *Nikko
Maru* steamed between the Heads into Sydney Harbour, perhaps the finest in all
the world.   Alexander could not help comparing this arrival with that of five
years earlier.   Then, he landed on Australian shores a lonely stranger, entirely
unknown—now, with his wife at his side, he was eagerly looking forward to meeting
thousands of warm-hearted friends, and of introducing his wife to them.   No
plans had been made beforehand, and few knew that he was coming, but it did not
take long for the news of his presence to spread like wildfire, and a visit which had
only been intended to last a few days between steamers, lengthened into four weeks,
packed with glorious occasions of praise and thanksgiving.

On reaching Melbourne, one of the first thoughts in Alexander's mind was for
the two young men he loved so well, Rupert Lowe, his former secretary, and Robert

Harkness, whose health had broken down, necessitating a voyage home. A re-union, which took place in the Federal Coffee Palace the first night was graphically described by Mr. W. A. S. Shum, Sub-editor of *The Southern Cross* :

"A gust of laughter, and a slow, soft voice drawling, "Does my ole man like chickun ? Why, my ole man, he's so fond of chickun that ef he cain't git 'em in the natch'l way, he—he—he'll *buy* 'em."' "Another gust of laughter, and then the same voice : ' Sa-ay,' and there's a sound of a book smacked on the table, ' that's the *best* book of Gospel songs I know." "Yes, it was Alexander —Charles M. Second-Timothy-two-fifteen Alexander—standing under the electric light with a red-covered hymn-book in his hand.

"At midday, he and Mrs. Alexander had stepped off the Sydney express. At three o'clock, wires were sent north and south, and as the upshot, here, at eight o'clock, was this gathering ' for rehearsal and reminiscence.' At the table, wielding a useful darning-needle, sat Mrs. Alexander. On the sofa reclined six feet one-and-a-half inches of J. J. Virgo, caught *en route* from Hobart to Sydney. Occupying the piano-stool was Robert Harkness, who had just walked in from the Bendigo train. At one side of the fire was Rupert Lowe, of Geelong, Mr. Alexander's secre-tary through a dozen campaigns abroad, and at the other—filling the easiest arm-chair in the room—was the journalist.

"There was no lack of material for reminiscence. During the five flying years since the same half-dozen—with the one notable exception—met in that room, much has happened. Mr. Alexander has girdled the world with his music, has set millions of voices singing the 'Glory Song,' has seen thousands of con-versions—and has married. Mr. Harkness has developed from a boy with a musical instinct and a boyish enthusiasm for dashing accompaniments, into a finished musician, with a gift for composition and the ability to play his own hymns as no one else can play them—and other people's as if they were his own. Now he was making little cascades of music run down the keyboard. ' That's right, Harkness, let us have No. —,' said Mr. Alexander, and sang softly :

> He bore it for you,
>   He bore it for me ;
> The curse has been all removed.

' Now listen to this chorus.' They listened, and it was an Alexander-Virgo duet that repeated it. ' Good music, good words ! If that's a fair sample, these are going to be good songs,' said Mr. Virgo. ' Good songs ? ' replied Mr. Alexander, ' they're soul-winners ! Now, Harkness, play " He will hold me fast." Listen :

> When I fear my faith will fail,
> Christ can hold me fast.

My ! If I had five hundred men here to sing the air of that song, I'd give something,' and he reached round, as if by some good fortune he might find them tucked away in his pocket. ' It's simple, but it has fine melody. Every note tells, and every line. I wish you knew the writer of those words—Miss Ada R. Habershon. She spoke to me after one of our London meetings, told me she wrote verse, and I persuaded her to try her hand at writing Gospel songs. She dropped me a note next day to say that she had prayed all night about it, and had decided to try. That was two years ago, and since then she has written hundreds of verses and looks like being the best Gospel-song writer in the world. She is an invalid nearly all the time, but those who suffer know best how to touch the heart. Think of the hymns that have been written by blind people, such as Fanny Crosby! Miss Habershon is well-read, too; has the Bible in her head as well as in her heart, and all her songs have a scriptural foundation. She is direct: makes a picture in every line.'

" ' He will hold me fast ' is a stirring piece. It brought Mr. Virgo to his feet to sing the solo of the verses. Mrs. Alexander beat time with her needle and supplied the alto to the chorus, Mr. Alexander singing the air, Harkness himself the bass; and even the journalist, who has a voice of uncertain quality and unclassifiable range, was swept along and forced to join in."

Within the next three weeks, in addition to the private gatherings in many homes around Melbourne, two big choir practices were held in the Melbourne Town Hall, with a final Song Service in the great Exhibition Building. In the intervals between, the towns of Ballarat, Geelong and Bendigo were visited, and, in each, Song Services were held. The Town Hall practices developed into enthusiastic Gospel services, at which many decisions were made for Christ. What a thrill of delight went through Alexander's soul as he looked out on hundreds of familiar faces, with their radiant smiles of welcome, and stood in the midst of tried and trusted friends upon the platform, such as the Hon. James Balfour, who filled the chair, Mr. Charles Carter, Mr. William Howat, Mr. G. P. Barber, and many others. In Ballarat a mayoral reception was given for the purpose of greeting Mrs Alexander, and in Geelong the couple received a hearty welcome from Mr. and Mrs. George Hitchcock and other leading Christians.

In Bendigo, far-famed for its gold-mines, the Harkness family overwhelmed them with loving hospitality. The manager of the " Red, White, and Blue " gold-mine, who was also an enthusiastic Sunday-school superintendent, arranged for the Alexanders to go below. Six hundred feet under the surface, as they were being piloted through subterranean passages, candle in hand and disguised in overalls and old caps, they stopped to sing the " Glory Song " to a couple of miners. In the middle of the song a moving light revealed another opening, and soon an old miner emerged, with candle aloft, lustily joining in the chorus. He begged for another verse, whereupon Alexander shook hands with him, asking him if he was a Christian man. " No, sir, but you almost got me last night. I was shaking from head to foot," he answered, referring to a meeting of the previous evening. Alexander pleaded with him to decide right there, telling him it made no difference to God whether a man was above or below the earth's surface, in church or out of it. The big Cornishman hesitated, saying he would come to the meeting two nights later, but Alexander continued his pleading. " Won't you accept the Lord Jesus as your Saviour, right here, and live for Him from now on ? " A moment's pause, and then came the words, firmly spoken, " I will." Down on their knees went the miners, with their visitors and the mine manager, while

Robert Harkness and Mrs. Alexander prayed and thanked God for this new-born soul. Next Sunday night—Easter Sunday—the Forest Street Church was crowded to overflowing. True to his promise, the miner was there in one of the side galleries. Charles Alexander told the story of his conversion, appealing to him for confirmation of it. The old Cornishman rose, and his tremulous but earnest confession of Christ thrilled the meeting, no doubt giving courage to some of those who took their stand later in the evening.

The final service was held in the Melbourne Exhibition Building. At four-thirty in the afternoon an eager crowd began to assemble for the meeting advertised at eight o'clock. By seven-thirty ten thousand persons had been admitted into the building, and no more being allowed to enter, the doors were closed upon hundreds of disappointed people. Assisted by Mr. J. J. Virgo, Robert Harkness, and the huge choir, Charles Alexander led a festival of Gospel singing, which seemed a very foretaste of heaven. Numbers of decisions were made for Christ, and with the stirring of old and tender memories came a new inspiration for future service.

The last Sunday of this visit to Australia was spent in Sydney. There had been no opportunity, as in Melbourne, to meet any choir for rehearsal, but out of the eight hundred men who gathered on Sunday afternoon in the Y.M.C.A. Hall, where twenty-four decisions for Christ took place, four hundred men volunteered to form an impromptu choir for the evening meeting. The crowds that gathered for this seemed almost appalling. The Sydney Town Hall accommodates over four thousand, and when it was packed beyond the limits usually permitted, the police sent orders for all the doors to be closed, and for announcements to be made that no one could be allowed to leave until the service was over, as they were embarrassed to know how to deal with the dense crowd that continued to gather on the outside of the Hall. A number of ministers and others volunteered their help, and soon several open-air services were in progress, which kept the crowds singing and happy until the police could disperse them. During the meeting, Alexander noticed the bright faces and hearty singing of three marines from a British warship in the harbour, and called on them to sing one of the new choruses by themselves. The great audience was thrilled as they responded heartily. About two weeks later, when the Alexanders spent a day ashore at Suva in the Fiji Islands, they noticed the same warship in the harbour there. Alexander received a letter from one of the three marines who had sung for him in Sydney, saying how much they had enjoyed the meeting in the Town Hall, and that out of the hundreds on their ship only ten were out-and-out Christians, but God was giving them strength to be true to Him, and they hoped to win some of the rest.

Mr. T. Shaw Fitchett, of Melbourne, who was making a business trip through America and Europe, was a fellow-passenger of the Alexanders on their voyage from Sydney to Vancouver. On April 27th, they touched at the cable station of Fanning Island, a mere coral reef in the great Pacific, only ten miles in circumference, thickly fringed with coco-nut palms, and having a shallow lagoon in the centre. It lies alone, like a circlet of emeralds surrounding a turquoise, in the wide azure waste of sea and sky, and at the time was inhabited by a lonely group of seventeen white men and three white women, besides a few coloured people. The

Alexanders gave to them a number of hymn-books, with an earnest prayer that the printed messages might reach souls for Christ. A day was spent amidst the perennial summer beauties of Honolulu. A week later in Victoria, in contrast to the autumn left behind in Australia and the tropical heat through which they had just passed, they were greeted with a breath as of English springtime in the daffodils, tulips, and bluebells. A memorable journey through the Rocky Mountains, broken by a stay over Sunday at Field, with its memory of Ralph Connor's pioneer work, and followed by days speeding across the never-ending stretches of prairie, brought them back once more to the rush and bustle of Chicago. Alexander was delighted to introduce Mr. T. Shaw Fitchett to his friends at the Moody Bible Institute and the Pacific Garden Mission, and soon afterwards to the dear old Water Street Mission in New York City. Here they waited expectantly for a telegram from Vancouver, telling of the safe arrival of the dear English mother and sister, who were on their way from South China, with three girl cousins who had joined them there. All were eagerly looking forward to the reunion in New York, and the voyage home together across the Atlantic. A telegram reached the Alexanders indeed, but it brought such tidings as caused them to lean hard upon the promise of the year-text they had chosen : " Let not your hearts be troubled : ye believe in God, believe also in Me." The message brought the news that half-way between Yokohama and the Canadian coast, the sweet English mother had all unexpectedly gone to join her beloved husband in the Saviour's presence. During a severe storm, a sudden lurch of the ship caused her to miss her footing while ascending a steep gangway to the writing-saloon, and she had been hurled to the foot of the stairway. The fall caused concussion of the brain, and she had passed away that same night without recovering consciousness. She had been spared all knowledge of pain or death, and in the midst of their grief, there was, for those who loved her so dearly, a triumphant joy in the thought of all that this sudden translation meant for her. For eight years she had borne her loneliness with sweetness and courage, and now had entered upon her reward. The presence of the Alexanders' friend and hers, Sir Alexander Simpson of Edinburgh, who was a fellow-voyager, made it possible to take the precious body home to the stricken circle in Birmingham, England, to be laid beside that of the loved husband, whose own body, eight years earlier, had been brought home from Jerusalem.

A hurried journey back across Canada brought the Alexanders into touch with the sorrowful little party near Winnipeg, and on June 5th, they sailed from New York by R.M.S. *Oceanic*. " Tennessee " had been closed during the long absence of its master and mistress, and they lived for a while with their sister at Uffculme. Upon Mrs. Alexander and Beatrice Cadbury, when the funeral was over, devolved the heavy task of breaking up the family home—a task which covered the next four months. Alexander had promised to help in some of the Bible Conferences in America, including Northfield. " My darling Mother," he wrote to his mother from England, " your sweet letters have been read by Helen and me with warm appreciation for all your love and thoughtfulness. You always say the right thing in the right way. I am coming over for the August Conferences and shall hope to have a glimpse of you. My girl cannot go with me, and it is going to be a great wrench to pull apart, even for a few weeks. We have been so constantly together almost every hour of the day through the past year. She never seemed so sweet and precious as now."

At the end of July he sailed for New York by the R.M.S. *Campania*. " I am glad that you and dear little Beatrice have each other for comfort," he wrote just before the steamer sailed. " Two familiar faces—Foxley and Fenn—were on Liverpool station to greet me. We have had a prayer-meeting together in my cabin, to dedicate it for the Lord on this passage. Rev. and Mrs. Stuart Holden are in a cabin near mine. He is to be one of the speakers at Northfield, so we shall travel there together. Mr. Holden told me just now about being in the home of Prince Bernadotte, where they gathered around the piano once each day, children and all, to sing hymns from our ' Red Book.' . . . How I shall be missing your wise counsel, but most of all that never-failing deep of affection that nothing can replace. Pray for me ; I never miss that part of my office for you, dear."

" I never wanted you so much in my life," he wrote some weeks later. " I have never had so many perplexing things to settle as in the last few weeks. I am sure you have been praying for me. There have been many business affairs to attend to, and a good many family affairs as well. I saw Dr. Torrey in Chicago, and had a good time of conference with him. Mr. Revell is to publish my new hymn-book. Mr. Davis and I sail for England next Wednesday on the *Adriatic*. How I wish I never had to be out of your sight again."

When Alexander reached England in September, the work of breaking up the family home at Uffculme was almost completed. Preparations had been made, involving some enlargements to the house at " Tennessee," so that Beatrice Cadbury might share the Alexanders' home, which also opened its doors to several of the dearly-loved household staff from Uffculme ; of these, three maids and two gardeners were still at " Tennessee " when the beloved master was called Home in 1920, and were reckoned among his valued friends. The affection which bound Alexander and his wife to their sister, Beatrice, grew deeper than ever during the next four years, in which she shared their home.

CHAPTER FOURTEEN

The Book he Loved Best

IN the log-house on the Alexander farm at Cloyd's Creek in the early 'seventies, a small boy might often have been seen staggering away from the bookshelf with a huge illustrated Family Bible. Laying the heavy book upon the floor, he would lie full length beside it, chin propped on hand, and hour after hour would ponder its pages with absorbed interest. So long and so diligently did he continue, that at last the book wore out from constant use, and another had to be purchased in its place. Unfortunately, this second one had no pictures, but still the boy pored over it, and his mother is the authority for saying that, at nine years of age, Charles Alexander had read the Bible through from cover to cover. "There was no prize offered to him for reading the Bible," she wrote to Charles's wife long years afterwards, in confirming this statement, "he just seemed anxious to know what there was in it for him."

Taught to use it in his first schooldays as a textbook from which he learned to read and spell, hearing it spoken of with reverent affection by his parents, and seeing its beneficent influence on the lives of those about him who believed it and obeyed it, it was little wonder that Charles Alexander grew to manhood believing it to be the inspired Word of God Himself. "To him," as Dr. Torrey stated at the Memorial Service held in New York in January, 1921, "the Bible not only contained the Word of God, but *was* the Word of God."

From his earliest evangelistic work, Charles Alexander felt the need of establishing those who took their stand for Jesus, so that they might not slip back, to their own injury and the hindering of the cause of Christ. He always insisted that there were three equally important essentials, to secure a growth in grace that would be constant and beautifying—communion with God, through prayer ; nourishment of the spiritual life, by feeding on the Word of God ; and development of spiritual muscle, through the exercise of soul-winning, for which the Bible must be the unfailing weapon.

It was in 1897, in Waterloo, Iowa, at the home of Mr. and Mrs. J. H. Leavitt, that Alexander established the Bible classes which were fruitful in producing some of the most forceful Christian leaders and Bible-teachers of the present day. Miss Grace Saxe, who was sent from the Moody Bible Institute of Chicago to take charge of the Waterloo Bible Class, had experienced a remarkable conversion. During her subsequent training at the Moody Bible Institute she showed great aptitude for Bible-teaching, and although, in her first public efforts at Waterloo, she was extremely diffident, she gradually gained confidence in her work, under the cheery, encouraging guidance of Charles Alexander. It was for Miss Saxe that he sent in 1903 to follow up the Torrey-Alexander missions in England with courses of Bible-study, and in later years she became a great power in similar work in connexion with the " Billy " Sunday meetings in the United States.

For years Alexander was groping for some practical, attractive method of bringing the lives of people into daily contact with the Word of God. He longed to persuade them to love it, and to lean upon it, and to find their joy in it, as he did himself. But he knew this could only come through inducing them, by some means or other, to read it for themselves continually, and to make use of it for helping others. Hundreds of Bibles were given by him to men, women and children, whom, in his own inimitable way, he unexpectedly called upon in meetings everywhere to sing a solo for him. His own burning conviction of the truth of the Bible compelled the attention of many, especially when they saw it exemplified in the character of the man who recommended it so urgently. " Here is a man who has no doubts," wrote Mr. A. J. Rees, during the 1909 Chapman-Alexander meetings in Melbourne. " He believes the Bible is the inspired Word of God. To those who are weak and vacillating, or are assailed by doubts, he is a rock of refuge. They have an instinctive feeling that no one could believe it so whole-heartedly as he does, if it were not true."

At the close of the three-years' Torrey-Alexander campaign in Great Britain, Alexander left a parting message in the pages of the *Revival Times* of December 15th, 1905, for the friends, converts, and workers of the missions. It showed his loyal regard for the Word of God. " First of all," he besought them, " fix your eyes upon Jesus. You will be disappointed if you fix them upon any man or upon anything on this earth. You can lift people no higher than you are yourself, and if you trust in man, you will get people no higher than man. If your hand is in the hand of Jesus, you can reach down and lift up another, and put his hand into the hand of Jesus ; but you can readily see how helpless you would be if your hand was in the hand of a man, and you had only his help to give to the man or woman down in sin. *Stick to the Bible, no matter what anyone else says.* They have nothing to give you in its stead. When any one wishes you to give it up or doubt any part of it, examine their life and see what the fruit of their teaching has been, whether they are becoming better men and more like Jesus, and whether they have power to go down and save fallen men and women and lead them definitely to accept Jesus Christ. Do not miss this point. You may measure them by their sweet, lovable lives, but that alone is not the test. They have no power to bring men and women definitely to accept Jesus Christ or to train them to be strong in Him. They have the wrong message. They are leaders you cannot follow. Take your ideas first hand : go straight to God and the Bible. Keep on singing, and get other people to sing. Share your good things with others, and you will find that as you share them they will grow larger. Learn new Gospel songs. If you cannot sing well yourself, get some one, who *can*, to sing them. Songs will carry the message many times where you could not speak. Be a peculiar people, zealous of good works. Don't forget ' Second-Timothy-two-fifteen.' "

Charles Alexander loved to approach the Bible as though it were a new book. Crossing the Atlantic at Christmas-time in 1905, he wrote back to his wife : " I have been reading my Bible quite a good deal. I began at the beginning, and approached it as though I had never read it before, to see how interesting it was from a story standpoint. I have found it most thrilling, especially the clear-cut way in which it makes statements of great events. In two verses it will give the history of a couple of men's lives—what they did, and how they died, which if a man should start to write, it would spread over several pages."

Never until he came to the simple plan of the Pocket Testament League did Alexander find any method that satisfied him as a means of binding a human life and the Book of God together in a way that should prove effective and fruitful. He was feeling for it when he said at a men's meeting at Dundee, Scotland, in February, 1903 : " Get hold of the Word of God, and freeze right on to it. Have a copy of *at least* the New Testament always in your pocket, not just in your Sunday clothes ; but when you change, let it change too." But although he was anticipating the **very** words of the Pocket Testament League pledge, afterwards adopted, and himself frequently carried a Testament or small Bible in his pocket, he did not as yet make an invariable habit of carrying it, nor seek, beyond words of general advice, to persuade others to do so. Consequently, like all other generalities, the good advice did not take hold. But in the autumn of 1907, when through force of circumstances, which were a definite leading of God, he had a little time of unaccustomed leisure at home, these vague thoughts began to crystallize into a definite plan.

The recent journey round the world, with its long sea-voyages, had been blessed of God, in spite of the sorrow and shock of her mother's sudden Home-going, to the complete restoration of Mrs. Alexander's health. Both husband and wife felt that this was a clear leading for him to follow once more, with her at his side, the call of God to the strenuous work of world-wide evangelism. The expectation of linking up once more with Dr. Torrey was, to the disappointment of both, no longer practicable. For Dr. Torrey had been obliged to continue his work through the long interval, and was now being gradually drawn back to some extent into the work of teaching, which had been his as head of the Moody Bible Institute, and which finally drew him to the position of Dean of the Bible Institute at Los Angeles, California. The tender bond of friendship between the two men was not loosened, though they could no longer carry on their old work side by side.

Mr. George T. B. Davis returned to England with Charles Alexander, from the summer conferences in America of 1907, to work with him on the production of a book telling of the triumphs of the Gospel round the world, and also to help in frequent incidental meetings in England.

Mr. Edward Roberts, a convert of the first Torrey-Alexander mission in Liverpool in 1903, came to some of these meetings to give the testimony of his conversion, which had made such a deep impression when first told, about a year after the event, at the Tournament Hall Mission in 1904. He had formerly been a referee at prize-fights, and a thorough sporting man. His Christian wife, with a little band of devoted friends, had been praying earnestly for his conversion for six long years.

She tried to get him to attend the meetings at the Philharmonic Hall, but in vain. At last, to satisfy her, hearing that at some of the meetings the floor was reserved for men only, the women being asked to go into the gallery, he surprised her by saying that he would accompany her.   His intention was to slip off to an impending prize-fight as soon as he saw his wife safely up the stairs to the gallery.   But at the moment of expected parting, she seized him by the sleeve.   " I want you to come with me," she said.   " I know you, Ted ! "   Ashamed to reveal his secret plan, he accompanied her, and although there was no outward sign, the Spirit of God began to lay hold of him that night.   To his wife's utter amazement he told her next day, without invitation, that he was going to hear Dr. Torrey preach, though he himself hardly understood the reason for his action.   Nothing in the meeting moved him, apparently, until Alexander began to lead the hymn, " When I survey the wondrous Cross."   As the third verse was sung—

> See from His head, His hands, His feet,
> Sorrow and love flow mingled down !

such a vision of what the Saviour had done for him came before the soul of Ted Roberts, that before he knew it, or could prevent it, hot tears were coursing their way down cheeks that had not felt such dew for many years.   Soon he was sobbing like a child, and made his way to the front of the meeting.   Here a good Christian worker made the Way of Life plain to him from the Word of God.   " Sir," said Ted Roberts, " do you know I have seen more of that Book in the last five minutes than in the past fifteen years."   With joyful heart he hurried home to bring the good news to his wife, who had been praying during his absence that he might accept the Lord Jesus Christ as his Saviour.   From that time his faith never wavered, and his whole life was revolutionized.   At the close of his testimony, Ted Roberts reached into his pocket, pulled out a Bible, and holding it aloft, said, " Friends, I love the Word of God so much that I like to have it always with me. *Whenever I change my coat, I change my Bible.*"   Impressed with this sentence the first time he heard it, Mr. Davis had started some " Testament Circles," in Philadelphia during the Torrey-Alexander Campaign in February, 1906.   Charles Alexander was much interested in these groups, the members of which pledged themselves to carry a Testament in their pockets.

It was during the quiet weeks at home in England, at the close of 1907, that he thought of systematically urging people to adopt the habit of carrying, as well as of reading the Bible.   As the matter was being discussed one day in the drawing-room at " Tennessee," Mrs. Alexander exclaimed, " That reminds me of our old Pocket Testament League at the High School."   She then, for the first time, told her husband and Mr. Davis of a plan she had organized among her schoolmates, soon after her conversion at the age of twelve.   The joy and peace which filled her soul was too good to be kept to herself, and she hungered to share it with some of the girls, from homes representing every phase of belief and unbelief, whom she met daily at the High School.   Trained by her godly father and mother, she was anxious from the first to make it clear to her worldly companions from professedly Christian homes, also to those with Jewish and atheistic surroundings, that she was not trying to force any private opinions upon them, but simply desired to direct their attention to the Word of God Himself. For this purpose she kept a Bible in her desk for constant, easy access, but discovered that even this was not a convenient enough arrangement. Opportunities often came for a few words out in the playground, or away from the class-room, which would be lost if a break were made to fetch her Bible, and she always found the impression deeper when the words were actually read together rather than quoted from memory. The Bible still remained in her desk, for needed references to the Old Testament, but a New Testament was not too heavy to be carried all the time, and became a far more usable and potent weapon, always ready for service. It was not long before a number of Christian girls in the school banded themselves together for soul-winning with the Word of God, and the original Pocket Testament League came into being. Through its agency a number of girls were led to Christ, but when the first organizers left the school it was gradually disbanded. Charles Alexander and Mr. Davis listened with interest to this story, and immediately determined to revive the Pocket Testament League. The first and most important change in the method of using it, was the thought of not confining it to those who were already Christians, but of seeking to enlist as members any man, woman, or child who would be willing to read a chapter a day and carry the Book constantly. A number of attractive illustrated Testaments, suitable for carrying, were obtained at once, and some slips, with the Pocket Testament League pledge printed upon them, were pasted inside the covers. Setting Mr. Davis free from other work, Mr. Alexander asked him to use his time to go into the streets, or anywhere, to test the new experiment. He was provided with Testaments so that he might make a free gift of one to any person willing to sign the pledge of membership, to carry the Book and read a chapter a day.

At the top of Moor Green Lane, on which " Tennessee " stands, Mr. Davis, on the first morning, met a tall, fine-looking policeman. After a few words of ordinary conversation with him, Mr. Davis produced one of the small Testaments, offering it as a gift, if the policeman would " sign on " to carry it and read a chapter a day. A month later, Charles Alexander was conducting a meeting in a small Mission Hall in Birmingham, in which Mrs. Alexander's secretary was interested. When the invitation was given, the first response came from a tall man at the back of the meeting, who marched boldly up to the front, soon followed by a number of young people from various parts of the hall. Struck by the first man's fine appearance and prompt decision, Alexander said to him, curious to know what point in the meeting had been used of God to bring him to decision, " Brother, I do not usually ask this, but I would like to know what led you to decide for Christ ? " The man, whom neither Mr. Alexander nor Mr. Davis recognized as a policeman in his plain clothes, pulled a small book from his pocket. " It was this Testament, sir, given me a month ago," he said. He proved to be the very policeman to whom Mr. Davis had spoken, and he had read himself into the Kingdom. This was a revelation of the power of God's Word, without human interpretation or guidance, to lead a soul to salvation through Christ. A decision was quickly made to seek out the other men belonging to the two local police stations of Moseley and King's

Heath, and to offer each man a Testament on the same terms.   So, as **Mr. Davis** often says when telling the story, " For a time I kept going after the policemen, instead of their going after me ! "   Marvellous results followed.   In five months eight policemen in one of the stations confessed Christ.   Five were confirmed at one time, and one became an elder in the Presbyterian Church.   It was a real revival, brought down from heaven by the Word of God.   For many months one man, on duty in a large park near by, scoffed loudly at the other men, who might often be seen sitting round the fire in the police station openly reading their chapter ;   but in the end he was led to join also.   At a gathering of a number of these policemen and their wives at " Tennessee," in the summer of 1910, this man gave the brightest testimony of them all, and told of the constant blessing he received as he read his precious Testament through and through, time after time.   About nine years later, during the latter part of the great world-war, a man walked into the Pocket Testament League office in London to purchase some Testaments.   He told a wonderful story of the joy he had experienced in leading fifty of his comrades in the Army to accept Christ.   On further conversation it was revealed that this was the Birmingham policeman who had scoffed so bitterly at first, and who afterwards became such an ardent soul-winner.

Convinced increasingly of the far-reaching power of this simple method of using the Bible, Charles Alexander determined that in the new work toward which his face was turning, it should never fail to be a prominent feature.   Among many attractive openings for future service the choice was not an easy one ;   but, after much prayer and correspondence and many interviews, Alexander determined that, as soon as Christmas was over, he would sail for the United States to confer with Dr. J. Wilbur Chapman on the question of taking up work together.   Two main questions had to be faced before any final decision could be made.   One was his concern to use the Pocket Testament League ;   the other was a promise given to his friends in Australia, to return there as soon as possible for a further series of missions.   Alexander himself they insisted on having, and such was their confidence in his judgment, that the Evangelization Society of Australasia had entrusted to him the choice of a preacher, saying they would be perfectly satisfied with his frank recommendation.   Of all the available men Alexander knew, he felt that the message of Dr. Chapman was the best suited for the conditions then prevailing in Australia, and practically decided that if Dr. Chapman should be willing and able to visit the Antipodes in the near future, he would take it as God's leading that they should become associates in evangelistic work.

December 28th, 1907, found Alexander on board R.M.S. *Lusitania*, bound for New York.   He wrote to his wife :—" While arranging my seat for the dining-saloon, a clergyman from Sydney, who had worked through our mission there, spoke to me, and I have arranged to sit with him and his friend.   Since dinner I have read a splendid article on Abraham Lincoln, also part of Lockhart's *Life of Sir Walter Scott*.   Feeling rather lonely, I began to talk to a quiet fellow sitting near.   He lives in Boston, and deals in Packard motor-cars, so I have industriously extracted all the motor knowledge I possibly could from him ! "

December 30th.—" The mission I am on is no easy one, but God knows how to solve problems. It is no profit to worry ; but let us together, dearest, earnestly, but in calm submission, beseech of Him to make the way so plain that there could be no doubt. Ask Beatrice to join us at the Throne for this. I have had a long quiet day to think, read, and pray. The Australian clergyman, his friend and I had a Scripture reading and prayer, after lunch, in their cabin. A young man from Toronto who is returning home from Brazil, where he has been representing his company in a great gas and electric power-plant for Rio de Janeiro, told me he was at the Canadian Club the day I addressed them. I have had some straight talks with one or two stewards, and gave each a copy of *The Traveller's Guide*. I have been going over a number of my hymns and making lists of them.''

December 31st, 1907, 11.47 p.m.—'' Only a few more minutes and I shall never be able to write that year upon a letter to you again. It is a solemn thought ! My friends and I have just had a time of prayer together, taking as our year-text 1 Corinthians xiii. 13. I am looking at my watch, and when it reaches next year, I shall put down the date. . . . *January 1st*, 1908. *I love Helen Cadbury Alexander better and better as the moments fly.* The New Year bugle has just sounded above the roar of the sea and the wind. My ' good night ' is borne across the waves to the dearest on earth to me.''

To Charles Alexander the month of January was a time of great heart-searching and earnest prayer for guidance. One of his first engagements after landing at New York was to spend a few days at New Haven, Connecticut, to assist Dr. Chapman, who was conducting meetings there, frequently attended by students from the neighbouring University of Yale. After conferring together, Alexander agreed to meet Dr. Chapman for a week in Philadelphia at the end of the month, after having, in the meantime, thoroughly weighed and examined a number of other pressing invitations for service. The days thus spent were not idle or unfruitful. Wherever he went he loved to join in the work, rejoicing to have a part anywhere in the winning of souls. During a week-end spent at Northfield with Mr. Harkness, who had joined him from England, he held a couple of memorable services with the men of Mount Hermon School in their chapel, in which fourteen came out for Christ, thirty-seven others taking their stand for full surrender. On the Sunday night, similar results were witnessed in a service in the Northfield Church, attended not only by the townspeople but by the Seminary girls.

On January 27th, Alexander definitely decided to join forces with Dr. Chapman. After spending the promised week in Philadelphia, nothing remained but to hurry back to England to settle private affairs there, and take his wife back with him to enter upon his new labours in continuation of the great Philadelphia Simultaneous Campaign.

CHAPTER FIFTEEN

A New Yoke-fellow

1908 to 1909

THE man with whom Charles Alexander was to be specially associated for practically the rest of his life, was a man of wide experience in the pastorate, with a genius for organization. His virile faith and intensely sympathetic nature made him ever on the alert, not only to win men and women everywhere to Christ, but to strengthen and encourage pastors and leaders of Christian work in facing the problems which he himself understood so well.

Unwavering in his personal loyalty to the Bible as the Word of God, Dr. Chapman had a disarming gentleness in dealing with ministers who were unfaithful to the Truth, and often won them back to Christ instead of antagonizing them. Neither sarcasm nor denunciatory epithets were employed either by him or by Alexander, for the sensitive kindliness of both men left no room for cynical feelings. They cared far more, on leaving a city, to have been the means of purifying and strengthening the life of the churches, than to gain a record of immense crowds and sensational popularity ; and their chief concern, for those who professed conversion during a campaign, was to attach them to some live Christian community, where they would be helped to grow in grace and in usefulness. Dr. Chapman knew how to sympathize with those in sorrow, and his thoughtful courtesy won friends to him and to his Lord, wherever he went. On the platform, as in private, there was an attractive charm in his simple, unostentatious manner ; and the musical quality of his voice stirred, and yet quieted, an audience. His words, clearly enunciated, could be heard without strain by an immense crowd, even when hushed to a dramatic whisper. Dr. Chapman's marvellous power of condensing much matter into few words was the continual delight of Alexander's quick mind and of his intelligent observation of the moods of a crowd. "Chapman is one of the greatest artists I have ever known," he would say, "in telling a story without wasting a word. He can condense it without making it seem like an unclothed skeleton, and tell it in a quarter of the time most other men would take. He is one of the few men in the world that knows how, and when, to stop ! In the noon-hour meetings, men, whose time is precious, can always trust him to let them out punctually, though they get so much good food in a twenty-minutes' talk from him, that they might almost think they had had an hour's sermon."

From the time when they first met in Bloomington, Ill., in 1900, Dr. Chapman and Charles Alexander had been drawn to one another. Occasional meetings held together, and their mutual affection for such men as D. L. Moody and Sam Hadley, strengthened the bond between them. The influence of Moody had been a great factor in Dr. Chapman's life. In his student-days he had gone to Chicago from Lake Forest University to hear Moody preach. Although a professed Christian, young Chapman had no joy of assurance, and went into the inquiry-room, where Moody himself came to talk with him, grounding his faith on the wonderful words of John, v. 24, " Verily, verily, I say unto you, he that heareth my word, and believeth on Him that sent me, **hath everlasting life,** and **shall not come into condemnation;** but **is passed** from death unto life."

When only twenty-seven, Chapman was called to be the pastor of the Dutch Reformed Church of Albany, New York. It was a flattering appointment for so young a man, and, gratified by his successful position, the number of empty seats in the church did not disturb him, till a visit from D. L. Moody broke into his complacence. The great-hearted preacher's blunt remarks first wounded the young pastor's pride, then broke him down before God, and aroused in him such a fervent evangelistic zeal that he lived, more or less, in the atmosphere of revival from that time onwards. Moody's shrewd suggestions about introducing " Ring the bells of heaven " and similar Gospel songs into the evening services showed the young minister, not only how to disarm the prejudices of his conservative church officers, but how to fill his empty church and make it a centre of evangelistic influence. Thus early did Dr. Chapman learn the value of Gospel music, rightly used, as an essential part of any effort to bring about a spiritual awakening, and it was the realization of this that made him long for Charles Alexander as a colleague. Wider experience was gained later in the pastorates of the popular Bethany Presbyterian Church in Philadelphia, and the aristocratic Fourth Presbyterian Church of New York City, which was his last. Mr. John Wanamaker and Mr. John H. Converse, two of America's leading Christian business men, became his firm and loyal friends.

In 1902, when the General Assembly of the Presbyterian Church appointed an aggressive Evangelistic Committee, with Mr. Converse at its head, Dr. Chapman became its corresponding secretary. The phenomenal success of the work, which soon stirred other denominations also, necessitated Dr. Chapman's resignation from the pastorate, so that he might devote his entire time to personal direction of evangelistic meetings. The calls for united effort became so loud and insistent, and, after joining forces with Charles Alexander, so world-wide, that the General Assembly's committee finally released Dr. Chapman altogether from denominational work. For some years before he and Alexander came together, Dr. Chapman had been evolving a wonderful organization of Simultaneous Campaigns, in which a large city with its suburbs would be divided into, perhaps, forty districts, in each of which meetings would be carried on simultaneously by preaching and singing evangelists. The plan has much to recommend it, but, when carried out on too large a scale, the multiplication of machinery and expense, the frequent overlapping of districts, and the difficulty of ensuring uniform quality of workers, outweighs its advantages. The burden which fell upon the central leaders of the campaign, also made it difficult for them to give full time and energy to their own meetings. By degrees Dr. Chapman was persuaded to abandon the simul-taneous plan in favour of a large central party, with specialists to undertake prison and rescue work, the training of personal workers, and the Pocket Testament League.

In the Philadelphia campaign from March 12th to April 19th, 1908, the city was divided into forty-seven districts, with more than fifty evangelists and Gospel-singers as leaders. About three hundred churches united. Noonday gatherings for business men and women were held each day in the Garrick Theatre, and meetings for men only, on Sunday afternoons. In addition to the simultaneous church services at night, other meetings through the daytime were held in factories, in public-houses, prisons, and in the open air, wherever a crowd could be gathered. There were five thousand singers in the district choirs ; five thousand personal workers ; two thousand ushers ; one thousand volunteer " door-bell ringers " for house-to-house visitation, and two hundred and fifty district leaders.

Occasionally the Academy of Music was taken for an " Old-Folks' Meeting," or other special gatherings. One afternoon the Pocket Testament League was officially launched there, following a private gathering at the Lincoln Hotel, where the League had been first presented to the co-operating evangelists, and unanimously adopted by them as an integral part of their work. Two great Gospel Song Ser-vices were also held in the Academy of Music, under the direction of Charles Alexander, assisted by all the song-leaders and a choir of over one thousand voices drawn from the district choirs. The hymn, newly written by Robert Harkness, entitled " He will hold me fast," captivated Philadelphia, and revival hymns were hummed and whistled and sung all over the city. Interspersing the songs, as he usually did, with effective anecdotes, Alexander one day told the following story, during the singing of " He will hold me fast " : " Just before coming to Philadelphia, Mr. Harkness and I went into the Belasco Theatre in New York on Sunday night to hear a friend of mine preach the Gospel. I had tried to keep out of sight, but some one recognized me, and we had to go to the platform. I knew the Lord must have some message for me to give in song, and decided to teach the people two verses, which I could remember, of ' He will hold me fast.' After singing the chorus three times, I asked if there was anyone in the audience who would stand up and sing it alone ; if so, I would send him the music next day. There was a moment of hesitation, and then a coloured man rose up in the audience and sang it beautifully. I called out to him, ' Are you a Christian ? ' He said ' Yes, suh ! ' Turning to the ministers on the platform, I said, ' We hardly need to ask that, do we ? Anybody could tell by his face that he was singing from his heart.' The man then called out to me, ' An' *my* name's Alexandah, too, suh ! ' which made everybody laugh. I asked him to come up to the platform, and bent down to shake hands with him, then asked him to face the audience, saying we two would sing an ' Alexander duet.' After we had sung, I asked him to pray, which he did very earnestly, and I felt the message was going home to some one in special need."

Not until months after the Philadelphia Mission was over, did Charles Alex-ander hear a thrilling sequel to this incident. A minister wrote him the story of a woman whom he had just received into his church. Filled with despair, she had been on her way that night to commit suicide, but passing the door of the Belasco Theatre, and seeing the brilliant lights inside, she decided to go in and have one more bit of fun before taking the fatal step, little thinking that a religious meeting was in progress. The crowd was just singing, "He will hold me fast," and the message of the hymn, and the words spoken from the platform, arrested her attention. Finally, the earnest prayer of the coloured man melted her to tears, and she resolved to give her heart to God, and with His help to face the struggle of life with new courage.

One of the co-operating district leaders of this Philadelphia campaign was Dr. Chas. W. Gordon (Ralph Connor), of Winnipeg, Canada. He was placed in one of the outlying suburbs, among a community largely indifferent to spiritual things and not easily moved. He had brought with him some carefully prepared sermons, but became much discouraged at the lack of definite results to his work. Night after night on returning to his hotel, where the Alexanders were also staying, he was invited to their little sitting-room to enjoy some fruit, and took the opportunity of pouring his difficulties into sympathetic ears. Sometimes Alexander accompanied him to his room, and there the two would talk till the midnight hour struck. At the close of the Philadelphia meetings, Dr. Chapman, Dr. Gordon, and Charles Alexander were the guests of honour at a luncheon in New York City at the Hotel Astor, where more than one hundred prominent ministers and business men assembled to hear reports of the Philadelphia work. In relating some of his experiences as an evangelist, Dr. Gordon told of an incident which had opened a new vision to him. One night in Philadelphia, discouraged with the results of his work, he had got out one of his best sermons and began reading it aloud to Alexander, inviting suggestions. He noticed that Alexander did not appear much interested, and seemed to be absorbed in some words he was printing on a clean sheet of note-paper. Dr. Gordon concluded that the Gospel singer probably did not know a good sermon when he heard one, but continued reading. When he had finished, Alexander quietly handed over the sheet of paper, which bore the words : SHOW THEM THE WAY OUT. Dr. Gordon said he saw the point at once, and through the rest of the campaign he kept that bit of paper stuck in his mirror, lest he might forget its message. He went on to tell the ministers that he had thrown aside his polished sermons, and had given simple Gospel addresses, with glorious results. He added that, if any of the ministers would like to have those sermons of his, they were welcome to them, for, though they were good ones, he had no further use for them himself !

An echo of these days came to Mrs. Alexander, twelve years later, in the following letter. "During the early part of the Philadelphia mission I was a very worldly church-member, but after having several personal talks with Mr. Alexander, and hearing him speak on the first Psalm, I decided to change my way of living, and have been much happier for so doing. Your husband was the one who helped me to make the surrender, and I shall ever thank him for it."

While in Philadelphia this time, Alexander added a new member to his personal staff. This was Ernest W. Naftzger, who had already done some work for him in the Summer Conferences, and now became his regular soloist.

Only one more Simultaneous Campaign was held before the summer, in Norfolk, Virginia, where there were many opportunities for reaching the naval men for Christ and enlisting them in the Pocket Testament League. From Norfolk the Alexanders went for a week's happy visit to the family home at Knoxville, Tennessee, and from there to meet Dr. Chapman at Kansas City for the Presbyterian General Assembly, in connexion with which some evangelistic services were held. Early in June, Alexander and his wife crossed the Atlantic once more, for a short visit to their English home. But by August 1st they were back in America, accompanied by Mrs. Alexander's sister, Beatrice Cadbury, Miss Perks, the secretary at "Tennessee," and an English cousin, all three of whom stayed for a month to enjoy the Bible Conferences at Northfield and Winona Lake.

Not a day's break was open to Alexander for rest, the only short interval being occupied in helping his brother Homer to move from Chicago and settle into a new home in Philadelphia, with his wife and little daughter. A week-end was spent with Dr. Chapman at Auburn, N.Y., where, on the Sunday, five meetings were held, one of them in the great prison. On September 30th they were in Orillia, Canada, for a two weeks' campaign. This was followed by a conference tour through Ohio, Kentucky, and Tennessee, from one to three days being spent in each place visited. One of the most interesting was Berea, Kentucky, where they stayed with Dr. Frost, at the great schools in which hundreds of young men and women, from their isolated mountain homes, were being educated. To Alexander, it brought a breath of his old days of wandering over the mountains of Tennessee and North Carolina, as he looked into the clear eyes of these *genuine* Americans, handicapped by their early surroundings, but quick to absorb education and refinement as soon as opportunity was given. The Pocket Testament League was enthusiastically received by these young people, and Alexander's heart overflowed with joy as he and his wife presented a gift of the little Book to each one who joined the League.

The last mission of the year, in the latter part of November, was held at Burlington, Vermont, almost on the borders of Canada, and not far from the waters of Lake Champlain. At the end of the month, Alexander, accompanied by his wife and Robert Harkness, crossed the Atlantic for the sixth time that year. Even now he could only have four weeks in the home he loved, and during these he went to and fro, holding meetings in Liverpool, Birkenhead, and Bolton, besides several in Birmingham. To spend Christmas in their own home was a rare delight to them both, but on the following day, Charles Alexander must needs sail again for New York, this time alone, his wife being obliged to stay behind in order to arrange affairs at home for the long absence which lay ahead. For the promised visit to Australasia was now definitely on the programme, though in the meantime three campaigns had been planned for Richmond, Virginia ; and Boston and Springfield, Massachusetts.

"We have had very bad weather," Alexander wrote to his wife from the R.M.S. *Lusitania*, on *December* 31st, 1908. "I have had you before me in imagination numberless times, sometimes with your burst of girlish laughter, another time with tears of farewell upon your dear cheeks, then again you are in the dignified capacity of adviser and inspirer. I love you *all* ways ! "

January 1st, 1909. " Mr. Philip Mauro, of New York, whom I met in London recently, is on board with us. He is a prominent Patent lawyer, who argues his cases before the Supreme Court of the United States. He told me how he was converted in 1903. He was walking down a street in New York City one evening, when, rising above the roar of the street, there came a little thread of Gospel song from a mission room. He says he never knew why he went in ; he was not favourably impressed, and went away, but some power drew him back again the next night, and he made a public confession of Christ as his Lord. We have spent several hours a day together, studying the Bible and talking of the things of God. Another gentleman I have met told me that he was converted five years ago, during a voyage on the Adriatic Sea, through reading an account of our English missions in *The Christian*. I found he had three of Philip Mauro's books in his cabin, and I was delighted to introduce him to the author. Several other men on board told me that they had been to the Royal Albert Hall meetings."

January 16th, Richmond, Virginia.—" We have a fine auditorium here which holds about four thousand people, and the choir platform is splendidly arranged after our old-fashioned style, rapidly-rising tiers of seats, curved in at the ends. The choir is doing splendid work, and Mr. Naftzger is singing better and more evenly than before. I am so sorry that you are not here to get the benefit of these Southern people. The old Confederate Capitol is close to where we are staying—historic ground for a Southerner. This morning we are going down to a big tobacco factory to hear the coloured people sing at their work. This is our rest-day, so-called, but we are invited out to two meals and this factory. You will remember this is the town of John Jasper, the wonderful old coloured preacher. The man who drives our carriage is a member of his old church. We went out to a Presbyterian Theological Seminary yesterday morning. Mr. Davis gave his talk, and Dr. Chapman spoke beautifully, and we had a rather remarkable service. The students were fine fellows and seemed to be in earnest. One of my old school-friends from Maryville College is in charge of a Methodist Orphanage on the edge of the city. She was disappointed not to see you, and she said she had heard you were not ' stuck-up.' In the eyes of a Tennessean that is one of the highest virtues ! At a luncheon the other day for three hundred and fifty business men, Governor Swanson was present and made a most telling speech. He said he believed in revivals of the old-fashioned kind, and was glad that the Southern people had not gone away from the ' Old Book.' " *January 19th.*—" Thank you for all of your lovely letters. I want you to reach New York about March 10th, as we are to close in Springfield on the 9th, and have a day or two in New York before starting for Buffalo, where we go for a Conference. Then we go to Minneapolis for another Conference, to Winnipeg for another and then to Vancouver. We shall not seem so far away from you when we get to Boston, where we are looking forward to great meetings and times of blessing."

January 28th, Boston, Mass.—" After a long, hard pull I am here from Richmond. Sweet precious girl, how I miss you and long to have you by my side to advise me." *February 14th.*—" This is the end of a busy day, half-past eleven, Sunday night. How glad I will be to see your sweet face on the *Mauretania*. I will see that you are met in New York City if anything should prevent my being there. I am sorry not to see little Beatrice for so many months, but must look forward to seeing her in China. We never had such a perfect time all together as those last few weeks at home. She is becoming so sweet and filled with the Spirit of God, that I can hardly bear to think of her leaving us for so long. Dr. Chapman often speaks beautifully of you, and it is hard to keep back the tears when I hear your name mentioned."

The great campaign at Boston, which in some ways stood related to the Chapman-Alexander campaigns in the United States, as did the London Mission to the other Torrey-Alexander missions in Great Britain, was held from January 26th to February 21st. It was carried out under the simultaneous plan, which was more successful here than in any other city. One hundred and sixty-six churches co-operated in the movement, and the meetings in all parts of the city were led by evangelists connected with the Chapman-Alexander organization, assisted by the Boston pastors. Dr. Chapman and Charles Alexander led the central meeting in Tremont Temple, which seated about three thousand people, but was never large enough to accommodate the throngs that came to the services. After the first weeks of simultaneous work, the Mechanics Building, the most spacious auditorium in Boston, was engaged for united evening gatherings.

Boston University suspended recitations for a week, and Newton Theological Seminary for several days, so that the students might experience the uplift, and study the secret, of evangelistic work.

Among the district leaders in Boston was one of Dr. Chapman's dearest and most intimate friends, Dr. Ford C. Ottman—author of some notable works on prophecy. Speaking later to an Australian audience, he told them : " Boston is the centre of many things. It is the centre of Unitarianism, and that spells spiritual death ; it is the centre of Christian Science, the most transparent absurdity ever foisted upon the minds of men ; the magnificent temple of that cult is in the heart of Boston. It is also the centre of spiritism, theosophy, esoteric Buddhism, devil-worship, and other aberrations. Even some of its Christian ministers dare to question the authority of the Bible. Boston was spiritually dead. Men said it was impossible to move it ; but all things are possible with God, and Boston's extremity was His opportunity. Of the two hundred ministers who welcomed us to the city in January, 1909, some were half-hearted, but they came out with full hearts in the end. The business life of the city was stirred, and the great noonday meetings in Tremont Temple were crowded. Those who could get there early began coming at 9.30 to be sure of a seat for the 12 o'clock meeting. The attitude of the newspapers was very remarkable. First they gave a column, then two or three columns, then the front sheet, and then three or four pages. The reporters were splendid. Some of them who came to scoff remained to pray, and some fifteen or twenty of them, including several Roman Catholics, presented both Dr. Chapman and Mr. Alexander with a Bible containing their signatures."

The crowds that endeavoured to get to the Mechanics Building on the last Sunday night of the meetings were extraordinary even for Boston. All the streets around the building were filled with people. Those who were fortunate enough to get inside forgot the crush and the hours of waiting, as the singing began, and they took their part in the chorus of praise. " It was the best simultaneous work I have ever seen," declared Charles Alexander afterwards. " The work has been deep, and the three best points in it, outside those who came out for Christ, have been the number who were striving to do personal work ; the many who have pulled down their dusty Bibles and begun to read them anew ; and the large number who have joined the Pocket Testament League, promising to carry a Testament or Bible wherever they go, and read a chapter daily."

Dr. A. Z. Conrad, pastor of Park Street Church, and chairman of the Executive Committee, wrote, in a report of the meetings : " Mr. Charles M. Alexander, with his beaming countenance, which seems to reflect the very love of his Lord, instantly wins the affection of the people he meets. His ardent temperament, splendid enthusiasm, and unquestioning consecration, give him a tremendous power over the audiences before whom he stands. He is nothing less than a genius in his abilities as a director, and gives power and pathos to the most ordinary musical composition. It would be impossible to conceive of two men more supplemental to each other than Dr. Chapman and Mr. Alexander. Each one needs the other for the largest effectiveness in his work. Mr. Harkness is as unusual and noteworthy in his work at the piano, as Mr. Alexander in his capacity as director. Mr. Naftzger captures all hearts by his simple manner and wonderfully musical voice."

" I simply cannot tell you," wrote Dr. Conrad to Mrs. Alexander in 1920, " how he filled my heart with love for him during those blessed weeks of the wonderful revival in Boston. I was much with him those days, and have often longed to see more of him, yet both of us have been overwhelmingly occupied in the Master's work."

Deep interest was manifested everywhere in the impending visit of the Chapman-Alexander party to Australasia and the Orient. Large numbers were enlisted, both in Boston and in the short campaign that followed in Springfield, Mass., to pray that they might be greatly used for the salvation of souls, and for the encouragement of Christian workers, especially of the missionaries in China, Korea, and Japan. On March 12th Alexander's wife landed in New York, and three days later the mission party began the tour of conferences across the Continent which brought them to Vancouver at the end of March, ready to begin their voyage across the great Pacific.

Just before sailing, a telegram from Boston reached the party :—" Two thousand five hundred additions to the churches, by profession of faith, on the first Sunday after the mission. We wish you God-speed."

SONG SERVICE IN THE MECHANICS BUILDING, BOSTON, MASS., FEBRUARY, 1909

"JUST
A
WHISPER,
NOW!"

DR. J. WILBUR CHAPMAN AND CHARLES M. ALEXANDER IN 1909

VARYING TIMES AND CLIMES

A GOOD JOKE

CHAPTER SIXTEEN

The Power of Print

FROM boyhood onwards, Charles M. Alexander always had an intense appreciation of the far-reaching power, for good or evil, of the printed page. It was to make use of this power that he was led into a unique venture on the voyage that took Dr. Chapman and himself with their party across the Pacific to Australasia in 1909. The Vancouver meetings over, the party was to sail on board the S.S. *Makura*, on March 26th, for Sydney. Before them lay a voyage of three-and-a-half weeks, touching only at Honolulu, and at Suva in the Fiji Islands. The call of Christ for service had come from Australasia, but here on the voyage was an opportunity not to be missed. Alexander tried to think of some way in which a message about Christ might be brought to every one on board, and a novel plan occurred to him. Hurrying away from an early breakfast in the hotel, he made his way into the city, to see whether it would be possible, in the short time, to purchase a printing-press, with type, paper, and everything complete, in time to get it on board the ship, which was due to sail an hour after noon. He rapidly calculated that it would probably be possible to cover most, if not all, of the cost, by selling the plant on reaching Australia. A young printer, whom he was consulting about his hasty purchase, entered with great animation into the novel project, and when the final arrangements were being made to ship it to the wharf, Alexander suddenly said to him, " Say, old man, several of the men in our party know something about running a press, but we ought to have one thoroughly experienced fellow, at least. Why don't you come with us ? " At first, taken aback by the sudden proposition, a wistful look came over the young man's face. "I have been trying to plan for a good holiday the last six months," he said, "for I need a rest." " Say, man," said Alexander, "if I pay your voyage one way, will you come with us and take charge ? " " Why, that would be impossible," was the reply, " my mother and sister would not hear of my running off at such short notice, and besides, I have nothing packed." " Come now," said Alexander, " if I see to this press getting on board, you would just have time to rush home in a taxi, pack a bag, say good-bye to your mother and sister, and get down to the wharf. Will you do it ? " " I will," came the reply.

Just before sailing-time there was a commotion on the wharf, as a big printing-press was hurried on board, accompanied by a young printer. The captain and crew and all the passengers were aroused to interest ; a space by the laundry was given freely for the erection of the press, and the ship's carpenter was soon busy fitting up an empty cabin as a printing shop. The purpose of it all was to print a ship's newspaper, and through this medium to reach every person on board, a thing that could not have been accomplished in any other way. Several members of the party knew something of the printing trade, and all were eager to help. Difficulties came in the way with the storms of the first week, and later on with the melting of the rollers in the tropical heat. But in spite of all, a number of interesting issues of the *Makura Herald* were brought out. Ladies helped in the folding, and boys and girls ran up and down the decks distributing the papers. A free copy was given to every person on board. Stokers and stewards, officers and crew and passengers, all eagerly looked for it. News of the voyage, prize poems, diaries of the sports, and articles of various kinds were in the paper ; but besides these, there was a short message from Dr. Chapman, a hymn with words and music, and stories of the Pocket Testament League by Mr. Davis. One day a special illustrated supplement, telling of the Pocket Testament League, its origin and its purpose, was slipped into the paper. The members of the party were all ready, when opportunity offered, to speak a word for Christ, and to gain members for the League, especially Mr. Davis, well-known in connexion with it. Many joined the League, among both passengers and crew, and the stock of Testaments which had been brought on board, to meet the needs of those who had none suitable for carrying in the pocket, was entirely used. Two results that came of this venture must be told. Three years afterwards, in February, 1912, Dr. Chapman and Charles Alexander were again on their way to Australia for a much longer campaign. During a month's mission in Sydney, the Committee placed at their disposal an automobile, to carry them over the long distances between the places of their various meetings. On the first day the chauffeur said, " Good morning, Mr. Alexander." " Do you know me, then ? " " Three years ago I was a stoker on board the S.S. *Makura* when you crossed from Vancouver. I joined the Pocket Testament League then, and have read and carried my Testament ever since. See, here it is," and he drew it from his pocket. A few months later, the party were voyaging up the Queensland coast on the S.S. *Wodonga* from Brisbane to Townsville. Mr. Davis, always busy for his Master, spoke to one of the sailors about joining the P.T.L. " Oh," said the man, " I have been a member for four years. Don't you remember how a number of the crew of the *Makura* joined the League when your party crossed from Vancouver ? I was one of the stokers, and joined because I wanted to get the Testament, though I had no serious intention of reading and carrying it. However, when I had signed the pledge, I felt ashamed not to keep it. As I read the story of the Gospel day after day, I was led to accept Christ as my Saviour." " Do you take your stand for Christ before the other men ? " asked Mr. Davis. " Oh yes, sir, they call me ' Holy Joe,' but I don't mind, so long as I can witness for my Master."

Charles Alexander realized that while many could be reached in the great meetings here and there, there were thousands outside who could only be reached through the medium of the printed page. This was one of the underlying purposes of his great desire to scatter Gospel hymn-books broadcast. Much as he loved to see the thronging crowds and massed choirs open their books in some great building, and pour forth a volume of praise under his leadership, his mind reached out to the many who could not be included in such gatherings, and to the scattered individuals left behind when the great missions came to an end. Then it was that he loved to picture the song-books, with their messages, being opened in thousands of homes, and the family circles gathering round the piano to sing and revive the hallowed associations of the great meetings. Best of all, he loved to think of the books being carried into dark and sorrowful places, lighting them up with all their messages of cheer and of hope, thus not only crystallizing, but carrying forward the work crowded into a few short weeks. How many thousands of books he gave away he did not know himself, for he kept no record of his gifts.

It was not only hymn-books that he gave away. All through his life, and with large increase in the later years, he gave away Bibles, Testaments, and Gospels, never carelessly, but in such a way as to make the recipient realize that the gift was not from him alone, but from God. Other books he loved to give also ; if ever a book gripped him with its message, he was eager to share it as widely as possible. Dr. C. I. Scofield's *Rightly dividing the Word of Truth ; Truth in a Nutshell*, by Harold Sayles ; *Many Infallible Proofs*, by Dr. A. T. Pierson ; numbers of Dr. Torrey's books, especially *What the Bible Teaches*, and *Talks to Men* ; books by Dr. Haldeman, Dr. Ottman, and Philip Mauro—these, with many others, were constantly being given, wherever faith in Christ and in the Word of God needed to be established. Occasionally, some book not widely known would grip him with the power of its message. He would recommend it wherever he went, until it reached thousands upon thousands of readers. Such was the story of S. D. Gordon's *Quiet Talks on Power*. It was very little known, even in the United States, but Alexander, who had procured a copy after hearing of the mark made upon University students by Gordon's lectures, was deeply impressed by the book. On reaching England for the first time, he persuaded the publishers to issue a new edition for which he wrote an enthusiastic foreword. Everywhere in the great Missions that followed, he recommended it, and in a short time the book was not only famous, but was waking up sluggish consciences and getting people to work for Christ. Another book that Alexander was bringing to the notice of the public at that time, was *Down in Water Street*, the story of the great Jerry McAuley Rescue Mission, carried on for so many years by his beloved friend Sam Hadley.

One of the greatest accomplishments in using the power of print, was the issue of *The Southern Cross* Souvenirs, published through the enterprise of Mr. T. Shaw Fitchett at the close of Alexander's Australasian Missions with Dr. Torrey and Dr. Chapman. These attractive illustrated records not only helped to preserve and stimulate the great work in their own land, but were a means of arousing interest in Great Britain. Mr. David Williamson, gives an interesting reminiscence :—
" I met Charles Alexander for the first time in a London hotel within a few hours of his first arrival in England. He had come from Australia in advance of Dr. Torrey, and was a complete stranger in London, feeling very lonely. When he had unpacked some of his luggage he showed me the remarkable Souvenir of the Australian Mission, with the largest photographs of audiences I had ever seen. I may add

that it was this Souvenir which made an instant impression on the editors of two of the greatest daily newspapers in the country. One of them said to me on seeing these splendid photographs of audiences numbering thousands, ' There must be something in these men. But why have we not heard of them before ? ' I explained that Dr. Torrey and Mr. Alexander had not purposed, in the first place, coming to this country, but that the marvellous success of their missions in Australia had caused them to be invited. ' Well, we must have an article about them ! Will you do it at once ? ' I consented, and went back to the hotel to tell Mr. Alexander. He was never an easy subject for an interview, and I recollect it was some hours before I extracted from him the story of his career and his association with Dr. Torrey. He was far more eager to relate stories of conversion than to talk about himself. But I realized that people must first hear a little about the personality of the evangelists before they would be interested in their missions."

At the close of each series of Australasian campaigns, the " Souvenirs " were sent by the people to ministers, isolated Christians and others in the " back-blocks " of the country, also to missionaries on the outposts of Christianity in heathen lands, spreading the cheering news, wherever they were sent, that God was still working miracles of conversion through His saving power.

In his campaigns everywhere, Alexander was successful in persuading the editors of the great dailies to devote a space each day to the words and music of a Gospel song, to which he added some telling stories connected with it, or with other hymns. " Alexander's Songs and Stories " came to be a looked-for feature of the missions. He would often urge people to cut these out of the papers, enclosing them in letters to their friends, so that the blessing might spread widely.

A vivid pen-picture of Charles M. Alexander, as a temporary editor of a big daily, is given in the Philadelphia *Evening Telegraph* of April 13th, 1906. Dr. Torrey and he were then holding great meetings in the North and South Armories.

" 'If only I had a couple of columns a day in a great city paper, how much good I could accomplish,' said this earnest and energetic young man a few days ago. And the *Evening Telegraph* promptly placed two columns at his disposal.

" These columns will be under Mr. Alexander's editorial management exclusively. In them he will publish his new songs, words and music, his stories, with which he enlivens his talks and makes his words sink home. He will use these columns with which to preach the Gospel in a form and language that will interest even an infidel or the worst scoffer at sacred things. Did you ever meet Mr. Alexander ? If you have, the secret of his success, the magic of his pleading, you can readily understand. If not, picture to yourself a young man of average height, smoothly shaven, a head growing bald, but it holds a brain that never sleeps ; a pair of bright eyes that sparkle and dance with the joy of living, a mouth that is ever smiling, lips from which come sympathy for the unfortunate, encouragement for the depressed, hope for the fallen, and words of truth and wisdom for all.

" Charles M. Alexander is a magnetic man. He is religious from the soles of his feet to the top of his head. He is so full of good thoughts and works that they bubble over. He exudes them from every pore. You cannot be in his presence sixty seconds before you are infected by his manner. He is a humorist too. He extracts the greatest pleasure out of his life and his work, and is quick to see the ludicrous. His laugh is the hearty laugh that goes with a clear conscience.

" Mr. Alexander has entered upon his editorial work with the same enthusiasm with which he attacks everything. ' I want to do this to help people,' he said, ' I want to make their way smoother, their burdens lighter ; I want to lead them to God. I believe in newspapers. The power of the press to do good is incalculable. I would be glad if people who have been converted through our work would write and tell me just how their conversion came about ; how it affected them ; and I will publish some of their letters to show others how they can be saved.' "

Not only did Alexander spend many hours between meetings, when rest was a real necessity, in planning ways to interest people in the things of God, but he also trained every one of his helpers, pianists, soloists and secretaries, to be ready at any time to write articles when needed. When there was any remonstrance on the ground of incompetence he would laughingly say, " Never mind, it's hard on the puppy, but it's the making of a good dog ! " Even his wife was pressed into the service at times. At the beginning of one of the large campaigns in a Southern city, Alexander had negotiated with the editor of one of the two leading dailies about issuing an exclusive series of " Songs and Stories," without charge. The editor was not interested in evangelistic work, and flatly refused. Thereupon Alexander approached the other paper, and his offer was accepted at once. The campaign had not advanced far before the " Songs and Stories " were in tremendous demand, and the editor of the first paper came to see Alexander, and earnestly requested that some similar matter might be supplied to him. " Too late, old man ! " said Alexander. " I gave the exclusive rights to the other fellow, as you refused them." But the editor persisted in his request. " I'll tell you what I'll do," said Alexander. " Here is a short verbatim report of part of an address given by my wife in a women's meeting. If you like it, and wish to insert it, she shall write you an article each day for the next three weeks until the campaign closes."

Not until the following morning did his wife know anything of the transaction, for he knew she would be far too diffident to undertake the task, if requested beforehand, but would rise to a dire necessity. When the morning paper was brought to their room at the hotel, Alexander exhibited to her astonished gaze a small paragraph which intimated that during the remainder of the meetings a daily article would appear from her pen. Protests were unavailing, and his rallying good humour and persuasive encouragement won the day. Though the next night was more or less sleepless, she settled to her task, and the articles duly appeared.

A striking instance of the way in which Alexander turned to account any opportunity for bringing the Gospel-song messages to the notice of people occurred during the great London Mission of 1905. As was often the case, malicious reports had been industriously circulated that both Dr. Torrey and Mr. Alexander were making a fortune out of their work. London was already ringing with the new melodies which had captivated the great throngs at the Royal Albert Hall day after day. The Gramophone Company approached Alexander with a handsome business proposition for the making of a number of records, which, with the additional royalties, would have brought him in a large sum of money. To their surprise

he definitely refused at first.   On further persuasion he said :   " I will not accept
one penny for myself, either now or later.   But I'll give you some records, both in
song, and in spoken incidents, if you will take a big space in one of the leading
London dailies, and print the " Glory Song " above your advertisement, also adding
that I am giving you the records free, without remuneration or royalty.   Astonished by the unselfish generosity of the proposal, and finding it useless to persuade
him to receive any payment, the conditions were readily acceded to, with the result
that the " Glory Song " entered hundreds of thousands of homes in Great Britain ;
while, by means of the gramophone records, the very voice of the singer carried its
message in song, and told incidents of the meetings to people even in far-off lands.
It was reported at the time that the sales during the first few days amounted
to ten thousand records.   In their distant journeyings, Alexander and his wife
met with some strange surprises at unexpectedly hearing the sound of his voice.

Although most unworldly in his thoughts and ways of living, Alexander
was keenly alert to every practical, up-to-date method of arousing public interest. He
knew the value of pictures, and photography became one of his chief hobbies. After
his journey round the world with his wife in 1907, he issued for three years, at great
personal cost, a weekly illustrated paper which he named *Revival Times*. Its
pages contained stories of missionary work, new Gospel songs, and incidents of
evangelistic campaigns, many of the illustrations being from his own photographs.

At the close of his third visit to Australia in 1909 with Dr. Chapman, who was
there for the first time, the evangelists made their memorable missionary tour
through China, Korea, and Japan. A few days before they sailed from Sydney,
Alexander was talking with his Australian publisher, Mr. T. Shaw Fitchett,
and the idea occurred to them of running a series of popular articles in one of the
Australian magazines, telling of the missionary work in the Orient, as seen by the
party on their journey. Alexander was anxious to have the articles illustrated,
but realized that it would be impossible for him to find time for taking the necessary
photographs himself. A flashlight expert from Melbourne, Mr. Norman A. Thomas,
had come to Sydney to photograph some of the meetings. Alexander agreed
to go half shares with Mr. Fitchett in paying travelling expenses, if it could be
arranged for Mr. Thomas to make the trip at such short notice. Mr. Thomas was
a man of infinite calm, but had the Australian love of sport, and the proposition
appealed to him. Within twenty-four hours the last available berth had been
secured on the steamer, and with the small bag with which he had left Melbourne
for a few days, containing little else than a clean collar or two and an extra pair
of socks, Norman Thomas went aboard, and entered into an association with
Alexander that lengthened into twelve years, and brought the two men into a warm
and lasting friendship. Not only did the missionary articles appear with illustrations, including flashlight interior pictures of Oriental gatherings which were
entirely unique, but a collection of pictures was formed which added wonderful
interest to all of Alexander's subsequent work.

During the busy summer conferences in America, Alexander often had
unexpected opportunities of touching a life whose influence through the printed
page would spread far more widely than he ever expected. One day, at Northfield,

AT NORTHFIELD, MASSACHUSETTS

A FAVORITE RECREATION

WITH CHARLIE BUTLER, AUGUST, 1905

WITH SAM HADLEY OF "DOWN IN WATER STREET"

GROUP OF SPEAKERS AT THE CHRISTIAN WORKERS' CONFERENCE, AUGUST, 1908

IN
THOUGHTFUL
MOOD

PHOTO BY F. GUTEKUNST

A
MARKED PAGE
OF
ONE OF
PHILIP MAURO'S
BOOKS

Miss Rachel K. McDowell called to interview him. Writing to Mrs. Charles M. Alexander on October 17th, 1920, Miss McDowell says: " I owe so much to Mr. Alexander. It is due to him entirely that I devote all my time to writing *religious* news. When just starting out as a reporter, I came first to Northfield. I had an appointment with him at the Northfield Hotel for an interview for the *Newark (N.J.) Evening News,* on which I was then employed as a reporter of women's activities. He invited me in to breakfast with him. He could not be interviewed like anyone else. He interviewed me. He asked me what I was doing with my life. I tried to tell him. He said, ' I want you to promise me something. I want you to promise me that you will never write anything except as unto the Lord.' I told him that sounded very beautiful, but I did not see how it could be done. I had to make my living, and that meant writing whatever I was assigned to cover." In spite of all the claims on his time, Alexander went into the question with Miss McDowell with sympathetic patience. He sought to show her that she could begin at once to follow a new ideal by writing anything assigned to her with care and accuracy, ever on the look-out for anything that might help her readers, and seeking to avoid everything that would have the opposite effect. Not only did he remind her that any work undertaken by a Christian must be done in the right way, but that the work itself must be of that sort that is pleasing to God, and that if this was kept as a prayerful aim, God would not fail to provide suitable opportunity. " It was this personal appeal to me which was my second conversion," writes Miss McDowell. " It was not very long until I got the *New York Herald* to create the position of ' religious editor,' and secured the same. Since last February 2nd, I have been religious editor of the *New York Times.* And it is all due to your husband. I could have made a finer living, and won greater fame, as a society editor or a theatrical editor, or most anything else. But I would not have been so happy, because I feel, in my line, there is a real opportunity for service."

It was his innate love of books, and his knowledge of the potent influence of print, that led Charles Alexander, from early days, to be careful in selecting the right food on which to feed his own mind, and that of others whom he could influence. He revelled in the study of biography, which was closely connected with his exhaustless love of " folks."

God's Word was, he knew, in a unique way, " spirit and life," but he realized that *all* books produced an active effect for good or ill on their readers. He was therefore always on the eager look-out for what would help. This led him into a habit of marking sentences or phrases which impressed him. A red and blue pencil was never very far away from him, and to follow his bold markings through a book, not only shows his thoroughness of reading and eager outlook for original thoughts, but gives light on the development of what Mr. David Williamson calls " his remarkable gift for putting conventional religious ideas in a strikingly fresh phraseology." Mr. Hugh R. Monro, of New York, was struck by the same characteristic, and wrote of Charles Alexander, " I think of him as one of those who, without irreverence, had escaped the trammels of our cant phraseology. He had, I believe unconsciously, built up a spiritual vocabulary so sweet, genuine, and full of meaning, that it was, in itself, an interpretation of a transparent soul."

CHAPTER SEVENTEEN

A Third Visit to Australasia

1909

THE S.S. *Makura*, on which the Chapman-Alexander party had sailed from Vancouver on March 26th, put into port twice during the crossing of the Pacific Ocean. In Honolulu a great service was held, to which many Americans came who knew the work of Dr. Chapman and Mr. Alexander in the United States. At Suva, nine days later, missionaries and native pastors met the party on the dock, and escorted them up the hill to a native church, which they found packed with Fijians, their dusky faces crowned with a thick covering of hair, sometimes black, and sometimes copper-coloured through the bleaching of lime. On the next morning two services were held : one at ten o'clock for Fijians, and one at eleven o'clock for Europeans. A large crowd of both peoples gathered at the wharf later in the day to give the party a magnificent send-off.

At last, on April 17th, the shores of Australia came in sight, and the party spent a few hours ashore at Brisbane, where they were welcomed by the Evangelistic Campaign Committee, including Rev. W. Sweyn McQueen, D.D., and Mr. W. J. Tunley. From this date, the mission party laboured for four months without a single day's break, except for the necessary journeyings from place to place. In each of the two chief centres of the Commonwealth, Sydney and Melbourne, a full month was spent ; in Brisbane two weeks ; in Adelaide ten days ; Ballarat had a week, and Bendigo four days. Single meetings were held, in passing, at Castlemaine, Albury, and Moss Vale, while a couple of extra days were given to Melbourne and to Sydney for farewell meetings.

The party was a large and efficient one. Of them all, only Robert Harkness was returning to his homeland. To all the others, except to Charles Alexander and his wife, Australia was a new country. Ernest Naftzger was the soloist, Mr. and Mrs. Norton had charge of the personal workers, while Mr. and Mrs. William Asher were sent out to take the Gospel to the poor and outcast. With Dr. Chapman were his two youngest children, Agnes and Hamilton ; and, early in the Melbourne Mission, Alexander's wife invited Clara Lelean, a young niece of Robert Harkness, to spend the next three months with them. Other members of the mission party were the two secretaries, Miss Breckenridge and E. H. Bookmyer ; also George T. B. Davis, promoter of the Pocket Testament League, who was accompanied by his sweet old mother. Four other men had come to Australia to carry on smaller meetings simultaneously with the central ones. These were Dr.

Ford C. Ottman, assisted by Mr. Frank Dickson as song-leader and soloist ; while Mr. J. Raymond Hemminger, the Gospel singer, took charge of the music for Mr. W. P. Nicholson, the " sailor evangelist."

With such a corps of workers, supported by the efforts of local ministers and committees, and with thousands of prayers going up from the United States and Canada, as well as from all parts of Australia, it would have been strange indeed if the blessing of God had not been poured out in abundant measure.

The spiritual life of Australia was at flood tide just at this time. The results of the Torrey-Alexander Mission seven years earlier had made themselves felt, and a fresh quickening had been brought by the short visit of Charles Alexander in 1907. The world-wide ebb of spirituality, which has caused multitudes to drift out into the sea of indifference and unbelief in the last few years, had hardly set in as yet, and throughout the four months of the Missions of 1909 such marvellous scenes were witnessed, and such widespread interest awakened in the things of God, that it was truly a time of Pentecost for the whole Commonwealth.

The party did not leave their ship until reaching Sydney on April 19th. Here a conference was held with the local committee, and then a railway journey of about five hundred miles brought them to Melbourne. A meeting and reception was held on the day of arrival at the Federal Palace Hotel in Collins Street, where the plan of campaign was laid before the evangelists, and its details decided upon. Rev. Alexander Stewart, Mr. G. P. Barber, and others, voiced the hearty welcome of Melbourne to Dr. Chapman and his associates, and the joy of Australian people in seeing Mr. Alexander once again.

Rev. A. J. Clarke, of Croydon, South Australia, who had worked in London with Moody and Sankey from 1874 onwards, and had gone through all the Torrey-Alexander Missions in Australia in 1902, was also present at the meeting. He wrote afterwards :—" All the praying people of Australia felt that Mr. Alexander was a God-sent man. I do not know who has impressed the country as he has ; neither Governor, nor Governor-General, nor politician has ever won and held the heart of this nation like Mr. Alexander did on his first visit, and has done ever since. He has been the means of keeping a thread of unity through all the Australian evangelistic work. At the close of his first visit those who were in the inner circle turned to him and asked him to come back and bring somebody with him for another big work in Australia. When he left we started to pray for him. No arrangement was made, but we left the choice to him, praying that God would guide him to the right man. When we heard he was willing to come back and that he would bring Dr. Chapman with him, we felt that it was of God, although we only knew Dr. Chapman by repute. We were all delighted to see Mr. Alexander back and to hear his words of cheer at the welcome meeting in Collins Street. When Dr. Chapman rose to speak we soon felt that he too was the God-sent man for Australia. He immediately established our confidence and got right into our hearts. The results of the subsequent Missions in Australia proved that the choice of Mr. Alexander was God's choice, and that our prayers had been answered."

The Australian people left no stone unturned in assuring the mission party of a hearty welcome from every quarter. After meeting the Melbourne Committee, a large general meeting of ministers was held in the Assembly Hall, that they might extend their greetings and come into personal touch with the evangelists before they met the general public. Anglicans, Methodists, Baptists, Congregationalists, Presbyterians and Salvationists, united for this purpose, and the rather gloomy old Hall was soon brightened by the warmth and cordiality of the gathering. Alexander told of a motto, which the well-known Southern preacher, Sam Jones, sometimes placed over the platform in his meetings. It read like this: *Withhold your decision till the evidence is all in.* " Now isn't that a mighty good sentence to ponder over, for those who feel like criticizing this mission? " he asked. An earnest prayer by Dr. Ottman, and the short, telling address of Dr. Chapman, made a deep impression. " You Australians are certainly the greatest welcomers I have ever met," were Dr. Chapman's opening words. " This is the third time I have been welcomed in two days. I appreciate what you have said about me, and even more your reference to my beloved colleague, Mr. Alexander. If my evangelistic ministry has been blessed of God, much of the credit belongs to him, because he has made it the easiest thing in the world for me to preach."

The same night a public welcome meeting was held in Melbourne Town Hall, and once more, with joyful enthusiasm, the " Glory Song " sounded out, bringing back many sacred memories. Rev. Alexander Stewart, the president of the Melbourne Executive Committee, was in the chair, and leaders of all denominations uniting in the work, gave addresses of welcome. Rev. S. C. Kent, representing the Anglicans, said: " I am greatly delighted that Mr. Alexander has come here again. I learned to love him in this hall, on his first visit, and I will tell you why. More than once when he had to sing, he drew me aside behind the organ, where we could be alone, and said to me, ' I am to sing, I want you to pray.' We are delighted to have Dr. Chapman with us, and on behalf of our Archbishop, who is away, I bid him a most cordial welcome."

During the next month Melbourne was stirred from centre to circumference by the great mission. For the first two weeks the Town Hall was thronged at noon and at night, and the King's Theatre and other halls and churches were also frequently filled. Through the last two weeks, the great Exhibition Building was used for the night meetings and for occasional afternoon services.

The first noonday service in the Town Hall happened to fall on Eight Hours Day, and was crowded with holiday-makers. Mr. Naftzger, the soloist, had not arrived when Alexander stepped on to the little red dais to begin the singing. His eye lit on his secretary, seated at the Press table, and he called him up to sing a verse. " Now," said Alexander, when the solo had been vigorously rendered in a powerful voice, " no one here has any excuse for not singing that song, because if my secretary can sing it, anybody can." There was a holiday freshness in the laughter that followed, and the admonition to " cut your words off short, just as if you were speaking them," was instantly appreciated and obeyed. Never was the response readier or the singing crisper, and it seemed as though not a single voice was missing, when in answer to a request from the back of the hall, the crowd burst into the chorus, " He will hold me fast." All listened intently to a short, strong address of Dr. Chapman's, as he spoke of the meaning of pre-

MEETING FOR MEN ONLY IN THE MELBOURNE EXHIBITION BUILDING, MAY, 1909

BUSINESS MEN'S NOONDAY MEETING IN MELBOURNE TOWN HALL, MAY, 1909

FAREWELL TO TOWNSVILLE, QUEENSLAND, AUGUST, 1909

A MEETING
IN THE
VICTORIA
INSTITUTE,
THURSDAY
ISLAND,
AUGUST, 1909
The Mayor of
Thursday Island
seated between
Dr. Chapman and
Charles M. Alexander

MELBOURNE FRIENDS SPEED THEIR PARTING GUESTS, MAY, 1909

sumptuous sins, and how to be kept from them. The hall might have been empty for the hush that reigned, while he spoke of the downward pull of sin, and the helplessness of the strongest will to keep from falling. Taking a penknife from his pocket, Dr. Chapman opened his thumb and finger and it fell to the floor. He picked it up, and, addressing it, said, " I command you not to fall ! " but again it slipped through the loosened fingers. Then he drew a magnet from his pocket, held it to the knife and let go again. The steel, drawn down by gravitation, was yet gripped and held fast by the upward pull of a higher power. A thrill went through the audience as the clear, musical voice quoted from the eighth of Romans : " The law of the spirit of life in Christ Jesus hath made me free from the law of sin and death." A word of benediction, and as the audience poured out of the building to the work-a-day world outside, the words of the song, "He will hold me fast," rang in their ears. The rest-day was Saturday, and two of these free nights were set aside for special services of song in the Exhibition Building. On the first, Alexander met the members of his great choir, comprising five hundred sopranos, three hundred altos, a hundred and twenty-five tenors, and two hundred and fifty basses, for a special rehearsal. A week later, he led an audience of over ten thousand in almost continuous song for three hours, which flew like minutes.

Mr. W. A. Somerset Shum wrote in *The Southern Cross* some of the most vivid sparkling descriptions of Charles Alexander at work that have ever been penned. This life-story would lose its most brilliant pen-pictures were they omitted. " At half-past six on Saturday, May 15th," wrote Mr. Shum, " three men were sitting at the foot of the choir gallery in the empty Exhibition Building, listening to the gurgle and splash of water running down the gutters and cascading from the spouts.

" ' I suppose this is good for the country,' said one, ' but do you think they'll turn out a night like this to a choir rehearsal ? ' The second shook his head doubt-fully, and turning up his coat collar, shivered. ' Come ? ' said the third, scornfully. ' You chaps don't know an Alexander crowd. They'd come if they had to swim.'

" It was not long before the choir members were pouring into the hall between or through the showers, and soon the rising tiers of seats were filled with singers. As St. Andrew's clock chimed eight, a figure in a topcoat appeared in the aisle, and there being no other topcoat like it in all Melbourne, the waiting choir burst into a cheer of welcome. ' A-amen ! ' responded the figure in the overcoat, and there being no other ' A-men ' like it in all Melbourne, there was another round of applause. Alexander cast aside the famous overcoat, and ran up the carpeted flight of steps to the conductor's stand, raised some twelve or fourteen feet above the level of the platform. He got into touch with his choir-members at once. ' You have come from a great many churches,' he said, ' but with a single purpose, I know.' And then as by a happy inspiration, ' What do you say ? shall we sing " The Church's one foundation is Jesus Christ her Lord " ? '

" They sang it, and ' I *like* you ! ' announced the leader emphatically, and immediately called for another old favourite, ' For all the saints who from their labours rest.' Here was a chance for the tenors to show their mettle, and as they swept up the crescendo in the first four bars Alexander's eye kindled, and he nodded approval to Mr. T. Hopkins, his choir organizer, who had promised him a tenor-strength that would probably surpass anything he had known in England or America. ' Now I want you to sing a Gospel song written by one of yourselves, an Australian born and bred. Play " He will hold me fast," Mr. Harkness ! ' Harkness played the air through the applause. ' Now listen ! I want you to sing as I *want* you to sing. Did you get that ? Remember, I'm depending on you, and if *you* don't stay by me when the crowd is here, I'm gone ! Be good now, and sing as I tell you, as if you were preaching. That's what we're here for.'

" Then the music-lesson began. The soloist mounted the steps and stood beside the conductor. ' Watch how Mr. Naftzger sings ; I want you to follow him closely. You know that when a man writes a song he cannot put on paper everything he would like to—he just writes it straight ahead, and leaves it to your common sense to know how to phrase it. So SING IT RIGHT, if you knock the music all to pieces. It's the easiest thing in the world to kill a Gospel song. Listen ——' and Alexander sang the music exactly as written, mechanically as a metronome. ' Now don't you see ? ' he asked quickly. ' Sing it like that, and there's nothing to it ; but get it right, and there's a sermon in it ! '

" Then Mr. Naftzger sang the first verse, and Alexander, with a hand on his shoulder, flung in a comment at the end of every line. The result was something like this :

When I fear my faith will fail,	(*Catch that phrasing ?*)
Christ can hold me fast :	(*Just like that!*)
When the tempter would prevail,	(*Do you see ?*)
He can hold me fast.	(*Now the chorus !*)

" ' SING IT ! ' It was a trumpet-call, and it thrilled the ranks. ' Come on ! Come on ! ' and a vigorous foot stamped the time on the floor of the stand. ' That chorus once more, just a little faster, and when you come to the last " hold," sing it as if you meant it. Tell the people that Christ can *hold* them.' As the chorus pealed out crisp and clear in spite of its pace and volume, Alexander's face, at first rigidly set as if he were pulling the whole twelve hundred, relaxed into one beaming smile. ' Bless your old hearts,' he exclaimed. ' Let's stay here for a week ! ' The music lesson proceeded, and a few of us climbed to the top of the organ loft, not only to hear the singing, but to watch the conductor. And as we watched, we realized the difference between a choir conductor and a choir maker. We recognized, too, a greater Alexander than of yore—greater in skill, in knowledge of human nature, and in spiritual force. He talked to that company of singers—strangers, most of them, not only to him but to each other—as if they were members of a family, and handled them with absolute confidence born of the experience gained in the seven years since he first stood—a comparatively unknown leader—before an audience in the Melbourne Exhibition Building."

Once more let Mr. Shum, by the magic of his pen, take you with him to the Exhibition Building a week later, for the great festival of song which he calls " Alexander's Night " : " The great concert hall is still in semi-darkness, but as if by an unseen magician, the vast building is filled with light, soft and white. It is now a quarter to seven. There are some hundreds in the building already, in addition to a large proportion of the choir. A restlessness is upon the people.

Ah, what is that ? The doors are open ! The crowd is coming ! Yes, the crowd *is* coming. It is like an immense moving-picture exhibited to the accompaniment of rumbling thunder. Thousands upon thousands are hurrying up through the murky, dust-filled atmosphere, as if their lives depended upon their speed. On they come. It is like the bore of a great tidal river. In one vast volume it rushes till it reaches the space beneath the dome. The main stream continues and surges up the central aisle, and distributes itself all over the concert hall area. Two side streams have disappeared ; but they burst up from the stairways like waves from underneath hollow rocks, and splash and gurgle along the galleries. At five minutes past seven an official reports, ' All the seats are full.' And orders are given for the doors to be closed. But what a throng it is ! Hundreds yet are at the now closed doors. For twenty minutes the audience tries to go through the process of ' settling down.' It doesn't succeed very well. It is a happy crowd and has come for enjoyment ; it is also a rejoicing congregation, and has come for worship. At twenty-five minutes past seven the vast audience is cheering at its fullest power. Alexander has come ! ' We are to have a three hours' sing,' are his first words, and he smiles gleefully at thought of such a programme. ' Get ready,' he cries, ' for a long, hard, delightful evening. We are all going to join the choir.' His hands are uplifted—those wonder-working hands. ' Let us pray first.' And he prays briefly and simply. ' " Abide with me." Everybody stand ! ' The three hours of singing have begun. The conductor leans forward, scanning the great company. ' The last phrase just in a whisper.' His direction is obeyed. Ten thousand voices are blending in one great whispered prayer, ' Abide with me,' which the choir follows with a full-volumed, well-balanced ' Amen,' and the effect is beautiful. Some enthusiasts call out for the numbers they want. ' Wait a minute. I'll tell you when you can have your choice. We're going to learn a new chorus while we are fresh. There's enough in this to save any man, no matter how deep in sin.' The sopranos of the choir sing it first. Then the whole choir. The audience listens. Heads are gently swaying and nodding as the melody becomes more familiar. ' I believe, I believe on the Son of God.' The conductor is insisting on clear enunciation. ' Let the words come clear-cut : I believe.' Turning to the audience, ' Now are you ready for it ? ' The audience isn't sure. Alexander won't try it yet. He has another plan. Pointing to one of the officials, he asks, ' Do you think there's enough in that chorus to save any man ? ' ' Yes, I do,' replies the official, promptly. ' Then you give a Bible to the first volunteer who will sing it.' A ripple of merriment runs over the crowd. Two ladies volunteer to make the effort. The first is very nervous, and her voice thins off in parts almost to silence. The second sings clearly and well. Both are to get Bibles. Then everybody makes the attempt. ' I believe, I believe on the Son of God.' ' Glory ! ' exclaims a Salvation Army officer, his eyes glistening.

" The eyes of the conductor are now upon a lady in a wheel-chair in front. ' And what hymn would you like ? ' he asks sympathetically. She chooses ' There's power in the blood.' ' We used to make this old building ring with that seven years ago. Sing the chorus, choir : " There is power, power, wonder-working power." ' The word ' power ' vibrates and echoes. ' Do you want another verse ?

and the invalid smiles back her wish. The verse is sung. 'You've got them to sing better than I did.' How many hours will be cheered for her in the long days by the memory of this night !

"A look of delighted anticipation is on all faces when it is announced that Mr. Naftzger will sing 'The Ninety and Nine.' The clear, cultured voice sounds right out to the furthest rim of the multitude. With each verse the feeling grows. The last line rings out as with a heavenly triumph, 'Rejoice, for the Lord brings back His own.' The choir takes up and repeats the great, glad word ' REJOICE ' again and yet again. Then the whole line 'Rejoice ! REJOICE ! REJOICE ! for the Lord brings back His own.' Then the right-hand gallery sings it. Then the left-hand. Then the people far off under the dome. Then the yet more distant and almost invisible ones in the galleries beyond. Then everybody stands, and sings ' REJOICE, for the Lord brings back His own.' And up, up, and away, the thankful strain rises as though challenging the rejoicing in the upper courts of God, where the angels sing the triumphs of the Lord who seeks and saves.

"A sharp-faced, youthful-looking man has mounted the stand, but not to sing. He is Mr. Davis, who, for a few moments, explains and advocates the Pocket Testament League. 'We want this League to spread all over the land. It will bring the greatest revival this Commonwealth has ever known.' ' A-a-men,' says Alexander, who is seated on the steps behind the speaker. And then we sing ' Take it wherever you go.' It is now ten o'clock. But the audience is as keen in its interest as it was at eight o'clock, while the conductor disciplines the choir to perfection in its rendering of ' Who could it be but Jesus ? ' One more solo, and then we bow in prayer. People are asked to make their decision for Christ, for this song-service is an evangelistic meeting. Many stand. Not yet is the programme quite complete. We sing, as those who know that never again on earth shall we all meet just in this way, 'God be with you till we meet again.' It is a mutual prayer and a common pledge, and the benediction is as the confirming voice of God. This night of song is ended, yet it will *never* end."

The Pocket Testament League spread like wildfire through Australia during the four months of the Chapman-Alexander campaign. Not only in the meetings, but on streets and tramcars, Mr. Davis was busy enlisting members, especially among the tramway men and policemen, many of whom decided for Christ and became active in service. First in Melbourne, and later in Sydney, groups of these men became remarkable soul-winners, gaining hundreds of League members.

During these busy days in Melbourne, Alexander was looking for a verbatim stenographer, to take down Dr. Chapman's sermons just as he preached them. A young reporter on the "Hansard" staff of the Federal Parliament, just then in recess, accepted the contract. He was the son of a Presbyterian minister in Melbourne, but although attending his father's church regularly, William W. Rock was far from being a Christian. A keen sportsman, popular among a gay, careless set of young people, his whole mind was bent on having what he thought was "a good time." The first straight talk Alexander had with him on spiritual matters probed deep, and although Rock tried to efface it from his mind, the arrow of conviction rankled, and Alexander's intense earnestness impressed him strangely.

Two weeks afterwards, in another business interview with Alexander, Rock was stirred afresh with wonder that a stranger should care so much for his soul's welfare. A few nights later, sitting at the Press table in one of the great meetings, he bowed his head in his hands, and gave his heart and life to the Lord Jesus Christ. At the close of the Melbourne Mission, Alexander engaged him permanently as his secretary, in which post he remained for the next six years. His younger brother, Robert Blair, also on the "Hansard" staff, afterwards became Dr. Chapman's secretary, and the two young men were constantly in touch with Charles Alexander in Australia and in America and in England. Both of them afterwards became Presbyterian ministers in the United States. From his Melbourne manse, years later, their father wrote to Mrs. Alexander :—" Your husband was a rare man. I shall never forget that he led Will to decision for Christ. He was divinely taught, and knew exactly how to handle that eldest son of mine. He was the most charming personality I have ever known."

The Rev. Frederic C. Spurr, pastor, in 1909, of the Collins Street Baptist Church, wrote in 1920 :—" Charles Alexander and Dr. Chapman came to Australia twice whilst I lived there. I saw a great deal of Alexander, and we had some beautiful fellowship in our own home. The more I got to know of him and Dr. Chapman the more I grew to love them. They were ideally mated for their work. The great missions owed quite as much to Mr. Alexander's genius as a song-leader as to Dr. Chapman's preaching. I was always impressed by Mr. Alexander's perfect honesty and wonderful humanity. He was transparently good ; that is why he was so much loved. And he knew men—their weaknesses, their anxieties, and desires. Men knew that he knew them ; that is why they responded to him."

The farewell meeting in the Exhibition Building was in some ways the most remarkable event of the whole month. Long before noon, a great silent crowd had gathered round the doors of the building, and before three o'clock the vast hall was occupied by an audience of at least nine thousand. There was no choir, yet there *was* a choir nine thousand strong, including at least five hundred ministers. When Alexander made his appearance, the singing seemed to have a sweetness, a fire, and a note of gladness unknown before. Dr. Chapman was plainly touched as he spoke his farewell message, and in spite of the month of incessant labour, his voice was clear and ringing, showing not a trace of fatigue. When the meeting closed, the mission party, who were all gathered upon the platform, were rushed to the station in taxis, and barely caught the train for Sydney.

Here, as in Melbourne, the whole city, with its far-flung suburbs, was stirred, and the revival fire spread from this centre into all parts of New South Wales. The Sydney choir was organized by Alexander's old friend, Mr. J. J. Virgo. Once more, as in 1902, the magnificent Town Hall proved altogether inadequate for the throngs that came, hoping to find a seat within its walls. It was not unusual for four or five churches in the near neighbourhood to be filled as well with eager crowds, and it was a sign of the true working of the Holy Spirit, that out of these throngs of disappointed people, unable to get into the Town Hall meeting, there were large numbers of decisions for Christ. Night after night, members of the mission party assisted the Sydney ministers in leading these overflow services.

Great interest was taken in the meetings by the Countess of Dudley, wife of the Governor-General of Australia. Her favourite hymn was "Looking this way." She requested it more than once, and her beautiful eyes would fill with tears as the voices of the choir floated in clear pianissimo tones through the hall.

On the last Sunday of the Sydney Mission, the throngs were so great that the police, fearing accidents among the waiting thousands, ordered the doors to be opened at five o'clock. Word was sent to the hotel where Dr. Chapman and the Alexanders and others of the party were staying, to come at once to the Town Hall. They hurried over and began the meeting at half-past five. An hour later, by arrangement with the police outside, certain doors were opened for the attenders of the first meeting to pass out, while at the other end of the building the waiting crowds poured in to fill it once more for a second service.

The morning on which the mission party began their long journey northwards again to Brisbane, will long be remembered in Sydney. At seven o'clock the Town Hall was crowded. For almost an hour the people sang and listened to words of farewell, and then streamed in a great procession after the motor-cars which conveyed the mission party to the station. Only a limited number were allowed to pass through the barrier, but the huge multitude thronged around the station, and the train steamed out amidst the rising and falling cadences of the sweet hymn of farewell :—

> We'll never say good-bye in Heaven,
> We'll never say good-bye.

The journey through Queensland was full of interest to the whole party, for except for touching at the port of Brisbane, it was the first time that any of them, including Charles Alexander, had travelled through that part of Australia. They were such a big, happy family amongst themselves, that all weariness after the strain of the arduous weeks in Melbourne and Sydney seemed to vanish.

Brisbane has also an Exhibition Building, a little way out from the centre of the town, and here again wonderful scenes of enthusiasm in the cause of Christ were witnessed, many taking their stand for Him. In every place some song seems to take special hold of the people. In Brisbane during this Mission the hymn, "Oh, listen to the wondrous story," seemed the favourite, gaining a new beauty under Alexander's skilful leading. At a sweep of those speaking hands, the sopranos and altos rang out the question, "*Who saved us from eternal loss ?*" answered by the strong assertions of the tenors and basses, "*Who but God's Son upon the Cross !*" "*What did He do ?*" demanded the women's voices. "*He died for you,*" breathed the men in reply. "*Where is He now ?*" asked the sopranos and altos again, with a rising note, and the whole choir answered the question with a shout of triumph, "*In Heaven interceding.*" Soon the crowd had learned to sing it, and joined in as though they were a part of the great choir. Without doubt, many gained a new conception of the condescension, sacrifice and tender provision made by the Son of God for those who trust Him.

From Brisbane, Mr. and Mrs. Asher sailed to the Philippine Islands for a month's evangelistic work. The rest of the party travelled, by stages, back to

A TRADE IN CAMERAS
Dr. Ottman as "go-between"

MISS BEATRICE CADBURY JOINS THE PARTY.

JAPANESE OFFICERS OF THE "KUMANO MARU" JOIN THE POCKET TESTAMENT LEAGUE, AUGUST, 1909

IN THE STREETS OF HONG-KONG,
AUGUST, 1909

MAKING FRIENDS WITH
THE CHINESE COOLIES

LANDING AT SHANGHAI, SEPTEMBER 7, 1909

FILIPINO CHRISTIAN STUDENTS AT MANILA, AUGUST 27, 1909
During one day ashore from 7 a.m. to 11 p.m., Dr. Chapman and Charles Alexander held seven meetings, with missionaries, Filipinos, American business men and American soldiers, besides attending a reception by Judge Gilbert, Acting Governor.

Sydney and to Melbourne, spending a day in each, to meet committees, receive reports, and hold at least one great service ; then on again, across the continent, to Adelaide, in South Australia. Here ten more days were devoted to constant labour for Christ. Christians were strengthened and many souls won. In the meantime, Mr. Nicholson and Mr. Hemminger were holding missions in Geelong and other places which could not be reached by Dr. Chapman and Mr. Alexander, who did, however, succeed in giving a few days each to Ballarat and to Bendigo. On August 9th, Melbourne was reached again for the last time. Marvellous services of final farewell were held, and everywhere the longing, insistent request was heard, " Come back to Australia soon."

A serious proposition was laid before the evangelists, asking them to return three years later, as the four months set aside for this visit seemed only to have touched the fringes of the great work that had opened up. With a promise to see what could be done in making future arrangements, the mission party reluctantly made their last farewells, and were soon speeding northwards to Sydney again.

The various States which form the Commonwealth of Australia were founded independently of each other, and the capital cities of each lie far apart, only connected in the early days by sea, until the railways were developed. There was a considerable amount of rivalry between the States in those formative days, and when there first arose a likelihood of being linked together by land communications, each State provided its own railway gauge. It was therefore impossible to go from Melbourne to Sydney without changing trains at the State boundary line. The little town of Albury, where the change takes place, determined to benefit by the necessity, and as soon as the mission party alighted upon the platform at eleven o'clock at night on their journey north, they were hurried by a welcoming committee of ministers to a great wool-shed near the station, which had been roughly seated for a meeting, and which was crowded at that late hour with hundreds of people, many of whom had come long distances to be present. Their faith was rewarded in the blessing poured out by God upon the meeting, and a happy crowd escorted the mission party to their train at half-an-hour after midnight.

The next morning, at seven o'clock, the train stopped for half-an-hour at Moss Vale, in New South Wales, to give the passengers time to alight for breakfast. Here, again, arrangements had been made for a service, this time in the open air at the back of the station. Buggies and carts had driven in from every direction. A piano, hoisted upon a lorry, formed a convenient platform, and while the rest of the passengers had their breakfast, there was time for some hearty singing and an earnest message from Dr. Chapman. Kindly, thoughtful hands thrust in baskets loaded with good things for breakfast as the train was starting, so that the mission party might enjoy the meal they had missed.

More farewell meetings in Sydney, more requests for a speedy return, and on August 11th, the mission party, on board the Japanese S.S. *Kumano Maru*, passed out through the magnificent harbour, past the frowning Heads, into the open ocean on their voyage to China, where the missionary tour through the Far Eastern lands was to begin. Three times the *Kumano Maru* put into port before the coast of Australia was finally left behind. At Brisbane a farewell meeting was arranged in the forenoon at the Albert Street Methodist Church. During the singing, Alexander's keen ear caught a note of unusual sweetness. When the service closed, a message came to the platform, asking the Alexanders to hasten into the vestry, where, to their surprise and pleasure, they found the Countess of Dudley waiting to greet them. Her Excellency and Madame Melba had been sitting side by side far back in the body of the church. Lady Dudley insisted on carrying Alexander and his wife off to Government House for a hurried luncheon, and there, in the privacy of her boudoir, she told Mrs. Alexander of the blessing that had come to her heart through the meetings in Sydney, especially through the songs. Together they knelt for a few moments of prayer, and then Alexander and his wife were hurriedly driven down to the docks to join the rest of the party on board the *Kumano Maru.*

A letter found its way back to Rupert Lowe, in Geelong, which showed Alexander's deep affection for his old-time secretary. " Dear, dear old Lowe,—My heart has been tugging for Lowe. Your kind face, and gentle, dependable ways, always, but more than ever this time, leave a delicate rare perfume floating through my memory. Thank you for your invaluable help on our last day in Melbourne. I am sorry to say good-bye. Take a good look at the inscription upon your locket. For ever, Charles M. Alexander—Second-Timothy two-fifteen."

At Townsville, and again on Thursday Island, interesting days were spent ashore, and crowded meetings held among the white dwellers of those almost tropical regions.

A wonderful voyage inside the Great Barrier Reef, on over the calm blue expanse of the Pacific, passing almost within sight of the shores of New Guinea, provided needed rest after the months of constant labour and railway travel. Again the Pocket Testament League formed a means of witnessing for Christ on board ship. Almost all the Japanese officers, and many of the stewards, stewardesses and some of the passengers accepted the Testaments offered by Alexander and other members of the party, agreeing to carry them and read a chapter a day. The Japanese barber, Nakai, became a most enthusiastic member, and gave his heart to the Lord, keeping in touch with Mr. Davis by correspondence for years afterwards. The Chinese Consul-General, whom the Alexanders had met at Pakhoi in 1907, was a fellow-passenger, accompanied by his wife and young daughter. The little girl was delighted to meet friends whom she had known in her Chinese home, and loved to pace the decks with Mrs. Alexander. Their long talks and times of prayer, though handicapped by the difficulty of language, bore fruit, for years afterwards, in America, word reached Mrs. Alexander that little Miss Liang had given her heart to Christ upon that voyage.

THE FIVE-STORY PAGODA, NEAR CANTON, SOUTH CHINA, AUGUST, 1909

THROUGH A CHINESE DOORWAY

CHINESE
MEETING
IN
MARTYRS'
MEMORIAL
HALL,
SEPTEMBER,
1909

DOORWAY OF THE SHANGHAI
Y.M.C.A.

GROUP
OF
CHINESE
PASTORS,
MOST
OF
WHOM
HAD
SUFFERED
IN
THE
BOXER
RIOTS

CHAPTER EIGHTEEN

Among the Missionaries

1909

A WONDERFUL opportunity now lay before the Chapman-Alexander mission party for the next three months. In seven Chinese cities, in the two chief centres of Korea, and in a chain of cities through Japan, the missionaries were looking forward to times of conference and inspiration. Special meetings had been arranged in each place, not only for the native peoples, but also for the "foreigners" of British, American and other nationalities, many of whom were in as great need of Christ as those who had never heard His name, seldom, if ever, attending any kind of Christian service. The first touch with the missionaries was at Manila, in the Philippine Islands, where the party spent a delightful, but exhausting day ashore. From seven o'clock in the morning, when they were met and whirled off in motor-cars to breakfast, till eleven o'clock at night, when they were safely deposited aboard ship, they conducted seven meetings and attended a reception given by Judge Gilbert, who represented the United States Government. Mr. and Mrs. Asher were happy to meet their friends again and reported a time of fruitful service, on the way to the first meeting at nine-thirty with the Filipino students of the Union Theological College and Normal Training School. Missionaries and Christian workers, some of whom had travelled long distances to be present, gathered in the Y.M.C.A. at ten-thirty for an hour of refreshing fellowship. At noon, the Empire Theatre was crowded by representative business and professional men of Manila, who sang with an enthusiasm, and listened with an intentness, worthy of Americans. The men and women of the party were entertained at two separate luncheon gatherings, and at half-past three the First Presbyterian Church was crowded with a meeting for Filipinos and foreigners. Then the evangelists and their friends were whisked away to Fort McKinley, seven miles out of Manila, where at half-past six the American soldiers gave an enthusiastic welcome to their fellow-citizens, and listened with attention to their message. The last hours of the long day were devoted to two meetings, first in the Y.M.C.A. for "foreigners," and then a massed gathering of Filipinos in one of the native churches.

At Hong-Kong, on August 30th, good-bye was said to the *Kumano Maru*, and the Alexanders were greeted by their sister, Beatrice Cadbury, who had been staying with the Bradleys at Pakhoi, South China, and was to accompany the party on their missionary journey through the three Oriental countries. The few days at Hong-Kong were partly spent in excursions to the beautiful Peak that overlooks the city and the harbour.   Many of the Europeans and Americans were away for summer vacations, among the mountains, or in far-away Japan, so that only one large general service was arranged in the Hong-Kong Theatre.   Other gatherings were held in the To-Tsai Church, or " Church of the Heavenly Doctrine," twice in an evening ; at seven o'clock for the Chinese Christians, and at eight for the missionaries and English-speaking foreigners.

One long day was spent in Canton, the voyage from Hong-Kong and back being made by night.   Here, again, several meetings were held during the day, and opportunity was given also for seeing something of the surrounding country, including a visit to the famous five-story pagoda, as well as a ride in carrying-chairs through the narrow streets of Canton, crowded with half-clad figures in the summer heat.

Another two days' voyage from Hong-Kong brought the party to Shanghai, where the ten days' stay had been mapped out for a series of meetings more on the lines of an ordinary campaign.

Each day, three regular meetings were held, in addition to occasional morning and noon services.   At five-thirty, in the beautiful Martyrs' Memorial Hall of the Y.M.C.A., Dr. Ottman conducted a Bible reading.   At eight o'clock, Chinese Christians and their friends filled the hall for a service led by Dr. Chapman and Charles Alexander through interpretation ; and at nine o'clock a meeting was held for missionaries and other foreigners.   One Sunday afternoon a memorable service was held for young Chinese men, about seven hundred of whom packed the hall. Alexander had prepared some huge sheets with a Chinese version of the hymn, " Don't stop praying," in large characters which could be read from all parts of the hall.   By the help of a few Chinese phrases, which put him in touch with his audience, and made them forget the language barrier, he talked to them as though they understood, which indeed they partly did, from his expressive face and gestures, almost before the interpreter quickly followed each sentence ; and soon he had the crowd of sturdy young Chinese singing lustily.

At the close of his message, Dr. Chapman called those who would accept Christ and acknowledge Him as Lord and Saviour, to come forward and take Alexander by the hand.   A wonderful scene followed.   Fifty-three men of various ages came forward.   Then Dr. Chapman again put the decision for Christ clearly to them through an interpreter, asking those who meant from that day to stand for Him, to say, " I will," in their own tongue.   The vigorous, decisive response that came from their lips was a thrilling sound.

Some interesting gatherings were held with the Chinese pastors, with whom both Alexander and Dr. Chapman enjoyed delightful hours of conference and fellowship.   Many of them became intensely interested in the Pocket Testament League, promising to take it up in their churches.   Reports filtered through in later years of some of the extraordinary revivals that followed the introduction of the " Sleeve Testament League," as it was called in some regions.   Mission centres, schools, and hospitals were visited.   One day, Dr. Newell, sister of the famous Bible-teacher of Chicago, showed the party over the women's hospital. In one of the wards were two pairs of twins, only a few hours old.   Dr. Chapman

AT
THE
SHANGHAI
WOMEN'S
MISSION
HOSPITAL.
Two
pairs
of
twins!

COOLIES INTERESTED IN A NOTICE OF THE SHANGHAI MEETINGS, SEPTEMBER, 1909

DR. CHAPMAN AND C. M. ALEXANDER, WITH DR. OTTMAN AND THE Y.M.C.A. SECRETARY, MEET VICE-PRESIDENT
AND MRS. FAIRBANKS FOR BREAKFAST IN SHANGHAI.

ON THE YANGTSE-KIANG RIVER, SEPTEMBER, 1909

A GLIMPSE OF FLETCHER BROCKMAN AT WU-HU ON THE YANGTSE

and Charles Alexander were greatly interested in them, and were snapshotted with a tiny Chinese infant, swathed in wrappings, lying on each arm.

When the Shanghai Mission closed, the party began a fascinating tour through the great Celestial Empire. A railway journey of one hundred and ninety-six miles brought them to the famous, ancient city of Nanking, with its population of 300,000 and its many hundreds of students. Here Alexander had the joy of meeting an old Moody Institute friend, Abram E. Cory, who insisted on entertaining him and his wife. After one of the earlier meetings, having noticed his old friend hesitating somewhat as he led the singing, and giving directions rather to him, as interpreter, than to the crowd of Chinese students whom he was leading in song, Mr. Cory said, " Go ahead now, Alexander, forget all about the interpreter, get after them just as you used to do in Chicago." Alexander followed his advice, which was amply justified by the heartiness of the singing.

Mr. Cory wrote some years afterwards :—" Charles's ability to make everyone feel that they were his intimate friends was greater than that of anyone I have ever known. One incident stands out clearly in my mind. I had tried to persuade him to lead the singing in our Chinese school at Nanking. He felt that he could not do it, but he sang a verse of " God will take care of you," and I think I have never seen anyone manifest more joy than he did when he found that the boys could follow him. Some of them spoke English, and as you will remember, he soon had the whole school singing those religious songs. It was my privilege to interpret for him in conversation with some of the boys who were not Christians, and his simple easy way soon won them to decision. That visit to China was one of the most outstanding things in all of our missionary history. Charles was one of the brightest, truest, and most wonderful men I have known in all my life."

Another missionary, Rev. W. Remfry Hunt, wrote :—" It was such a joy for me to interpret for Mr. Alexander in Nanking, and I specially remember the fine meeting at the Drum Gower School, and his message to the Chinese girls. His love and sympathy, as we were parting with our dear children at that time, helped us greatly to bear the trial."

The temptation to linger on the many thrilling incidents of that memorable journey is well-nigh irresistible, but the marvellous river-voyage of five hundred miles up the great Yangtse-Kiang to Hankow ; the days of blessing spent in fellowship with that veteran servant of God, Rev. Griffith John, and other missionaries ; the six hundred miles of railway journey that followed, bringing the party from Hankow to Peking, can only lightly be touched upon. The week spent in the Imperial city was filled with happy activities and striking incidents. Each day, two or more meetings were held in various parts of the city for the Chinese, and at least one for foreigners, with extra gatherings of various kinds. To step through a gateway into the beautiful Methodist compound, transported in a moment from the glare and noise and dust of the Oriental city to the peaceful quiet of an American scene, with sunlit lawns bordered by pretty vine-clad houses, and the great church and University Building, was refreshment indeed, after a busy day's work. Delightful fellowship was enjoyed with the patriarchal missionary family headed by

Dr. H. H. Lowry, who had given forty years of fruitful service to China, and rejoiced in having children and grandchildren around him to share in his work.

From Peking the party travelled by rail to Tien-Tsin, where a busy day was spent, including five meetings, the party being rushed through the city from one service to another in rickshaws. On October 3rd, a small launch carried the mission party from the port of Tong-Hu eighteen miles out into the gulf of Pi-chi-li, where they boarded a Japanese coast steamer.

One more glimpse of China was given, in a memorable day spent ashore at Che-foo, where, after a visit to the Industrial Mission, they were entertained for lunch at the China Inland Mission schools, in which about three hundred boys and girls, almost entirely the children of missionaries, enjoy an education amid happy, healthy surroundings. Dr. Chapman, who was not well, had stayed aboard ship, but in the one hour of service with the bright-faced children, Charles Alexander accomplished a bit of work with far-reaching and long-lived results. With his genius for bringing others into service, he not only taught the children three new songs, and heard them recite Scripture verses, but made an opportunity for six others to take part, including his wife and sister and Mr. Davis. After they had listened to the story of the Pocket Testament League, Alexander told the children that he and his wife and sister would send a beautiful leather-covered Testament back from England to every boy and girl who would like to join. Every child, teacher, and missionary in the room seemed to rise in response, and the Testaments reached them a month or two later. How faithfully the little books were read and carried, will be seen in the following incidents.

Two years afterwards, Alexander and his wife, lunching at the China Inland Mission House in Toronto, Canada, met some missionaries whose children had been at school in Che-foo in 1909. "Are they carrying the Testaments, and still reading a chapter a day?" queried Alexander. "Ask them yourself. They will be in from school in a moment, and do not know that you are here," was the reply. A few minutes later a bright-faced girl of fourteen and her younger brother entered the room. Their delighted surprise at seeing the Alexanders left no time for the question to be asked, for both children, uninvited, pulled their Testaments out of their pockets with pride. The little boy, running off to his room, returned in a moment with one of his treasures—the hymn-sheet used at the meeting two years before. In Glasgow, in 1914, two of the Che-foo boys, grown into fine young manhood, and acting as ushers in the Chapman-Alexander meetings, were still carrying the same Testaments given to them in 1909.

After the signing of the Armistice, at the close of the world-war, Alexander and his wife, having returned to England, were holding a Pocket Testament League meeting in Bath in the autumn of 1919, when a note was passed up to the platform. It read as follows :—"Dear Mr. Alexander, Do you remember a visit you paid to Che-foo some years ago ?—Well, you gave Testaments to about three hundred of us then, and I had one of them. Some time later, when reading it in a few odd moments in the midst of a busy morning, I found the 'peace which passeth under-standing.' My little Testament was a great help to me during those first days of trusting in Christ. My eldest brother has his still. At the beginning of the war

WAY-
SIDE
BEGGARS

"GOD
WILL TAKE
CARE OF YOU."

GOOD-BYE TO THE MISSIONARIES ON SHANGHAI STATION, SEPT. 17, 1909

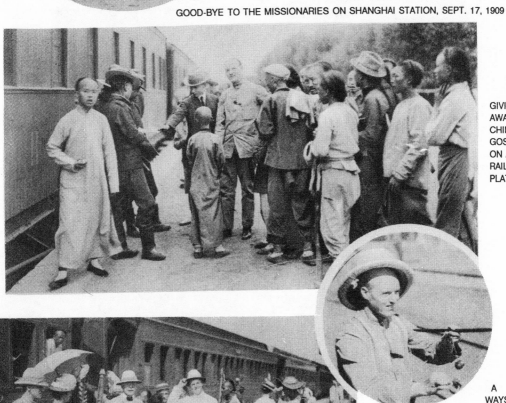

GIVING
AWAY
CHINESE
GOSPELS
ON A
RAILWAY
PLATFORM

A
WAYSIDE
PURCHASE

A
HOT DAY
EN ROUTE
TO PEKIN

JOINING THE P.T.L. ON TOP OF THE
WATER TOWER AT HANKOW, SEPT., 1909

CHINESE
CHRISTIAN
STUDENTS
AT
PEKIN
UNIVERSITY,
OCTOBER 1,
1909

MISSIONARIES' CHILDREN WHO JOINED THE POCKET TESTAMENT LEAGUE AT CHEFOO SCHOOLS, OCT. 4, 1909

In Toronto (Canada) in 1911, in Glasgow (Scotland) in 1914 and in Bristol (England) in 1919, Charles Alexander met some of these boys and girls still faithfully reading and carrying the same leather-bound Testaments sent to Chefoo in 1909 by himself and his wife and Miss Cadbury.

he gave it to me to keep, with a handful of things he valued, until he came back. (He carried a khaki one in France.) The other day he was ' demobbed,' so asked me for the same little old one again. He loves his as much as I love mine. I just *had* to write a line and say ' Thank you.' Yours sincerely, Eva M. McCarthy,'' At the close of the meeting, the Alexanders met the writer of the letter, a charming, bright-faced young woman. A few nights later, in Bristol, Alexander read her letter aloud, laying emphasis on the way in which faithful reading and carrying of God's Word had led to decision for Christ. Hearing footsteps on the steep flight of stairs leading up to the pulpit platform, Alexander looked down and saw a young woman, in deaconess dress, mounting towards him, holding out something which he soon saw was a little Testament. " I, too, was one of the schoolgirls at Che-foo in 1909," came from the eager lips, " and when I heard you reading that letter I felt I must let you know that I am still carrying and reading the little Testament you gave me then." Needless to say, each girl was soon the recipient of a beautiful new Testament, to save the first one from being worn out.

From October 9th to 20th, some busy weeks, full of fascination, were spent in the old hermit-land of Korea, opened up at last to the outside world, but not as yet under the sway of Japan, although it had been the unhappy ground on which the Chinese and Japanese armies had met in bitter conflict.

A wonderful week of conference was spent in Seoul, attended by missionaries from every part of Korea. Some of the party then travelled northwards to Pyeng-Yang, but Dr. Chapman, who had an attack of serious illness, travelled straight on to Japan with Dr. Ottman. It was a marvellous sensation to meet the many radiant Korean Christians in that great northern city, where seventeen years earlier not a ray of light had brightened the darkness of heathenism, but where in 1909, by God's blessing on the labours of Dr. Samuel H. Moffett and other missionaries, the Christians numbered eight thousand. So true and genuinely sincere were the Christian lives of these new believers, that fellowship with them carried Alexander and his party back, in spirit, to the days of the Apostles. The wonderfully organized system of Bible Schools particularly interested Alexander. At intervals throughout the year men and women who wished to study the Bible, but could not leave their occupations for long periods, travelled great distances, at their own expense, for a week's Bible Study in Pyeng-Yang, carrying back to their villages what they had learned, till another opportunity came for learning more. A journey on the primitive little Japanese train back to Seoul, where the Alexanders were the guests of Dr. and Mrs. Horace G. Underwood; another journey, stopping for a night at Song-Do, where they met Miss Cordelia Erwin and other missionaries, brought them once more to the port of Fusan, and across the shimmering streak of ocean to Shimonoseki, in Japan. In this land of Oriental charm and natural beauty, three-and-a-half busy weeks were spent in the cities of Kobe, Osaka, Kyoto, Nagoya, Yokohama, and Tokyo; with two delightful days of enjoyment amid the glorious scenery of Nikko and of Lake Chuzenji, whose waters, far above sea-level, mirror the stately splendours of the sacred mountain, Nan-Tai-San. Day after day was filled by Christian fellowship with missionaries and Japanese Christians, with opportunities for singing and preaching the Gospel, and with marvellous instances of decision for Christ. Again only a typical incident can be given. One night in Nagoya, in a crowded Japanese church, the power of the Holy Spirit seemed so great that Alexander, who was leading the meeting, turned to one of the missionaries, and asked him to slip into the vestry with one or two others, to translate into Japanese the chorus, which he had used so effectively elsewhere ;

> I surrender all,
> I surrender all,
> All I have I bring to Jesus,
> I surrender all.

He asked to have the Japanese words written out in Roman characters, easy for him to read. A few minutes later, while Mr. Davis was speaking, the chorus was brought to the pulpit, and a few whispered instructions given. When Mr. Davis had finished, Alexander told the assembly, through an interpreter, that he wanted to teach them a new chorus. To the delight of the Japanese, immediately expressed by the surprised smiles that spread over their countenances, Alexander sang to them in their own tongue, and was delighted in his turn, when, with low bows and expressions of assent, the Japanese congregation assured him that he had been clearly understood. In a few moments the whole church rang with the song of consecration and surrender. A hush followed some words of earnest prayer, uttered by one of the missionaries. It was broken by the voice of a little man, with a heavy, dark moustache, who leaned over the gallery, tears streaming down his face, his hands gesticulating, his voice rising and falling in tones of earnest entreaty. Alexander's inquiring look brought a quick interpretation from a missionary sitting near. " He is saying that the wonderful song has laid hold of him, and wants permission to come down to the front of the meeting and tell his story," was the whispered explanation. " Tell him to come at once," said Alexander ; and soon, in the hush of listening expectation, the click-clack-clack of Japanese shoes was heard coming up the central aisle. A stocky little figure faced the audience, and making a low bow, with head sinking below the level of the stiffened knees, upon which his hands rested, he was answered by the low, courteous bowing of everyone present. Then came the surprising story, told with a fervour and emotion that Alexander had never expected to see displayed by a Japanese. Sentence by sentence was interpreted in whispers by one of the missionaries into the ear of each of the Alexander party. The man was a blacksmith by trade, and told of his lifelong antagonism to the Gospel of Christ, and to the efforts of missionaries to bring the good news to his people. Ten years earlier, the Rev. Barclay Buxton had given him a Bible, which he had torn to pieces in fury and trampled under foot, vowing that he would never enter a place of Christian worship. Some power that he did not understand, but now acknowledged as the power of God, had led him into the church that night. The message had laid hold of him, and when the chorus, " I surrender all," was being sung, the Holy Spirit revealed Jesus to him, and, sitting there in the gallery, he had received Him as Saviour and Lord. He told of his drunken ways and violent habits, and that he was now going home to lead to Jesus the wife whom he had often beaten in a fit of temper, and to start

WITH DR. JAMES S. GALE, AUTHOR OF
"THE VANGUARD," IN SEOUL, KOREA,
OCTOBER, 1909

WITH DR. GRIFFITH JOHN IN HANKOW, CHINA, SEPTEMBER, 1909

A VISIT TO DR. AND MRS. HORACE G. UNDERWOOD AT SEOUL, KOREA, OCTOBER, 1909

KOREAN SCHOOL-
GIRLS AT PYENG
YANG

KOREA,
OCTOBER, 1909

WOMEN'S MEETING IN "THE CHURCH ON THE HILL," PYENG YANG, KOREA, OCTOBER, 1909--
DR. SAMUEL A. MOFFETT IN THE FOREGROUND

MEN'S MEETING IN THE YOUNG MEN'S CHRISTIAN ASSOCIATION AT SEOUL, KOREA, OCTOBER, 1909
(The horse-hair top-hats mark the married men.)

KOREAN SCHOOL-BOYS AND BIBLE STUDENTS AT PYENG YANG, KOREA, OCTOBER, 1909

Charles Alexander said this was the only group of people he had ever met in any country where everyone pulled out a Testament on being unexpectedly challenged.

AN OPEN-AIR SONG SERVICE WITH KOREAN BIBLE-CLASS WOMEN AND SCHOOL-GIRLS AT PYENG YANG

Many of these women traveled long distances at their own expense for a week or more of study at the Pyeng Yang Bible School. On returning to their own villages they taught what they had learned, until another opportunity came for learning more.

A VIEW OF PYENG YANG, KOREA, THROUGH ONE OF THE CITY GATEWAYS

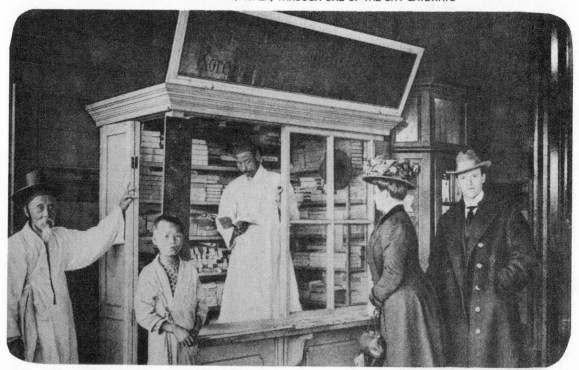

AT THE BRITISH AND FOREIGN BIBLE SOCIETY'S BOOK-STALL ON PYENG YANG STATION, OCTOBER, 1909

family worship with her and his three children. Letters received later brought Alexander the welcome news of a transformed home, in which Jesus was honoured, and the whole family became members of a Christian church.

One of the meetings in Tokyo was a great gathering of Japanese schoolgirls from a number of the missionary schools. Most of the girls spoke at least some English and seemed to drink in the message intelligently, even before the interpreter followed. On this day, Alexander was seeking to impress his audience with the call to Christian service and soul-winning. He had found, among the Japanese Christians, some who regarded Christianity as an educational advantage, bringing increased culture, knowledge of the world and fellowship with the West, but who had not grasped the thought of the obligations involved by the acceptance of Christ and His salvation. Alexander taught the girls the chorus:

> Can the Lord depend on you ?
> Can the Lord depend on you ?
> Does He find you ever true ?
> Can the Lord depend on you ?

When the chorus had been sung a number of times, enunciated with surprising clearness in the English tongue, he called for a volunteer to sing it as a solo. In the flutter and girlish whispering that followed, heads turned towards a black-haired girl in European dress, who was soon the centre of nudging elbows and whispered calls of, " Sing it, Haru ! " " Haru can do it ! " With a word of encouragement from the leader, the girl rose and sang the chorus more than once in a clear, ringing voice. It was the beginning of a new outlook upon life for her. Brought up as the ward of an American Presbyterian missionary, she had been trained in Christian knowledge and had joined the Presbyterian Church, but more as a matter of form than as the outcome of genuine faith in the Lord Jesus Christ. She had earned to look to God for the supply of her needs, and to depend upon Him, but now she determined that her life should be one of service. God accepted her offering, and led her step by step to her present position as a pastor's assistant in the city of Philadelphia.

In Yokohama came a time of parting. Some of the mission party travelled to New York over the long ocean roads by way of Europe. Mr. Davis, accompanied by his mother, returned to Korea, at the request of the missionaries, for three months' work in promoting the Pocket Testament League over the whole country, to stimulate the marvellous revival which had broken out. Beatrice Cadbury returned to the Bradleys in Pakhoi ; while Dr. Chapman, with his children, the Alexanders, Robert Harkness, and Dr. Ottman, sailed on November 15th, on board the *Empress of China,* for Vancouver.

CHAPTER NINETEEN

Constant Outpourings of Blessing

1910 to 1911

THE first glimpse of the rocky, pine-clad coast of Vancouver Island was welcomed by the mission party on November 26th, 1909. During the eight months' trip, seventy-seven nights, or the equivalent of two-and-a-half months, were spent aboard ship, while twenty nights were passed on trains. Yet with all the thousands of miles of travel, by sea and by land, there had been no accident of any kind. With thankful hearts they looked back over the long journey through which they had been safely brought, and which had afforded such unique opportunities for the service of Christ. On the way back from Vancouver to New York, short conferences were held in Minneapolis, Pittsburg, Boston, and Springfield, Mass. Glowing reports were given of the great work of God in Australasia and the Orient, and thanksgiving was manifested, especially in joyful song, over such answers to the many prayers that had gone up from thousands of hearts in America.

The first three months of 1910 were occupied with simultaneous campaigns in the New England cities of Bangor and Portland, Maine, and at Dayton and Columbus, Ohio, and in each much lasting good was done. But with every new experience it became clearer that the best results, in proportion to time and effort spent, were not to be gained on the simultaneous plan ; at least, not with such a large number of leaders and so much subdivision of districts.

The power and inspiration of the singing was a blessing everywhere. It was in Portland, Maine, that cold, snowy January, that Robert Harkness wrote the chorus " Travelling Home." One Sunday afternoon a meeting was being held in a large church off Main Street. Some three hundred travelling men, who were holding a business convention in Portland, were gathered in a hall near the church. Some of the Christians amongst them had begged Dr. Chapman and Charles Alexander to come over for a little while as soon as the afternoon service closed in the church. Hearing that few of the men were in sympathy with religious things, Alexander, taking Harkness with him, slipped out of the church as soon as the Song Service was over and Dr. Chapman had begun to preach. His plan was to break the ice, before Dr. Chapman should arrive at the hall, by getting into personal touch with the men through some informal singing. As they walked across the snowy street, Robert Harkness said, " I believe I have a chorus that will just suit these travelling men." " Good for you, old fellow," said Alexander, " we'll try it." The

A MEETING IN KYOTO TOWN HALL, JAPAN, OCTOBER 29, 1909

A MEETING OF JAPANESE SCHOOL-GIRLS AT YOKOHAMA, NOVEMBER, 1909

BY LAKE CHUZENJI, JAPAN, NOVEMBER, 1909

THE GREAT TORI AT CHUZENJI
VILLAGE, JAPAN

THE SACRED MOUNTAIN, MAN-TAI-SAN, FROM THE SHORES OF LAKE CHUZENJI, JAPAN, NOVEMBER, 1909

air of the hall, when they reached it, was thick with tobacco smoke and buzzing with noisy conversation.

One of the men who had invited the evangelists soon introduced Alexander and Harkness to a number of the others. Then, in his easy, natural manner, Alexander sprang on to the platform, and standing by the piano, called out to the men, " Say, fellows, I've got a young man here who told me, as we were crossing the street just now, that he has a song he thinks you will like. What do you say ? Shall we have him play it over, and see whether it is any good ? " " Sure, sure," came back the reply. Harkness played it, and then sang it :—

> Travelling home, travelling home,
> Led by Jesus, we are travelling home.

He struck a strange, weird, pathetic chord at the word " home " in the second phrase of the chorus as he repeated it, and Alexander's face lit up with a smile of appreciation. " I like it, don't you ? " he said, turning to the men. " Now I'll sing it, and then we'll try it all together." In two minutes the crowd of men had caught the tune, and as they sang, pipes and cigars were pulled from their lips, and went out without being noticed. Again and again they sang, listening, in between, to Alexander's telling stories and informal words that drove home the claims of Christ. The atmosphere of the room cleared, the power of God began to be felt, and when Dr. Chapman slipped in at the door, they were ready, without realizing that a meeting had begun, to listen to his message. A number of men took a stand for Christ, and again and again they sang the chorus, with its sweet, haunting strain. Next day the convention ended. The men spread far and wide over the United States, and before the chorus had been put on paper, they were humming it, singing it, whistling it, wherever they went. Letters came back from some of the Christian men, saying how often it had cheered and helped them on their long railway journeys as they went about their business.

An event that was to mean much to Dr. Chapman, and also to the Alexanders, was a visit to Dayton and Columbus, Ohio, during the campaigns there, by Miss Mabel Moulton, of Providence, Rhode Island. Some years before, she had taken a great interest in Dr. Chapman's simultaneous campaign in her own city, and before the Columbus meetings closed they were betrothed. Within a few days the party sailed for England to conduct a month's mission in Cardiff, South Wales ; and the engagement was not announced until Dr. Chapman's return to America.

From the beginning of April until May 2nd, 1910, a wonderful work of God was experienced in Cardiff. For the first time, Dr. Chapman heard the Welsh singing of which Alexander had given him such glowing accounts. Again four thousand voices rose and fell on the cadences of " Aberystwyth," and again the people quickly caught up the hymns, many of them written since the Torrey-Alexander Mission of six years earlier. One of the special features of the Cardiff Mission was a series of noon-day meetings held in the Stock Exchange, where a great impression was made on the commercial men of the city. At the last meeting, a prominent member of the Exchange said : " During the last few days we have listened to the straight, earnest preaching of religious truth ; Mr. Alexander has cheered our hearts by the stirring songs he has given us ; Dr. Chapman has dispelled many a doubt, and has strengthened the faith of many by his direct statement of the Gospel." The hymn " He will hold me fast," and the choruses " Travelling Home " and " I am included," were called for at almost every meeting of the mission. They were translated into Welsh, and spread through the hills of South Wales, and were sung in the villages and coal-mining towns throughout the Principality.

On May 7th, after a great Rally in the Sun Hall at Liverpool, the mission party sailed again for New York. Alexander left his wife behind this time, as his stay was to be short—chiefly for the object of taking part in the Presbyterian General Assembly in Atlantic City. Here he was taken seriously ill, but recovered sufficiently to return home and attend the World's Missionary Conference in Edinburgh in June. But the illness recurred, necessitating an operation for appendicitis, from which he made a splendid recovery. At the beginning of September, Alexander and his wife rejoiced in welcoming Dr. Chapman and his bride to " Tennessee." Together, the four, accompanied by pianist and soloist, made a tour of conferences through the British Isles. Inspirational gatherings, for praise and stimulation in soul-winning, were held in Ipswich, Cheltenham, and Newport ; in the Scottish cities of Edinburgh and Dundee ; and in Merthyr Tydfil and Cardiff, South Wales. On this tour, Mrs. Chapman had her first introduction to public work for Christ. On Sunday afternoons, when Dr. Chapman and Charles Alexander usually held mass meetings for men, their wives met gatherings of women in some church or hall. Mrs. Chapman's womanly, unassuming manner won affectionate respect everywhere ; and, gaining confidence with experience, her part in the women's services became, from that time onwards, a blessed ministry which endeared her to the women of Great Britain and her own land, and afterwards, to those of Australasia. Her tact and faithfulness in personal work were the means of winning many to Christ, and her unselfishness and wifely devotion doubtless saved her husband for years of service. The strain under which these two devoted men of God laboured, would surely have broken down their strength even sooner than was the case, but for that heart-satisfaction, and the constant, tender care given them by the wives whom God had honoured with the joy of such a happy privilege.

On October 4th, the company of six sailed from England for the United States, in time for a six weeks' campaign, once more on the simultaneous plan, which had been arranged for the city of Chicago. On reaching New York, Alexander sent forward the following message : " I am coming to Chicago with the deep, strong conviction that God is going to send a revival of Gospel song upon the city, and through this sweep thousands into His Kingdom. Our dependence is absolutely upon Christ's power to save sinners. Dr. Chapman and I have seen the same old message bring floods of joy and blessing, within the past two years, to ten different countries. Two hundred thousand people have covenanted to pray for the places where we preach and sing. Since last April we have visited England, Scotland, and Wales, and everywhere the Christian people were deeply interested in your great city movement. Psalm 57 : 7, is my Scripture message—' My heart is fixed, O God, my heart is fixed ; I will sing and give praise.' Charles M. Alexander, Second-Timothy-two-fifteen."

Chicago, with its two million inhabitants and its far-flung suburbs, was

A JAPANESE BEGGAR AT NIKKO

WITH HIS PHOTOGRAPHER, NORMAN A. THOMAS,
AT KOBE

A RICKSHAW RIDE THROUGH KOBE

IN JAPAN, OCT.-NOV., 1909

"SAYONARA"

MEETING AT WHITE CITY, CHICAGO, OCTOBER, 1910

GROUP OF EVANGELISTS AND SINGERS IN THE CHAPMAN-ALEXANDER SIMULTANEOUS CAMPAIGN IN CHICAGO.
OCTOBER, 1910

mapped out into many districts, with a preacher and song-leader in charge of each. For the first two weeks, the great Auditorium at White City was set aside for the central meetings led by Dr. Chapman and Charles Alexander. For the next two weeks, their meetings were transferred to a huge wooden tabernacle erected on the north side of the city ; and for the last two, they were again transferred to a similar tabernacle at Austin—six miles to the west. Leaders from all the districts met daily in the great noon meeting in the Opera House, and this helped to unify the work.

But again, overlapping of districts and the changes of the central meetings from place to place just as the work was beginning to take hold, caused the permanent results of the great campaign to be less than Dr. Chapman and Charles Alexander had hoped and prayed for, though the crowds were immense. Yet in each of the three large centres, as well as in the smaller districts, the meetings were full of power, and many decisions for Christ were recorded.

A short mission in Fort Wayne, Indiana, was followed by a break for Christmas, which the Alexanders spent in Columbus, Ohio, with their brother Homer—now pastor of a Presbyterian church there—his wife, and three-year-old daughter.

The first month of 1911 was devoted to a vigorous campaign in Toronto, Canada. The evening services were held in Massey Hall, and here Alexander delighted in meeting once more the " Alexander Choir " which had held together as an organization since the Torrey-Alexander meetings five years earlier. February was spent in Brooklyn. Here two hundred churches took part in the movement, the central meetings being held each night in the great Clermont Avenue Rink. As in Boston, the reporters, many of them quite indifferent to religious matters at the beginning of the mission, were deeply impressed, and several of them were converted.

On March 1st, Dr. and Mrs. Chapman and the Alexanders, with their immediate helpers, set sail once more from New York for a series of missions in the British Isles. A month in Swansea, South Wales, was followed by three-day conferences in Belfast, in Leeds, and in Birmingham.

The Chairman of the Swansea Committee was the Hon. and Rev. Prebendary W. Talbot Rice. Writing to Mrs. Alexander in 1920, he said : " We shall never forget the wonderful time in Swansea, and the great songs of the Gospel of God's grace. Those glorious songs will be echoing for years to come, and will be a light and guide for many. It is an uplift even to think of that time of grace and blessedness. Your beloved one has not lived in vain, and multitudes will rejoice for him for ever."

The season's work closed with a short mission in the old English town of Shrewsbury. The first days of the mission, which was held in the Presbyterian church of which Rev. B. Harvey-Jellie was minister, seemed strangely lacking in spiritual power and results. Suddenly, in an evening service, the cold indifference seemed to melt. People were stirred by the singing and by the sermon, and decisions were made for Christ. It was found afterwards that into the town had come a man of insignificant appearance, but of mighty power with God. He was a missionary from India, known in the Punjab as " Praying Hyde," and was on his way home to America, when he saw that fellow-countrymen of his were leading Gospel services in Shrewsbury. Finding that he had time to spend a few days there before his boat sailed, he visited the town, and entered one of the meetings. Sensing a curious spiritual opposition, he left the church, and, in a quiet room, went down upon his knees to pray for the evangelists. It was at that time that the break came, and for the few days that remained, wonderful blessings were poured out upon the meetings. " Amongst the happiest and most inspiring memories of my life," wrote Mr. Harvey-Jellie some years afterwards, " I cherish those of the wonderful days in Shrewsbury during the great mission conducted by Mr. Alexander and Dr. Chapman in connexion with my church there. There must be thousands who are grateful to God for the uplifting and inspiring influence of Mr. Alexander."

When the Shrewsbury Mission closed, Alexander carried off Mr. Hyde for a night at " Tennessee," but his guest was taken seriously ill, and the sailing for America had to be postponed. The best specialists were consulted, and Mr. Hyde was told that his condition of high blood pressure, due to long years of strain in India, was a clear indication that his life might end at any moment. The doctor was astonished at the steady calmness with which his verdict was received. A month's care and nursing so restored Mr. Hyde that he was able to go to his sisters in America, though he went home to Heaven within a few months. The lessons he taught, around the fireside at " Tennessee," of the meaning and power of praise, will never be forgotten by the Alexander household.

The autumn months of this year were spent by the Chapman-Alexander party in the north of Ireland ; first in Belfast and Bangor, then in Londonderry and Dundalk for two short missions in December. Once more, as in the Torrey-Alexander Mission at Belfast in 1903, Charles Alexander had the great joy of mutual work and fellowship with his old friend, Dr. Henry Montgomery. Great interest was taken also in the meetings by Sir Robert and Lady Anderson, and by Mr. and Mrs. W. H. McLaughlin. Towards the end of the Belfast Mission an interesting romance culminated in the engagement of Mr. E. W. Naftzger, Alexander's soloist, to Miss Ruth McLaughlin.

The approaching marriage of Beatrice Cadbury made it necessary for Mrs. Alexander to spend part of the time in England, only making occasional trips to Belfast for a few days in the meetings. " How precious and true you have always been," ran the little note which Alexander slipped into his wife's hand as she left him after the opening days in Belfast. " You are my dear teacher, comforter, sweetener, uplifter, my Gibraltar. When you read this my face will not be with you, but my heart will. I must loan you to our Beatrice for a while." A few days later, he wrote : " We have had many wonderful meetings this first week. Last night ninety confessed Christ, the night before there were seventy, and I think there must have been fully seventy again to-night."

From the many warm testimonies given of the work in Belfast only a sentence or two can be selected. A minister, referring to a Sunday morning service in the People's Hall, said, " I was astonished at the way Mr. Alexander got hold of my congregation. We had at least ten decisions, seven of them from the choir. I could never conduct a choir as Mr. Alexander did on Sunday. He appealed to them personally, and did not leave them till the seven had decided."

Tennessee

"TENNESSEE," BIRMINGHAM, ENGLAND, IN WINTER DRESS

AT WORK ON A NEW HYMNBOOK IN THE DEN AT "TENNESSEE"

"Have you ever heard of the
Pocket Testament League?"
"Oh, yes, sir, here's my Testa-
ment! I joined three years ago."

CHARLES M. ALEXANDER'S HYMNBOOK LIBRARY IN THE DEN AT "TENNESSEE," 1910

Rt. Hon. Thos. Sinclair, D.L., declared : " I have been much struck with the great sanity with which this mission has been conducted. We sometimes associate such movements with extravagances. There was absolutely an absence of anything of the sort in these meetings." Rev. W. H. Brownrigg, of the Church of Ireland, said : " The time through which we have passed has been one of marked spiritual revival such as I have never before been connected with."

The five weeks in Belfast were followed by ten days in the adjoining coast town of Bangor, where the rising tide of blessing overflowed again into the larger city. Here an instance of Alexander's tact occurred, during a visit to the home of a Christian family whose members were church-workers. While looking in a drawer for some photographs, a pack of playing-cards was discovered. Said the lady of the house : " I hope you do not think we play for money. We have a friendly game now and then amongst ourselves, or when the young folks have friends to visit them." Alexander replied, smiling, " I didn't say anything about the cards. Why do you apologize for them ? " " But surely you do not think there is any harm in playing, do you ? " was the question asked after a short interval. " Do you think it would help you to get your friends to surrender to Christ ? Would it be easy, after a game of cards, to start a conversation which would lead them to Jesus ? " " Well, perhaps not, just at that particular time." " Then you might lose the opportunity." " I believe you think we ought not to have them at all," said the hostess. " I don't want to say what *you* must do about it. I always ask myself a question about these things : ' Will it help me in winning others to Christ ? ' " " I have never looked at the question quite so closely as that, I fear," said the lady. After a few days the two met again, when, with a look of deep satisfaction, the lady said : " I have burnt those cards : they were in the way." The next day, in order to save Alexander time and trouble in reaching a distant appointment, the lady loaned him her motor. At the conclusion of the journey he had a talk with the chauffeur, who came out with a clear acceptance of Christ. When thanking the lady over the telephone for the loan of her car, the news of the chauffeur's conversion was added to the message. " Perhaps this blessing has come to your house to make up for the loss of those cards," was the last sentence in the conversation.

Ten days in Londonderry and a week in Dundalk completed the work in the north of Ireland.

A note from Alexander to his wife says : " We closed our wonderful week at Londonderry last night. There were almost one thousand people who made vocal confession of Jesus Christ. It would have done your true heart good. Mrs. Chapman has been doing personal work as I never dreamed that she would, and Miss Ruth McLaughlin brought twelve girls to the front one night. Naftzger acts like a new man. He often speaks of what he owes to you and ' Tennessee.' "

The Chapmans returned to their own land for Christmas, and Charles Alexander to his home in England, to make final preparations for the promised return visit to Australasia.

CHAPTER TWENTY

Summer Days in England

1910 to 1914

THREE miles from the heart of Birmingham, that great manufacturing centre of the English Midlands, lies a district round which the city has stealthily crept, but which still holds an atmosphere of country freshness. It was once composed entirely of a number of large estates, with their sloping lawns and majestic avenues, their woods, and lakes, and open fields. But with the growth of the city, some of these estates were broken up by new intersecting roads, lined with suburban houses. Right across Moor Green, winding and twisting for a mile in length, runs the lane which was its main thoroughfare in olden days.

Hawthorn, lilac, laburnum, and early fruit-blossom told that April had come. A grocer's boy, dashing down Moor Green Lane on his bicycle, turned in between some gate-posts on which were carved " Tennessee." He looked with surprise at the arches and festoons of laurel, and at numberless flags, gaily fluttering in the breeze, which lined the drive-way to the house. " Are yer expectin' Royalty ? " he asked the cook, as he delivered his goods at the kitchen door. She laughed happily. " No, but the family is coming home to-day," she said. Not long afterwards a hansom-cab rounded a bend in the lane. As it turned in under the arches at the gate, passing up the drive to the gaily-decorated porch, a loud, shrill whistle from within it was heard in the house. The front door opened, showing a bevy of happy-faced girls and older women in white caps and aprons, while from a side gate hastened two or three gardeners. A hearty laugh rang out, and two people stepped from the cab. Then followed a time of handshaking and an exchange of cordial greetings.

It was the long-anticipated homecoming of Charles Alexander and his wife in 1910 after an absence of sixteen months, part of which had been spent on the other side of the world. They had journeyed through seven countries, and voyaged over nine thousand leagues of ocean, and now once more they were back in " dear old Tennessee." A day or two later, Beatrice Cadbury returned from China by way of Siberia, Russia, and Europe, and the family circle was complete. Meanwhile, Dr. Chapman and eleven others of the mission party and friends had joined them at " Tennessee," and shared their happiness. But only four days could be enjoyed together in the longed-for home, before all were on their way to the mission in Cardiff. Then again Charles Alexander must hurry across the Atlantic for a few

PARTY
OF
LOCAL
POLICEMEN
AND
THEIR WIVES
AT
"TENNESSEE"
IN THE
SUMMER
OF 1910.
All the men are
members of the
Pocket Testament
League

DR. AND MRS.
J. WILBUR
CHAPMAN
VISIT
"TENNESSEE,"
SEPTEMBER,
1910.

A GROUP OF
AUSTRALIANS AT
"TENNESSEE" IN
THE SUMMER OF 1910.
Dr. W. H. Fitchett, of
Melbourne, between
Charles Alexander and
Robert Harkness, with his
grandson, Alan Fitchett,
standing behind him

A
STROLL
ROUND
THE
GARDEN

FOURTH
OF JULY
AT
"TENNESSEE"
TEA
IN THE
LOG HUT,
1914.
Senator and Mrs.
Simon Fraser
of Melbourne,
on the right

MR. AND MRS.
FLEMING H.
REVELL
AT
"TENNESSEE,"
1914

A HOUSE PARTY AT "TENNESSEE," MAY, 1914

important engagements in his own land. But in June he was home once more, welcomed by the wife and sister whom he had left behind.

For the first time in his life, with the exception of that anxious summer of 1906, when his wife lay for weeks at the point of death, Alexander looked forward to a whole summer in England. And now for four summers in succession, divided by fifteen months more in the Antipodes, he was to have the enjoyment of being in his own home. Many events of joy and of sorrow marked these rarely sweet seasons of private life. Not least among the pleasures was the fellowship with the constant stream of guests who filled " Tennessee " to overflowing, whenever the hospitable head of the home was there. Amongst them were missionaries from China, Korea, and India, from Syria and Egypt. Visitors came from Australia, New Zealand, South Africa, from Holland, Canada, and the United States, and others from nearer home. Many an old friendship was linked up, and memories were renewed of mutual service for Christ in other places. Among the first guests in 1910 were Dr. Samuel A. Moffett, of Korea, and his brother, Mr. Thomas Moffett, of New York, director of missions among the North American Indians, Mr. Sherwood Eddy, of India, also Dr. Ross Stevenson, President of Princeton Theological Seminary, with his wife.

During his short return to America in May, Charles Alexander had been taken seriously ill with an attack of appendicitis. He recovered temporarily, but intermittent attacks proved that an operation was necessary, in spite of the benefit derived from a two weeks' holiday at the Lizard, Cornwall. His wife had often told him of the beauty of the rugged Cornish coast, the frowning black cliffs with their crown of emerald grass, and the azure water breaking into foam on the rocks and on the smooth white sand. From this first visit Alexander loved and enjoyed it as much as she.

On July 17th, on the eve of the operation, Alexander wrote to his mother in America :—" Your lovely letters with the solicitude for my health touched me greatly. There are no eyes like a mother's. I had not noticed there was much the matter, but I suppose there was something wrong when you saw me last. The doctor thinks that after the operation I shall be stronger than I have been in years. The trouble that arose from the accident to my spine has almost disappeared, and I am surprised that I could walk twelve miles a day over the cliffs in Cornwall."

Another short note was slipped into his wife's hand just before she walked with him into the temporary operating-room at " Tennessee," to stay while the anæsthetic was given :—" My precious Helen, I love you, and can never tell you the hundred thousand ways you help and make me. It is heaven to live with you. . . . You are my best adviser. As wife, honey, I always think of the Scripture verse, ' Exceeding abundantly above all that we can ask or think.' You have made it so easy to approach this solemn event." Weakness and pain could not keep Alexander's loving heart from its constant ministry. Both nurses were led to the feet of Christ, and were gained as members of the Pocket Testament League. The helpful Christian spirit of the household staff aided in forming the atmosphere at " Tennessee," which to the thankful delight of the Alexanders, caused one guest to describe it as " such an easy place to pray in." The presence

M

and sweet influence of the dearly-loved sister was another helping factor ; to her, as well as to Alexander and his wife, home was a gift of God, to be used for His glory and for the winning of souls, as earnestly as the opportunities of an evangelistic campaign.   Ten years afterwards one of the nurses, Miss Marjorie L. Summers, whose kindly services were so valued at this time, wrote to Mrs. Alexander :— " Perhaps you have forgotten me.   Yet you and Mr. Alexander are to me one of the dearest memories I have of human kindness and love, and never shall I forget the time I spent with you.   It was like living at the very gates of Heaven."

Under the blessing of God the operation was entirely successful, and con-valescence was completed by two more happy weeks in Cornwall.   Hardly had they returned home from Cornwall before they were welcoming guests from Australia, and, a few days later, Dr. Chapman and his charming bride.

Adjoining the original gardens of " Tennessee " were some farm buildings and some spacious, brick-built pavilions named " The Tea-sheds," bordering a small field and plantation which Alexander and his wife had purchased from the Uffculme estate.   These " Tea-sheds " were erected by Mrs. Alexander's father to provide covered shelter, in case of rain and stormy weather, for the summer parties of ragged children, or Sunday Schools, Mothers' Meetings, and similar organizations, to whom he freely lent the fields round Uffculme for their annual picnics.   The " Tea-sheds " could no longer be put to their original use without the surrounding fields, and two fine rooms had therefore been made at one end, one of which was called " The Den," and the other, facing towards the sunset, the " West Room."   In " The Den " Alexander kept his unique library of hymn-books and his wonderful collec-tion of lantern slides.   A piano was also there ; great cupboards for his many photographs ; and shelves for the marvellous albums full of cuttings, containing detailed records of his evangelistic campaigns.   Many a new hymn was composed in " The Den " ; hundreds of other hymns—new and old—were tried over, criticized, and selected from, to form new editions of hymn-books.   Often the sound of singing —solos, duets, quartets, and choruses—would stream through the open windows, causing people passing down the near-by road to stop and listen.   In the adjoining " West Room," the walls were lined with bookcases and cupboards filled with hymn-books, Testaments and leaflets for use in meetings ; with blocks, photographic materials, and all the apparatus of a literary workshop.   On the big central table —once a nursery table in his wife's old home—two or three typewriters were often busily clicking.   At the other end of the " Tea-sheds " were two small rooms : one containing copper boilers, originally built for making tea in large quantities, was adapted to form a capital washing- and drying-room for photographs ; while the other, used in the old days for cutting up hundreds of cakes, and the slicing and spreading of countless pieces of bread-and-butter, was now transformed into a dark-room, with storage for the thousands of photographic plates.   It may easily be imagined what a scene of busy activity the " Tea-sheds " became, when Alexander and his staff of assistants had a few days or weeks to spare between missions for the comparative rest of work at home.

A new experiment was entered upon in the summer of 1910, which proved a source of much enjoyment and blessing.   Up to this time the group of young men assistants, with whom Alexander always loved to surround himself, had been entertained at " Tennessee," or in lodgings near by. Many of the young men were American and Australian, and were far from their own people. In 1910 Alexander rented and furnished a house near " Tennessee " for the purpose of making a real home for his " boys." To give it distinction, this annex to " Tennessee " was named " Kentucky," suggested by the neighbouring States of the South, and all who lived there were known as " Kentuckians." They were frequent guests round the festive board of " Tennessee," and filled the days with pleasant activity in the work carried on at the " Tea-sheds." Now and again, soon after eight in the morning, a succession of young men might be seen hurrying after each other down Moor Green Lane, buttoning coats and fixing ties as they ran, to join in the circle at " Tennessee " for family worship and breakfast. Then would come a morning of song and story, during which the guests of the household were introduced to new hymns, or enjoyed revived memories of Gospel songs that had first grown familiar under Alexander's magnetic leadership in crowded song-services held in lands beyond the sea. Sometimes " Kentucky " would return the hospitality of " Tennessee," and a brilliant programme would be provided, of original recitations, songs, and pictures, specially prepared for the occasion Miss Elinor Stafford Millar was one of the guests at " Tennessee " to share in the first " Kentucky " party in the summer of 1910. She was also present at a memorable gathering of local policemen, who had joined the Pocket Testament League, and who were entertained at " Tennessee " with their wives. " Visions of a beautiful past come before my eyes continually," she wrote from Chicago long afterwards. " New Zealand, America, and beloved ' Tennessee ' are among the places of happy days, when the charm of Mr. Alexander's personality and devotion seemed ever to beckon me on to fuller service for the King. I never forget that I am in this country, with all its opportunities, because of him. Such true and loyal friendships are rare, and I thank God for this one."

An earlier memory of Alexander in his home is given by Rev. W. Talbot Hindley, M.A. :—" Do you know that when I first came to ' Tennessee ' I almost dreaded coming, lest I should be disappointed, for I loved and admired Charles so much, and I had so often been disappointed by those whom I saw on platforms. The first thing I noticed in the drawing-room was the little motto ' Each for the other, and both for God.' I soon found that it was true, and Charles in the home was an infinitely bigger man to me than even Alexander on the platform. He was never once a disappointment to me."

Dr. W. H. Fitchett, of Melbourne, visited England in 1911, and was a guest at " Tennessee." In an Australian magazine, he said : " Almost everybody in Australia knows Mr. Alexander as he stands on the platform with radiant face and uplifted arms, kindling thousands of people into song, himself an embodied song ; but not many can know him in private life under the roof of his own hospitable home. Yet he is exactly the same man on a platform before five thousand people, as by his own fireside with a single friend. He is probably the least ' professional ' man in the world. With him, religion is woven into the texture of body, brain and heart. It is as natural for him to talk about religion, or to sing about it, as it is to breathe. And so under his own roof he produces exactly that atmosphere of radiant piety—a piety that sings, and that sets other people singing—with which Australia is familiar in him.

"England is a land of happy homes, but there is certainly none happier than that of the Alexanders. A night spent in this home will be a fountain of happy memories for the rest of one's life. Mr. Alexander, even after the strain of such campaigns as those at Chicago and Brooklyn, seems hardly a day older. His tall figure is as erect as ever, his face as youthful, his laugh as mellow. He is an American, but with the Southerner's gentleness, his soft humour, and his open-handed generosity. For all his half-boyish mischief and simplicity, he is one of the shrewdest of men. He is not merely one of Nature's gentlemen ; he has a touch of chivalry, not to say knightliness, which makes love, in those that know him best, take an accent of profound respect.

"He is supposed to be resting just now after recent great missions in America for what we all hope will be a still greater mission in Australia next year, but, as a matter of fact, he is hard at work in his own special realm of music. He collects hymn-books as other people collect postage-stamps or ancient china. The latest addition to his library is from the collection of Ira D. Sankey, and includes some of his MSS. and copies of some of his publications, as prepared for the press, with his notes. This library of evangelistic music resembles a collection of flowers gathered from every soil and from under every sky in the world, and from these Mr. Alexander, with Mr. Harkness to help him, is distilling the honey of a new Gospel hymn-book, which will be published in Australia next year. He is also busy preparing a book of hymns arranged for male voices.

"The process of evolving a Gospel hymn-book is by no means so simple as some persons imagine. It is a science that means wide knowledge. It is an art that requires expert skill, and it needs money, much money. Mr. Alexander has brought both science and art to the process, and he has spent with a most unselfish spirit much money upon it. Copyrights, even of hymn tunes, are properly fenced round with legal guards. They must be bought before they can be used, and Mr. Alexander has already spent many thousands of pounds in the purchase of copyrights for the tunes used in the hymn-books already published. Of course to the amount spent in the purchase of copyrights must be added the cost of what we may call his staff. The whole profits on these hymn-books are expended in maintaining and carrying on evangelistic work, and not for private purposes. That is a fact upon which some critics, always ready to suspect motives of other men, may well meditate. Mr. Alexander's home in Moor Green Lane is really a little colony of workers, one-half of them at least being Australians. A more delightful evening than one spent in this company could hardly be imagined. Fragments of hymns were sung, and some of the new tunes tried over, singing of course being the principal charm of the evening. Then talk took the place of song—talk spiritual enough for a revival meeting, and yet lit up with laughter, humour, and pleasant stories. Then followed prayer and a farewell song, and a night to be remembered for many a year came to an end."

The summer of 1911 was very full of events of private import to the Alexanders.

A busy winter had been passed in the United States, followed by spring campaigns in South Wales and in England. In the month of June the British nation was full of rejoicing, as they celebrated the Coronation of King George V and his English-born Queen. It was more than a superficial rejoicing, for the nation, as a whole, built up upon reverence for the Word of God, which had been mightily strengthened under the long rule of Queen Victoria, rejoiced in having at their head not only sovereigns ably fitted to rule a great Empire, but a man and woman who exemplified in their private family life the strength and beauty of a Christian home.

About a week later than the great event which drew the feet of British subjects to London, and the hearts of them all from every part of the world, a coronation of another kind was looked forward to in the happy home of " Tennessee." That crowning and completion of married life, for which the Alexanders had hungered and hoped for seven years, was about to be given them. The pride and joy of Charles Alexander knew no bounds. The anticipation of fatherhood had brought upon his face a radiance that several had remarked upon who did not know the cause of his overwhelming happiness. But God had a severe trial in store, by which in His love He saw fit to test the faith of His children and their willingness to let Him choose their path through life. Many a time in past days, putting aside all mention of his own heart-hunger, Alexander had comforted his wife with the pleading words of Elkanah, " Am I not more to thee than ten sons ? " And when in the bounty of the heavenly Father the gift was granted, the little life was dedicated to Him as sincerely as that of little Samuel by Elkanah and Hannah. But at the moment of crowning joy, the precious treasure, given by God that His children might have a priceless gift to present to Him, was safely taken into the strong Hand which can keep as well as save. The first words that fell from the grief-stricken lips of the bereaved mother when she knew that the little son had been taken to serve in the heavenly temple, were : " The Lord gave, and the Lord hath taken away. Blessed be the name of the Lord." With an unselfish devotion that could only be appreciated by those who knew his passionate love for children, Charles Alexander turned aside from all self-pity in the loss of the proud, joyful hopes and the plans that he had been building, to expressions of thankfulness that the one precious life had been spared, and to the rebuilding, with her, of a new life of service, emptied of so much that had seemed to fill its horizon. Only those who love each other as did these two, can fully know the consuming desire to trace the beloved features and ways in a new life that is part of both. But even in after-years this joy was not granted, and husband and wife learned to walk more humbly before their God, bound to each other in a new bond of tender sympathy and love that drew them nearer to Him.

During these months, two other sorrowful events touched the Alexanders' lives—the sudden death, after an operation, of Homer Alexander's young wife in Columbus, Ohio, which left him the bereaved father of two little girls ; also the sudden death of a young English nephew, the eldest son of Mrs. Alexander's brother, Richard Cadbury. The little fellow, only ten-and-a-half years old, had visited " Tennessee " five months before, and had joined the Pocket Testament League. He had faithfully carried and read the small Testament given him by his Uncle Charles, and when a sudden accident took him into the Saviour's presence during the autumn term at school, Arthur had the little book in his pocket. He had persuaded many of his schoolfellows and teachers to join the League, and his love for the Bible and for Christ was a great comfort to his godly parents in the shock of their sorrow. To them both the Pocket Testament League gained a new and sacred significance. For his sake their interest in it as a means of soul-winning grew deeper, and wherever the story of little Arthur has been told, it has been a blessing. The child " being dead, yet speaketh."

In spite of these shadows of sorrow, there were many days of sunshine in the Alexander household. It was a joy to be called upon to enter into the joy of another, although it meant a personal loss to them. For during this summer their sister, Beatrice Cadbury, became engaged to a young Dutchman, Cornelis Boeke.

Her wedding six months later, in December, 1911, was a time of family reunion. A few days beforehand, Dr. and Mrs. Neville Bradley and their three children arrived on furlough from China, spending eight weeks at " Tennessee," before settling into an English home of their own for a while. In January, 1912, Beatrice and Cornelis Boeke started on their way to their missionary labours at Brumana, on Mount Lebanon, and a month later the Alexanders set sail for Australia. Quiet and loneliness reigned at " Tennessee " till their return in June, 1913. Then again for two summers the Visitors' Book at " Tennessee " records names from every part of the world. " Kentucky " and the Tea-sheds became hives of industry once more, and music, song, and laughter were the order of the day. Through it all Charles Alexander never swerved from the main purpose of his life—the winning of souls to his Saviour. From hundreds of incidents a single one is selected. Mr. Ted Roberts, the sporting man who had been so marvellously converted during the Torrey-Alexander Mission at Liverpool, wrote the following reminiscence :—

" Do you remember the evening in the summer of 1913 when I called at ' Tennessee ' to see you and Mr. Alexander ? I found a number of guests were there, amongst them a young doctor from Australia. After a few minutes, Mr. Alexander said to me, ' Stand just there, and tell these people in five minutes how you were converted.' I did so in as few words as I could. Then I had to hurry to the Conference for which I had come to Birmingham. Mr. Alexander came to the door to let me out, and said, ' I wanted that young doctor to hear the story of your conversion. We do not know him well, but some friends of his were anxious about his spiritual welfare, as he had been thrown into the company of sceptics and atheists, and they asked us to have him here with us, that the atmosphere of our home might be an influence for good.' I thought I knew Mr. Alexander fairly well, but I can scarcely describe my feelings at his words. I knew that his whole life was a consecrated one, and that he was always looking out to win souls ; but the thought that he and you took a young man as your guest so that the influence of your lives and the holy atmosphere of your home should have the desired result, was something new and wonderful to me."

AT POMPEII, FEBRUARY 10, 1912

WITH A PORT SAID CUSTOMS OFFICIAL,
FEBRUARY, 1912

THE SS. "OTRANTO" AT PORT SAID, FEBRUARY, 1912

THE MELBOURNE EXHIBITION BUILDING FROM THE LAKE, APRIL, 1912

A SERVICE IN THE MELBOURNE EXHIBITION BUILDING. LOOKING TOWARDS THE CHOIR
FROM BENEATH THE CENTRAL DOME.

CHAPTER TWENTY-ONE

Fourth Journey Round the World

1912 to 1913

CHARLES M. ALEXANDER was an American through and through, a Southerner at that, and a native-born Tennessean. He treasured the privilege of his birthright as a priceless possession. His loyalty and love for his own land never flagged, and his gratitude to God for the part she had been called to play in the family life of the nations was ever a source of thankful pride to him. Yet to few men has been given so strange a sense of being at home in so many parts of the world. It is of course, in a measure, the common heritage of all the children of God by faith in Christ, to rise above distinctions of nationality or race. A foretaste of the family union of heaven may be enjoyed on earth, even by those who do not understand each other's language. But to Charles Alexander were given unique opportunities of coming into constant personal touch with Christians in various lands, and it would be hard to say whether he was more at home in New York or in London, in Philadelphia or in Melbourne, in Chicago or in Sydney, in Glasgow, Belfast, or Toronto. The warm-hearted Southern temperament with which he was endowed, his fresh, keen interest in his fellow-beings, and his marvellous capacity for friendship, built up around him a circle almost like that of a family wherever he went. To leave any place was a wrench, and if he had once been for any length of time in a city, it was like a home-going to return to it.

It was therefore with the joyful expectation both of meeting old friends and of renewed opportunities for the winning of souls, that he and his wife left their English home again on February 6, 1912, for his fourth journey round the world. He sent forward a message of greeting through the pages of *The Southern Cross* :—

" Since we left Australia, Dr. Chapman and I have had some wonderful experiences in various lands, seeking to win for Christ men of many races and colours. Besides our visit to the Philippine Islands, China, Korea, and Japan, we have worked in two of the largest cities of the United States, and in Canada and Great Britain.

" We have been planning for our return to Australasia ever since we left you. My part of the work, of course, has been in prayerfully and carefully selecting, from every source, the best hymns available for our new campaigns. Dr. Chapman wins the hearts of the people wherever we go, and his message grows even stronger as the days go by. His preaching carries the same telling force and tender compassion that characterized it in Australia. We have been drawn still closer together as fellow-workers, and are looking forward to a time of great blessing with you·

As a party, our constant fellowship in service during the past two-and-a-half years has helped, under the blessing of God, to increase the effectiveness of our work.

"The importance of personal soul-winning cannot be overestimated. A genuine concern and definite effort on the part of individuals to reach individuals, and win them to Christ, will be the greatest factor in the success of any mission. The Pocket Testament League is spreading all over the world far more rapidly than we had ever anticipated, and the striking and convincing fact is, that wherever it has been promoted souls are being won for Christ.

"I am coming back for my fourth and longest visit to the country I love so well, with an all-consuming conviction of the power of Gospel song to reach and save. I still hold to my phrase that A GOSPEL HYMN IS A SERMON ON WHEELS. To the people of Australia I would say, KEEP ON SINGING ! A few minutes spent in teaching or singing these Gospel hymns, no matter in how humble a sphere, is time well spent.

"A Gospel song, with a prayer behind it, may reach to the furthest corners of the earth. If you have received a blessing, sing it out. 'Singing with grace in your hearts to the Lord' (Col. iii. 16). One of the new hymns we are bringing to Australia expresses this sentiment in the following beautiful words :—

> I've something in my heart which Jesus gave to me,
>   It makes me feel like singing glory all the day ;
> He found my captive soul, and gave me liberty,
>   And now I feel like singing glory !
>
> My Saviour loosed my tongue that I might sing His praise ;
>   Since then I have been singing glory all the day ;
> I love to tell the lost of Jesus and His ways,
>   And oh, it keeps me singing glory !
>
> *Chorus :*
> He makes the path grow brighter every passing day,
> He makes the burden lighter all along the way ;
> His Word is my delight, His will I now obey,
>   And all the time I'm singing glory !

After journeying across France, Alexander and his wife joined their ship, R.M.S. *Otranto*, at Toulon. On board they found a party of friends who were travelling to Australia with them. Sir Robert and Lady Anderson, of Belfast, also Mr. and Mrs. W. H. McLaughlin, had been so greatly stirred by the work in the North of Ireland, that they desired to take part in the great Australasian campaign. The same was true of Mr. A. Hope Robertson, of Glasgow, who had first met Dr. Chapman and Mr. Alexander in Scotland, and, as a guest of Mr. McLaughlin, had helped in the Irish missions. Mrs. McLaughlin's sisters, the Misses Warren, of Dublin, were travelling to Australia to visit their brother, Dr. W. Warren, of Melbourne. Norman A. Thomas, the photographer, was also on board. His share in the missions, though a quiet one, had much to do with stirring up interest in the work through the pictures he took with such skill and care. Most of those which illustrate the present volume are the result of his work. The two secretaries, W. W. Rock, and his brother, had left England in advance of the others. E. W.

CHARLES M.
ALEXANDER
AND HIS WIFE
ON THE GROUNDS
OF THE
EXHIBITION
BUILDING,
MELBOURNE,
APRIL, 1912

WITH
MR. W. H.
McLAUGHLIN
OF BELFAST
AND
ERNEST W.
NAFTZGER
AT
NEWCASTLE,
N.S.W.,
AUGUST,
1912

WITH
CHARLES
CARTER,
OF THE
EVANGELISATION
SOCIETY OF
AUSTRALASIA,
DECEMBER,
1912

WITH SOME OF "THE OLD GUARD" AT MELBOURNE, ON THE STEPS OF "WINDELLA," KEW
RESIDENCE OF HON. JAMES BALFOUR (third from left in front row). APRIL, 1912

AT BROKEN HILL, NEW SOUTH WALES, JUNE, 1912

SEEING THE CHAPMAN-ALEXANDER PARTY OFF AT MIDNIGHT, JUNE 17

A SERVICE BELOW GROUND

READY TO GO DOWN THE MINE
"DO YOU KNOW US?"

A DAY OFF AMONG THE CAMELS
AT BROKEN HILL, N.S.W.,
JUNE, 1912

READY FOR A RIDE,
BROKEN HILL, N.S.W.,
JUNE, 1912

"STEADY NOW!"

MAKING FRIENDS WITH A DINGO, CHARTERS TOWERS,
QUEENSLAND, OCTOBER, 1912

MEETING IN AN OPEN-AIR PICTURE THEATRE AT KURRI KURRI, NEW SOUTH WALES, AUGUST, 1912

Inset--On Dr. Chapman's shoulder

Inset--In a Kurri Kurri crowd

NOONDAY MEETING AT ALLIGATOR CREEK, NEAR TOWNSVILLE, SEPTEMBER, 1912

THE TOWN HALL, SYDNEY, AUSTRALIA

CHAPMAN-ALEXANDER MEETING FOR MEN IN SYDNEY TOWN HALL, JULY, 1912

CAUGHT BY
THE TIDE
AT MACKAY,
QUEENSLAND,
OCTOBER, 1912.

AUSTRALIAN
ABORIGINES
IN THE
BACKGROUND

As J. Wilbur
Chapman, Junior,
carried Charles
Alexander across
he was offered a
pound to drop his
father in the
middle of the
stream.

Alexander was
laughing in merry
anticipation, but
Wilbur hesitated
and finally carried
his father safely
over. "You rascal,"
said Alexander,
"you took my
offer!" "Yes," said
Wilbur, "but Father
whispered in my
ear, 'I'll give you
two pounds if you
don't drop me!'"

AMONG THE KANGAROOS AT GOULBURN, NEW SOUTH WALES, JULY, 1912

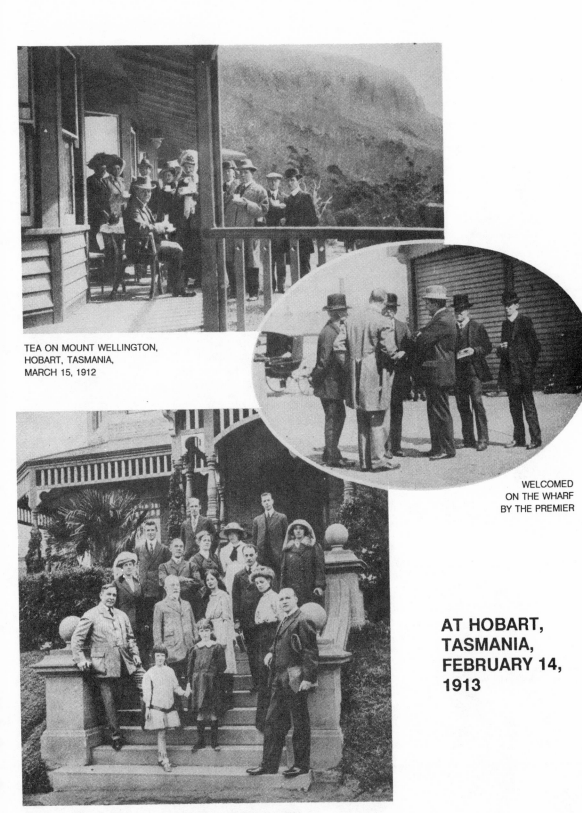

TEA ON MOUNT WELLINGTON,
HOBART, TASMANIA,
MARCH 15, 1912

WELCOMED
ON THE WHARF
BY THE PREMIER

AT HOBART,
TASMANIA,
FEBRUARY 14,
1913

WITH ADMIRAL SIR GEORGE KING-HALL

WITH SIR ROBERT AND LADY ANDERSON OF BELFAST,
IRELAND, AT DUNEDIN, NEW ZEALAND, APRIL, 1912

AT CHARTERS TOWERS, QUEENSLAND,
SEPTEMBER, 1912

THE CHAPMAN-ALEXANDER PARTY AT BRISBANE, QUEENSLAND, SEPTEMBER, 1912

Naftzger, whose marriage to Miss McLaughlin had taken place in Belfast in January, took his bride by way of America, to visit her new relatives there ; while the marriage of Robert Harkness to Miss Ruth Langford, of Adelaide, took place in that city some weeks before the mission party reached Australia. The two young brides were warmly welcomed into the circle, and entered with eager interest into the work.

The *Otranto* put into port for a long day at Naples, and here Alexander and his friends took the opportunity of visiting the fascinating ruins of Pompeii. On returning to the boat at night, a happy reunion took place with Dr. and Mrs. Chapman, who had travelled direct from New York to Naples. With them were Mr. and Mrs. Ralph C. Norton, and Mr. Charles H. Denison, of Saginaw, Michigan, an old friend of Dr. Chapman's.

The long voyage to Australia provided, as usual, the chief opportunity given to Dr. Chapman and Charles Alexander for a real rest between their seasons of strenuous labour. Surrounded by such congenial companions, the weeks spent on board were full of delight as well as of physical refreshment, and many opportunities occurred for holding services, and for witnessing for Christ in various ways. The few cold days in the Mediterranean soon melted into warmth, as the *Otranto*, after touching at Port Said, passed slowly through the Suez Canal and out into the Red Sea. At Colombo a day was spent ashore while the ship was coaling, giving time for a meeting in the Y.M.C.A. Hall, to which missionaries from various parts of Ceylon had gathered for a short time of fellowship and conference with the men of whose work they had heard so much. The next stopping-place was Fremantle, in Western Australia, which was reached on March 5th. The party was taken up the Swan River to Perth, where a luncheon was provided so that the evangelists might meet the local ministers and other friends. This was followed by a conference in which final arrangements were made for the mission in Western Australia, which was to take place in November.

The *Otranto* reached Adelaide forty-eight hours behind time, in consequence of a severe cyclone in the Great Australian Bight, which almost stopped the progress of the ship. All arrangements had been made for the great welcome meeting in the Melbourne Exhibition Building, on Monday, March 11th. The only way to arrive in time was taken. The party left the ship at Adelaide and were hurried by special train across South Australia and Victoria, through Ballarat and Geelong, to the great capital city.

An immense programme lay before them. Nothing but reliance upon the supporting power of God could have enabled ordinary human beings, with their limited powers and capabilities, to face it fearlessly. For fourteen months, almost every day was planned in advance, with hardly a break between the missions, great and small, except the time required for necessary journeying from place to place. For reasons of climate, the first month's work was to be in Dunedin, in the south of New Zealand. This was to be followed by a great campaign in Melbourne and the Adelaide Mission. Then there were to be five shorter missions in smaller towns, long distances apart, on an average of a week each, interspersed by single days in towns passed en route. From July 13th to August 9th, the capital of New South Wales was to be the scene of another great campaign, then further meetings of a week each in three smaller towns, and a number of passing services as the party should slowly work their way northwards into Queensland.

The Brisbane meetings were to take the first two-and-a-half weeks of September. In 1909, Brisbane had been the furthest north of any Chapman-Alexander Mission, although the party had gone ashore for a day of meetings both at Townsville and at Thursday Island on their way to China. But on this tour, a week's mission had been planned for Townsville, from which point they were to travel by rail seventy miles inland to the mining town of Charters Towers, for eight days of meetings. Another week further down the coast was to be given to Mackay, a sugar-growing centre, unconnected with any other place except by sea. A few days at Toowoomba, to the south of Brisbane, completed the programme for Queensland. From October 24th to November 12th, Victoria was to claim the party again, with a short mission at Albury, and almost a couple of weeks at Ballarat. The last six weeks of the year were to be given to Western Australia, including the voyage of a week each way.

A short break was arranged for the midsummer holidays, which in this part of the world occur at Christmas-time, and are usually accompanied by almost unbearable heat. This was to be followed at the end of January by the last Australian Mission in Geelong, and by three days of monster farewell gatherings in Melbourne. Three months were then to be devoted to New Zealand, the party travelling by stages from the Bluff, at the southern tip of South Island, to Auckland, in the north. Only a few days each were given to Dunedin, Queenstown, and Timaru, the first regular campaign taking place in Christchurch. A mission in Wellington was to be followed by a few days' holiday in the Roturua District, and the final campaign of the whole series was to be held in Auckland, closing on May 10th, 1913.

On the evening of March 11th, 1912, the great Exhibition Building at Melbourne was crowded once more, as it had been so often during the Chapman-Alexander meetings of 1909. Mr. T. Hopkins, who had kept the Alexander Choir together through the interim period, had gathered a splendid company upon the platform for the Welcome Meeting. Long before eight, an eager crowd had filled the building and Mr. Hopkins started them singing. Slowly the hands of the clock worked round towards the appointed hour, but there was no sign as yet of the Chapman-Alexander Mission party, for whom all eyes were looking. The empty seats on the front of the platform gradually filled with ministers, some of whom had come from distant cities to share in giving the welcome. Eight o'clock struck and the singing continued, still under the leadership of Mr. Hopkins. At last Rev. Alex. Stewart, M.A., chairman of the meeting and of the Evangelistic Council of Australasia, stepped forward to make an announcement. "The sea has not been behaving itself well," were his first words. Then he asked for a little more patience until the special train, which was bearing the party rapidly towards Melbourne, could arrive.

At five minutes to eight the train steamed into Spencer Street Station. A number of taxis, held in readiness, dashed the principal members of the party through the streets to the Exhibition Building. The brothers Rock were at the station to meet their respective chiefs, and to take charge for them of all trunks and baggage, so that not a moment need be wasted.

THE MELBOURNE EXHIBITION
CHOIR, APRIL, 1912

ROBERT HARKNESS AT THE PIANO

"SING IT!"

130A With his Australian publisher, Mr. T. Shaw Fitchett, and Mr. W. A. S. Shum,
sub-editor of *The Southern Cross*, Melbourne, April, 1912

LEAVING HOBART, TASMANIA, ON THE SS. "WARRIMOO," MARCH 15, 1912

"GOOD FOR YOU!"

A CAREFUL SHOT

DECK BILLIARDS ON BOARD THE SS. "WARRIMOO," MARCH 16, 1912

The people in the Exhibition Building were beginning to get a trifle restless, though the hour had not long passed. Suddenly the choir and the great audience rose to their feet, bursting into the Doxology, as Dr. Chapman was seen upon the platform, followed by Charles Alexander and other members of the party. It was some time before quiet reigned again sufficiently for the meeting to proceed. Then a prayer of thankfulness and petition by the Rev. F. C. Spurr, and the reading of Scripture by the Rev. D. M. Deasey, were followed by some announcements given by Mr. W. Gordon Sprigg, organizing secretary of the Australasian campaign. Letters and telegrams from all parts of New Zealand, Tasmania, and Australia, had been sent to express a welcome and the spirit of happy, prayerful expectation. These were read aloud by Mr. Sprigg. Then followed a number of short speeches from representatives of New South Wales, South Australia, and Queensland, intro-duced by the chairman. " We know Dr. Chapman and Mr. Alexander, and we trust them," was the central theme of his message of welcome. " We have been beside them in their work, and understand how God uses them. They have come again to Australia, that Christ may be lifted up and glorified. Then will their hearts and ours glow with a great thanksgiving." Once more, when the speeches were over, this representative throng of Melbourne people gave themselves up to the delight of singing under Alexander's leadership. " His magic presence is resist-lessly felt," says a report of the meeting. " Time seems annihilated. We are back in the old mission again. The familiar strains of the ' Glory Song ' greet us. A peculiar solemnity passes over us, as the words—

Friends will be there I have loved long ago

are sung softly. ' Hands up, those of you who have been helped by the " Glory Song ",' cries Alexander, and in all parts of the building hands are uplifted. ' You started that song in Australia. You wouldn't like to kill it, would you ? ' And the sound of many voices comes back, ' No, No.' ' Then sing it ! ' and every-body joins in the old, but ever new, refrain—

When by His grace I shall look on His face,
That will be glory, be glory for me.

The ' Glory Song ' has the life of youth in it yet ! "

One more day was spent in meeting committees and gatherings of ministers, and on Wednesday, March 13th, the mission party sailed from Melbourne by the S.S. *Warrimoo* for New Zealand. A rough passage to Tasmania made the few hours ashore at Hobart, and the excursion up Mount Wellington, doubly welcome. At noon the following Monday, the *Warrimoo* drew alongside the dock at the Bluff. A stop-over at Invercargill gave time for a luncheon, a Y.M.C.A. meeting in the afternoon, an evening meeting in the Theatre, and a few hours' sleep. An early start by the 6.15 train brought the party to Dunedin in time for a Welcome Luncheon. Grace was said by Bishop Neville, Primate of New Zealand, and the Moderator of the Presbyterian Church of New Zealand pronounced the Benediction at the close. A Dean, an Archdeacon, a Canon, University professors, professional men, editors, and merchants were seated round the luncheon tables, as well as ministers and laymen from all the churches. The Mayor of Dunedin expressed a civic welcome, followed by a number of ministers and others, whose faces as well as their words told of their joy that the looked-for time of special effort for Christ had at last begun in their midst. A preparatory meeting of workers was held that first night in Burns Hall, which was used throughout the mission for the business men's meetings at noon.

Day after day, until April, the meetings continued every noon and every night, with many extra services in the mornings and afternoons. Brydone Hall proved, as was so often the case with the largest buildings, inadequate for the crowds, and, especially on Sundays, numbers were unable to gain entrance.

Through all of the longer campaigns in Australasia, Dr. Chapman followed a plan, gradually evolved by himself and Alexander, of setting aside one week, which they called " Home Week," for special consideration of matters connected with family life. A sermon on the Prodigal Son made its appeal to young men. On another night, an address on Rahab was the occasion of a special call to the young women, as daughters, sisters, and wives, to give their lives to Christ. The subject for a third evening was the pathetic cry that rang in the ears of Joseph in Egypt : " How shall I go up to my father, and the lad be not with me ? " This emphasized the responsibility of parents to their children. Another sermon was on the broken family circle, with a plea to those away from God to make their own family circles complete in Christ.

On one afternoon during the " Home Week," a meeting was held for aged people and for invalids who could not ordinarily venture into the crowded services. Christian people who had carriages or automobiles were asked to lend them for the purpose of bringing these elderly and infirm friends to the meeting, which was always a time of tender sweetness. From many an old man and woman the years rolled off, as Alexander would invite all those over seventy to rise and sing some hymn of childhood, such as " Jesus loves me, this I know." A bit of fun was usually introduced in finding out the age of the oldest man and the oldest woman present, who were often invited to the platform, and some small presentation made to them. Sometimes Alexander would persuade a septuagenarian to stand beside him and lead the old people in a verse of a hymn familiar to them. Frequently a committee of ladies, interested in the meeting, would provide a cup of tea for the old folks, after the service, to refresh them before their journey home. One of the beautiful elements, in this old people's service, was the opportunity it often afforded for enlisting the sympathetic interest of people who had hitherto held aloof from the mission. The appeal for their practical help, which was rarely refused, was often the beginning, not only of an interest in the meetings, but in spiritual matters concerning their own souls.

On one of the evenings of the " Home Week," Dr. Chapman made a practice of pleading with the young men and boys, who were already professed Christians, to offer their lives to God in service, ready, *if God should call*, to enter the work of the ministry or the foreign field. In Dunedin, one hundred and eighty-three boys and young men answered the call, and a great crowd of young women and girls came forward later, in response to a similar appeal, to surrender for definite service under the leading of God. This special night of the " Home Week " reached, perhaps, its most impressive climax in the great Melbourne Mission, which extended from April 20th to May 17th, of 1912.   Never will those who were present forget the great company of young men and boys filling the space in front of the Exhibition Building platform, and reaching down into the side aisles, as they stood with bowed heads, offering their lives to the service of the Lord Jesus Christ.   Equally affecting was the sight of hundreds of young women that stood in their places a few minutes later.   Afterwards, the young men withdrew to a side hall, where Dr. Chapman had a further talk with them, while Alexander carried on the big meeting.   The young women also passed into another hall, where Alexander's wife spoke to them, assisted by Mrs. Chapman and the other ladies of the party.   Looking down from the rough table on which she stood, into the upturned, earnest young faces of the densely-packed crowd of girls around her, Mrs. Alexander's eyes grew moist as she saw amongst them a girl of seventeen, whom she and her husband loved to call their " Australian daughter."   This was Clara Lelean, of Bendigo, who had, three years before, spent some months under their care, and was now visiting them again.

Every day incidents occurred of far-reaching power and influence.   But the space of these pages is too limited to record more than a few of them.   One afternoon, at a great meeting for mothers, at least two thousand women, fashionable and simple, old and young, gathered in the Exhibition Building.   Many of the younger mothers had brought their little ones with them.   Scattered among the rest were grandmothers, and here and there lonely figures, dressed in mourning.   Both the singing and the preaching touched all hearts deeply.   Before the meeting closed, Dr. Chapman came down from the crimson-covered dais to the main platform. " I want those of you who will dedicate yourselves to Christ, to come right down the aisle and stand here with bowed heads."   After a moment's hesitation the aisle was thronged.   " Now," said Dr. Chapman, " I want those of you, who can say the words sincerely, to repeat after me, ' With God's help, this afternoon, May 9th, 1912, I specially dedicate myself to Christ as a mother ! ' "   In the solemn hush, hundreds of trembling voices repeated the words.   " Write the dedication in your Bible when you get home," said Dr. Chapman, and led in an earnest prayer.   The stillness was broken by a burst of song.   Alexander had started the hymn, " When He cometh," and as the women returned to their seats, the joyful words which rang in their ears pictured their hope for their children—

> Like the stars of the morning,
> His bright crown adorning,
> They shall shine in their beauty,
> Bright gems for His crown.

These sound-pictures, vividly colouerd by many tender associations, can never fade from the memories of those who have heard them.   The music of the world, at its most magnificent best, fades into insignificance by this music, used surely for the purposes intended by God for His gifts of melody and harmony.   Who could forget, for instance, the comforting sweetness of the strains issuing from the choir, as, borne aloft on the music, the words floated out over the listening crowd—

> O House of many Mansions,
> Thy doors are open wide ;
> And dear are all the faces
> Upon the other side

Dr. W. H. Fitchett, who was present at many of the Exhibition services, describes the singing of the refrain :—

> Jesus will give you rest,
> Jesus will give you rest.
> Turn from your sin, call now on Him,
> For Jesus will give you rest.

" Mr. Alexander called, now upon the choir to sing it, then upon one gallery or another, then upon the people beyond the dome. It was deep calling to deep, the galleries challenging the floor, the floor rolling back in a wave of sound to the galleries. And always the words ran through them—

> Jesus will give you rest.

A working man sat near the present writer, his dress rough, his face unshaven. His lips were parted in surprise, wonder looked out of his eyes ; and as these waves of music burst upon his ears, his face softened, his lips presently began to sing. A blind girl sat a little beyond him, the blind eyes wearing a strangely pathetic look. The words—

> Jesus will give you rest

stole into her brain through the listening ears, and then broke out in music on her lips. She too was singing ! "

The Adelaide Mission was begun on May 18th with a handicap. Ernest Naftzger, the soloist, was ill, and Dr. Chapman, who had been laid low in Melbourne with a severe cold, could not use his voice for the first few days. But Rev. Henry Howard, with Mr. McLaughlin, of Belfast, and Dr. Warren, of Melbourne, stepped into the breach, and assisted Charles Alexander in carrying on the meetings. One of the most striking services of this mission was that held at the close, for the special purpose of greeting and encouraging those who had taken their stand for Christ during the three weeks. Almost a thousand of these converts gathered in reserved seats in the centre of the Adelaide Exhibition Building, surrounded by perhaps eight thousand friends, who had succeeded in gaining an entrance. Invitations had also been sent out to the converts of the Adelaide Mission of three years earlier, and many of them came to the meeting. In spite of the fluctuations that come with passing years, the personal letters which Dr. Chapman held in his hand accounted definitely for more than four hundred who were known to be living lives of faithfulness to Christ. Some were scattered throughout the State and the Commonwealth, others were in the foreign mission field, or preparing to go there. Some were training for the Christian ministry, a larger number serving the churches as office-bearers and Sunday-school teachers. After an earnest address by Dr. Chapman on the necessity for open confession of Christ and consistent living, the whole body of converts of this and the previous mission were invited to come down the aisles to the front. Each was presented with a Gospel of St. John, and a specially printed card with the text John iii. 16 upon it, having a blank space instead of the word " whosoever," so that each might write his or her own name in its place. There was a reverent hush upon the crowded audience as the converts came forward. After they had returned to their seats, a fresh invitation was given to others who would decide for Christ, to which there were many responses.

As the outcome of this mission, a Chapman-Alexander Bible Institute was established in Adelaide. Its purpose was to provide spiritual training for the young people who had taken a stand for Christ, and had definitely surrendered their lives to Him for service. Mr. and Mrs. R. H. White volunteered the gift of their own beautiful home as the headquarters of the Institute ; afterwards giving an additional piece of land adjoining it. Mr. and Mrs. J. M. MacBride, of Kooringa, gave the sum of four thousand pounds to provide the necessary equipment. A letter written from Melbourne, a little later, by Dr. Chapman and Charles Alexander, showed how spontaneous the gift had been. "The Bible Institute now being established in Adelaide," they said, "has our sincere confidence. We believe there is a place for such an institution in the Commonwealth, and we are of the opinion that no better location could be found. We were not instrumental in any way in establishing this Institute, except as it is said to be an outgrowth of our mission in Adelaide ; nor did we suggest the name to be given to it." During the following five years, in spite of the difficulties caused by the war, two hundred and fifty-three students were trained in the Chapman-Alexander Institute, many of them having gone into Church work, and others into foreign missionary service.

The next mission in Broken Hill, from June 8th to 17th, was a great contrast to that in the cultured city of Adelaide. Broken Hill is entirely a mining town, on the edge of the great central desert. It is within the border of New South Wales, although the only approach by rail is from South Australia. There is a short season following the heavy rains, when the grass seed, lying under the dry soil, suddenly sprouts, sending up tall shoots, which wither quickly under the burning sun. But for the greater part of the year Broken Hill itself, and the great, wide plains stretching away towards the centre of the continent, are parched desert, sprinkled with grey-green tufts of sage-scrub. The only greenness that the town can boast is provided by the graceful, feathery pepper-trees, with their tassels of crimson berries. In the rather pathetic attempt at a park, avenues of pepper-trees mark the lines of what elsewhere would be roads or walks across the greensward. In one small, railed-in circle, constant care and watering succeeds in producing a few flower-blooms, and on Sunday afternoons the miners will carry their babies to take a look at the only flowers in Broken Hill. Ten miles over the desert is the reservoir which supplies Broken Hill with water, and near by is a large camel camp. From this point long trains of camels, heavily loaded, are the only means of supplying the great inland stations of New South Wales with their necessities. To watch the camel trains, with their Afghan leaders, slowly winding their way over the dusty desert, seemed more like a scene in Arabia or Egypt, than Australia, to the mission party, who hitherto had only known the cities of the coast.

Port Pirie, and Mount Gambier, in the extreme south of South Australia, where further missions were held, were each unique and interesting places. The beautiful pines and fir-trees, and weird crater lakes of Mount Gambier, form a strong contrast to the surroundings of Broken Hill. Many wonderful stories could be told of those who found Christ in these places, and in the five towns of New South Wales—Goulburn, Bathurst, Newcastle, Maitland, and Armidale, as well as in the great mission held in Sydney, but space does not allow.

Triumphs, as well as failures, are a test of character, and this is specially true in the spiritual realm.   Perhaps none but those engaged in work of this kind can fully understand the deep need of close, daily touch with God, and of ceaseless, humble dependence upon the Holy Spirit, and the blessed Book, for true inspiration in their task.   The constant travelling, with its natural interests, the meeting of old friends, the forming of hundreds of new acquaintances, the continual publicity, and the fame given by association with God's wonder-working power, could easily draw the leaders of such work aside from its true purpose.   The responsibility of caring for, and directing, a large party of fellow-workers, and with them seeking, in place after place, to raise its spiritual tone from indifference into genuine love for Christ, is a drain on every part of a man, which comparatively few experience.   Wherever they went, Dr. Chapman and Charles Alexander were intensely conscious of, and grateful for, the support of prayer from thousands of their friends in other lands.

With but few slight breaks, physical health and strength was given them to carry on their work, and in a marvellous way they were kept from becoming in the least mechanical or professional in their untiring efforts to bring men to Christ.   Yet, while to tell the story of their work in detail would seem like a monotonous repetition of meetings and crowds, and methods employed, there was, in the work itself, no monotony.   To Charles Alexander, every new soul with whom he came in contact thrilled him with an ardour as fresh as if it were the first whom he had ever sought to lead to Jesus.   The women of the party were also marvellously blessed with physical strength and endurance, but to the anxiety of Charles Alexander his wife was laid low in some of the missions in Queensland, and at Ballarat, with sharp attacks of appendicitis.   Two days spent in Melbourne, before the party sailed for Fremantle, provided an opportunity for obtaining expert advice, and it was found that an operation would be necessary after a period of entire rest.   Alexander was therefore obliged to depart for Western Australia, which was at that time unconnected by rail with other States, without his wife—leaving Miss Beatrice Atcherley, of Geelong, and Clara Lelean, of Bendigo, to be her companions in his absence.   The mission party sailed from Melbourne on November 13th, Alexander joining them on board at Adelaide.

S.S. " Otway," Outer Harbour, Adelaide, November 15th, 1912.—" I am thankful to have received your telegrams, and am sure you are in good hands with the two girls to take care of you.   Mr. Rock and I had a good night's rest on the train. We have just had lunch on board with the rest of the party, and delivered your telegraph message to them.   Some friends came down to the boat with flowers for you and were sorry to hear that you were ill."

Fremantle, November 19th.—" We have had a remarkably smooth trip, and only needed you with us to make it perfect.   We have been a jolly party, sharing one big table in the dining-saloon, except Mr. and Mrs. Davis, Mr. Rock, and Mr. Thomas, who were at a small table close by.   The committee at Fremantle are greatly disappointed that you are not here.   We have splendid halls for the meetings, both here and at Perth.   It is a hard pull to be away from you, but these people have been working hard, and I think it was right for me to come.   Mr. Davis signed up a large number of Pocket Testament Leaguers on the boat ; several of

LOOKING ACROSS THE SWAN RIVER TO
PERTH, WESTERN AUSTRALIA, FROM
KING'S PARK, NOVEMBER, 1912

BOUND FOR
WESTERN AUSTRALIA

"I DARE YOU TO SING IT ALONE!"
A SERVICE ON THE WHARF, FREMANTLE, W.A.,
NOVEMBER 15, 1912

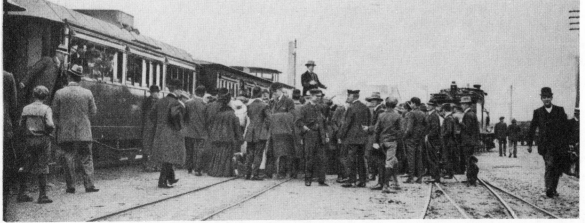

A FAREWELL SONG ON THE RAILWAY STATION AT PORT PIRIE, SOUTH AUSTRALIA, JUNE, 1912

HAPPY DAYS
AT DUNEDIN

NEW ZEALAND,
APRIL, 1912

NOONDAY MEETING AT ADDINGTON RAILWAY WORKSHOPS, NEAR CHRISTCHURCH,
NEW ZEALAND, MARCH, 1913

TRAIN STOPS TWENTY MINUTES FOR REFRESHMENTS! NEW ZEALAND, APRIL, 1913

them accepted Christ. There is to be a civic reception in the Town Hall this afternoon and our first big meeting is in the Skating Rink to-night."

November 22nd.—" We have been having good meetings. Last night twenty-three accepted Christ. I am continually meeting people who were in our missions in England. Several were in the Royal Albert Hall, Strand, and Brixton missions. The ministers here are good fellows, splendid personal workers, with ability and consecration, but the town reminds me of Port Pirie, in the large number of drinking men about everywhere. We close here next Monday night, and have a choir practice and workers' meeting next day in Perth. I miss my darling all the time. How good it will be to see the dear face and hear the voice that always brings sweet peace to my heart. I pray for you many times each day, and am asking the Lord to give us and the doctors wisdom in every move we make."

On December 10th, Charles Alexander returned to Melbourne about ten days ahead of the rest of the party, Mr. Naftzger taking his place as song-leader for the closing days of the Perth Mission. Alexander found his wife much benefited by the month's complete rest, and after three days he took her to ' St. Ives,' a private hospital in East Melbourne, where the operation was to be performed on December 16th. Before returning alone to the hotel he left a little note of comfort with her :—" How I should love to have you in our beloved ' Tennessee,' where we would not be away from you one moment. Our year-text must include this in one of the ' all things ' working together for good. I know that this new set of people amongst whom you have gone will feel your strong, love-filled personality, and some may be saved as a result. I must not be too selfish, but lend you to other needy ones for a time. . . . *He* loves you, and I know His power is enough. I shall love the hymn ' 'Tis I, be not afraid ! ' since your sweet voice has hallowed it." Sunday—the day before the operation—was a sacred time for both. Part of his note left at the hospital that night ran, " A stream of prayer is reaching the Throne, and victory is in your soul as a result. I leave you in the gentle care of our heavenly Father, and I know you will be strengthened by His Spirit."

The operation, though long and severe, was entirely successful, and by January 17th Alexander had the joy of taking his wife for a few days to Macedon, a beautiful mountain resort some forty miles from Melbourne. The Christmas and New Year season was exceptionally hot and trying this year. Dr. and Mrs. Chapman enjoyed the benefit of a delightful holiday at Mole Creek, in Tasmania. Dr. Chapman's eldest son, J. Wilbur Chapman, Junior, and his young bride, were with them, adding greatly to their happiness. A trip round the world, with the marvellous opportunity of sharing in the great meetings in Australia, had been part of the parental wedding present to the young couple. They had joined the party early in the campaign, and had travelled with them through Queensland and Western Australia, and the holiday at Mole Creek marked the close of their visit to the Antipodes, for from Tasmania they travelled to Java, and on towards home.

Other members of the party were enjoying a short time of rest in various places, but Charles Alexander, staying at his Melbourne hotel through these hot days of Australian midsummer, was hard at work, between his daily visits to the hospital.

N

Early in January he invited all the men of the great Exhibition Choir to meet him in a church in Swanston Street, that they might spend an evening together rehearsing a number of items from the new " Alexander's Male Choir " book. Busy days had been spent at " Tennessee " during the previous summer preparing this collection. The plates were barely finished when the party left England, and it was necessary for some one to bring them out to Australia by the following boat. This was done by Mr. F. S. Turney, of London, who had been Charles Alexander's assistant in the technical work of preparing his English hymn-books, since his first arrival in England with Dr. Torrey in 1902. Mr. Turney's association with Gospel hymns was a long one, dating from the early days of the Moody and Sankey missions in Great Britain. In addition to services rendered to Ira D. Sankey, he came into touch with James McGranahan, Geo. C. Stebbins, J. H. Burke, and other Gospel singers, before beginning his association with Charles Alexander. The hymn-plates reached Australia safely, and the book was shortly afterwards published by Fitchett Bros., and became a source of pleasure and profit to many.

On Saturday, January 11th, Alexander arranged, at very short notice, a great Reunion Song Service in the Exhibition Building. This was preceded in the afternoon by a gathering in the Exhibition Oval, to which he invited the choir members. Over eight hundred of them accepted his invitation, a fine tribute of affection from sport-loving Australians on a Saturday afternoon in the middle of the midsummer holiday month. In the brilliant sunshine, they were arranged in group after group, and photographed, for Charles Alexander desired to carry away with him permanent records of his wonderful Melbourne choir. Mr. and Mrs. Harkness came from Adelaide for the occasion. Other helpers assisting Alexander on the great day were George T. B. Davis, W. W. Rock and his brother, and F. S. Turney, while Mr. T. Hopkins, organizer of the choir, and Mr. W. Gordon Sprigg, secretary of the mission, did everything in their power to make the occasion a memorable one. During the taking of the photographs, a lorry with a piano upon it was driven to the front of the crowd, and an enthusiastic open-air song service was held, Alexander standing on the driver's seat of the motor-lorry to conduct, with shining face and coat-tails flying. Later, he presented to the men members of his choir a copy of the *Male Choir*, in memory of the happy hours spent together in the service of Christ. At the evening song service, within the familiar walls of the Exhibition Building, the only sermons consisted of pithy stories told by Alexander between the singing, a short talk by Rev. Alex. MacCallum, and another by Mr. Davis on the Pocket Testament League. A description of this song-service, written at the time by W. W. Rock, says, " Music dominated the meeting—the music of Gospel songs that Australian audiences have learned to love. Through it all, the song-leader on the high stand, his tall, commanding figure silhouetted against the white dresses of the ladies in the choir, swayed and moved the crowd, moulding it to the spirit of the meeting. Without stint he spent his energy, and his quaint phrases, his buoyant humour, his ever-ready smile, lifted his audience out of themselves. The keynote of the service was sounded by the song-leader when he said, ' We are hoping that somebody will find the way to God to-night.' Throughout the meeting he never lost sight of that purpose, nor allowed it to be

MEETING IN THE EXHIBITION BUILDING, ADELAIDE, SOUTH AUSTRALIA, MAY, 1912

A GIFT OF "MALE CHOIR" BOOKS TO MEMBERS OF HIS MELBOURNE CHOIR, JANUARY, 1913

A MIDSUMMER SONG-GATHERING WITH HIS CHOIR IN THE EXHIBITION GROUNDS AT MELBOURNE, JANUARY, 1913

FAREWELL TO AUSTRALIA, FEBRUARY, 1913

FAREWELL SERVICE AT THE MELBOURNE EXHIBITION BUILDINGS, FEBRUARY 11, 1913

Leading the singing from the deck of SS. "Moeraki"

Leaving Melbourne behind for New Zealand, Feb. 12

"GOD WILL TAKE CARE OF YOU."

"GOOD-BYE, OLD MAN!"

submerged by other things. The singing continued until after ten o'clock, and the fact, that this was the last time the big choir would come under those compelling hands in the Exhibition Building for many a long day, lent a touch of pathos to the closing scenes. It was the pathos of farewell." Unknown to all, it was indeed farewell, for this was the last service ever conducted by Charles M. Alexander in the Melbourne Exhibition Building.

At the end of January, Dr. and Mrs. Chapman returned to Melbourne from Tasmania, and on January 29th the whole of the party gathered in Geelong for the last mission in Australia. Perhaps at no other centre was the disappointment at the shortness of some of the missions so keenly felt as in Geelong. The ten days allotted were but the beginning of a rising tide of blessing. The ministers and workers were anxious to see every church and Sunday-school penetrated by it, and in order to conserve the results of the Chapman-Alexander meetings the main features of the work were organized into a three months' continuation campaign. Dr. Chapman and Charles Alexander were more than ever impressed with the need for longer missions, but the fifteen months available had been spread over as many towns and cities as possible, and many invitations for even short periods had to be refused.

Three days, February 9th, 10th and 11th, were devoted to farewell meetings in Melbourne. Stirred by the parting with his own and his wife's friends, Robert Harkness had written a chorus, which was sung over and over again at the final meetings in the Town Hall. Through the days of war that came afterwards, it has since been sung in many a camp and navy-yard :

> Good-bye, God bless you one and all,
> Until we meet again.

On February 12th, the Melbourne dock rang with the sound of Gospel hymns, for a great crowd had gathered to say good-bye to the mission party, as they sailed for the last time from the city where they had become such familiar and well-beloved figures. On this occasion, the gangway of the ship provided a platform sufficiently high to raise Dr. Chapman and Charles Alexander above the heads of the crowd. A farewell message was given by Dr. Chapman, a word of prayer uttered, and then those well-known, wonderful hands, that had drawn such volumes of song from the people of Melbourne, led them once more in singing.

As the ship moved away from the dock, paper streamers were thrown by friends on board, and still for a few moments kept them in touch with each other across the ever-widening space. But a closer bond, which did not snap asunder like the frail paper ribbon, bound those together who commended each other to God in the chorus of song that floated back and forth over the water.

Once again it was necessary for Alexander and his wife to be separated by the ocean. The first part of the work in New Zealand was to include much hard travelling, and it was thought best that Mrs. Alexander should join the party two months later at Wellington.

When the *Moeraki* put in port at Hobart, the party was welcomed at the wharf by the Premier of Tasmania, afterwards being hospitably entertained by Admiral Sir George and Lady King-Hall, who had already taken a deep interest in the work of the Sydney Mission a few months earlier, and had frequently entertained the party at Admiralty House.

A stormy voyage brought the party to the Bluff, to begin their journeyings through New Zealand. Dunedin and Queenstown were visited, with a few meetings in each ; and a short five days' campaign was held in Timaru. Then came the mission in Christchurch, from March 4th to 24th. Here the afternoon services were held in the Y.M.C.A. building, or a large theatre, an enormous tent having been specially erected for the mass meetings at night. " I have been doing all kinds of things," wrote Alexander to his wife from Christchurch on March 9th, " to keep me busy until I have you back with me. The days drag drearily with you away, but it will be a bright day when I see your face. You will see by my long, dictated letter what a stretch we have been on, and we have had to be satisfied with poor accommodation and anything we could get to eat. Here we have a perfect place to stay in, a clean, homelike boarding-house. We are staying away from hotels with a licence whenever possible ; the liquor fight is so keen and we want to help all we can. I am keeping a photographic history of our journeyings for you when you come. The big tent here is a beauty. Almost two hundred and fifty people publicly confessed Christ yesterday."

On March 25th, the party arrived in Wellington, at the extreme north of South Island. Wellington is the capital of the Dominion and the seat of Parliament. Hon. W. F. Massey, the Prime Minister, presided at the opening service on the following day, and welcomed the mission party on behalf of the people of New Zealand. This mission, which had seemed less likely of good results because of some lack of co-operation on the part of the local ministers, proved, through the blessing of God, to be unexpectedly fruitful. A letter written by Charles Alexander on March 28th, reached his wife in Sydney just before she set sail across the thousand-mile strip of water that separated them :

" How glad I shall be to have you once more by my side to sympathize and consult with. Do not be afraid of the voyage alone. It will be calmer and warmer than ours was by way of Hobart. We are having splendid results here, and our party has been most harmonious. This Town Hall is much like the one at Sydney and almost as large. The days are packed with work, and I am thankful that I am keeping strong through it all. . . . Good-bye, sweet wife, until I see you at the Wellington wharf."

On April 9th, the looked-for meeting took place, and Alexander rejoiced that his wife was able to enter with him into the work of the closing meetings in Wellington. Then came three wonderful days of holiday in the Roturua district, where the presence of the Earl of Liverpool—the new Governor of the Dominion—gave exceptional opportunities for seeing the Maoris, in their native dress, giving exhibitions of old-time customs and war-dances. The marvellous natural phenomena were also a source of great interest. The hissing steam, issuing in many places from cracks and fissures in the ground, the heat underfoot, the pools of boiling mud, and the steaming geysers, proved the thinness of the earth's crust in these regions.

This short rest enabled the mission party to begin their last and very important campaign in Auckland with freshness and vigour. Unusually thorough and earnest

LOOKING OUT OVER THE REES VALLEY, NEW ZEALAND, FEBRUARY, 1913

A MAORI HOUSE NEAR ROTORUA, NEW ZEALAND,
APRIL, 1913

A REST DAY NEAR DUNEDIN, N.Z.,
APRIL 6, 1912

THE BIG MISSION TENT AT CHRISTCHURCH, NEW ZEALAND, MARCH, 1913

SERVICE IN THE TOWN HALL AT AUCKLAND, NEW ZEALAND, MAY, 1913

preparation had been made, much individual prayer on the part of the Church members had been enlisted, and numbers of prayer-meetings had also been held in churches and homes. It was therefore not to be wondered at that the blessing of God came down upon the city. Before three-and-a-half weeks were past, almost two thousand persons had accepted and publicly confessed Christ as their Saviour, and several hundreds of young people had dedicated their lives to Him for service.

On May 10th, the long series of campaigns in Australia and New Zealand came to an end, and the party set sail for Vancouver on board S.S. *Niagara*.

During the voyage across the Pacific, delightful, short visits were paid once more to Suva and to Honolulu, and the life on board ship was full of physical refreshment. Friendships were formed among their fellow-passengers, and the witness of Charles Alexander to his Lord was as constant and true as ever. An echo of the voyage came to Mrs. Alexander from Christchurch, New Zealand, in January, 1921. " Perhaps you will remember," wrote Mrs. R. M. Fergusson, " your trip on the *Niagara* eight years ago. I was on board with you, and I want to tell you what a comfort your dear husband and you were to me in my loneliness, travelling by myself. Mr. Alexander's kindly manner and inspiring personality I can never forget. His personal touch with the Master was keenly felt in his intercourse with others, and many a lonely feeling was swept away by his kindly word and smile. The Bible-readings on board were also most helpful. The Chapman-Alexander Missions are still often spoken of and remembered by many as the greatest spiritual uplift New Zealand ever experienced, especially your dear husband's singing and leading of Gospel songs."

The journey across the Rocky Mountains in early June was delightful, especially a stay, over Sunday, at Banff. A few days spent in Chicago gave an opportunity for memorable services, conducted by Dr. Chapman and Charles Alexander, in the Moody Church on Chicago Avenue. Busy hours were filled with the pleasure of meeting hundreds of old friends and of telling the good tidings of God's work on the other side of the world. Another highly-prized opportunity was also given to the Alexanders of spending a few days with their family in Ohio. His only sister, Ida, had been married, and was settled in her own home in a northern part of the State, a few miles distant from her brother Homer, who was now pastor of a Presbyterian church in Fostoria, Ohio. The home in Tennessee had been broken up some time before, and the loved mother had come northwards to look after the home of her son, and care for his motherless little girls. The youngest brother, Leo, also shared the family home in Fostoria.

It was hard to break away from such a happy reunion, but other duties claimed Charles Alexander and his wife. On June 11th, they landed in Plymouth, England, from the great steamship *Olympic*, which had borne them across the broad Atlantic, and on June 12th they passed once more beneath the portals of " Tennessee," their beloved English home in Birmingham.

CHAPTER TWENTY-TWO

Scottish Missions, Interrupted by World War

1913 to 1914

THE delight of Charles Alexander in spending another summer with his wife in their quiet English home, after the long, long months of travel and of incessant labour in the midst of crowds, may well be imagined. Before him lay the prospect of an extended period of service in Great Britain. Almost eight years had elapsed since the close of the three years' British Campaign with Dr. Torrey, and, during the interim, his large campaigns both with Dr. Torrey and Dr. Chapman had been chiefly in the United States, Canada, Australasia, and the Orient. Chapman-Alexander Missions had been held in South Wales, and in the North of Ireland, in 1910 and 1911, but none in England, except a few days in Shrewsbury, although Alexander himself had conducted meetings in various places.

He had kept in close personal touch with many of the Scottish friends made ten years earlier in his work with Dr. Torrey, and during the short visits paid to Edinburgh and Dundee in September 1910, he had introduced Dr. Chapman to many of the Christian leaders of Scotland. These men had followed the work of the Chapman-Alexander missions with deep interest. Urgent invitations had been sent out to Australia in 1912, and plans had been made for campaigns in Glasgow and Edinburgh, which would occupy the season from the autumn of 1913 to the Spring of 1914. Hundreds of people who loved Alexander and who remembered the great Song-services of 1903, were looking forward eagerly to his leadership. A fresh hymn-book, including many of the beautiful new pieces by Harkness and others, was a necessity, and during the summer of 1913 Alexander was hard at work at " Tennessee " with his band of helpers, preparing his " No. 3 " book, which was barely ready in time for the opening of the Scottish Campaign.

The first meeting in Glasgow was held in St. Andrew's Hall on October 5th. For three months Dr. Chapman and Charles Alexander moved from one district to another of the great, widespread city, bringing a message of joy and hope to its toiling thousands. To one of Dr. Chapman's impulsive and generous disposition, the reception at the beginning might have seemed to lack warmth, for Scotsmen are proverbially cautious and undemonstrative, and only give themselves lavishly to a man after he has proved himself. But their friendship and trust, once given, are never withdrawn. Ere many days had passed, all barriers were gone. First Glasgow, and then Edinburgh, opened their hearts to the friends new and old, and poured out upon them a wealth of deep affection.

THE SS. "NIAGARA" AT SUVA, FIJI, MAY, 1913

WITH THE FIJIAN POLICE

A CALL TO CHURCH SERVICE. The hollow logs were formerly used to summon the people to cannibal feasts.

CASCADE MOUNTAIN FROM BANFF, CANADIAN ROCKIES, MAY, 1913

During the Christmas holidays some changes took place in the personnel of the mission party. Albert Brown, of Nottingham, a fine Christian man, with a magnificent, well-trained baritone voice, was definitely appointed as Alexander's soloist in the place of E. W. Naftzger, whose health had temporarily broken down. Robert Harkness, who had been Alexander's right hand as pianist for twelve years, felt that he must settle into a home of his own, and took up business in London. The parting was a severe wrench after so long a time of intimate association in the Lord's work. Alexander tried for a time to obtain another pianist through the ordinary means of advertising. Several men of high ability and with wide experience as church organists endeavoured to fill the position, but the standard of the work needed was too severe a test. It required a peculiar adaptability of temperament, a quickness of resource, an exercise of memory powers, and of fine intuition, rarely possessed by even experienced musicians who have been trained along mechanical lines.

The curiously rigid, cut-and-dried attitude of many of the British people towards the music of hymns and sacred songs often causes a misunderstanding in the use of " Gospel Song " music, the rhythm of which is distinctively American. Because it is unfamiliar, it is sometimes treated with scant courtesy. The phrasing, which is the soul of " Gospel music," and which would be accorded to any other kind of musical composition, is often entirely disregarded, the piece rattled off without thought, and contemptuously thrown aside as a " mere jig." Unfortunately, some who love Gospel songs, and the message they contain, murder the music of them just as much, through ignorance of right phrasing, and by playing them all at a uniform high rate of speed. Another cause of misunderstanding arises in the use of syncopation, which, when properly employed, is not only effective in musical expression, but often helps to bring out the force of the words, which, after all, is the main purpose of religious music. The " coon-songs " which often pass in England for the music of the coloured people of the South, and the modern use of " rag-time " often cause a similar rhythm to be applied to Gospel songs, and this introduces a cheapness and levity that destroys all beauty in the song. But it takes time to learn and understand the right way of using this form of sacred music, and Alexander realized that the kind of double-harness work which twelve years had developed between himself and Harkness could not be immediately accomplished by one strange to his particular methods. But although never impatient, he was quick to see whether the ability was latent or not, and, after testing several applicants, he came to the conclusion that the usual avenues of advertisement were not of much value in finding him the right pianist.

Going one day into the London Headquarters of the Y.M.C.A. to call on his old friend J. J. Virgo, Alexander asked whether any of the young men were specially fond of piano-playing. " We are rather short of good musicians just now," replied Virgo, " but there is one fellow who is always playing around on the piano—' Barrie,' the others call him. I believe he is here now. Shall we go and see ? " Mr. Virgo opened the door of his office, and the two entered the Lounge. A gust of laughter, and the sound of men's voices in song, greeted them. Seated at the piano was a short, stocky young man, with dark hair and spectacles, playing a rollicking song for the group of young fellows crowded closely around him. They were all enjoying themselves immensely, and at the sound of Mr. Virgo's voice the pianist turned with a broad and beaming smile. " I want you to meet Mr. Alexander," said Virgo. After a general handshake all round, Alexander asked the young men to go on singing, and finally arranged an interview with Mr. Barraclough. Finding that he was on the point of resigning from his position as secretary to a member of Parliament, Alexander invited him to come to Scotland for a week or two as his guest, to help him with stenography, piano accompaniments, or anything that was needed. Mr. Barraclough gladly consented, and spoke of the desire he had always had to make more use of his music, and to give his time more definitely to Christian work. " He is a fine fellow, is Barrie," Virgo had remarked to his friend. " There's only one thing you won't like. He smokes like a chimney-stack ! " During the interview, Alexander referred to the habit of smoking, asking Mr. Barraclough if he would feel able to try and drop it. No further word was said on the subject. But after Mr. Barraclough's visit in Scotland had lengthened out to several weeks, and he had undertaken an increasing responsibility at the piano, Alexander asked him how he was succeeding in getting over the smoking habit. Mr. Barraclough looked up at him with astonishment. " Why, I have never touched tobacco in any form since the day you spoke to me in London, Mr. Alexander ! " The young man's natural musical ability was shaping itself for the special work required, but perhaps this indication of a strong character helped Alexander's decision to offer him the position of pianist.

On January 14th, 1914, the mission party gathered together again in Edinburgh. Dr. and Mrs. Chapman had taken a flying trip home to New York during the Christmas holidays, and the others had scattered to various points of the compass. Mr. Barraclough was now the new pianist, and Mr. Brown the soloist, assisted by a Scottish tenor, Mr. William Andrew, of Glasgow. The Olympia Building in Edinburgh, seating six thousand people, was thronged day after day until early in March, and the conservative Scottish capital rang with the sound of Gospel hymns. It was pathetic to see the lines of men and women waiting out in the street long after the doors of Olympia had been closed by orders of the police. Sometimes so many were still there when the service had closed, that Alexander stayed, with all of the choir who could assist him, to give them a special song service. The Rev. George Shaw, of Williamsburg, Pennsylvania, was studying in Edinburgh University at the time. " I was trying to get into the Assembly Hall one after-noon," he wrote to Mrs. Alexander long afterwards, " but was refused admittance because of its crowded condition. While I was trying to get in, Mr. Alexander came along. ' What do you want, Indiana ? ' he said in his cheery way, knowing I came from that State. ' I want to get into the meeting.' ' Come along with me,' he said, and took me to the platform, giving me a seat near his own. I did not know him well, but that incident has enshrined him in my heart for ever."

Returning to Birmingham for a few days to entertain some friends at " Tennessee," and having a quiet hour on the Sunday afternoon, Mrs. Alexander wandered across into the grounds of Uffculme, her old home. She wrote to her husband : " It is exactly ten years by the date since thou and I wandered round the grounds at Uffculme, alone together for the first time, and passed where the snowdrops were pushing up through the snow. This afternoon, I took Kelly (a fine Irish setter) with me for a walk round the dear old garden, so altered in many places, but almost the same at that spot, except that the little pool and the summer-house, where we sat and talked so sedately, are now shut off by tall iron railings. The snowdrops are coming up in the grass, and I picked a few for ' auld lang syne.' As I stood there in the quiet, I thanked God for all that the ten years have brought us—precious joys and sacred sorrows, wealth of love and friendship, and above all, unique opportunities of winning souls to Christ, of circulating His Word, and of carrying joy and comfort and encouragement to thousands of hearts in many parts of the world through Gospel songs and hymns. Beloved, my heart is too full to utter my thanks to God for thee, and for all He has given me in and through thee, but He knows that I thank Him ' upon every remembrance ' of thee. It was about four o'clock as I stood by the snowdrops, so I prayed specially for the men's and women's meetings in Edinburgh, and knew that my prayer was being heard for a great outpouring of the spirit of decision for Christ."

The mission in Edinburgh touched all extremes of the population, from the poorest to the richest, the most intellectual to the most ignorant. One night the Corn Exchange in the Grass Market was crowded out with a company of about four thousand of the poorest from the Edinburgh slums. On other occasions Dr. Chapman preached, and Charles Alexander sang, in some of the old aristocratic churches of the city. A signal mark of honour was paid to Dr. Chapman by the invitation to preach the University sermon in St. Giles' Cathedral. Day after day at Olympia three venerable and striking figures might be seen upon the plat-form : Principal Alexander Whyte, and Dr. George Wilson, representatives of the two great sections of the Presbyterian Church in Scotland, and Sir Alexander Simpson, so well-known and beloved. All three had passed through the great revival movements of the past half-century, and were men sensitive to spiritual atmosphere. " It has been an inspiration to thousands," wrote the editor of *The Life of Faith*, " to see their faithfulness to this movement, and their intense loyalty to the missioners. One day, about this time, a ministerial friend met Dr. Whyte in Princes Street, and stopping for a chat, said it was a pleasure to many to see him so regularly at the Olympia meetings. He replied, ' *I cannot keep away !* ' and in saying that, the famous preacher spoke for a vast multitude." Indeed, so great was the interest throughout the city, that a proposition was seriously made, that if, as was hoped, the evangelists should return to Scotland in the autumn, a movable wooden tabernacle, accommodating five thousand people, should be provided for the meetings. So insistent were the present claims of Glasgow, that other plans gave way for a return mission there during the month of March. This time the meetings were held in the great Zoo Building, usually the scene of exhibi-tions of various kinds.

During these days of strenuous evangelism in Scotland, Dr. Chapman had serious indications that his health was suffering from the strain of the past years. He frequently preached, both in Edinburgh and Glasgow, in direct opposition to his doctor's orders, but although for several days he was confined to the house by a severe attack of illness, he was back at his post long before he should have been.   Both he and Charles Alexander were in the work they loved, for God, and not for selfish aims ; and together they gave themselves to it, without stint, courageously, and with self-sacrifice and consecration.

At the close of the Edinburgh meetings, Dr. George Wilson, with others, published his impressions in a special edition of *The British Weekly*.   The last sentence of his message ran : " As an old man, I rejoice to have been spared to see what I believe to be the most wonderful spiritual movement since the days of Whitefield and Wesley."   Invitations from many other Scottish cities poured in upon the evangelists, but for this season all that was possible to arrange was a conference tour, during which eight towns were visited for two or three days' meetings.   From Falkirk the Chapman-Alexander party travelled northwards, through Perth, and Aberdeen to Inverness.   To this last town, beautifully situated at the head of the Caledonian Canal, three busily-occupied days were given.   Ministers from all parts of the Highlands and Islands had been invited to a special conference, in addition to the meetings for the general public.   At this ministers' conference representatives of separate branches of Scottish Church life met for the first time, and the blessing of unity and mutual sympathy, that resulted, was felt throughout the north of Scotland.   Visits to Paisley, Kilmarnock, Ayr and Dumfries brought the mission party southwards again, and on April 11th, Dr. and Mrs. Chapman sailed for America, while Alexander and his wife and others of the party returned to Birmingham, England.

During the sunny days of June and July, the Alexanders spent three wonderful weeks amid the beauties of Cornwall, at Kynance Cove, a lonely cleft between the cliffs, two miles over the moors from the Lizard Point.   They stayed at Thomas's Hotel, an old mill adapted as a dwelling house, the only building in the Cove.   Here, among the rocks and the boisterous waves and the calling sea-gulls, they enjoyed another span of the honeymoon that continued through all their years of married life.   Part of the mornings, spent in the quiet little room that had once been the mill-room, or sitting on the rocks outside, were given to Bible-reading.   With the new light of the times upon it, they studied the book of Daniel together, and were impressed more than ever that the time for the return of Christ must be drawing near.   Fellowship together with the precious Book of God strengthened and fitted them for the difficult service so soon to come through the troublous years of war, of which no shadow lay upon them in those peaceful June days.

Another interest occupying the days at Kynance Cove was the formation of an advisory committee of the Pocket Testament League in England.   In a sense, this movement had never been a cut-and-dried organization, nor did Charles Alexander wish to make it so.   He felt that the simple plan of getting people everywhere to promise to carry at least the New Testament in their pockets, and read a chapter from the Bible daily, would reach further, adopted by other Christian institutions *as a method*, than by constituting a new organization.   However, he realized the need of a definite headquarters for the work, in a central office where the methods of the Pocket Testament League, instead of being a side-issue among other interests, should be the chief object of thought and effort, with

THE ALEXANDER
FAMILY
AT
KANSAS, OHIO,
JUNE, 1913

LANDING AT
PLYMOUTH FROM
R.M.S. "OLYMPIC,"
JULY 11, 1913

THE CADBURY
FAMILY AT
"UFFCULME,"
BIRMINGHAM,
ENGLAND,
AUGUST, 1913
(*Inset*--Dr.
Neville Bradley,
absent
in China)

CONFERENCE
OF MINISTERS
FROM
THE HIGHLANDS
AND ISLANDS,
AT
INVERNESS,
SCOTLAND,
APRIL, 1914

GLASGOW
EXECUTIVE
OF THE
CHAPMAN-ALEXANDER
MISSIONS,
DECEMBER, 1913,
AND MARCH, 1914.
Sir Joseph P. Maclay,
chairman, standing by
Charles Alexander

OLD FRIENDS
AT
EDINBURGH,
MARCH, 1914
Standing outside
Sir Alexander Simpson's
home at
52 Queen Street,
in which the
discovery of
chloroform as an
anesthetic was
made by his uncle,
Sir James Simpson.
Dr. Alexander Whyte
in front of
Sir Alexander Simpson
and Dr. Chapman

one purpose, and one only in view—the winning of souls to Christ.   For this reason he had already, at his own expense and on his own initiative, rented a small upper room in Paternoster Row, near St. Paul's Cathedral.   He and his wife had furnished it and dedicated it to God with prayer, hardly knowing what the next step was to be.   They felt that the most important need was the personality and conse-cration of the one who should have charge of the office.   For this matter they looked to God alone for direction, and in a wonderful way were led to Miss E. Wakefield MacGill, of Glasgow, who, since 1914, has been the honorary secretary in charge of the London office.   From the first, Miss MacGill realized the unique possibilities of the League as an instrument for soul-winning.   Her experience as secretary of the Grove Street Institute, in Glasgow, founded by her father, had given her training and experience in business matters and in organizing.   At first it was not clear how the new office could best be used to stimulate the work of the Pocket Testament League.   But Charles Alexander had felt impelled to take this step forward in the dark, and it was not long before the purpose of the Holy Spirit in thus leading him was made abundantly manifest.

A few days at the end of July were spent at Keswick, in the English Lake District, during the Convention.   Here Alexander had the opportunity of meeting a group of Christian men from Cambridge University.   One day he invited them all for an excursion on Lake Derwentwater.   He also conducted them in a delightful hour of song on Friar's Crag, presenting each man with a copy of his hymn-book. An informal talk by Mr. Davis interested them in the Pocket Testament League, and on the return trip in the launch, more hearty singing echoed across the waters of the lake.   How little any of the company realized that within a few weeks, practically every man amongst them would be facing the serious issues of war— and that many of them would be called to give their lives for their country.   The Pocket Testaments and the songs were to be more precious to them than they knew.

After a flying visit to Scotland, the Alexanders settled into their home in Birmingham with happy anticipations of some weeks of peace and enjoyment before beginning the next winter's campaign, which was to be the second stage in an extensive evangelistic movement throughout the British Isles.   Missions were planned for Hull, Dundee, Aberdeen and other places, chiefly upon the east coast of England and Scotland, beginning with a short mission, especially for young men, to be held in the Y.M.C.A. headquarters in London.

News of the assassination of the Crown Prince and Princess of Austria stirred England as well as the Continent, but brought no general presentiment of the thunderbolt of war, which fell so soon afterwards.   At the time, " Tennessee " was overflowing with guests, and the daily delights of Christian fellowship amid the charm and refreshment of Gospel music seemed like a foretaste of heaven. Right at the centre of it all was the radiant presence of Charles Alexander, guiding and directing, entering into the fun and games of the young people, and inspiring home services of song, which in joyful intensity, if not in size, rivalled the great meetings which he had conducted around the world.   The thought of actual warfare seemed to the happy homes of England a dim and far-away thing.

But when the war-clouds broke upon the continent of Europe and a bitter

cry for help rang out from the little martyr-nation of Belgium, a thrilling change
passed over the British Isles, and the waves of it spread to every quarter of the
globe.   Stories of horrors being perpetrated across the narrow strip of water
shocked men like a great explosion out of their ordinary course of life, and drew
them in thousands to the recruiting stations.   As the cry of agony increased and
drew nearer to the homes and the women and children of their own land, volunteers
flocked in greater numbers still.   The spirit of jingoism was entirely lacking.   These
volunteers offered themselves with a resolute quietness, as of men who looked
straight into the eyes of death for the sake of those they love.   Squads of
marching men in training began to parade the streets of the cities, beautiful parks
became military encampments, and on many a stretch of lovely open country
the white tents of training camps seemed to grow like mushrooms in a night.

Within a month or two of the outbreak of war, the vast expanse of Salisbury
Plain began to be covered with canvas cities.   You might motor for hours over
the wind-swept hills without altogether losing sight of the white tents, and every
now and again you would pass sunburned, active men at drill, horses in training,
guns being drawn into position for practice.

At the railway stations near by, trainloads of horses and men were constantly
coming and going.   It was all so real and grim that the awful fact of war was
brought very close to a country which for generations had not known its presence.

These new conditions presented a new call to the servants of Christ all over
the country.   The Y.M.C.A., already at work amongst the Territorials, was immediately permitted by the Government to enter the new military camps and to put
up a big marquee or to use any convenient local hall for their work.   Writing-tables
and stationery were provided for the men's use, and games and musical instruments
for their recreation, also a lunch-counter where they could get tea and coffee and
light refreshments, and also purchase stamps, postcards, and other conveniences.

In the large cities, these lunch-counters were almost entirely staffed by
voluntary helpers, many women of means and position volunteering to give hours
a day to stand and serve the men with tea and coffee.   In the huge camps, away
from the cities, numbers of business men, and men of leisure, gave their time for
weeks or months, as they were able, to help in the same work.   Everywhere the
influence of these Y.M.C.A. centres was wholesome and helpful, and to some extent
acted as a counter-attraction to the canteen and the temptations of liquor.   But
some of the Christian workers found themselves confronted with a great problem
whenever they tried to go further and present the definite question of personal
salvation.   Some with hearts on fire to win the men to Christ became disheartened,
finding that Gospel services of any kind were poorly attended, and efforts at soul-
winning made little headway.

Right into the heart of this difficulty God sent the Pocket Testament League.
But for the new office just established in London, the work would have been difficult
to begin, and could never have developed in the marvellous way it did.

Through the pages of the *Record of Christian Work*, three years later, Charles
Alexander told American readers how the simple plan of getting men pledged
to carry a Testament in their pockets and read a chapter a day took hold of the

A HOLIDAY IN CORNWALL, JUNE, 1914

CLIMBING UP FROM KYNANCE COVE

THE LIZARD HEAD, CORNWALL

A HELPING HAND
(The Lizard Head in the distance)

"STAND
UP
STRAIGHT,
HONEY!"

THE MOORLAND WALK OVER THE CLIFFS
TO THE LIZARD FROM KYNANCE COVE

AT KESWICK, JULY, 1914

A CHAT WITH
GEORGE CLARKE

A MORNING
STROLL WITH
LORD KINNAIRD

EXCHANGING NOTES WITH

DR. W. GRIFFITH THOMAS

A SONG SERVICE WITH CAMBRIDGE STUDENTS ON LAKE DERWENTWATER

British soldiers and sailors, leading hundreds of souls to God :—" In September, 1914, the National Secretary of the British Y.M.C.A. asked me to hold meetings in some of the great tents they had set up in the new encampments. He said the men loved to sing, and it would be a great opportunity. Salisbury Plain was the first place selected for our campaign. I had with me four young men. One of them is an American, who carries a revival flame wherever he goes. His passion for the Word of God, and his ability to secure interest in the Bible, surpasses anything I have ever known. Another is a big, tall Englishman, with a cultivated baritone voice and a heart consecrated to God. A fair-haired Scotchman, with a high tenor voice, melted many a hard heart as he sang the hymn, ' Will the circle be unbroken ? ' These two sang duets most tellingly. Then came our pianist, a Yorkshireman, always on time, anxious as any of us to reach and save these men who were so soon to face death. With constant prayer going up to God, we set out, taking with us four thousand Testaments, six thousand Gospels of John, and five thousand hymn-books, mostly the small ' words ' edition. The Gospels included hymns, both words and music, three stories and a form of decision at the end. On arrival at Salisbury we looked around for an automobile to take us the fifteen miles to the Plain. We were fortunate in finding a Salvation Army man who carried the mails and who knew all the country round. We engaged him for the five days we were to be there, and with our great packages of books we started for the camp, reaching it late in the evening. The tent was packed full of soldiers. Perched high upon a table, I offered the men a copy of the combination khaki-covered-vest-pocket-hymn-book-Gospel-of-John-tract-Decision-card if they would come and get it ! They all rushed for them, and we were soon singing new choruses. Then came some touching solos and duets. When the soldiers' hearts were warm, I asked them to listen a few minutes to ' the man with a Bible.' You should have seen the eager listeners in that dimly-lighted marquee ! The speaker held up a book and said, ' Men, the little book of songs and Gospel of John, given you a while ago, you may keep without any strings to it, but here is a beautiful little Testament which only weighs two-and-a-quarter ounces, waterproof cover, with fifteen coloured pictures of Palestine. The first three pages are taken up with an arrangement of Scripture, so clear that you can find the way to become a Christian. Then come two songs, words and music. Another page tells you what the Pocket Testament League is, and how it was started. Over on the inside of the back cover you will find a statement of decision for Christ. There is a blank space in John iii. 16, where you can sign your name, if you will decide to accept Christ as your Saviour and confess Him before others. Any one of you may have this beautiful Testament if you promise to do two things : read at least one chapter each day, and carry it with you wherever you go, changing it when you change your clothes. On the inside of the front cover you will find a membership pledge. If you will honestly sign it with ink or indelible pencil, the book is yours.' Then he told of policemen, railwaymen and others who had joined the League, and had soon found Christ through the regular reading of God's own Word, and in a few sentences he made the Way of Life clear. Duplicate cards, with the League pledge upon them, were then passed through the crowd, to secure the names of those ready to join. A large number passed in their signed cards that night, receiving Testaments in exchange. Many of the men had also responded to the invitation to accept Christ, given earlier in the evening. These were asked to write the words ' I accept Christ ' on the back of their cards. A Christian Colonel said a few words, and a closing prayer ended our first meeting.

" The Colonel told us that he wanted to introduce us to a business man who had volunteered to give his time to help the Y.M.C.A. in its work in the camps, and said he was one of the best men he had ever known. His name was Henry J. Lane, a big, warm-hearted, open-faced man. I had only spoken a few words with him, when I decided that he would be the very one to stand behind the tea-counter and give the Pocket Testaments to the men who desired to join the League. So we made a public announcement that Mr. Lane would have a supply of Testaments to give away, and any man interested could come and talk with him about it. We left two hundred Testaments with him, and the next afternoon as we came by in our Salvation Army automobile, his face was radiant. He said his Testaments had all been taken, and he had had some wonderful experiences with the men in conversation about their souls. He said the plan of the Pocket Testament League was the most marvellous instrument for winning souls that he had ever known. Mr. Lane was the proprietor of a motor garage in a Cornish town, but had left his business to help the younger men who were answering their country's call. He had been working on Salisbury Plain for two weeks and had almost decided to leave, as he had only been able to lead two men to Christ, and felt he could do more at home. Then he saw the notice of our meeting, and wondered if this might be the beginning of a revival with the men. When he heard the Pocket Testament League explained, he felt convinced it was the very thing to reach them. We left him more Testaments to work with. That night we went to another tent, where we had a longer time. A large number of men not only joined the League, but publicly confessed Christ.

" The next morning our friend Lane came into Salisbury on his motor-cycle for several hundred more Testaments. He said the men were becoming more eager and more interested each hour. Then we began to hear day by day of the wonderful results he was having in leading people to Christ as he served them at the tea-counter. I stood behind to help him one day when men passed by in little groups. While comic songs were being played at the other end of the tent, he would be in solemn conversation with a group of men, talking over the Pocket Testament League, and showing them the Way of Life. Then he asked those who would accept Christ to remove their caps, and one little prayer-meeting after another took place there. It was one of the most beautiful sights I have ever seen. This continued day after day. We kept sending him Testaments and receiving the good news, until at the end of six weeks three thousand men had signed the Pocket Testament League pledge at that tea-counter, and sixteen hundred had said they would openly acknowledge the Lord Jesus Christ.

" One morning a Sergeant came to Mr. Lane and asked him if he had not a Bible, or book of some kind, with which he was working. ' Yes, why ? ' said Mr. Lane. Then the Sergeant told this story. He had two tents of thirty men,

WITH THE MEN ON SALISBURY PLAIN, SEPTEMBER, 1914

STARTING OFF FROM SALISBURY WITH BUNDLES OF TESTAMENTS AND HYMNBOOKS
(Charles Alexander with Albert Brown and William Andrew, soloists; Henry Barraclough, pianist; and
George T. B. Davis, secretary of the Pocket Testament League)

THE TABERNACLE IN ATLANTA, GEORGIA, MARCH, 1915

STANDING BY HIS FAVORITE TEXT

FAREWELL MEETING IN THE GROUNDS OF FIRST PRESBYTERIAN CHURCH AT CHARLOTTE,
NORTH CAROLINA, APRIL, 1915

MEETING IN THE CHAPMAN-ALEXANDER TABERNACLE AT WILMINGTON, NORTH CAROLINA, MAY, 1916

fifteen in each tent, and the discipline had grown worse and worse, until he had almost decided to tear off his stripes. He said it was impossible to keep discipline. The men would come in late, drunk, fighting, using filthy language, and often had to be sent to the guard-room. One night, when the men were going to retire, one of them opened a little book, and, by the light of a candle which he held in his hand, began to read it. Another man across the tent shouted, 'What are you reading, old man?' He replied, 'I am reading a Pocket Testament. I have joined what they call the Pocket Testament League, and I promised to carry this with me wherever I go and to read a chapter a day.' A stillness fell on the tent, and another man called out, 'Don't be stingy. Read us some out of it.' The next night five men pulled out their Testaments and read their chapter one after another, passing the candle round, and the other men were quiet and orderly. Now every one of them in both tents has joined the League, and they are in every night on time, there is no filthy language, they are never drunk, and I believe I have the best discipline on the Plain in my squad. This morning just after roll-call, when they fell out, my men gathered round me. One of them said, 'Sergeant, do we have better discipline than we used to have?' 'We certainly do,' I replied. 'Well, do you know what made it?' I asked him what it was. Every one of them held up a Pocket Testament and said, 'This is what did it. We have all joined the Pocket Testament League, and it has changed our lives, and Sergeant, it's up to you now. Won't you join us?' 'What could I do, sir, but come down here and join the League?' He signed the pledge of membership, and then Mr. Lane turned to the back page, where the decision form is, and began to show him the Way of Life. After making it as clear and definite as he could, Mr. Lane asked the Sergeant if he would decide that very day for Christ. He said, 'Certainly, I expected to go the whole way to-day,' and he did.''

At the end of the first four days of Alexander's work on the Plain, two thousand of the men in training had become members of the Pocket Testament League, and four hundred had accepted Christ. The last meeting of the last day promised to be the most difficult of all. Through the previous days the work had been among Territorials and Kitchener's Army, but the final meeting was among the regular cavalry troops, men who had seen years of service all over the world. Everything seemed unfavourable at the beginning. The two hundred or more men present were seated at writing-tables. Alexander swung himself up on the counter to lead them in song, but for the first ten minutes most of the soldiers appeared critical and indifferent. Many kept on writing letters, but gradually, as the meeting progressed, joking ceased, writing stopped, and the men began to drink in the message in hymn and story. God's Spirit was working mightily. Sacred song under a master-hand had triumphed. While the Pocket Testament League was being presented and the Gospel message given, the men listened with rapt attention. When the appeal for decision was made, a thrilling scene followed. Right before their comrades, a large number of regulars boldly rang out the words, "I accept Christ as my Saviour, my Lord, and my King."

Once the flame was lighted, other workers kept it burning, and, two months later, news reached the Pocket Testament League office in London that in six camps alone, nine thousand seven hundred and eight soldiers had joined the League, and over two thousand six hundred men had declared their acceptance of Christ.

On September 29th, Dr. and Mrs. Chapman arrived in London from America to begin the mission for young men in the Y.M.C.A. that had been planned previously. The new circumstances that had arisen, and the strange conditions imposed by the war, had caused the cancellation of the programme for future Chapman-Alexander missions in Scotland, but Mr. J. J. Virgo, who was at this time installed at the head of the Y.M.C.A. work in London, and had arranged the London meetings, insisted that these should not be cancelled, and had cabled Dr. Chapman, earnestly pleading with him to come as arranged.

From September 29th to October 11th, Dr. Chapman and Charles Alexander carried on a wonderful series of meetings with men of all ages in the Y.M.C.A. Headquarters at Tottenham Court Road. During the noon-hour, remarkable services were held day after day in the historic Guildhall, in the heart of the City. It was the first time this building had ever been used for Gospel services of any kind, and it was an impressive sight to see the building packed with men representing every possible business and profession, the gallery at the back, between the gigantic figures of Gog and Magog, being filled with women. The beautiful old hall echoed with the unaccustomed sound of Gospel hymns, sung with tremendous enthusiasm ; and then, amidst a tense silence, the voice of Dr. Chapman pleaded with men to consider the claims of Christ upon their lives. The following two weeks of October were given to a series of meetings at the Metropolitan Tabernacle, where Dr. A. C. Dixon was the pastor. For a few more weeks the evangelists went hither and thither to various training centres and camps in and around London. Some fruitful services were held with the naval men in training at the Crystal Palace. Everywhere the Pocket Testament League laid hold, and the Word of God came into prominence in the everyday life of men and women, who were not ashamed to be seen reading it in public. Finding the doors closed for their regular work in Great Britain, and having many urgent calls for work in their own land, Dr. Chapman and Charles Alexander felt that it must be the leading of God to step into the opportunity that was offered, although they hoped that the British programme might only be postponed for a while. Few realized, even then, that it would be possible for so destructive a war to continue long. Before leaving England, Charles Alexander laid the need for responsible supervision of the Pocket Testament League before his old friend, Dr. J. Louis Fenn, of Liverpool, asking him to assist Miss MacGill in every possible way during his absence. Dr. Fenn removed from Liverpool, and accepted the call to become the rector of a Reformed Episcopal Church in London, and here he was better able to help the work of the Pocket Testament League office in Paternoster Row. Later, as the work increased, Dr. Fenn became Field Secretary of the League, having an office adjoining that of Miss MacGill, and gave more and more of his time to the work.

On December 16th, with many earnest prayers for the work he was leaving, as well as for that to which he was going, Charles Alexander sailed for New York with his wife, on board the *Lusitania*. With them went Albert Brown and Henry Barraclough, the singer and pianist.

CHAPTER TWENTY-THREE

American Campaigns with Dr. Chapman

1915 and 1916

ONE of the most difficult lessons which the Heavenly Father often has to teach His children, is to walk by faith and not by sight. Human nature desires to see ahead and to know the future, but the more closely a soul comes into touch with God through Christ, the more he is satisfied to leave the future with Him.

The next few years were, for Charles Alexander and his wife, a time of deep study in the school of trust. One plan after another was broken and changed, and yet whenever God closed a door of opportunity, another was unexpectedly opened. Year by year, Alexander learned, even more than in the past, to have no personal ambition apart from the will of God. He learned to love God's will more completely, and as his marvellous personality continued to develop, and his influence over men increased, his spirit became more and more like that of a little child, in trustfulness and humility.

For two years the Chapman-Alexander campaigns were continued in various cities of the United States, the first of this period beginning in Lima, Ohio, on January 5th, 1915. During this campaign a touching incident occurred, that was used of God to melt many hardened hearts. At one of the first meetings, Alexander was teaching the chorus written by Mr. Barraclough :

> Shine, shine, just where you are,
> Shine, shine, just where you are ;
> Send forth the light,
> Into the night !
> Shine for the Lord, where you are.

Seeing a number of bright-faced boys in the meeting, he called them up to the platform. The faces of the people lighted up with a new interest as the little fellows, standing in a row, rang out the chorus. Alexander's quick ear caught the sweet tones of a boy's voice at the end of the line. Calling him up beside him on the raised dais, and putting his arm round the little shoulders to give confidence, Alexander asked the boy to sing it alone. There was something so stirring in the tones of the clear young voice, that the audience broke into spontaneous applause. Hushing it quickly, Alexander asked the boy to sing the chorus again and led in a word of prayer for him. About a week later, news came that the little lad had met with a serious accident, being thrown from his bicycle and rendered unconscious by the fall. Finding that the family were not in affluent circumstances,

Dr. Chapman and Charles Alexander sent for the best nurse that could be obtained, and they and their wives visited the home. This boy of ten was the only child of his parents, and the only grandchild on both sides of the family, the hopes of which were wrapped up in his little life. But in spite of all that was done, the Good Shepherd, in His wise and loving purpose, bore the little lamb safely into the heavenly fold, giving grace to the bereaved parents to trust Him in their sorrow. Dr. Chapman and Charles Alexander conducted the funeral service. Less than two weeks from the day when the boy had stood, well and strong, singing the chorus of " Shine," the little form lay quietly upon the same platform in its simple casket, surrounded by flowers, in the centre of which was a large white star with the word " Shine " in gold letters across it, the gift of the Chapman-Alexander party. There was a tender pathos in the meeting that none who were present could ever forget. Alexander's strong voice trembled with emotion as he led the people in song. After Dr. Chapman's earnest appeal, many decisions were made for Christ. " My little shining star," breathed the mother, as she looked upon the smiling, upturned face for the last time, until the bright eyes should greet her own again in the dawn of " the first resurrection."

Several short conferences followed the Lima campaign, and during these weeks Alexander was able to see much of his beloved mother, who was now settled with the rest of the family in Northern Ohio. On February 9th, the Chapman-Alexander party gathered their forces in Atlanta, Georgia, to begin the first of a series of great campaigns in the South. A large Tabernacle had been erected on Peachtree Street between the Governor's mansion and the University Club. Atlanta is proverbially a difficult city to move to enthusiasm. Life in that southern climate is easy and comfortable, and even poverty is mitigated by the kindliness of nature. Time and leisure seem more abundant than in the bustling cities of the North, and few matters seem of sufficient importance to be unduly disturbing. Sin does not wear a glaring garb, but subtly veils itself under a cloak of indolence and indifference. Among the Christian people there is a greater reverence for the Bible than in the northern cities, and a fairly general habit of formal churchgoing. But the easy conditions that hide from view sharp contrasts of sin and holiness, are apt, even among Christians, to encourage a lukewarm faith and a blindness to the spiritual danger of the unsaved, that checks soul-winning ardour.

In such a soil the weeds of false religion grow apace, and it was no surprise to find that deceptive doctrines like those of Christian Science and Theosophy had taken deep root in Atlanta. Only the power of God Himself could shake the lethargic complacency induced, and make it tremble in repentance before Him. Many of the ministers in Atlanta had been longing for a breath of God's power in their midst, and welcomed the coming of the Chapman-Alexander party as an opportunity of uniting under the leadership which God had so richly blessed in other places. In addition to the regular meetings in the Tabernacle, countless morning and afternoon services were held in homes, in churches, in club buildings, and wherever a Gospel invitation could be given. Much emphasis was laid upon the glad news of the Resurrection, and the truth was marvellously used of God to counteract the baleful influence of Christian Science. Towards the middle of the meetings there came a time of great discouragement, but faith triumphed. The messages in sermon and song won their way, and two months later, news reached the evangelists that the accessions to the churches had increased to four thousand six hundred and twelve, and that over five thousand members had been gained for the Pocket Testament League.

The strain of the work told a good deal on the health of Dr. Chapman, and Alexander, with his usual quick sympathy, laid himself out to cheer and encourage his colleague as much as possible. Saturdays were the rest-days of the campaign. On some of the Saturday mornings, the two evangelists with their wives, would set out for a motor drive to a primitive country boarding-house some miles from Atlanta, and here they would rusticate for the day. The coloured waiter, Mirl Nuckles, provided plenty of amusement, and was much flattered by being constantly photographed. Alexander renewed his boyhood among the Southern surroundings, and delighted in showing his wife the cotton-fields, and in talking with the picca-ninnies. One day, when they had driven out to see an old-fashioned cotton-gin, he noticed a coloured man laboriously pushing a plough, drawn by an old mule. Flinging off his coat he called out, " I'd like to see whether I can still plough a straight furrow." A moment later, the astonished darkey felt the plough-handles taken from him, and saw his old mule, with a new briskness in his movements, urged up the furrow by a gentleman who had just alighted from an automobile. Away up the field went Alexander till he had laid off his furrow, straight as a dart, to the far end. Then, dexterously turning, he urged the old mule back again in double-quick time. Perspiring and breathless, but gaily triumphant amidst the applause of his friends in the motor, he added to the surprise and delight of the coloured ploughman by the gift of half-a-dollar and a little red-bound copy of St. John's Gospel.

The Chapman-Alexander party next made their way to Charlotte, North Carolina, where another inspiring campaign was carried on from April 3rd to May 15th. Here again a special Tabernacle was erected, and the meetings went with a rush of enthusiasm, especially on the part of the younger people. The whole city seemed to be singing Gospel songs. One day, a Charlotte conductor on an in-coming train, announced : " All out for Charlotte ! Don't forget your umbrellas or your Pocket Testaments, and shine just where you are ! " Alexander formed the boys and girls into a " Sunbeam choir," who did yeoman service, especially with the short choruses. A corner section of the great Tabernacle was reserved for the coloured people, and Alexander would often get them to rise and give a few verses of their inimitable music. " I want you to teach these white people how to sing Gospel songs," he would say to them. One memorable night was given up to a mass service of the coloured population, white folks being allowed in the reserved section only. Both Dr. Chapman and Charles Alexander abandoned themselves to the occasion. When song after song had been sung, and many had come forward, amid the rumble and thunder of heartfelt ejaculations, to yield themselves to God, Alexander called up an old coloured Bishop to start them off singing some of their old-time melodies. Who, that heard it, could ever forget the intensity of the fervour, and the swing of the rhythm, as with swaying bodies, punctuated by ejaculations that somehow worked themselves into the rhythm of the music, without marring it, they sang :—

> Oh ! I caint stay away,
>   I caint stay away,
> I gotta go to Heb'n to see my Jesus,
>   Caint stay away ! "

Among the many remarkable conversions in Charlotte, none was more striking than that of Vance Fite. This man owned a grocery store, which was the headquarters for the rough men and boys of the town ; he was, moreover, a far-famed professional " chicken-fighter," owning some magnificent game-roosters. One night he came up to the platform when the meeting was over, greatly moved, and begged Alexander to pray for him and his three brothers. Alexander called a band of workers together, and all prayed earnestly. Vance Fite made no decision then, but the next night he asked one of the ushers to reserve a whole row of seats at the front for himself and his family ! As soon as the invitation to accept Christ was given, he and his mother, and his three brothers, with other members of the family, came forward and occupied the seats reserved for them. As the good old lady looked round at her sons, she gave a shout of joy that attracted the attention of all the people in the Tabernacle. The following evening Dr. Chapman called on Mr. Fite for a testimony, and the people were thrilled as he told his story. Sixteen years earlier, beside their father's death-bed, his children had promised to meet him in Heaven, and to live happily together. But the promise had not been kept, and the family had been split up, some of the brothers not speaking to each other for years. Gambling on game-roosters had drawn Vance Fite into bad company, in spite of the influence of his Christian wife. He was, in fact, on his way to a chicken-fight when he had slipped into the Tabernacle, and Dr. Chapman's first sentence, " Prepare to meet thy God," shot him through the heart.

As soon as the news of his conversion became known, his telephone bell rang all day with the congratulations of his friends. In giving his testimony he said, " I've not had so much attention paid to me since the day I was married. I've just *busted* into society ! " At the close of his testimony, many people came forward to greet him, at Alexander's invitation. One kindly, but rather formal, minister shook him warmly by the hand, saying ceremoniously, " I hope the Lord will bless you richly, my dear brother." " He's done *done* it, sir ! " replied Vance Fite with a beaming smile. As he himself said, Vance Fite lost half his vocabulary when he was converted, but he acquired a new one, and began giving his testimony everywhere. He set out at once to bring to Christ the men and boys whom he had helped to ruin—and, with a group of other men, went into all parts of Mecklenburg County, on three nights each week and all day Sunday, testifying for Christ in the small country towns and villages. At Davidson College, some twenty miles from Charlotte, where a series of remarkable meetings were held several months later, Alexander sent for Vance Fite, who spoke to the students, making a profound impression. The change in him, the happiness of his home, and the convincing power of his testimony, were nothing short of a miracle to the people of Charlotte.

During the meetings in Charlotte, Alexander's secretary, W. W. Rock, decided to study for the ministry, and left in the middle of the campaign to pay a visit first to his Australian home. A good-bye letter from his beloved " chief " was slipped into his hand as he was leaving, and shows Alexander's spiritual concern for those who worked with him : " It is very hard to say good-bye to you after these long years of working side by side, but it is the greatest joy to know that you are closer to God than when we began. I hope the memories will be sweet, and, above all, helpful. Our talks and confidences in difficult places have been more interesting as you grew in wisdom and discretion and balance. Now that you have begun to have a genuine passion for the souls of lost men and women, I can let you go with an easier feeling than I could if our prayers for this had not been answered before we parted. ' HE THAT WINNETH SOULS IS WISE ' : (Prov. xi. 30). That is quoted from the highest and final authority. God bless you, my boy. I love you fondly, and shall often bear you up to God in my prayers."

In his reply, Mr. Rock wrote :—" I have just read your letter, and the water in my eyes and the lump in my throat are the result of it. There is no one like you in all this world. The first real live impression I had of you, you were doing some personal work, and the work was with me. You know the result of it. The last impression I got of you in a meeting, you were doing personal work, and again —although quite unknown to yourself—the personal work was with me. Just before I left the meeting to-night, as I was passing through the front rows, I heard some one say, ' Go the whole way ! Why don't you go the whole way ? ' The voice was yours, and immediately two people stood up and went the whole way. It flashed on me that that was a message for me also, and I want to tell you that I am now ' going the whole way ' with God's help. You came into my life and changed the whole course of it. I know that the memory of you will keep me winning souls."

Plans had been practically made for Alexander and his wife to return to England in June, and passage had been tentatively reserved on board the *Lusitania*. But on May 7th, a week before the Charlotte meetings closed, the country was electrified by the news that the dastardly threat of the Germans had been actually carried out, in defiance of the whole world's outraged feelings. The *Lusitania*, with her freight of human lives, including numbers of defenceless women and children and unarmed men, had been deliberately sunk by submarines. This awful deed and the unsettlement of everything, caused a hesitation in the plan of going back to England for the summer, during which Alexander had expected to find opportunities of bringing cheer and spiritual help to the men in the British training camps.

Hearing that there was a possibility of his remaining in the United States, leaders of the various Summer Bible Conferences, which he had been unable to attend since 1908, sent him urgent invitations to take part in them. Assured that this must be God's leading, Alexander decided to stay and give the best that was in him to these calls from his own land, and the summer months were devoted to Bible Conferences and to meetings in Ohio, and in Chicago, New York and Philadelphia, also to the preparation of a new hymn-book. In October he joined Dr. Chapman again for a five weeks' campaign in Asheville, North Carolina, and this completed the work of the Chapman-Alexander party in the South for a while. Through December, 1915, they were in Brattleboro, Vermont, and after a short break for Christmas, in New York, the party met at Springfield, Illinois, for a campaign which lasted until February 12th, 1916.

A striking incident that occurred in Springfield was the conversion of Dr. J. A. Wheeler, Sheriff of Sangamon County, which resulted in a marvellous revival among the inmates of the county jail. The bold and fearless stand taken by Dr. Wheeler in the meetings, when he publicly confessed Christ as his Saviour, stirred the whole city and made a deep impression. Dr. Chapman and Charles Alexander were invited to come and speak to the prisoners, of whom there were a large number. So many men were converted that the whole atmosphere of the jail was changed. Several nights a week, headed by the Sheriff himself, the whole company of prisoners, each accompanied by some man responsible for his security, but without handcuffs or other mechanical safeguards, filed into seats reserved for them in the Tabernacle. Among the number who were converted were seven convicts, who a few days after the close of the campaign, had to go to the State Penitentiary to work out their sentences. No effort was made by the men themselves, or by others, to interfere with the course of the law, but the revival was such a true work of the Holy Spirit, that these men determined to shine for Christ in the Penitentiary. As a help in making their position unhesitatingly clear as Christians, they expressed a desire to be baptized, if permission might be granted. Without guards of any kind, except the company of the Sheriff, these seven long-sentence men came to a Baptist church in the city, where in the presence of Dr. and Mrs. Chapman, Mr. and Mrs. Alexander, and a small company of other friends, who were permitted to know of and to attend the service, they were publicly baptized and received into the Church. As one of the men was about to enter the baptistery, he was seen to draw back, after whispering something to the minister who was waiting to baptize him. He had been convicted under an assumed name, and he was anxious that the name which was to appear on the church roll should be his true one, desiring that the last piece of deception should be cleared away before his baptism.

The Rev. Donald C. MacLeod, D.D., Chairman of the Springfield, Ill., Committee, said in his report of the campaign : " The Chapman-Alexander meetings were hindered by every possible adverse condition of temperature and health. They opened in a blizzard, with a temperature below zero that lasted most of the time. An epidemic of influenza almost caused the cancelling of the meetings, and an outbreak of smallpox kept some of the schools closed at the opening of the campaign. In spite of these conditions the results have been wonderful. Over thirteen hundred were received into the membership of the twenty churches engaged in the campaign, and the ministers and Christian workers feel that the gain will be more than usually permanent. Instead of being something abnormal and sensational, creating a temporary enthusiasm which could not afterwards be sustained by the churches, this campaign, while intense and evangelical in spirit, was sane and conservative in its methods ; aiming to bring the best into modern church life, and enabling the churches to move forward upon a higher plane of efficiency. The financial phase, which is sometimes an unpleasant feature of professional evangelism, was conducted by Dr. Chapman and Mr. Alexander with such utter disregard for self-interest and in such a fine Christian spirit, as not only to disarm criticism, but also to win for them the enduring esteem and praise of all associated with the work. The Chapman-Alexander party have left many delightful memories, and not a single unpleasant one, in Springfield."

On February 19th, a five weeks' campaign was due to begin in Washington, Pa.—" little Washington," as it is called, to distinguish it from its important namesake in the District of Columbia. Early that Saturday morning, Alexander and his wife arrived in Pittsburg, intending to spend the day in the city before going out to Washington in time for the preliminary meetings in the evening. As they were on their way from the station to the hotel where they intended to breakfast, the steering-gear of their taxi suddenly broke, and it dashed into an iron post on the edge of the sidewalk. Alexander, who was thrown violently forward against the glass screen, was severely cut about the head by the broken glass, an artery being severed. One of the best surgeons in Pittsburg happened to live in the hotel to which they were going, and under his wife's tender nursing, and the skilful care of Dr. Baldwin, Alexander's precious life was spared, in spite of severe septic trouble which caused a time of grave anxiety. God had further work for His servant to do, and at the end of two weeks the wound began to heal. On Sunday, March 5th, somewhat pale, and with a large plaster patch across the top of his head, Charles Alexander was in his place in the Washington Tabernacle at the three o'clock service for men, and at the general meeting in the evening. The welcome he received was a real ovation. There were many in Washington who remembered the wonderful meetings twenty-three years earlier, when, as a young man of twenty-five, Alexander had led the singing for Dr. Smiley's meetings, winning all hearts by his fire, consecration, and lovable personality.

Once again the Chapman-Alexander party turned southwards for a campaign in Wilmington, North Carolina, through April and May. Here, as in each of the other cities, the Pocket Testament League played a great part in the work. Among various groups of people influenced, were the firemen of the city. Practically all of them became members of the League, and many of their waiting hours were spent with the Word of God. With his helpers, Alexander held some remarkable meetings with the High-School boys, who specially fell in love with Mr. Barraclough's song, " Ivory Palaces," and also took up the Pocket Testament League with enthusiasm. The two men at the head of the Wilmington Committee were Mr. James Sprunt, and his brother, cotton merchants, and enthusiastic Christian leaders. An interesting event occurred on one of the rest-days, when Mr. James Sprunt took the members of the party down the river in his launch to spend the day on his magnificent plantation, Water Orton. Upon it are the ruins of an old English church, built of bricks which had been carried across the Atlantic in ships' bottoms. Some of the party were taken in canoes through the cypress swamps, and paddled their way between the smooth grey trunks which grew straight up out of the water, and the festoons of moss which drooped from the branches. In the weird, shadowy quietude, crocodiles were occasionally seen gliding under the clear, brown water, while a clapping of hands startled great flocks of gay-plumaged cranes from their nests in the high trees, to whirl in noisy circles before settling down again. But the event of the day was the dedication of a chapel which Mr. Sprunt had built, in memory of his wife, for the coloured people on the plantation. The opening had been deferred until Dr. Chapman and Charles Alexander could come, and the service in the little chapel, crowded with dusky faces, old and young, was full of pathos and fervour.

Keene, New Hampshire, was the centre of activity for the Chapman-Alexander party from May 20th until June 20th, 1916. Rev. W. O. Conrad, brother of Alexander's friend in Boston, was chairman of the executive committee in Keene. A sentence or two from his report reads : " Dr. Chapman and Mr. Alexander have conducted a most wonderful work in Keene. It has made Christ more real to us, the Bible the greatest book, the Christian life the one life worth while. Our churches are aroused, our ministers encouraged, and our community stirred. The finances are no burden, the freewill offering for the party is that, and nothing more. Dr. Chapman and Mr. Alexander eliminate all possibility of the charge of commercialism from their work. The presentation of the Gospel by these men is wholesome, vigorous, persuasive, sane and dignified, and the results of the meetings are sure to be lasting." Four years later, Rev. W. O. Conrad wrote to Mrs. Alexander : " You will never know here on earth how much good the entire Chapman-Alexander company did to the Christian forces of Keene. It was refreshing to hear men of such unshakable faith, reinforced as they were by their wives. Your husband was one of those rare men who had a genius for friendship, and the faculty of attaching to him those who came under the spell of his personality. I never knew a man to give all his powers in a more completely devoted way to the service of Jesus Christ."

Up to this time, as in the early days of the Pocket Testament League in England, there had been no distinctive and independent headquarters for the work in the United States. Since the launching of the League in Philadelphia in 1908, the Presbyterian Board of Publication had generously given assistance by arranging for large orders of Testaments, and by providing space in their own offices as temporary headquarters, under the enthusiastic supervision of Mr. Allan Sutherland. Through the eight years, the League had spread into many parts of the United States, largely as a result of the Chapman-Alexander campaigns and the work of Mr. George T. B. Davis, and local secretaries had taken up the work in the churches and communities of many cities.

Early in the summer of 1916, the same irresistible impulse that had led Charles Alexander, in bare faith, to open an office for the Pocket Testament League in London, impelled him to rent a large room in the Presbyterian Building on Fifth Avenue in New York City. As yet there was no clear indication as to the work that should be done through it, but, alone in the empty room, he knelt in prayer and dedicated it to God, asking for guidance. His first step was to enlist, as a member of the League, the superintendent of the building from whom the room was rented, presenting him with a beautiful little Pocket Testament. By degrees the room was furnished and Alexander began to look for God's provision in the matter of a secretary. By ways as strange as a fairy tale, he was brought into touch with the one whom God had been preparing for the work in His own way.

Mrs. Besse D. McAnlis, who had just graduated from the Bible Institute of Los Angeles, California, of which Dr. R. A. Torrey was Dean, was introduced to Alexander by a mutual friend. After the death of her young husband, Mrs. McAnlis, with God-given courage and sunny trust, had devoted her life to aggressive Christian service. She became immediately enthused with the Pocket Testament League, as soon as she saw the efficacy of its method in leading souls to Christ. After a few days of prayer and serious consideration, she was appointed secretary. The office was again dedicated with prayer, and now the question arose as to how the work was to begin. "You are a stranger in New York, Mrs. McAnlis, but the Lord will open the way for you and we shall be praying," said Alexander. "I want you to begin right here in this building. There are dozens of offices with people coming and going, representing all kinds of religious work. Make it your aim to see how many of them you can get to carry a Testament and read a chapter a day. Have a daily prayer-meeting to which any of them may come. Let our office be known as a place where anyone can come to be shown the Way of Life, or to find sympathy and some one who will pray with them, and where anybody that wants to, can learn to win others to Christ." Within a few weeks, at least one hundred people in the building had been enrolled as League members, including six or eight elevator boys and other employees.

Some meetings of the New York Tent Evangel, which Dr. McPherson had invited Alexander to conduct, gave an unexpected opportunity for presenting the Pocket Testament League, and for introducing Mrs. McAnlis to representatives of many of the city churches. Invitations began to pour into the office, asking Mrs. McAnlis to present the League and its methods in various parts of New York City. In a very short time an office assistant was needed, but the right one was difficult to find. No one but a sincere Christian, and one who was not addicted to worldly amusements and ways of living, could uphold the spiritual atmosphere of the office. One day a young woman came in to purchase some Testaments, and while she was looking over the various styles and bindings, the office telephone bell rang. Having heard part of the conversation that ensued, she said, "Will you excuse me asking whether you are needing an office assistant?" Mrs. McAnlis replied in the affirmative. The young woman was a graduate of the Northfield Seminary and had recently resigned from a good position in a commercial office on account of its irreligious atmosphere. Drawing a worn little Testament from her pocket, she told how she had joined the League in February, 1911, during the Chapman-Alexander campaign in Brooklyn, and spoke of the disappointment of her wish to become a foreign missionary. Before leaving the office that morning Miss Jennie A. Johnson had been engaged as assistant.

Only a few days of this busy summer of 1916 did Charles Alexander manage to put aside for complete rest, and these he and his wife spent on a delightful motor trip, through the most beautiful part of the State of New York, to Fremont, Ohio, for a short visit to the family home.

Leaving New York City on Thursday, September 21st, they planned to stay over Sunday somewhere en route. Just before reaching Olean, N.Y., on the Saturday morning, the car broke down, and they were obliged to make this their stopping-

place. Next morning they attended a service in one of the churches. A very
earnest plea was made by the minister, in his sermon, for a genuine spiritual revival.
With much pathos he spoke of the evanescence of many revivals because they
were not founded upon the Word of God. Then he told of his prayers and efforts
through the past six years to get his congregation interested in the Bible, and of
his disappointment in the little he had been able to accomplish. Alexander's
sympathy was too deeply stirred, to leave without offering help. He was sitting
at the back of the church, and had been picturing what might be accomplished
through the Pocket Testament League. As the Benediction was about to be pronounced, he rose and asked permission to say a word. Surprised, and somewhat
hesitating, the minister gave consent. In a few simple, direct words, Alexander
told of the breakdown of his automobile, adding that the Lord must have planned
it all, as he had a message of hope to bring, along the very line of Dr. Gates' plea.
Then he told briefly of the Pocket Testament League, saying that he and his wife
would be delighted to send the gift of a Testament to anyone, present in the congregation that morning, who would agree to carry the Book in their pockets and
read a chapter of the Bible every day. To the astonishment of the minister and
of Alexander himself, people began rising all over the church. When the names
and addresses were taken on slips of paper, it was found that more than a hundred
desired to join the League. Meanwhile Dr. Gates had been puzzling over something
familiar in the speaker's face. " May I ask if your name is Alexander ? " he said,
as the stranger took his seat. Alexander nodded assent. " I thought I knew his
face," said Dr. Gates, turning to the congregation. " This is Charles Alexander,
the Gospel singer, of whom many of you have heard. If he will consent to take
our evening service, how many of you will come, and seek to bring others with
you ? " A forest of hands went up, and at night the big church was crowded to
suffocation. Again Alexander presented the Pocket Testament League, also
teaching the choruses of some new hymns. After his wife, at his request, had
told the story of her conversion when a child of twelve, he called for decisions.
Several came forward to accept Christ as their Saviour, and others to surrender
their lives for service. The revival for which Dr. Gates had prayed and worked
so earnestly, came to his church. In a short time more than four hundred had
joined the Pocket Testament League, and a new interest in the Bible and in the
winning of souls was manifested.

On September 30th, the autumn campaigns of the Chapman-Alexander party
opened in Galesburg, Illinois. Although the work had many blessed results
in the salvation of souls, it was an uphill fight, chiefly on account of the strong
Universalist influence that had crept in unawares, through a member of the
committee. During the fifth week of the meetings, Dr. Chapman was taken
seriously ill, recovering sufficiently to preach at the final service, in spite of the
doctor's warning. His journey to New York was managed safely, but his physician
there discovered the need of an immediate critical operation, which took place
on November 9th.

CHAPTER TWENTY-FOUR

War Work in American Camps

1917 to 1918

A CHAPMAN-ALEXANDER campaign had been planned for December, 1916, in Charleston, West Virginia, but this and several later campaigns were of necessity postponed on account of Dr. Chapman's illness. In the meantime, urgent calls had been coming from the British National Council of the Young Men's Christian Association, who were planning an extensive series of evangelistic campaigns for Great Britain and France, and who begged Dr. Chapman and Charles Alexander to return to England and give their assistance. Dr. A. C. Dixon, then pastor of Spurgeon's Tabernacle, had also written, saying: "I most earnestly hope that you and Alexander will accept the invitation to come over for a campaign among the soldiers. It is such an opportunity to save men as may never occur again. The churches in America ought to release you for this." Dr. Chapman had replied, saying that engagements made for the winter season of 1916–17 were too definite to be cancelled, but hoped that he and Mr. Alexander might be able to come to England later. Now, through his sudden illness, work on either side of the Atlantic was made impossible for him, and Alexander felt that he must not desert his colleague at such a critical time. The burdens which fell upon Alexander's shoulders, with a large party to be responsible for, were extremely heavy, but during Dr. Chapman's slow recovery, he was led into new work. Retaining his three special helpers, he visited churches, schools, colleges, factories, and homes, with the message of Gospel song and the Pocket Testament League. Invitations poured in so fast that he could hardly keep up with them. First in New York City and its environs, then for a week in Atlantic City, where Dr. Chapman was enjoying a gradual convalescence under the benefit of the invigorating ocean breezes, and afterwards in Philadelphia, Alexander and his party were hard at work, carrying sunshine and new spiritual energy everywhere, and leading many souls to Christ. A sudden dangerous illness of Mrs. Alexander's sister, Mrs. Bradley, who, with her five children, was living at the time in Victoria, British Columbia, broke into this work, and called Alexander and his wife across the Continent. But Dr. Bradley, on furlough from China, was able to postpone his return, the dangerous crisis passed, and the Alexanders hurried back to Philadelphia.

In the meantime great changes were at work. The terrible war in Europe had been growing more and more savage and destructive, and it became clear that, before long, the United States must be drawn into it. The sympathies of the whole country had been deeply stirred by the world-struggle, and help of all kinds had been poured out for the war-sufferers in Europe. Not only much money had been given, but also the service of many devoted men and women. The life of the nation was not, however, deeply affected by the war until neutrality was laid aside.

Almost the first engagement undertaken by Alexander, after returning from the West, was at State College, Pennsylvania. This great college, from which the little town and the railway station take their name, is a centre for training in scientific agriculture, among other branches of study. On April 6th, 1917, the United States had at last, officially, as well as with unofficial sympathy, thrown in her lot, as a nation, with that of the Allies in the great World War. As in other lands, university life was immediately affected, although the colleges were not broken up and emptied of students to the same extent as in England. Everywhere military uniforms began to be seen, and every college campus echoed to the tramp of marching feet. On his first visit to State College a month or two earlier, Alexander had won the hearts of the men, and it was with general delight that he was welcomed back for an intensive campaign of three-and-a-half days. He was accompanied not only by his wife, Mr. Brown, and Mr. Barraclough, and Mr. Mills, but also by Mrs. McAnlis, secretary of the Pocket Testament League in New York. From morning till night each one of the party was hard at work. Mr. W. R. Moody, director of the Northfield Schools, was also at State College for two of the days to address the students. Whole Fraternity houses joined the League, and the entire college was stirred. Mr. Horner, secretary of the College Y.M.C.A., continued the work with enthusiasm after the Alexander party had left, and by the end of the term in June, twelve hundred and forty-four men and women students of State College were enrolled as members of the Pocket Testament League. Not many weeks passed by before a number of these students were on their way to France, to test, as their fellow-soldiers from Great Britain and elsewhere had done, the value of God's Word, and the comfort of His promises, in times of crisis.

From the beginning, the churches of America realized that they had a heavy responsibility towards the men who were being drawn into the maelstrom. A month after America had declared herself to be in a state of war with Germany, the great Presbyterian Church of the United States met in General Assembly at Dallas, Texas. It was an indication of the sense of need in the direction of evangelism, as well as a tribute to the work accomplished through Dr. Chapman's leadership, that he was appointed Moderator for the ensuing twelve months. Hearing that there was some probability of the choice falling upon him, and insisting that he was sufficiently recovered from his operation to take up active work again, Dr. Chapman had talked the matter over with his colleague beforehand. Alexander fully agreed that in the changed conditions that prevailed, Dr. Chapman should accept the call if it came, even though it would necessarily mean the putting aside of their usual work together.

The long years of travelling and mutual association had drawn the inner circle of the Chapman-Alexander party into a real family relationship. Many a joke and allusion was shared between them, that conjured up some past adventure or experience, or some story known to them all, largely drawn from Alexander's inexhaustible store. Dr. Chapman's announcement of his election as Moderator was characteristic. Alexander had a Southern anecdote of a little country town where the post of bailiff was an honour greatly sought after by the inhabitants. One day the newly-elected bailiff went home to his wife and family in triumph, to tell them the news. "An' now," he said pompously, "ef the jedge wants anything, he'll jest turn to me an' say: ' Bailiff, bring in the prisoner,' or ' Bailiff, get me a glass of water,' and there ain't nobody has the right to do it but me.' " Crowding round him with awe-struck faces, one of the children piped up: "Is we all bailiffs now, Paw?" "No," cut in the mother, "shet yo' mouth! They ain't nobody bailiffs 'ceptin' me an' yo' Paw." Dr. Chapman's telegram to Alexander from Dallas read simply: "We are all bailiffs now!"

At this time the National Service Commission, appointed by the Presbyterian General Assembly, extended an urgent invitation to Charles Alexander to take up special work for a year in the camps and navy yards in various parts of the United States. With the Pocket Testament League and his marvellous gift of song, he went forth to meet the new opportunity. Occasionally he and Dr. Chapman met for a service together. The work that Dr. Chapman accomplished, necessitating so much strenuous travel, was little short of a miracle to those who knew the condition of his health. In spite of temporary breakdowns, he seemed so full of physical energy and spiritual zeal, that few guessed what his work was costing him.

Early in 1917, Alexander did some splendid work in the Philadelphia and Brooklyn Navy Yards and in the officers' training camp at Plattsburg, N.Y. This was done in connexion with the War Work Council of the Young Men's Christian Association. One of the earliest of these meetings, in the Philadelphia Navy Yard, took place in the dining-saloon of the U.S.S. *De Kalb*. The sailors sang lustily, and listened hungrily as the Way of Life was presented in song and address. At the close, many joined the Pocket Testament League, and a number signified their willingness to accept Christ. The *De Kalb* was a converted German cruiser and raider, formerly the *Prinz Eitel Friederich*. As the meeting proceeded, it was impossible not to conjure up the scenes which that dining-saloon must have recently witnessed, crowded as it had often been with companies of passengers and crews taken from raided ships of the Allies. On May 28th, the last night of this series of meetings, a general service was held in the Naval Y.M.C.A. Hall. It was crowded with marines, naval reserves and sailors. A deep sense of the Holy Spirit's presence quieted the gathering from the first few minutes. The songs seemed to go straight to the hearts of the men, many of whom were fresh from their homes, with no previous experience of naval life. At the close of an ardent appeal by Mr. James Whitmore, an earnest young Y.M.C.A. speaker, one hundred and forty-six men boldly took their stand for Christ. Two hundred and eighty-seven joined the Pocket Testament League, making four hundred and seventy, in all, for the seven nights' work. Equally wonderful days were experienced at the Brooklyn Navy Yard, and at Plattsburg.

From June to September, Alexander was busily engaged in summer Bible Conferences, the autumn's work beginning with the Pennsylvania State Sunday

School Convention in Pittsburg, Pa., from October 8th to 15th, at all the gatherings of which he conducted the music.

At this time a new pianist took the place of Henry Barraclough, who, in September, was drafted into the American Army. Leonard C. Voke was a young Englishman, eighteen years old, who had come over to the United States three years before. As a little fellow of five, in Brighton, England, he had heard glowing accounts of the singing under Alexander's marvellous leadership, and of the wonderful piano accompaniments of Robert Harkness, when his parents came home, night after night, from the Torrey-Alexander meetings in the Dome. A great ambition had sprung up in the boy's heart, gifted as he was even then, that someday he might grow up to be a great pianist, and play for Mr. Alexander. By what might seem like a series of strange coincidences, his wish was brought about. Before there was any thought of Alexander losing the services of Mr. Barraclough, Mr. Brown had become acquainted with young Voke, and, finding that he was thinking of going into concert work, pleaded with him to devote his talents to the Lord. Mr. Brown spoke from deep personal experience. Himself an Associate of the London Royal Academy of Music, he had put aside many temptations to use his wonderful baritone voice, with its great range and powerful tone, on the operatic stage. Finding that even concert and oratorio work brought him into constant fellowship with the artistes of the stage, he had relinquished music altogether as a profession, until the opportunity had occurred of becoming Alexander's soloist. Voke also faced the issues, yielding himself to God, Who had thus been preparing him for the offer that came within a month or two.

The new season's work had been arranged after a conference of the Y.M.C.A. War Work Council and the National Service Commission of the Presbyterian Church, who worked in complete co-operation in sending Alexander and his party to the various camps. The Rev. Frank W. Sneed, D.D., of Pittsburg, and Mr. J. Lewis Twaddell, of Philadelphia, were respectively the chairman and secretary of the Commission's committee on the Pocket Testament League.

Immense, newly-erected cities of wooden huts, intersected by long streets, sprang into being all over the country like magic, usually in some wild, unfrequented spot, far from other towns or habitations. The long motor rides in all kinds of weather, at all hours of the day and night, the frequent uncertainty in knowing where the nights were to be spent, the constant travelling from one State to another, made this work such as would try the health and endurance, even of those possessing great physical strength. Add to this the responsibility of arranging for a party of helpers, and of carrying constant supplies of Testaments, Gospels and hymnbooks, and to all this again the burden of spiritual effort, and some idea will be gained of what this year of strenuous service meant to Charles Alexander. But his joy in the Lord not only carried him through, and communicated itself to his co-workers, but was infectious wherever he went as a veritable " apostle of sunshine."

From October, 1917, until the end of May, 1918, with the exception of a few weeks spent with Dr. Chapman in Elizabeth, New Jersey, Charles Alexander travelled incessantly from State to State, and from one camp or navy yard to another. With him went Albert Brown and Leonard Voke, also a new assistant, George C. Cooke, a tenor singer and skilful trombonist.

Before Christmas, 1917, the following cantonments had been visited : Camp Upton, at Yaphank, on Long Island, and Camp Dix, near Wrightstown, New Jersey. The next three were in the State of Illinois—Fort Sheridan, the Great Lakes Naval Training Station, and Camp Grant, near Rockford. Through the latter part of November and the month of December the Alexander party turned southwards to Fort Benjamin Harrison, near Indianapolis, Indiana, and Camp Meade, near Petersburg, Virginia. Christmas was spent in the little home at Larchmont.

Then followed the Chapman-Alexander campaign in Elizabeth, New Jersey, from January 6th to February 3rd, 1918, the only one which he and Dr. Chapman had been able to arrange on the old, familiar lines. The meetings were followed by splendid results. Many found Christ during the five weeks, and the churches were built up and strengthened. The enjoyment of the two leaders in working together once more was not marred by any realization that this was to be the last of the Chapman-Alexander campaigns.

The work of the camps was resumed on March 23rd, when Alexander and his party held meetings in Fort Mont, New Jersey, another day being given to Fort Dupont, near Wilmington, Delaware.

On March 25th, they went to New York for a week of meetings in the Brooklyn Navy Yard. One of the most faithful helpers during these meetings, which were held in the Naval Y.M.C.A. Building, was a young sailor who had been led to Christ, a short time before, by a volunteer lady-worker in the post office department. One day she had been sorting a large pile of mail, and the sailors were filing past to receive it. She handed a letter to one of the boys, but when he saw the hand-writing upon it his expression changed. Handing it back to her, he said, " Say, lady, I haven't the heart to open that letter. It's from my old mother, and I've just got a telegram in my pocket to say that she is dead." The lady was a member of the Pocket Testament League herself, and beneath her post office counter she had a stock of Testaments ready for business. Taking one out, she opened it to the fourteenth chapter of John, and handing it to the sailor-boy, she said, " I have no time to talk with you just now, while so many are coming for their mail, but you take this over to that quiet corner, and read it. I think it will help you to open your letter. I will be praying, and you can come back to me later to have a talk." Half an hour later, the rush at the counter was over, and the sailor returned. " Say, lady," he said, " that chapter you gave me was my old mother's favourite chapter. She often used to read it to me. It did help me to open my letter, and while I was reading it, I made up my mind that my mother's God should be my God too." Alexander did not know where the incident had occurred, but he had heard the story and had already told it in a number of his meetings in the camps. On his first night in the Brooklyn Naval Y.M.C.A., he had just finished telling it again, when a big, sturdy-looking sailor stood up, and lifting his hand to attract Alexander's attention, called out, " I know that story is true, because I am that sailor." Alexander's face beamed with surprised delight. " Good for you, old man ! " he said. " Come right up here by me and give your testimony." Greeting him with outstretched hand, followed by a hearty slap on the back, Alexander pulled him to the front of the platform. There they stood together, and, with Alexander's arm thrown around his shoulders, the sailor told his story. The impression upon the audience was so great, that after a word of prayer, Alexander gave an invitation to accept Christ. Quietly, men rose to their feet in all parts of the audience, and when the Pocket Testament League had been presented, and membership cards passed around, those men who had made their decision were asked to add the words, " I accept Christ," on a corner of their cards, before handing them in. Each night after this the sailor was on hand, eager to help, in giving out hymnbooks, Gospels, or League membership cards. His shining face was a sermon in itself, and doubtless helped many others to decide for Christ.

From April 3rd to 6th, the Alexander party were in Camp Dix again. Mr. Philip E. Howard described one of the meetings in Camp Dix for the *Sunday School Times* of Philadelphia :—

" When the motor halted in front of the General's headquarters, the little village seemed very silent, after the two hours' run over truck-ravaged roads. A man in overalls came out from behind the barn, and whistled his way along the shaded street. The afternoon sun spread its glow over the brown and gold of the oaks, and mellowed the sombre green of the pines. War ? Surely not here. Only a sleepy, comfortable village all around us. But in the near distance, at a turn of the road under cover of the trees, I caught a passing glimpse of a brown shadow slipping across the way. I looked intently, and the shadow was a file of men in khaki, disappearing into the woods even as I looked. That shadow is war.

" We tarried in the village until dark, and then we took the road to the camp— a short run of three miles. The night was black. The lights of many cars bored into the darkness as we sped along a crowded road. We had reached a corner of the great Cantonment, and the lights in the buildings were gleaming fitfully through the trees, when Alexander called for silence in the car, and said to one of us, ' You pray.' It was a time for prayer. Who were we, that we should adventure the evangelizing of a Cantonment, without talking it over with the Captain ? I am sure He was with us as we swung into the rough maze of roads, half-roads, and no roads at all, that constituted the ways of the big new camp, and He gave us a guide who piloted us past flaring fires, and lumber piles, and rocking trucks, and ditches, and marching men, soldiers and artisans, straight to the Y.M.C.A. building of wood, and windows, and crowded rooms.

" You must see it, to understand the grip the whole thing gets on your heart. You are on a platform overlooking the length of an oblong room of plain boards and rafters, with six or seven hundred boys in khaki on wooden benches. Along the entire length of each side of the room is a writing-shelf, but the boys, who are writing there, soon turn towards you when the meeting begins. At your left, a piano ; at your right, you have helped to spread out, from a big box lugged in from the car, a stack of red-bound Gospels of St. John, with several hymns bound in, and still in the box is a store of Testaments. That's your ammunition. You at once discover what song can do. For the boys are singing as soon as the little red Gospels are scattered, and Alexander has smiled at them, chatted with them, started them off. Keep still if you can—but you won't, for before you know it you'll be singing, ' Give your heart to Jesus, He is calling you,' with that eager, full-toned, vital crowd of fellows. Then watch the interest and the fun, when one fellow rises, at the promise of a Testament, to sing it alone—and so, until four have done so, at once brought forward as a quartet by Alexander. And when one of the four, evidently a foreigner—turns all his big lung power entirely loose on the last phrase, and shouts, ' Give Him your heart to-day,' you burst out with the whole crowd in wild applause. Well, the quartet deserved it !

" You won't be able to see so very clearly, when Alexander or Davis makes the appeal to the boys to accept, to carry, and to read the Testament. Some of the faces in the crowd will come to you clearly through the mist. That mere boy over there is not seeing with his frank eyes just what's going on around him. What is he seeing ? And another chap, rough-hewn out of gnarled timber, is simply lost in wonder, as the leader gives us a glimpse of what the Gospel message is. And when you go down the aisle afterwards, with your pockets full of Testaments, and your dignity all broken up into brotherliness, just notice the hands that reach out to you the little pledge cards of the Pocket Testament League, all signed up with names finding their origin in numberless Homelands. You wish you had a dozen hands to use in gripping, and in filling those stretched out to you, because you know that back of the eager gesture, the willing response to the invitation, is hunger, hunger for what Christ gave you to pass on.

" Clamber up the platform, now, and look ! The leader is going to call for a show of Testaments. And then a whisper to the secretary, instant silence over the room, and the sharp, clear words : ' Any non-commissioned officers of Company —— are to come over at once ! ' Three young fellows near the front rise up, and step quickly into the aisle. ' Hold on, boys, you didn't get your Testaments, did you ? ' calls out the leader. ' Don't stop them,' says a secretary quietly, ' you see they are under orders.' And nothing does stop them. They march swiftly out, and that night, perhaps, are on their way to—well, we all know where our hearts are turning nowadays. Oh, the obedience of it, the suddenness, the imperative demand of that swift order breaking in upon the meeting !

" And so they are slipping away. Did the three get their Testaments ? I don't know. What I do know is that, as we picked our way out of the Cantonment that night, and the lights fell away behind us on our way through sleeping villages and the October woods, I saw a great host of young men with their faces toward the sunrise, breasting into the thick of the world's black night for us of an older generation, and for generations yet unborn. And I made covenant then, that as God may give strength to my hand, I shall do what may be done to put into the outstretched hands the living Word of God."

On April 7th, Alexander and his party held meetings on Governor's Island, New York ; next day, on the battleship *Columbia*, outside Philadelphia ; and the day following, at Fort Slocum, near New Rochelle, on Long Island Sound. From April 10th to 13th, they visited Camp Merritt, the great embarkation camp behind the Hudson River Palisades, near Tenafly, New Jersey. George T. B. Davis, who had crossed from England the previous summer, after three years in the Scottish

P

camps, had been steadily working in Camp Merritt for some time, and was delighted to have a few days with his " chief " once more. From Camp Merritt, Alexander and his party of workers turned northwards. A full week was given to Camp Devens, near Boston, and the exceptionally warm spirit of co-operation on the part of the Y.M.C.A. secretaries, in this camp, made the work easy and delightful. The next stop was at Fort McKinley, near Portland, Maine, and on April 27th a night's visit was paid to Popham Beach, far north at the mouth of the Kennebec River, where a small gun-station guarded the approach. Here the party slept in a weird, old, empty, country house, said to be haunted. Their cots had been placed all together in one room, bare of other furniture except for a stove, red-hot with a blazing fire. The room was stifling, in spite of the clear, cold night of that northern region. Alexander opened one of the windows in the ghostly hall, propping up the broken sash. Just outside, in the brilliant moonlight, the waves were lapping over the sand. In spite of the comfort of each other's company, the youngest member of the party was affected by the solitude of their surroundings, and Cooke, especially, enjoyed teasing him. " You'd better stop, Cookie, or something really *will* happen," called out Voke from his cot. A gale of laughter shook the rickety cot on the other side of the room, on which Alexander was trying to sleep. For a few moments silence reigned. Then came a terrific crash, which echoed through the empty halls. It sounded as if some heavy object had been thrown down the staircase. Like a shot, Alexander was out in the hall to discover the cause, but it was only his prop that had given way under the broken window!

The next day the party went to Newport, Rhode Island, and here they were joined by Mrs. Alexander, who came from New York to share a few weeks of her husband's work. In Newport and at New London, Connecticut, the work was almost entirely among naval men and marines. Trips were made to islands guarding both harbours, and the meetings were doubly appreciated by the men thus cut off, on their lonely stations, from the outside world. A letter from Mr. Harry J. Schulman, written to Mrs. Alexander on October 18th, 1920, brings a reminiscence of those days. " It was a peculiar honour to meet Mr. Alexander in the spring of 1918, when I had an opportunity of seeing his sterling Christian life. You may recall that when travelling in the interests of the Pocket Testament League, you came to the New London district of the Y.M.C.A. Huts, and after a stormy trip from New London, came to a small hut on an island named Fort Michie. I was the Y.M.C.A. secretary who had the pleasure of welcoming you. Mr. Alexander and his co-workers held a wonderful meeting at night, and after you left, many of the boys, in comparing various entertainments which we had held for them, affirmed that the meeting you gave them was the best. That night Mr. Alexander and I had a wonderful time together, and he gave me an autographed Pocket Testament which I have always cherished. After he left us, I felt that to have met him was one of the red-letter days of my army life."

The last of this war work was in Camp Sherman, near Columbus, Ohio, from May 13th to 27th, broken by a few days spent in Columbus, to attend the Presbyterian General Assembly, at which Dr. Chapman's year as Moderator closed. Reports were given, to the Assembly, of the work accomplished by the National

Service Commission, including that of the Pocket Testament League Committee. One night a huge banquet was arranged for the delegates attending the sessions of the General Assembly, of whom the larger number were ministers. While the banquet was being partaken of, Alexander and his party sang to them, started a few choruses, and told stories of the work in the camps. Using the little red Gospels, a typical camp service was reproduced, ending with the same presentation of the Pocket Testament League that had been constantly made to the men of the Army and Navy. With his usual enthusiasm, Alexander pleaded for volunteers to carry the Word of God as a constant companion and weapon, and to read it much and frequently. As a result, seven hundred and eighty-nine of those attending the banquet joined the Pocket Testament League that night.

The methods which Alexander had adopted for his war work in America had been just the same as those which he had tested out on Salisbury Plain at the beginning of the war. They " did the business," to adopt his own descriptive phrase. Some of the deepest and most fruitful work of his life was this with the young soldiers of the old and new worlds. For he was always a man's man, and in their company was the central and dominating figure. He never faced an audience of soldiers without realizing that many of them might be hearing the Gospel invitation for the last time. No wonder he pressed home, with eloquent persuasion, the claims of his Master, both in his personal dealing with the men, and in his talks from the platform. He longed that before meeting the full blast of the hurricane on the battle-front, they should know the joy of salvation. That was his reason for toiling so strenuously.

And not only did his own time, and energy, and money, go ungrudgingly and gladly into this splendid service, but he pressed upon others the duty of helping in similar ways. Through his personal efforts, many friends were brought into touch with the movement, and liberally assisted in providing Testaments for the fighting forces. That the supply should be maintained was his constant concern. To provide for this, the Business Men's Council of the Pocket Testament League had first been inaugurated in Philadelphia.

The work which he had set in motion in England went steadily on, reaching out to every corner of the widely-separated war areas. Every week he received a report from the office in London—not a stereotyped statement of facts and figures, but a living, throbbing record of achievement and blessing, a story of souls saved, of spiritual victories in trench, and hospital, and camp. The boys in khaki told of what God's Word meant to them in the firing-line ; bereaved mothers often told, through their tears, of the comfort that had come to them, when receiving the little bag containing their boys' possessions, they found a small Testament among them, with the beloved name signed on the Decision page. If the story of those busy war years could be fully told from the standpoint of the Pocket Testament League, it would add a glowing chapter to the Acts of the Apostles.

From Camp Sherman, Alexander went to Philadelphia, to direct the singing in the great and memorable Conference on the Second Coming of Christ, which was held in the Academy of Music from May 28th to 30th. Early in June, a letter reached him from Dr. Chapman, saying that the troublesome wound from his first operation in 1916 had not yet healed.   Now that his year of service as Moderator of the Presbyterian General Assembly was over, his physician declared that another operation was necessary at once, but gave hope, through this, of complete recovery. As soon as the ordeal was over, Dr. Chapman began to gather strength in a way that encouraged them both to go forward with tentative plans of work together for the ensuing winter.   In the meantime Alexander entered into his busy summer's work in the Bible Conferences.   But as the weeks passed, it became evident that Dr. Chapman's return to health was not as sure or rapid as had been hoped at first, and, for a time at least, the strain of long campaigns was out of the question. Alexander, therefore, went on for a while, independently, with his Pocket Testament League work and Song Services.   The bond of affection between himself and Dr. Chapman caused him to hold back unselfishly from making any larger plans which might take him too far away from his beloved colleague.

On November 11th, 1918, the Armistice was signed, bringing to an end the daily holocaust of human life.   The joy and relief of all the nations was expressed in wild abandon.   The outlook began to brighten, and it seemed as if new opportunities might now be found for preaching the Gospel of Christ.

From November 25th to 28th, Alexander led the music at all the sessions of a great Prophetic Bible Conference held in Carnegie Hall in New York City.   Among many marvellous addresses that were given, the most impressive message of the whole conference was felt to be that delivered by Dr. Chapman on " The return of the Lord Jesus Christ," for Whom he was looking with joyful expectancy.   No message could have been more tender or effective, if he or his audience had realized that it was to be his last public utterance to so large an assembly.   From December 7th to 9th, the two evangelists and their wives spent a delightful week-end together at the home of Mr. and Mrs. Charles L. Huston, at Coatesville, Pennsylvania.   Three meetings were held on the Sunday, Dr. Chapman preaching at each of them.   Mr. Brown, Mr. Cooke, Mr. Voke, and Mr. Geo. Davis were all there, to help in the meetings, and in the presentation of the Pocket Testament League, in the cause of which Mr. Davis had already been spending some fruitful weeks in Coatesville.

The fellowship which Dr. and Mrs. Chapman and the Alexanders enjoyed amid the surroundings of that lovely Christian home, brought back happy memories of many such days spent in the years that had passed.   It revived the hope of future days of service together ; but God's will was otherwise.   On December 23rd, Dr. Chapman was suddenly obliged to undergo a third most serious operation, from which he barely recovered consciousness.   Very early on Christmas morning he passed into the light and glory of Heaven.   The blow fell heavily upon Alexander, for the two men had been as brothers through the past eleven years, and no other man could ever fill the place which Dr. Chapman had held in his life and work.

It had previously been planned that Alexander should accept a long-postponed invitation from Dr. Torrey for a two months' campaign in Los Angeles, beginning in January, and tentative plans had already been made for the Chapman-Alexander party to begin their usual work again in April, with a campaign in Indianapolis.

Now, once more, the future was hidden from Alexander's sight, but he decided to carry out the visit to Los Angeles as arranged.

AMONG HIS BELOVED NORTH CAROLINA MOUNTAINS, NEAR MONTREAT, N.C., MAY, 1915

"WAY DOWN SOUTH"

BUGGY-RIDING
IN THE
NORTH CAROLINA
MOUNTAINS,
MAY, 1915

"STILL ABLE
TO
MAKE A
STRAIGHT
FURROW"

"I SHO'
DON'T LIKE
BEIN' TAKEN
WID DAT
CHICKUN,
MISTAH
ALEXANDER,"
PROTESTS
MIRL NUCKLES.

CHAPTER TWENTY-FIVE

Services of Song in Summer Conferences

1915 to 1918

NO story of the life of Charles M. Alexander would be complete without a picture of him in the summer Bible Conferences of his own land. Thousands of people look back to days of recreation amidst the beauties of nature, woven through and through with memories of Gospel song. With the song comes the vision of a radiant personality. They see once more the shining eyes and happy face of the man who not only taught them how to sing, and gave them the joy of hearing Gospel music at its best, but who, through the music, and by his own lips and life, led them to a place of full surrender to Christ. At Winona Lake, Indiana; Montrose, Pennsylvania; Montreat, North Carolina; and at Stony Brook, on Long Island, New York, he was a familiar figure. But the place visited by Charles Alexander more often than any other, through these summer days of conference, was Northfield, that beautiful spot among the hills of Massachusetts, where D. L. Moody had founded the Seminary for girls and young women, and the Mount Hermon School for young men. The purpose of these Northfield schools, four miles apart, and divided from each other by the Connecticut River, is not identical with that of the Chicago Bible Institute, where men and women are trained in knowledge of the Bible, and in the use of music and every other method of Christian service for bringing souls to God.

The Northfield schools, first opened in November, 1879, were founded with the object of providing for the sons and daughters of ministers, missionaries, and Christian workers of small means, a good, general education amid healthy surroundings, and in a Christian atmosphere in which the Word of God was loved and honoured. One by one, handsome college buildings have been erected on the campus both of Northfield and of Mount Hermon, each of which has also a fine chapel for religious services. Not less than from six to seven hundred students fill the dormitory buildings on each side of the river. The constant provision for the varied needs of this army of over one thousand young people is a heavy burden, and it rests chiefly upon the shoulders of the president, Mr. W. R. Moody, elder son of the great evangelist. The responsibility is most ably shared by his wife, a daughter of Major D. W. Whittle, and other members of the Moody family assist in various ways. In addition to the schools, there are the great conferences to be planned for, which, according to D. L. Moody's economy of purpose, make use of the school buildings during vacation time. Northfield possesses a splendid auditorium building, where, through the school terms, gatherings and entertainments of various kinds are held, in which the boys from Mount Hermon frequently participate.

At the beginning of the long summer vacation there is a general exodus of students from Northfield. The dormitories are emptied. The sloping lawns of the campus no longer echo to the sound of girlish laughter. But silence has hardly settled down, and there has scarcely been time to clean the buildings, before trainloads of people are coming into Northfield for the summer conferences. Not only is the spacious Northfield Hotel filled to overflowing with guests, and every dormitory building upon the campus turned into a summer boarding-house, but in various open spaces between the trees, groups of white tents appear. Conferences of young men and of young women, home and foreign missionary conferences, and others, follow each other in rapid succession. Among the pines on the thickly-wooded slopes above Northfield, is a boys' camp, and all along the Ridge, for a mile or two, the roofs of rustic cottages peep out between the trees. The crowds for the various conferences come and go, but the houses along the Ridge are filled through the hot months of the year with people who make Northfield their summer home.

The climax is reached in the General Conference for Christian Workers, which comes in August at the close of all the others. From nine o'clock in the morning until noon, three consecutive services or lectures are held in the Auditorium, and usually there is one short afternoon service. Before seven o'clock, streams of people may be seen crossing the campus from every direction, and converging upon a smooth, grassy hillside, which has sacred associations for all lovers of Northfield. On the crest of Round Top, as it is called, are two simple graves, side by side, bearing the names of D. L. Moody, and his wife. To this spot Mr. Moody had loved to come and commune with God, as he gazed over the glorious scene before him, with the wide, shining ribbon of the Connecticut River winding through the midst of it. Some of the most delightful memories of Northfield are of these sunset services on Round Top, the slope of which forms an almost perfect natural amphitheatre. Stories of rescue missions, and of adventures for Christ in many lands, have been poured into listening ears amid the whisper of the wind through the maple trees. At eight o'clock the Round Top audience joins the crowd that streams into the Auditorium for the final service of the day.

Whenever Charles Alexander was able to be at Northfield for the General Conference, he gave himself, heart and soul, to the effort of bringing every one within reach into touch with Christ. Many a time he would be the guest, for eight o'clock breakfast, at one or other of the dormitory buildings, leading the family worship, and starting the day with praise. On other days, with his singer and pianist, he would spend the early morning hour with the boys in their camp among the pines. Before the evening address began, he conducted a half-hour or more of song in the Auditorium, closing the day as he began it, with vocal praise and thanksgiving.

But Alexander's special hour of the day was from ten to eleven in the morning. This hour was his own, to be used in any way he wished. It was a veritable feast of Gospel music, for besides his own pianist and soloist, he would gather round him a group of other singers, as well as organizing a choir of adults in the raised seats behind the platform, and of children in one of the side galleries. It was almost the only hour of the day in which the children flocked with their elders to the Auditorium. Few of the lectures and addresses were attractive enough to them in their vacation days, to draw them from the delights of the open air, but when the song service began nothing could keep them away. This unique hour was carefully chosen by Alexander at a time of the day when the students, who were working through the summer months as waiters, and waitresses, and cooks, in the various dormitory buildings, could steal away for a little while and have a share in the gatherings of the conference. "Alexander's hour" was more than a song service; one of its chief delights was its utter unexpectedness. Sometimes Bible stories would be told, by some master in the art, between the singing. At other times marvellous testimonies of conversion, or of God's guidance in times of perplexity, or of His deliverance from temptation and danger, would be forthcoming from varied sources. In later years, the Pocket Testament League was a constant theme.

Alexander's visit to Northfield, after his journey round the world with Dr. Torrey in 1903, had first led W. R. Moody to invite him to direct the music at the General Conference the following year, and when 1904 arrived, Alexander did not go to Northfield alone, but took with him his English bride. For five summers in succession, until 1908, he led the conference in song. Then came a break of seven years, during which either Australia, the Orient, or England, had claimed him through the summer days, and the summer of 1915 had come, before his happy face was once more seen at Northfield in the Christian Workers' Conference.

One Saturday morning in August, 1907, Alexander was on the platform of the Northfield Auditorium, with Robert Harkness at the piano, and Charlie Butler, of Macon, Georgia, as singer. The "man with the orange-blossoms in his voice," as Alexander had named Butler, sang a solo. "Now I am going to do something new," said Alexander. "I want to organize a Sunbeam Choir in the gallery up there on my left. There are a lot of you young people who like to sing. All of you boys and girls, who are under seventeen, can leave your mothers and fathers for a little while, and come up here—the little boys in the front seats, the girls behind them, and the big boys right at the back. I want you all to be here on Monday before ten o'clock. Be sure you look your best, now; and shine up your faces!" Some two hundred children made their way to the gallery, and meanwhile Alexander kept the audience singing. "Who said that there were no young people in Northfield? You older folks will have to sit up straight. You have some rivals up there. Now let's sing 'Don't stop praying.' Sing the first verse, Butler, so that they can learn it." Soon the whole audience was singing the first verse. Then the children tried it, and did well. "I see a Scotchman back there from Philadelphia, singing without a hymn-book," said Alexander. "Give us the next verse, brother." The Scotchman fumbled for his glasses, and borrowed a book from his neighbour. Then he sang the verse. "How's that, Brother Stebbins?" said the leader, turning to his old friend upon the platform. Mr. Stebbins said it was fine! "'Don't stop praying for every need.' A man told me that was all nonsense, but bless your heart, I prayed for a suit of clothes once when I needed it, and I got it. At that time it meant as much to me as a whole row of brick buildings. Now look at the third verse, 'Don't stop praying when led to sin.' That's just the time the Devil wants us to stop praying. When the house is on fire, that's the time to call for water! Mr. Stebbins will remember a story Dr. A. J. Gordon used to tell, about an old coloured saint. They asked him what he did when the Devil tempted him. 'Bress yo' soul, chile, I draps right down on my knees and say, 'You betta look out, Lord, yo' property's in danger.'"

Later in the meeting Alexander taught the people the chorus, "Can the Lord depend on you." Then the leader turned to his Sunbeam Choir. "If any one of you boys or girls will sing the chorus alone, I'll give you a beautiful Bible, and it won't be a dollar-and-a-half one, either!" There was a moment's hesitation, and then a small boy got up and sang the chorus in his piping treble. "Bless your heart," said Mr. Alexander, "you ought to be a preacher! You've got more courage than some of these grown-up folks."

So deep was the interest, that it was a surprise to find the hands of the clock pointing to the closing hour. "Where's 'Bishop' Trotter?" said Alexander, looking round the platform. A big man with a beaming face rose in the audience, and came a step or two forward down the aisle. "Stand right where you are and ask God's blessing upon this meeting and the songs." And Melvin E. Trotter, the famous Rescue Mission worker, whom Alexander was introducing at Northfield that year, led in a closing prayer. "Turn and say a kind word to the person next you," was Alexander's benediction, as he stepped down from the platform, making way for the lecturer whose hour followed his own.

In August, 1915, Mr. Stebbins, who had directed the singing since 1908, welcomed Alexander warmly after his seven years absence from Northfield. The younger leader would not let his beloved friend stay in the background. Knowing his difficulty in hearing well, Alexander placed a chair near to the piano, at which Henry Barraclough was presiding, and where Mr. Stebbins would easily catch the words and tones of the solos by Albert Brown or William Andrew. Meanwhile, Mrs. Alexander took pains, each day, to see that a comfortable chair was reserved in the front row of seats below the platform for Mrs. Stebbins, whose upturned face glowed with pleasure, as Alexander spoke with loving appreciation of the work her husband had done, through long years, in the realm of Gospel music. Alexander made a special point that year of choosing as many songs as possible written by Mr. Stebbins, and aroused a new appreciation and love in the hearts of many of the younger people, who had not known the famous singer in his early years. Mr. and Mrs. Stebbins were staying at the Northfield Hotel. A few days after the close of the conference, they gave a small dinner-party to some of their friends, including Mr. and Mrs. W. R. Moody, and Charles Alexander and his wife. The guests of the hotel had been begging Alexander to give them a night of song. He decided to combine the two occasions, saying that it would be a "Stebbins" night, and no hymns by any other composer would be used. After dinner, a large company assembled in the spacious parlours of the hotel to enjoy the musical programme.

Mr. Brown, Mr. Andrew, Mrs. Moody, and others, sang solos. But the event of the evening, which caused the greatest enthusiasm, was a duet by Mr. and Mrs. Stebbins. Hand in hand, as in the olden days, they stood to sing the best-known of all his hymns, " Saved by grace." The trembling voices gave little hint of the strong, sweet tones that had thrilled many an audience in India, as well as in Great Britain and America. But there were few dry eyes in the audience, as all voices mingled in the last chorus :

> And I shall see Him face to face,
> And tell the story : Saved by Grace.

The ovation they received filled Mrs. Stebbins with delight, as she looked proudly up at her tall, handsome spouse. " This summer has been one of the happiest of my life, and to-night has crowned it all," she said to Mrs. Alexander before retiring.

Barely a week later, at the Northfield Hotel, dear Mrs. Stebbins was taken seriously ill in the middle of the night. Twenty minutes afterwards she entered " the palace of the King," and saw Him " face to face." Mr. Stebbins bore his grief with the patient dignity that has always distinguished his noble character. The loving sympathy of his friends, and his association with Alexander in the preparation of a new hymn-book, helped him to pass through some of the first hard days of loneliness. " Charles was one of the loveliest and most valued friends I have ever had," he wrote to Mrs. Alexander, when in a few short years she, too, was suddenly left alone. " He was the most gifted and honoured leader in the history of sacred song. My relations with him were of a close and intimate nature, and he gave me many reasons for holding him in deep and abiding affection."

The Conference of 1916 came at a time when all hearts were in great anxiety at the course of the war in Europe. None had expected that it could linger on so long, nor even then dreamed of how much longer it would continue. The wreckage of civilization carried with it to destruction the faith of many wrongly-taught young people. That moral system, which had been built up for them by teachers, who owed all that was best to the Bible, and yet denied its authority, had gone to pieces before their eyes. The theories of social evolution, at least, had proved so utterly false, that those who believed it to be compatible with the teaching of the Bible, were thrown into confusion and despair.

The only people whose faith never shook, as the signs of the end of the age began to manifest themselves, as foretold in the Scriptures, were those who believed the Word of God. It was a time when faith needed strengthening, and when those who had been trained in false theories by unreliable teachers, needed to be pointed to the Lord Himself, and to His unshakable Word. Alexander chose the phrase, " We trust in the living God" (1 Timothy iv. 10), to be the key-note of his song-service hour throughout the Christian Workers' Conference. Day after day, as the crowds gathered in the Auditorium, he would have them repeat the words : " We trust in the living God." Sometimes he would call upon the Sunbeam Choir to rise and say it together ; sometimes the adult choir. Then he would ask the ministers all over the audience to rise and ring out the words, " We trust in the living God."

One day, about the middle of the conference, Mr. Barraclough brought Alexander a chorus, which was soon being sung all over the campus :—

Trust in the Living God.

W. W. Rock.   Henry Barraclough.

International Copyright by
Charles M Alexander

Before the conference closed, many a waverer had been led back to Christ, and a large number had surrendered themselves, mind and body, to Him. There were two testimonies used by Alexander in his hour of song which made a special impression upon the conference. One was that of Mr. James Kerr, of Philadelphia, who had found Christ as his Saviour a little while earlier. The joy of salvation beamed from his face whenever he gave his testimony, and his happy exuberance of spirit thrilled the whole gathering. He was only able to be in Northfield for a few days, and before leaving, asked the prayers of the meeting for a brother still unconverted. The Pocket Testament League appealed to him as a wholesome, practical method of winning men to Christ, and Mr. Kerr determined to gain members for the League, and, through it, lead them to Jesus. Within a few days of his return to Philadelphia he attended a small banquet of business men. About twenty-five were present. As soon as the business was over, but before anyone had risen from the table, Mr. Kerr rose and said : " Gentlemen, if you will pardon my speaking of an outside matter, there is a little book in which I am greatly interested, and it would be a great pleasure to me to present one to any of you who would care to carry it in your pocket, and read a chapter a day." Quickly slipping a beautifully-bound Testament in front of each man at the table, Mr. Kerr, in a few short words, told of his conversion, and of what God's Word meant to him. He asked any who cared to accept it, to sign the membership pledge inside the front cover, and those who did not care to do so, to leave the book lying on the table. Instantly fountain-pens were busy, and only one book was left upon the table when the company withdrew. Before leaving, Mr. Kerr signed up the head-waiter and his assistants, and also a messenger boy who had brought him a note. Amongst those present at the banquet was his brother, for whose salvation he was so earnestly praying. The brother, to his great delight, had accepted the Testament, and had signed up as a member of the League. Not long afterwards he accepted Christ, and both brothers now work together for the same Lord, using the Pocket Testament League as one of their greatest aids in soul-winning.

The other testimony, which made so deep an impression at Northfield, was that of Miss Haru Inoguchi, a young Japanese student from a Christian Workers' Training School in Philadelphia. With several other students, she had been sent to Northfield for a few weeks to enjoy the conference. When she saw Charles Alexander, her joy was unbounded, for she was the very girl who had sung the chorus, " Can the Lord depend on you," for him at one of the schoolgirls' meetings in Tokyo seven years before, and had remembered him with loving gratitude ever since. She told him of the new joy that had come into her spiritual life a month or two earlier, during a " Victorious Life Conference," where she had first learned the secret of victory over sin through the indwelling Christ. Pride and a hasty temper had held the mastery over her, in spite of her struggles to overcome, and now she was learning that in her own strength she could do nothing, but, like Paul, must say, " I live, yet not I, but Christ liveth in me." Alexander was using the hymn, " Christ liveth in me,"—by Whittle and McGranahan—frequently that summer. One morning he turned to Miss Inoguchi, who was helping in the choir, and said, " Tell these people what you told Mrs. Alexander and me about your experience along that line." After a short hesitation, the girl arose, and speaking in clear English, with her pretty accent, she poured out such a glowing, heartfelt story of Christ's power to deliver, that the audience was completely melted. One minister said afterwards that her testimony had helped him more than anything in the whole conference.

Alexander's serene trust in God coloured everything he did, and if he felt a conviction that God was leading him in any direction, and had carefully tested this conviction by the Word of God and with prayer, no difficulties in the way ever discouraged him. He loved to tell the story of an old coloured man who was being twitted by his friends for his simple readiness to attempt anything he felt the Lord wanted him to do, in face of any obstacle. " Now come, Uncle Mose," said one of them, " look at that solid brick wall. Do you mean to say, if the Lord told you to jump right through it, you'd jump ? " " Bress de Lawd, honey," said the old man, " *Ef de Lawd tole me to do it*, I'd sho' jump, for I knows by de time I got thar there'd be a hole." The hundreds who left Northfield that summer went back to their winter's work with a new courage, and the words ringing in their ears, " We trust in the living God."

The lonely Japanese girl was tenderly cared for by her Heavenly Father, for Alexander's wife was led to invite Miss Inoguchi to stay with them the following summer to recover from a serious operation, and the visit lengthened into three years. About that time, the work in the camps, which absorbed Alexander's energies, made it necessary for Mrs. Alexander to settle into a temporary home for a year or two. A pretty, furnished house was found at Larchmont, twenty miles from New York City, on Long Island Sound, and here it was a comfort to Mrs. Alexander to have the daughterly companionship of Miss Inoguchi, who on her side frankly adored her " Otō-San " and " Okā-San," as she called her friends. Another temporary " daughter " was soon added to the family, in the person of Clara Lelean, of Australia, who also came to recover from a long, serious illness. The short times of home-life at Larchmont refreshed and strengthened Alexander for his strenuous work in the camps and navy yards. He was never happier than when surrounded by a crowd of young folks. The merry Christmas seasons with his wife, the two girls, and the young men who sang and played for him, with Mrs. McAnlis and other young people who frequently joined the family circle, were days to be long remembered. Through the whole of the summer of 1918, his niece, Helen, elder daughter of his brother, Rev. Homer J. Alexander, was with them in New York. She was at that time a sunny-faced child of thirteen, and was immensely happy to see so much of the uncle she loved, and to enjoy the happy home-life at Larchmont, and the great Bible conferences at Northfield and other places.

That summer, Alexander and his wife acted as host and hostess for Mr. and Mrs. W. R. Moody, at Revell Hall, where the speakers of the conference were entertained. Through Mr. Moody's generosity, the whole " Alexander family " was invited to stay at Revell. Although not able to express itself quite in the same way as in his own home, the genius of Charles Alexander as a gracious host, and the delightful atmosphere of family life with so many of the young people present, made the summer of 1918 at Revell Hall a time to be remembered. It was a fitting crown to the days at Northfield, though no one realized that it was to be the last time of singing under Alexander's leadership, or of being stirred to action by his insistence on soul-winning.

The spontaneity of his work upon the platform, his daring simplicity, and lack of formality, gave little indication of the careful and prayerful preparation he gave to his work. In one of his Bibles was found a paper, headed, " Suggestions written out for guidance before the Northfield Conference."

> Have short expositions of the Bible daily. Have a poem each day, or frequently. *One definition each day*—Faith, Obedience, Castaway, Trust, Redemption, Sin, Temptation, Victory, Prayer, Guidance, the Gospel. What is meant by preaching the Gospel ? What the unpardonable sin is, and what it is not. A clean heart. One day take up trouble and worry. What is the difference between them ? What to do when they come. Have several people tell what they do individually with them.
>
> Line up all our crowd. Tell them everything must bend and break before the ten o'clock hour. Each fellow must guard his every look, act and thought. Win every person in reach not already a Christian. Not to stop with that, but watch vigilantly to say a kind word, or lend a hand wherever there is an opening. If no opening, make one. Tell them to be careful to get good rest, and be in prime condition to meet every call with a virility that will grip. Make no moves without asking God's guidance. Tell them, in a place like this, one sentence or one look may neutralize a week's work. People know we are together. Let us be loyal to each other to the backbone.

In the summers of 1915 and 1917, Alexander led the singing at the great Southern Presbyterian Conference at Montreat, North Carolina.

It was at Montreat, when Dr. Chapman and Charles Alexander were there together in 1915, that Mr. Barraclough's famous song, " Ivory Palaces," was written. Each morning in the Auditorium, Alexander's hour of song was followed by an

AT NORTHFIELD, MASSACHUSETTS

CAMP SERVICE AT 8 a.m. AMONG THE "CATHEDRAL PINES," AUGUST, 1916
(Albert Brown singing, H. Barraclough at organ)

AT WORK ON A NEW HYMNBOOK
WITH GEORGE C.
STEBBINS,
SEPT.,
1915

ON THE STEPS OF THE MOODY HOMESTEAD WITH
DR. SCOTT (of China), MR. W. R. MOODY,
MEL TROTTER AND DR. ZWEMER.

THE LIGHTER SIDE OF NORTHFIELD

UMPIRING AT A   BASEBALL GAME, AUGUST, 1908

A MORNING RIDE,   AUGUST, 1918

address from Dr. Chapman. One day the subject of this address had been the poet's picture of Christ, as given prophetically in Psalm xlv. 8 : " All Thy garments smell of myrrh, and aloes, and cassia, out of the ivory palaces." That afternoon, Alexander and his wife, with Mr. Brown and Mr. Barraclough, took a long motor ride through the woods clothing the beautiful North Carolina mountains, which Alexander loved so well, to the summer headquarters of the Southern Y.M.C.A. As they drove back between the over-arching trees, through which the setting sun was sending long shafts of light, Mr. Barraclough, sitting quietly in front with the chauffeur, was lost in reverie. When they reached Montreat again, he drew a small card from his pocket, and, pulling out his fountain-pen, made some hasty notes upon it. Turning to Alexander, he said, " I believe I have the words and music of a hymn on the subject of Doctor's sermon this morning." Soon afterwards, the Alexander party were gathered round the piano, trying over " Ivory Palaces," with its beautiful chorus :—

> Out of the ivory palaces
> Into a world of woe,
> Only His great, eternal love
> Made my Saviour go.

It is written in duet form, and as Mr. Brown and Mrs. Alexander tried it over together, the tender strains of the music almost brought tears to the eyes of the little company. The new hymn was sung at the evening gathering of the conference, and was called for every night afterwards. Alexander realized that a message had been given in song which would bring joy and salvation to many a heart. In later conferences and evangelistic campaigns, it became one of the greatest favourites among the new songs.

Two other conferences, in which Alexander took a prominent part through these latter years, were Montrose, and Stony Brook. Montrose is beautifully situated among the mountains of northern Pennsylvania, and the summer Bible Conference is under the direction of Dr. R. A. Torrey, Dean of the Los Angeles Bible Institute, Alexander's teacher and colleague of earlier days. Montrose stands four-square for the fundamental truths of Christianity, with a special emphasis laid upon prophecy, fulfilled and unfulfilled, and the " blessed hope " of Christ's return. The same may be said of the Stony Brook Conference. The little town of Stony Brook, on Long Island, is within easy reach of New York City, and provides summer attractions amid beautiful scenery, looking across the waters of the Sound towards Stamford, Connecticut. Dr. John F. Carson and Dr. Ford C. Ottman are directors of the Stony Brook Assembly, and wonderful progress has been accomplished in a few years. A sandy piece of hilly woodland has been transformed into a conference centre, with a fine auditorium and beautiful halls of residence.

Mr. and Mrs. John H. Wyburn, who had carried on the Water Street Mission since the time of Sam Hadley's death, had a summer cottage at Stony Brook, and, with their daughter Bessie, enjoyed the various conferences. But they, like many others, looked forward most of all to the days when Alexander was there, to lead the music and inspire those about him with his sunny faith, his joyous heart, and his steadfast zeal.   Wherever he went, Pocket Testaments soon began to be in evidence.   He constantly spoke everywhere of his conviction that the form of revival most needed in these latter days, and which he believed was beginning to take place, was a " Bible Revival."   Perhaps he hardly realized to what extent he himself was the instrument of God in bringing about the thing he prayed for.   Yet known as he is the world over for his message in song, and for his genius in setting whole communities to singing the Gospel, there are few who do not even more intimately connect the name of Charles M. Alexander with a burning zeal for the Word of God, and for the method of using it for which the Pocket Testament League stands.   To Miss Bessie Wyburn, in her schooldays, anxious to find a suitable way of helping her parents in the difficult rescue work among poor drunkards, he had suggested the Pocket Testament League.   She became enthused with the idea, and set to work to gain every man, who professed conversion at Water Street Mission, as a member of the League.   Her first Testaments were provided by Alexander.   By degrees her list of members grew, until in 1919 she wrote in triumph, to tell him that she had gained her thousandth member !

A letter from her to Mrs. Alexander in 1920, says : " Dear Mr. Alexander has meant so much to me.   It was through him that I first made my decision for the Lord, and all through my Christian life he has been an inspiration.   I have many memories which will be a blessing to me."   Her mother and father wrote : " We feel that the best way we can honour Mr. Alexander's memory is by continuing our efforts to further the work of the Pocket Testament League, which was so dear to him, and to increase the membership."   While these pages have been in course of preparation, Mr. John H. Wyburn has gone to join his friend in the Glory-Land !

Another young girl, to whom Alexander was a beloved inspiration, was Miss Winnie Griffith Thomas—daughter of the famous Bible-teacher.   This family also had a summer cottage at Stony Brook, and Miss Griffith Thomas helped in the music with her clear, sweet voice.   After Charles Alexander's Home-going, she, too, wrote to his wife : " The remembrance of what he has done for all of us— even the little children—will remain with us all our lives.   My cherished dream of one day perhaps being with you and Mr. Alexander, to have my share in spreading the Gospel message in song, is now shattered.   But I mean to carry on, and, if it is the Lord's will, to use my voice at home, or if I can go out as a missionary I shall be ready.   I like to think that Mr. Alexander knows this and is glad.   I shall never forget the wonderful times we used to have at Stony Brook."

One more letter, from Miss Elizabeth D. Strong, must be quoted from : " I last saw you all at the Auditorium at Stony Brook, where I had the privilege and joy of singing under Mr. Alexander's leadership.   I have dates marked in my Stony Brook *Hymns of the Assembly*, and short sentences with which Mr. Alexander introduced the hymns, and I feel I have many precious memories stored up for the future.   He showed me not only how to ' sing with the heart ' unto the Lord, but how to work for Him more efficiently.   Mr. Alexander has long figured in my mind as ' Mr. Great-Heart ' in our *Pilgrim's Progress* of the twentieth century."

CHAPTER TWENTY-SIX

Bible Revivals in America and England

1919 and 1920

IN all his journeyings round the world, Charles Alexander had never seen the beauties which are to be found in that perpetual summerland of his own country, Southern California. On Tuesday morning, January 14th, 1919, he and his wife left New York to begin the long journey of three thousand miles across the continent, from the Atlantic seaboard to the Pacific.

They were accompanied by Mrs. B. D. McAnlis, who was in need of a change after two-and-a-half years of faithful work in the Pocket Testament League office in New York, and who looked forward with a happy heart to meeting her old friends in Los Angeles. The deserts of Arizona and New Mexico, with occasional glimpses of the Indians, were full of interest to the Alexanders, who had never been so far south in the States before. On January 18th, the end of the journey was reached, and a warm welcome was given by Dr. and Mrs. Torrey, and by Mr. T. C. Horton, Superintendent of the Bible Institute, and Mrs. Horton. In the centre of the magnificent pile of buildings is a large auditorium, seating over four thousand people On each side is a hotel building, thirteen stories high, one for men and the other for women, somewhat on the plan of Young Men's and Young Women's Christian Associations, with the lower floors reserved for the students. In the basement of the men's building is a large cafeteria, a modern restaurant system in which customers wait upon themselves. Alexander enjoyed repeating the story of a man in San Francisco who was greeted by his friend with the words, " I see you've been in Los Angeles." " Who told you ? " said the first man, in astonishment. " No one," replied the other, smiling, " but I see you've rubbed a button off your vest (waistcoat) carrying trays in the cafeterias ! "

High up on the tenth floor of the Women's building is a pretty suite of rooms reserved for special visitors, and here Alexander and his wife were hospitably lodged.

Los Angeles is some twenty miles from the ocean, and the surrounding country, with its palm trees, its countless roses a-bloom, its orange and lemon groves full of fruit, its eucalyptus and pepper trees, its sandy soil, and growths of cactus, reminded the Alexanders of southern Italy, or parts of Australia, or Palestine. Circling about the distant horizon are the snow-capped mountains, which guard this paradise from the cold winds of the north.

The new campaign began on January 25th, and Dr. Torrey and Charles Alexander were carried back in memory to the days of their earlier work together. They were assisted in the meetings by Albert Brown, George Cooke, and Leonard Voke, who had followed westwards by a later train.   A splendid choir of students gave Alexander a fine instrument in leading the singing of the crowds that assembled in the auditorium every evening throughout the following six weeks.   Various meetings occupied many of the afternoons and occasional mornings.   But the only other regular meeting each day was held, from noon until one o'clock, in Biola Hall, an old down-town picture-theatre, rented by the Institute for its work.   Sunday was always busy, with meetings from morning till night, Monday being the rest-day.

Dr. and Mrs. Torrey's home was in South Pasadena, from which the Doctor came over daily to Los Angeles for his classes and meetings.   During the first week, the Torreys' only son, Reuben, who had been home on furlough, sailed for China with his wife and two dear little children.   His delight at seeing his beloved " pal " of olden days was unbounded.   The fifteen-year-old schoolboy, present at the Alexanders' marriage, had grown into a tall, handsome fellow ; but his dignity as a missionary, a husband, and a father, dropped from him, as in the approved fashion of other days, he hurled himself upon his old friend with a bear's hug.

Day after day the meetings in the auditorium increased in size and in power, and many took their stand for Christ.   Alexander's leadership in song was a new experience to many in that Western land, and the joyousness of his presence brought a foretaste of Heaven here as elsewhere.   Among the new hymns, taken up with enthusiasm, was " The King's Highway," of which both words and music were written by Leonard Voke.   Another hymn much used at these meetings, and one of Albert Brown's favourite solos at all times, was " One Day," the words of which had been written by Dr. Chapman, and set to music by Mr. Charles H. Marsh, Professor of Music at the Los Angeles Bible Institute.

The noon meetings in Biola Hall gave Alexander more individual scope than any others.   He was entirely responsible for them, and made out of them one of the unique opportunities of his life.   Beginning with a small attendance, the meeting steadily grew, day by day, and week by week, until towards the end of the six weeks the theatre was crowded daily.   Best of all was the extraordinary growth in interest and in spiritual power.   The whole hour was devoted to singing and to the Pocket Testament League.   The plan was a new one, and in some ways the most fruitful kind of meeting Alexander had ever conducted.   He and his wife purchased a large number of Testaments, so that they might be able to make a gift of one to each person, present at the noon meeting, who desired to become a genuine and sincere member of the Pocket Testament League.   Those who did so were asked to sign the membership pledge, promising to make a regular habit of carrying the book with them everywhere, and of reading at least a chapter from the Bible daily.   This gave an opportunity for presenting the League without any accusation of commercialism being possible, and yet the work was so carefully done as to run no risk, on the other hand, of lavish and wasteful distribution of books to those who did not intend to carry out the pledge faithfully.   The gift was a heavy drain upon Alexander's pocket, for a far larger number availed themselves of his offer than ever he had ventured to hope, in spite of the rigid conditions.   But his joy was never greater than when giving that which cost him something, and he was

SONG SERVICE WITH AMERICAN SAILORS
AT NORFOLK, VIRGINIA, MAY, 1915

POCKET TESTAMENT LEAGUE MEMBERS AMONGST
WOMEN STUDENTS AT STATE COLLEGE, PA

MEETING IN AN AMERICAN PENITENTIARY

"When God forgives He forgets," was written in such a meeting after Dr. Chapman had preached on Divine forgiveness.

POCKET TESTAMENT LEAGUE MEMBERS AT STATE COLLEGE, PENNSYLVANIA, 1917

A NIECE PARTY AT "TENNESSEE," BIRMINGHAM, ENGLAND,
SEPTEMBER, 1919

OUTSIDE THE BIBLE INSTITUTE
OF LOS ANGELES, APRIL, 1919

WITH FRENCH E. OLIVER AND HIS WIFE (CAROLYN
WILLIAMS) AND DAUGHTER: IN CALIFORNIA,
FEBRUARY, 1919

A "POCKET TESTAMENT LEAGUE" HOUSE PARTY
AT "TENNESSEE," SEPT., 1919

WITH DR. TORREY IN CALIFORNIA,
MARCH, 1919

CHARLES M. ALEXANDER AT THE HOME OF MRS. LOUIS P. NOTT,
BRISTOL, WITH HIS POCKET TESTAMENT LEAGUE HELPERS,
OCTOBER 29, 1919

richly repaid in seeing the new spiritual vivacity and zeal in service that developed from it. After a time of hearty congregational singing, interspersed with solos and duets, Alexander would call on Mrs. McAnlis, or his wife, or others, to explain the Pocket Testament League, and give incidents of its working, and of the power of God's Word used in this way. Then he would make his offer of a Testament to any man or woman who would " sign up," then and there, to carry the book and read a chapter a day. After this had been done, and the Testaments presented, the new members were asked to rise, that they might be welcomed, and answer their first challenge by producing their books and holding them aloft. Then the whole company would sing the chorus of the rally-song of the League :—

> Take it wherever you go.
> Take it wherever you go.
> God's message of love,
> Sent down from above,
> Oh, take it wherever you go.

All members of the League were asked to hold their books high during the singing of this chorus. It was interesting to watch how the numbers of upraised hands grew from day to day—first just a few scattered here and there, largely members of the party itself, then more and more, until towards the end of the six weeks, a forest of hands with a Testament grasped affectionately in each, went up without even an invitation, at the first notes of " Take it wherever you go." The next step was to set these new members to work. Alexander reminded them of the bookstall in the lobby, and urged them to purchase one or more Testaments as they were able, and seek at once, outside the meeting, to win other members. Just as he himself never failed to draw attention to the decision form at the back of the Testament, so he urged these new workers, after securing members who would sign up to " read and carry," to turn to the back page and seek to win to Christ those who had not yet decided for Him. He asked them to return, bringing definite reports of what had been accomplished. Each day at Biola Hall these reports were called for, under stipulation that they must not be more than twenty-four hours old. The only exceptions to this rule were on Tuesdays, when the report might go back as far as the previous Friday or Saturday. The extraordinary freshness and unexpectedness of these reports acted like a spiritual tonic, and each day a larger slice of the hour had to be given up to them. From homes and from churches, from offices and places of business, from hotels and from the streets, tidings were brought of those who had promised to carry and read God's Word, and of souls surrendered to Christ. It brought an element of constant joyful surprise, and the people found it hard to wait from one meeting to the next. A lady told of approaching the manager of the hotel where she was staying. He refused, somewhat contemptuously, to accept the book. Nothing daunted, she went to work amongst the clerks, waiters, and other hotel employees, gaining many of them as members of the League and for Christ. One day the manager came to her, apologizing for his rudeness. He said he had been struck by the number of employees who were carrying and reading the little books, and said he would be very glad to accept one himself if the offer was still open. Though not able to report his acceptance of Christ, the lady asked prayers for him, and a spirit of confidence pervaded the meeting that God would speak through His own Word. Touching incidents occurred daily. One little woman, working as a dressmaker, told how, after purchasing a few Testaments, she had no money left, and was unable to reach some friends whom she specially desired to win for Christ. Then, unexpectedly, a lady, for whom she had done some work, had insisted on paying her two dollars more than the charge. She had brought the two dollars in triumph, as a gift from the Lord, to purchase the four Testaments she specially wanted. Almost immediately, some one rose in the audience to say, " If the lady who has just spoken can use them to advantage, I shall be delighted to give her six more Testaments." The offer was gratefully accepted. From that day, in an extraordinary manner, hearts were opened, and gifts of Testaments were constantly made by those able to purchase them, to others without money who were able to use them for God.

Outside these meetings, the Pocket Testament League began to catch fire everywhere. In an Army and Navy Academy near Los Angeles, where Alexander had held a meeting with his helpers, a great number of the cadets joined. Several weeks afterwards, Alexander had a letter from the Head Master, saying that the practice of reading at least one chapter a day seemed to have become a settled habit with the boys. In fact, the boys and the instructors had begun so regularly using the short intermission at dinner-time for their reading, that the authorities had established an order of " at ease " for that period.

Before leaving Los Angeles, an energetic branch of the Pocket Testament League was formed, with headquarters at the Bible Institute. For over two weeks, in the latter part of March, Dr. Torrey and the Alexander party held meetings at Redondo Beach, a sea-shore resort, some twenty miles from Los Angeles. One striking conversion that resulted was that of a Jewish proprietor of a large dry-goods store. After much spiritual struggle, he yielded himself to Christ, and with his wife, who had formerly been a Romanist, he came to the great closing services in Los Angeles. Here they both publicly confessed Christ and were received into the church.

In the little hotel at Redondo Beach, the Alexanders had been thrown into close daily contact with Dr. Torrey, and with his wife, who came over occasionally from South Pasadena. Among the many letters that poured in upon Mrs. Alexander in October, 1920, none was more tender, and none more highly prized by her than one that came from Dr. Torrey. In it he said : " For you, dear child, for you seem almost like my child to me, what can I say ? Every one who knows you knows how you loved him, but very few knew all the romance of it, and the wondrous depth of your affection for him, as I do. I always regarded it as one of the most beautiful things I ever saw in all my life. I remember that I said, on the day when you were married, and Mrs. Torrey and I took the place of father and mother for Charlie, ' You think you love one another to-day, but you do not know what love means, as you will when years have passed by.' And I know you found it so. I was so glad to be with you in Redondo nearly two years ago, and to see how love had blossomed and ripened."

After the journey east from California, during which the Alexander party had a glimpse of the mysterious grandeur of the Grand Canyon of Arizona, three busy months were given to directing the music at conferences on " Christian Fundamentals " in Baltimore, Philadelphia, and Buffalo, and to numberless other meetings in the furtherance of the Pocket Testament League.

The little home at Larchmont, which had been such a haven of rest and peace during part of the long absence from " Tennessee," was given up, and arrangements were made for leaving the two girls in America.

At last, it was possible for Alexander and his wife to turn their faces once more towards England. The Alexander party was broken up. Geo. Cooke entered upon new work elsewhere ; Albert Brown was soon afterwards married, and took up a position as assistant pastor and musical director of a church in Wilmington, North Carolina. Only Leonard Voke went to England. Alexander would not be without a pianist, and was also anxious that his youthful helper should enjoy a happy reunion with the parents whom he had not seen for six years.

If other welcomes at " Tennessee " had been full of delight, it may well be imagined what this homecoming was, on July 18th, 1919. But this time the joy was tempered with the realization of the solemn and sorrowful events that had occurred since leaving England at the end of 1914. It was a surprise to find how much the country had recovered in many ways from the effects of the war. Everywhere was a noticeable dearth of men, and a manifest difficulty and slowness of adjustment in the effort to return to pre-war conditions. A novel experience was the necessity of reporting to the police as aliens, and of securing " identity books." To Alexander's wife especially, it was strange and somewhat amusing to realize herself an alien in her own home in her native town. Both alien officers were extremely courteous, and Alexander found that one of them had been on duty at the Bingley Hall Mission in 1904, while the other had done similar duty for his meeting at the Hong-Kong Opera House in 1907 ! The home at " Tennessee " seemed unchanged, and the loving hearts that had waited long and patiently for the return of their beloved master and mistress, were warmer than ever. The joy of meeting the Cadbury family circle was not marred by the loss of a single life, although the three eldest nephews had been actively engaged ; one in ambulance work, one in the navy, and one in the air service ; the last of the three having escaped death, as by a miracle, in an aeroplane accident. The five years had wrought a great change in the nieces and nephews, most of whom had been mere children at the outbreak of war, and one of the first things planned by the Alexanders was a house-party of nieces, to take place at " Tennessee " at the end of the summer holidays.

During August, they paid a short visit to their sister, Beatrice, in her new home in Holland. It was hard to tear themselves away from the beloved family, and the four little nieces with their fascinating chatter—half of English, half of Dutch— but there was need to hasten back for the niece-party at " Tennessee."

From September 4th to 8th, a bevy of girls filled the house with laughter and merriment. Norman Thomas, the photographer, whose health had been almost shattered in the war, and who had been slowly recovering at " Tennessee " since the previous Christmas, added greatly to the fun by his good nature and humorous recitations. Happy memories of these days were crystallized in numerous photographs, which were afterwards made into albums and presented to each of the nieces. Leonard Voke's music added much to the pleasure of the house-party, and many hours were spent in singing hymns, new and old. It will readily be imagined what lay deep in the heart of Charles Alexander for these girls, so dear to him and to his wife. Everything was planned, not only to give a happy time, but to draw all nearer to Christ. The last day—Sunday—was filled with enjoyment. After attending the Friends' Morning Meeting together, the afternoon and evening were given up to reading and singing, with a pleasant break for tea out-of-doors in the log-hut. Early in the afternoon, Uncle Charles called the whole party into the drawing-room, asking them to do something for him. He gave to each a pencil and piece of paper, saying, " I want you to take a quarter of an hour to write down your own answer to the question, ' What is a Christian ? ' The room was very quiet for the next few minutes, except for the sound of pencils gliding over paper. When all were finished, and the unsigned sheets handed over to Alexander, he read the definitions aloud one after the other. They gave a beautiful revelation of the high ideals, held by each, of what a Christian should and might be, and brought a new desire that the ideal might be realized through the Holy Spirit's power. That evening there was singing in the drawing-room. Then one of the elder nieces read aloud, in her sympathetic voice, a tender poem called " The Hebrew Mother." It is the story of Abijah, the little son of Jeroboam.

All were deeply stirred by the tender story with its lesson of trust, and in a few moments Uncle Charles had suggested the words of a chorus, that has helped to strengthen the faith of many a sorrowful heart. Then all bent their heads in prayer, asking that the right musical setting might be given. In a minute or two Leonard Voke began softly playing the following melody :—

No. 436. I'll Trust Where I Cannot See.

The first time this chorus was used, outside the home circle, was at a welcome meeting given to Mr. and Mrs. Alexander, arranged by the Pocket Testament League. It was held at Sion College, on the Victoria Embankment in London, on September 16th. Dr. J. Louis Fenn, Field Secretary of the League, was chairman at this meeting, and the first prayer was led by the Rev. Barclay F. Buxton. In a few words Dr. Fenn offered a hearty welcome to the guests of the evening, expressing gratitude to God for the blessing He had granted, through the war years, to the work of the League on both sides of the Atlantic. He then briefly outlined the campaign which had been planned for the coming autumn, to further a " Bible Revival " in England. The soloist that day was a young Dutch lady, Miss Toti van Leeuwen, a guest at " Tennessee," who, after a little practice under Alexander's instruction, had mastered the English pronunciation, and the proper phrasing of a Gospel hymn, with wonderful rapidity. Rupert Lowe, of Australia, in his uniform of a trooper in King Edward's Horse, was also present. Alexander was in his element among his old friends, many of them tried and trusted through the years. After some hearty singing, he told story after story of God's working through the Pocket Testament League in America. He also told the following incident :—

"About six years ago at 'Tennessee' I happened to think that I had never spoken to a young fellow who worked in our garden about joining the League. One Sunday morning I went to speak to him as he was feeding our dog 'Kelly.' 'Harry,' I said, offering him a nice, leather-bound Testament, ' I would very much like you to carry this book with you, change it when you change your clothes, and read a chapter a day.' 'All right, Mr. Alexander, I will do it.' I just wondered if he was promising in order to get the book, but I signed him up. Be sure to get people's names down, it means a lot ! The other night, somebody told me that Harry had been 'demobbed,' and had called to see me. I found a well-set-up looking fellow, who looked me straight in the eyes, and said, ' Mr. Alexander, you know that Testament you gave me six years ago ? ' I said, ' Yes, what happened to it ? ' And he said, ' Here it is, sir ! I have been four years in the army.' The Testament was nearly coming to pieces, eight or ten leaves just worn clean off from the cover ; I wish I had brought it to let you see. ' Mr. Alexander, they put me in the burying-squad. That's what I had to do all through the war, and this book was the only thing I got any comfort out of. I never missed reading it.' I said, ' Have you had that with you these six years ? ' The marks of perspiration were on it, but it had been a real good Testament, and you could still read it. I said, ' I will give you a nice new one if you will let me keep this ; it will be very precious to me.' That shows you what a talk of five minutes can do—six years of carrying and reading God's Word. What a good return ! Why should we give away poor Testaments ? It is the Word of God. You would not give away other cheap things to anybody, and yet people with the most money often want the cheapest Testaments. ' Can't we get it any cheaper ? ' they are always asking. Why should you want the Word of God cheaper ? I used to do that way myself when I was your age, but I have quit it now, and I get just as good Testaments as I can. It's better to give away fewer good ones, than so many poor ones that won't last. Many a man who has signed up was first attracted by the beauty of the League Testament. There's no end to this work ! It just *goes* in every direction. The Lord will use you in ways that you never thought of. Let us get to work. Time is flying, souls are dying ! "

The rest of the autumn, and the early part of January, 1920, was kept busy with a series of Pocket Testament League meetings. The first were in the neighbourhood of Birmingham, at Oldbury, West Bromwich, King's Heath, and

Summerfield, with numerous small gatherings at " Tennessee." Miss van Leeuwen remained in England until November, and helped greatly with her solos, especially " The Land where the Roses never Fade." For several weeks, also, Miss Jenny van der Mersch, Secretary of the Pocket Testament League in Holland, was visiting " Tennessee," and accompanied the Alexander party to all their meetings, giving her testimony, and telling of the League work in Holland, in clearly-enunciated English. Meanwhile, Alexander had found a new soloist, Lieut. Theodore B. Atkinson, who had been converted during the war, and was anxious to devote his voice to the service of God. Miss MacGill, Dr. Fenn, and others joined the team of workers, and great blessings followed their short visits to Bath, Bristol, Ipswich, Colchester, London, and Southampton. Many of the meetings were held in public halls, some in churches, and amongst the most remarkable and unusual were some song services held in Episcopal churches, where the Pocket Testament League was also presented. Everywhere a fire was kindled for God and for His Word. Mr. A. Fraser-Harris, of the Manor House, Millbrook, who had helped in the Torrey-Alexander missions at the Royal Albert Hall, at the Strand and Brixton missions, and later in the Chapman-Alexander mission in Cardiff, wrote to Mrs. Alexander in October, 1920 : " I had an intense admiration and great affection for your husband, and was one of those who welcomed him and you at the meeting held at Sion College, about a year ago, on your return from America. The last time I saw his happy, beaming face was in Southampton, when he conducted a meeting in his own vigorous way in the interests of the Pocket Testament League, of which I then became a member. My life will bear the impress of Mr. Alexander's wonderful, manly, and uplifting influence for ever. I delight to think that this is also true of thousands of men all over the world. I thank my God upon every remembrance of him."

It was felt that England was on the eve of wonderful blessing, and the necessity of Alexander's return to America was deeply regretted. But a strong call for a " Bible Revival," which Alexander felt must be responded to, had come from Detroit, Michigan—a great centre of the automobile industry—and plans were made to leave England again in January.

Among the many visitors to " Tennessee " that autumn was Mrs. W. R. Moody. For years she had been spending her strength of body, mind, and spirit, for the girls in the Northfield Seminary, and in sharing her husband's burdens. The complete rest in the happy home of her friends proved an effective tonic, and helped to restore the needed strength. When the news reached Mrs. Moody, a few months later, that Charles Alexander had suddenly been called away to heaven, she wrote to Mrs. Alexander : " All night I lay with the memories of those seven precious weeks in your home. If God's grace is sufficient to uphold you now, I shall dread nothing in the future. Never was there a more ideal love than yours and Charlie's. . . . I loved him like an own brother. His loving kindnesses to me, while with you, and in London, will be amongst my sweetest memories."

The opportunity of spending Christmas at home was a great pleasure to the Alexanders, who little realised that this would be their last Christmas together.

The happy days were shared by Miss Frances D. Shaw, an old college-friend of Mrs. Alexander, and a great-niece of Frances Ridley Havergal. A reminiscence of hers gives a beautiful picture of Charles Alexander in his home. " My Christmas visit to ' Tennessee ' is an unforgettable memory. Just previously I had been through a time of trouble and anxiety, and I arrived on that bleak afternoon of December 23rd, 1919, a little tired in mind and body. Almost as soon as the hall door opened, a cheery voice said, ' Come in, come in, Miss Fan. When you once come in here you will leave all your troubles behind you.' A warm glow, physical and mental, enwrapped me at once. It was one of those wonderful flashes of intuition for which Mr. Alexander was noted—for he knew nothing at all, then, of my circumstances.

" What impressed me chiefly about him in that happy visit, was the extraordinary blend of devoted religious feeling and shrewd judgment, combined with charming kindliness and courtesy. Here was no visionary wrapt away from earthly affairs. He brought his love for God into every-day doings, weighed practical problems in the light of a sound common sense, and with his keen insight and quick grasp of another's mind diagnosed the trouble and the remedy in a flash.

" Of his wonderful charm as a host one need hardly speak, as it must be known to many. It was the attention to little things, the thoughtfulness in ways that would escape the ordinary man's attention altogether, that struck me most. He knew by instinct what would please best, save you most, help your cast of mind. Nothing was too much trouble, too small to matter. A perfunctory and shallow politeness was foreign to his nature. He wanted you to have as good a time as he could possibly give you.

" On Christmas Eve we went a short walk together, and a fast-trotting pony in a light buggy passed us, which we paused to admire. ' Ah, Miss Fan,' he said, ' there are two things I love most—a good Gospel song, and a good horse.' On those Christmas evenings I realized his charm as a story-teller, enhanced by that wonderful voice of his. On Christmas Day I went with my host and hostess to two large family gatherings. There Mr. Alexander was at his best, the centre of life and fun, entering into every one's pleasure, radiating happiness and love. At the end of the Christmas evening party, when the fun and games were over, we sang that exquisite song, ' We journey to a city,' led by his beautiful voice. The festivities ended by his prayer to the heavenly Father, giving thanks for the Christmas happiness and family love."

A few days later, Mr. and Mrs. J. Kennedy Maclean, with their daughter and young son, came to " Tennessee " for a New Year's visit. " We all sat up to see the old year die," says Mr. Maclean. " There were games for all, Mr. and Mrs. Alexander entering into the enjoyment of the occasion with a whole-hearted joyousness. A bran-tub contained a fine variety of presents, no one being omitted. The joy of my twelve-year-old boy, when a handsome camera bearing his name was uncovered, can easily be imagined. Soon after our arrival, Mr. Alexander had talked cameras to his young namesake, and seeing the sparkle in the boy's eyes, determined to give him an up-to-date Kodak. Then, slipping out of the house without being observed, he made the journey into town, returning as quietly as he had departed. Camera and developing apparatus were all complete, and arrangements made to give the boy a day's instruction under a sympathetic expert.

"Everybody under the kindly roof of 'Tennessee' lived and served in the stimulating atmosphere of love ; it was love that made the wheels go round. 'We can't get on here without love,' said the housekeeper on one occasion to a new cook, to whom the conditions at 'Tennessee' were a perplexing puzzle. And that was perfectly true. You felt it as soon as you stepped over the doorway, and like a mantle it wrapped you round in its gracious influence at every turn.

"To the personal comfort of his guests Alexander devoted himself with the tenderest care, his face glowing all the time with that infectious joy that spread like a shaft of sunlight to all within its sphere. And then, when the day was hastening to its close, he would gather his friends into the drawing-room, and sing with them those delightful songs of Zion with which his name will ever be associated. Often he would tell them stories of the negro men and women of the Southern States, told in the inimitable dialect none but a Southerner could reproduce ; stories that he had collected on his frequent travels ; stories sad, and stories gay ; one following another in the most delightful variety, until sometimes the enchanted listeners, sore with laughing, had to plead with him to desist. As the hour for retiring approached, he would bring the company back to the things of God, and as all dropped upon their knees, he would lead them in a prayer as simple and beautiful as that of a little child

"At one with him in all his enterprises and activities, Mrs. Alexander shared with her husband the throne of their home. There, as in the larger world outside, they thought and acted together, and even in the simplest matters sought each other's advice and judgment. Thus, as the years passed, it became impossible to think of either of them in any relationship without also thinking of the other. More and more they blended into a perfect oneness, each depending upon and requiring the other ; and within the sacred circle of their own home this closeness of heart and aim shone with a radiance that lifted the married state into an exalted sphere. With them, married life never degenerated into a commonplace or humdrum relationship ; it was the supreme expression of earthly felicity, never shadowed by a doubt or a misunderstanding. Lovers to the end, they walked together in shining garments down life's pathway, hand in hand, and heart in heart. Of all the endearing terms that fell from Mr. Alexander's lips, nothing ever sounded so charmingly appropriate as the name " Honey," as he often called his wife. It is frequently used among the warm-hearted people of the Southern States, but the word can be uttered without expression, and we may hear it a thousand times without being impressed. To hear it, however, as he used to say it, suggested a tender affection that had no end."

On January 19th, 1920, Alexander left his English home to sail to America for the last time. He seemed especially full of buoyant health and energy, and looked forward with eager anticipation to the campaign in Detroit, which was to be held through February and March. On leaving Southampton, he wrote a little note to the housekeeper at " Tennessee," which reflects the enjoyment which the past few months had brought him : " The days we have spent in our God-given home have gone by so swiftly that it seems almost a dream. My happiest days with Mrs. Alexander have been spent while we were surrounded by all that makes our home. You have been a part of it all, and we have prayed for you each day through all the years you have given your loving, splendid service—to think of home and happy times is to think of you, and the maids and the men who have made it all possible. Thank you for the special care that you have taken this time of my precious wife. I am glad you all love to read and talk about the Bible and good things. Encourage this all you can. We shall be delighted to have letters, any length, from any of you."

Mr. Theodore Atkinson, the soloist, had sailed to America, some weeks earlier, to enjoy the benefit of a time of study in the Moody Bible Institute in Chicago, but on board the *Mauretania* with Alexander and his wife were a young niece, Miss Betty Butler, and Leonard C. Voke, his pianist. After a few days in New York City, Philadelphia, Coatesville, and Northfield, Mass., Alexander and his party entered upon the great "Bible Revival" campaign in Detroit, on February 12th.

In some ways this work was along different lines from any of which Alexander had ever before been the leader. The invitation to Detroit had come from a very large Methodist church, with a membership of over three thousand, and many more attenders, having also flourishing Sunday schools and young people's societies. There were two co-pastors at the head of it, one devoting himself chiefly to the preaching, and the other chiefly to the pastoral work. These men, Dr. M. S. Rice and Dr. Charles B. Allen, were assisted by a large board of trustees and church officials, numbering about fifty men, many of whose wives took an active part also in the work of the church.

Dr. Rice had been in England and France during the war, and had become most enthusiastic over the marvellous power of the Pocket Testament League as a means of reaching and holding the soldiers for Christ. This was the reason for the urgent, insistent invitation to Charles Alexander, who was felt to be the man, above all others, whom God might use to lead a Bible revival in Detroit. It was, in fact, the last extended movement led by him, and was in some respects as wonderful as any of even his great and varied experiences. It is therefore of special interest to have some account of the work in his own words. "For years," he said, "a group of friends, few at first, but now a great host, have been praying with me for A BIBLE REVIVAL WHICH WOULD REACH ALL AGES AND ALL CLASSES IN A GREAT CITY. Here in Detroit we have at last seen our prayers answered. At the present time a Bible revival is sweeping over this great commercial centre such as has never been known in the history of the city. Everywhere one goes, on street-cars, in factories, in schools and commercial houses, one sees the little brown or green Testaments which mark the owners as members of the Pocket Testament League.

"The centre of the work was a big Methodist Tabernacle where Dr. M. S. Rice and I have been holding meetings for the past seven weeks. From the very first night we determined to have a Bible revival. In a short time the people there were on fire with love for God's Word, and with zeal for using it in soul-winning. Then I addressed a general meeting of ministers, and calls began to pour in for some one to spread the fire to their people.

"Mr. George T. B. Davis, a member of our party, was sent out to visit churches and Sunday schools and various gatherings of Christians, telling how they could be made over, by getting every one to read and carry God's Word, and to use it in winning others to Christ. We know that sixty-nine churches have already been reached by the Bible revival, and over twenty-four thousand Testaments have been placed in the pockets of the people.

" From first to last, the Bible revival has been a soul-winning movement, backed by a great volume of intercessory prayer. From only partial records that have come to hand, one thousand eight hundred and twenty-nine have been reported as having accepted Christ thus far. A group of about twenty-four business men, from one church, lunch together each week. They saw the great possibilities of the Pocket Testament League as an agency for soul-winning. They themselves first enlisted, then started to sign up others in their places of business, and among their friends, and in outlying churches. At the close of their first week they reported seven hundred and thirty-eight League members, and one hundred and thirty-nine decisions for Christ. As the results were read out, the men themselves were greatly astonished, and one man remarked that he had never heard of such a thing being done by a group of business men in Detroit.

" Here are some examples of the way in which the movement is reaching the commercial classes. In one of the leading banks of the city nearly one hundred officials and employees have become daily Bible-readers, and are carrying God's Word in their pockets. One of our party called at a newspaper office in Detroit. He was told that several of the staff wished to join the League, and in a few minutes the news-editor, a feature-writer, and two copy-readers were enlisted. Four more of the staff were enrolled at other times, including an editorial writer, who insisted on buying Testaments to give away.

" Detroit is the centre of the motor-car industry. One woman employed by the big Cadillac Motor Company attended the Tabernacle meetings and listened night after night to the stories of soul-winning with the Bible, told by members of the Pocket Testament League. She secured a few Testaments and began to work in her office. Thus far, she has enrolled one hundred and eighty-two in the Pocket Testament League, including the factory manager ; and five of them accepted Christ. Another young lady signed up eighty-two in her brother's factory, and became so enthused over the work that she is thinking of going to the Moody Bible Institute. A high official of the Maxwell Motor-Car Company bought one thousand Testaments and offered one to any employee who would join the League, and at the first meeting two hundred and sixty-three were enrolled. A minister told me his daughter was employed in another great motor-car factory. The foreman in her department used such bad and insulting language that she reported the matter to higher officials. Recently the girls noticed a great change in the man. They could not understand it until one of them said, ' Why, don't you know ? He carries a Pocket Testament.' That was sufficient explanation.

" The work of the boys and girls in connexion with the Bible revival has been most striking. Large numbers have faithfully attended the meetings, and have been intelligent workers, spreading the movement in the public schools and among their friends. On our closing night, a special service for the young people was conducted by my wife while the main meeting was in progress. About two hundred boys and girls were present. Mrs. Alexander carefully questioned them regarding their work throughout the campaign, and secured the following astonishing figures; nine hundred and ninety-seven had been signed up in the League by those boys and girls, and of this number six hundred and twenty-six were reported as having made their decision for Christ."

Hand in hand with love for the Word of God went the joy which was so infectious in Alexander's life, and which found natural expression in song. The solos of Mr. Theodore Atkinson, and the playing of Mr. Voke, brought a new appreciation of Gospel hymns, while the singing of the fine choir of five hundred voices, under the same inspiring leadership that had made the Royal Albert Hall and the Melbourne Exhibition Building ring with melody, filled the great Methodist Tabernacle with heavenly music, which was wafted out over the whole city of Detroit. A " sunbeam choir " of some hundreds of boys and girls grew out of the small beginning of five or six lads whom Alexander called out of the audience, one of the first nights of the campaign, to come to him on the platform and sing a chorus. The Sunbeam Choir sat in the great gallery, facing the platform, and were always given a special part in the service. Among the many choruses which they sang, with a vigour that stirred the whole meeting, was a new one written by Mr. Voke:

I Would Be Like Daniel Bold.

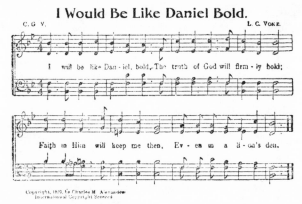

Copyright, 1909, by Charles M. Alexander.
International Copyright Secured.

The Pocket Testament League appealed to them as much as to the older people, and many of them became enthusiastic workers. Each night when " Carry your Bible " was sung, Alexander asked all the members of the League to hold their Testaments high. At first the upraised hands, each holding a Testament, were scattered sparsely over the Tabernacle, but towards the close of the meetings, as at Biola Hall in Los Angeles, a forest of hands would be raised, and the unanimous response of the choir upon the platform was only equalled by that of the eager crowd of boys and girls that faced them in the gallery, with Testaments held as high as little arms could stretch, and bright eyes shining.

An added source of happiness to Alexander during the weeks spent in Detroit, was the opportunity of seeing much of his beloved mother. His brother, Rev. Homer J. Alexander, had been called to the pastorate of a Presbyterian church in Trenton, Ohio, some twenty-five miles from Detroit. The family home was transferred there from Fremont just at the beginning of the Detroit campaign, and mother, brothers and nieces were able to share in many of the meetings. During an afternoon service especially for older people, the hearts of all present were deeply stirred, when at Alexander's persuasion his little mother stood by his side upon the platform, his arm around her shoulder, and joined her sweet faint treble to his softened baritone in her favourite hymn of the South:

> There'll be no sorrow there,
> There'll be no sorrow there,
> In heaven above
> Where all is love,
> There'll be no sorrow there.

After leaving Detroit, some busy weeks in Chicago brought Alexander into close touch once more with his old friends at the Moody Bible Institute. " He was our best-known alumnus," wrote Dr. James M. Gray, Dean of the Institute, " and his every visit to his Alma Mater met the warmest welcome. In the summer of 1920, negotiations were in progress for his addition to our faculty and the staff of our Extension Department, because we so highly valued his inspirational qualities and his example as a soul-winner."

Alexander gave one or two illustrated lectures to the students on Gospel music, and how to use it, and many remarked on the apparent buoyancy of his health and his overflowing energy. " It was my rare good fortune," wrote the secretary of the Alumni Association, " to be present at Mr. Alexander's last service with our Institute students. I shall never forget it. As I think of it now, it seems that, had Mr. Alexander known it was to be the last, and had planned for it, it could not have been more appropriate. One who was present expressed his appreciation, and, as we went out, said, ' I have never known such a bundle of sunshine and inspiration to be gathered together in one package.' How we do thank God for his wonderful ministry."

Rev. Samuel Chadwick, Principal of Cliff College, near Sheffield, England, and successor to Rev. Thomas Champness, was in Chicago at this time, lecturing to the students at the Moody Bible Institute. " We met at the Institute," wrote Mr. Chadwick later, " and had lunch together afterwards. He was just the same happy soul, and as keen as ever about the salvation of others. I have never known a more lovable man." " He came to our hotel to be our guest," added Mrs. Chadwick, " but became our host, out of his usual generosity and goodness, and we shall never forget that meal."

Through June, July, and part of August, Philadelphia became Alexander's headquarters. Mr. Atkinson, the soloist, had gone home to Australia from Detroit, and only Mr. Voke accompanied Alexander to the various conferences and Pocket Testament League services, during the final weeks in his own land. One of the most memorable occasions was the State Christian Endeavour Convention at Columbus, Ohio, from June 22nd to 25th, in which Alexander had three Song Services a day, and set the young Endeavourers on fire with love and enthusiasm for the Word of God, and the desire to win souls to Christ.

CHAPTER TWENTY-SEVEN

From the Earthly Home to the Heavenly

1920

THE busy weeks in Philadelphia, which Alexander had devoted largely to work upon his hymn-books, and in preparation for the " Bible revival " campaigns he was expecting to undertake, first in England, and then in America, drew to a close.

One of the last matters to occupy his careful and prayerful attention before sailing for England, was the appointment of a committee of strong Christian business men to care for the work of the Pocket Testament League during his absence from America. He expected to be away for about a year, if the " Bible revival " in England developed as he prayed it might.

On hearing the almost incredible news a few weeks later, that the man who had seemed in the flood-tide of his strength and usefulness on earth, had been called to other service, Mr. Alwyn Ball, chairman of this committee, wrote to Mrs. Alexander : " We thank God for granting us even a little fellowship in his sunshine. How wonderful that he should have arranged matters here before leaving. We pray that our blessed Lord may show us His will, and how to extend this service for Him." The treasurer, Mr. G. H. Gudebrod, said, " I only met him personally at the Eighth Avenue Mission about a year-and-a-half ago, when I first became interested in the Pocket Testament League. I do not think I ever learned to like a man as much on so short an acquaintance. I believe he was the most sincere and devoted Christian worker I have ever met, and, with it all, the most happy man in his work that I have known. I shall always consider it a great privilege to have known him, even for so short a time." Mr. Hugh R. Monro, the vice-chairman, expressed the same tender regard : " We who were privileged to know Mr. Alexander and feel the warmth and spiritual passion of that great heart of his, find it difficult to become adjusted to the thought of a world without him. Of no other do I seem to cherish so many tender impressions—impressions of the kind that stir the soul with holy purpose. I recall how he used to call me ' Bishop,' using the term in a more discriminating sense, I believe, than is common, for did we not both belong to the spiritual bishopric, which in Scriptural terms includes every ministering servant of Christ ? "

The last Sunday before sailing, Alexander was alone in New York City, having gone over from Philadelphia on Pocket Testament League business. Rev. J. J. Ross, D.D., of Chicago, who was preaching in Dr. Haldeman's church that Sunday, and who had frequently seen Alexander upon the platform, met him personally for the first time. " I want to tell you of my unique and happy experience in meeting your husband," wrote Dr. Ross to Mrs. Alexander the following October. " I was preaching in the First Baptist Church of New York City on August 15th, and Mr. Alexander came to attend the morning service. At about 10.40 he came round to the pastor's room, to meet and greet me before the service began. I can see his happy face now. ' What brought you here this morning ? ' I asked. ' When we are in New York over Sunday, and I am free from other engagements, my wife and I always come here to worship,' was his quick and happy reply. ' Dr. Haldeman is a great and wonderful preacher and teacher of the Word, and I knew he would not have any scrub in his pulpit, so I have come to hear your message. You are in the apostolic succession, brother ! so take care how you preach about Christ. He will be present to hear what you say.' With a warm grip of the hand, and a smile that was almost heavenly, he turned to go into the auditorium. I gazed after him as he went down the hall-way, and noticed that after a few steps he stopped as if he had forgotten something. Turning round, he called back, ' While you are preaching, I will be praying.'

" He seemed to enjoy the service that morning, and his presence was an inspiration to me. After it was over, he came forward to speak to me, and his eyes were sparkling through tears of deep feeling, as he said, ' God bless you, brother ! You are no scrub-preacher ! Your message has blessed me through and through. I have real joy in putting you on my prayer list, and will pray for you always.' I felt strengthened when he told me that, and I do not think that, because he has gone Home, he has taken me off his prayer list. Our Lord prays there for us, and Mr. Alexander is with Him, and I feel confident that he is praying for us still, along with his Lord. Nothing would do that Sunday, but I must accompany him to the Belmont Hotel and have lunch with him. We spent about two-hours-and-a-half together in fellowship over the things of Christ, talking, praying, and singing. To me it was a wonderful time. Mr. Alexander told me of his plans for the future in the Gospel, and as he talked of preaching and singing Christ, he would say, as only he could say it, ' What a *wonderful* Saviour ! ' " On October 11th, Alexander's last day but one upon earth, Dr. Ross was writing to him from the office of his church in Chicago : " I have not forgotten your great kindness to me in New York City. It seems peculiar to me that one like yourself could entertain a stranger as you did. I had often heard you sing, and had witnessed you leading great congregations in song. Your spirit and manner were always a help to me, and I have thanked God a good many times for such a life." When the letter reached England, the one for whom it was intended had been in Heaven for several days !

Friday evening, August 20th, was the eve of sailing for England, and, in the way he loved, Alexander gathered around him a group of a dozen young people, including the Rock brothers, both ministers of churches in New Jersey, and several other former helpers, for a delightful farewell time of fellowship and song.

Ten days later, the last day of August, found the English home of " Tennessee " a-flutter once again with the joyful excitement of welcoming home the beloved master and mistress. Alexander's correspondence file was full of invitations for work in his own land and the British Isles, and some urgent messages from Australia and New Zealand, where many were longing for a sight of his happy face and the inspiration of his presence. But while he had visions of a great " Bible revival " in England, and expected to remain there for nine months or a year, he had a strange sense of being unable to make any definite promises beyond the coming winter. A few weeks earlier, in replying to an invitation for a campaign in Louisiana for June, 1921, he had said, " As yet I have no definite dates or plans for the future. My present intention is to stay in England until next summer at least, unless the Lord makes it very plain that I should do differently. Things are so uncertain I could not promise you a date, so I had better not be counted on." For a few days after his return, he gave himself up to family visits and to work at home in his delightful " Den," where he continued the sifting and selecting of hymns for the new standard book he was preparing. A five-seater motor-car which he had brought back from the United States, as a gift to his wife, was a great delight to them both. Day by day, through the glorious sunshine of those September days, they explored the country roads round Birmingham, towards Stratford-on-Avon, Evesham, Warwick, Worcester, and other places. It was all new to them, as they had never had a car in England before, and they revelled in the pleasure they were able to give their friends. Alexander, though able to drive himself, had great pride and confidence in his wife's driving, and loved to call her his " chauffeur." Side by side they drank in the loveliness of the country-side, Alexander, map in hand, guiding and directing.

Among other visitors during that month were, as so often happened, some of the new friends made on board ship. Mr. and Mrs. Spencer Kellogg, of Buffalo, New York, spent a night or two at " Tennessee," and, on one of the evenings, Alexander took them down to his " Den," where he showed them some of his thousands of beautiful lantern-slides, proudly displaying them himself on the electric lantern given him by his wife. A few days later, startled by a short announcement in *The Times*, Mr. Kellogg wrote : " Mr. Alexander was seemingly in such wonderful health and spirits, we are in absolute ignorance as to what can have happened. We feel as if we had known both of you for years. Personally I felt so acutely his wonderful personality and great magnetism, that I fell in love with him. The second time I talked with him, on the *Caronia*, I was astonished at the feeling that welled up from my heart."

Several others who met Charles Alexander during those summer months of 1920, were struck with the heavenly radiance that seemed to surround him. Because he seemed to be in need of a rest, before beginning the winter's programme of meetings, plans were in the air for a motor trip with his wife in October through Cornwall or the North of Wales. In the meantime, Alexander made several journeys to London and elsewhere, and held one or two meetings. At Coventry, on one of the journeys up to London, two men entered the railway compartment in which he and Mr. F. S. Turney were seated. One of them was a stout, well-built, fresh-faced man, with a cheery, pleasant manner, the other, by way of contrast, was thin and short, a jockey, without doubt. " Well, what is on to-day ? " asked Alexander. " Coventry Races, sir, just over," was the reply. Alexander's companion, knowing his tireless manner of reaching every available man for Christ, and his tact in doing it, wondered what was coming. " Have you won anything ? " " Well, no, sir ! You see we are not betting men, but sell what is called a ' tip ' for half-a-crown, as to what we think is the most likely horse to win." " How do you get your crowd and attract people's attention ? " was the next question. After some further talk, Alexander threw in, with a laugh—" Ever try a cow race ? There's more fun in that than any horse-race ever run ! " Some more pleasant banter, and talk that showed Alexander's knowledge of the " points " of a good horse, put the two men entirely at their ease. Then, reaching slowly into his back pocket, a beautifully-bound Testament was produced and handed over for inspection. " Do you know what that is ? " said Alexander to the older man. Unhesitatingly came the reply, " A Testament." After the pictures and handsome binding had been examined, the man slowly read the membership pledge of the Pocket Testament League. " If you care to sign that promise—and I suppose you can find time to read a chapter every day if you want to—you may keep that Testament." " I'll sign it, sir," said the man, with an earnestness in his tone quite foreign to his racing talk. Accepting the loan of a proffered fountain-pen, he boldly signed his name and passed the book across to show what he had done. At Euston station, while Mr. Turney called a taxi, there was time for a few earnest words in private. " Well, what did you make of our friend, in the finish ? " was Mr. Turney's question as they drove to a hotel. " One of the greatest surprises of my life ! He told me he used to be an evangelist on the race-course, but before that he was a racing man ; the temptation had been too great, and he had slipped back into his old life. He says he no longer drinks as he used to do, and that his mother is a good Christian woman. He seemed much impressed, and I believe he will get back to the Lord."

The last meeting ever held by Charles Alexander, was a Young People's Meeting at the Friends' Institute, Greet, a suburb of Birmingham, on Tuesday, September 28th. He and his wife were accompanied by Mr. L. C. Voke, his pianist ; Miss Jenny van der Mersch, the secretary of the Pocket Testament League in Holland, some members of the staff from the League headquarters in London, and other friends. Only about eighty persons were present, but Alexander gave himself as unsparingly to a small as to a large gathering. Before the evening was over, all had joined the League, promising to read a chapter from the Bible daily, and to carry a Testament with them wherever they went.

A day or two before this, Alexander and his wife had called on their cousin and lawyer, Mr. Walter Barrow. " I never thought," he wrote a few days later, " that the evening you motored round to Lawn House was the last time I should see him in this world. Charles was a real, strong man—there was nothing weak about him. I always felt that he faced life with open-eyed bravery and sanity. I thought he looked rather worn since he came back from his last trip to America, but he was just his own charming self, bright and cheerful, and full of thought for others."

On Wednesday, September 29th, Alexander went to Southsea, near Portsmouth, on Pocket Testament League business. At Southsea station, with Dr. Fenn, he spent some time examining the contents of the bookstall, for books and publications

NOONDAY SERVICE OUTSIDE AN AUTOMOBILE FACTORY AT DETROIT, MARCH, 1920

CHARLES M. ALEXANDER AND HIS EVANGELISTIC PARTY AT DETROIT, MICHIGAN,
FEBRUARY 12 TO APRIL 6, 1920

G. T. B. Davis *(Pocket Testament League)*   Edwin H. Bookmyer *(Secretary)*
Miss Haru Inoguchi *(Girls' Worker)*   Mrs. C. M. Alexander   Miss Betty Butler *(English niece on a visit)*
Mr. Theodore B. Atkinson *(Soloist)*   Mr. C. M. Alexander   Leonard C. Voke *(Pianist)*

AT HOME AGAIN IN ENGLAND, SEPTEMBER, 1920

AUGUST, 1919

AS BEST MAN
AT THE WEDDING OF
MR. J. J. VIRGO,
OCTOBER 12, 1920

GOING TO "THE DEN," SEPTEMBER, 1920

WITH DR. LYNN H. HOUGH

of every kind always had for him an irresistible fascination. Then he got into conversation with the manager. It was not long before the inevitable question was asked, " Are you a Christian ? " The man replied that he was. " What are you doing at it ? " was the next question. The answer this time was not quite so ready, nor was it altogether satisfactory. But there passed between the men one of those sacred exchanges of experience that sometimes change the whole current of a life, and it brought back to one of them the glow of a fire that had been steadily waning. Alexander then spoke of the advantages of the Pocket Testament League, and challenged his newly-made friend to speak to his minister about it, and have a branch started in his church. If he would, Alexander promised that on his next visit to Southsea, he would make him the present of a handsome Testament. The two men never met again ; it was the first and the last time they were ever thrown together on the sea of life ; but a month or two later Mrs. Alexander was at Southsea, and introduced herself to the bookstall manager. Finding that the challenge had been met, and that there was now an active branch of the Pocket Testament League in the church he attended, Mrs. Alexander gladly gave him the promised Testament. It had a sacred value to the man who received it, as he thought of the blessing that had come to him through the passing visit of this man of God.

The next afternoon, Thursday, September 30th, Alexander reached home again, feeling unaccountably weary, but bright as usual. Only one guest was at " Tennessee," Miss Jenny van der Mersch, and as she was much like a daughter in the house, she shared a cosy supper upstairs with Alexander and his wife. During that night he was awakened by a sudden heart-attack, that almost took him Home, and caused agonizing pain. Medical aid was at once summoned, and after some hours the pain slowly yielded, but his strength seemed sapped to its foundations. Careful examination appeared to contradict the thought of heart trouble, for the pulse was full and strong and regular. The doctor was puzzled, but the thought of serious danger receded, especially as the pain disappeared entirely. Several engagements for the next few days were cancelled, but in a day or two, since he longed for the fresh air and more of the delightful motor rides through the open country, he was able to enjoy them again. Once more, for several days in succession, he and his wife sat blissfully side by side, gazing out upon the glories of the autumn foliage, glowing in the bright sunshine, as they sped along. Only his strength seemed strangely slow in returning, and they began to plan for a longer holiday. On one of these days some cousins called just as the motor ride was to begin, and were taken home in the little car. " I shall always love to think of you two," wrote one of the cousins a few days later, " as you came into the drawing-room at ' Tennessee ' that bright afternoon Cousin Charles looked so absolutely content and to have such confidence in thee. The radiant peace and happiness of his face has abode with me ever since."

Alexander had promised to act as best man for his friend, J. J. Virgo, whose marriage was to take place in Birmingham, on Tuesday, October 12th. As it was to be a very quiet wedding, with only a short service at the church, the doctor gave his permission for the plan to be carried out. On Monday morning, October 11th, Miss van der Mersch left for Holland, and that evening Mr. Virgo arrived at " Tennessee." Alexander seemed so much stronger, and more like his natural self, that the burden of anxiety lifted from his wife's heart. That evening he was radiant, giving himself up entirely to making his old friend happy. Mr. Voke was also at " Tennessee," and the four spent a delightful evening round the piano, Alexander and Virgo joining their voices in some of the old songs they had sung together in Melbourne and Sydney. Then Alexander tried over some of Mr. Voke's recently-written hymns, especially a favourite new one—" Redeemed by the precious blood of Jesus." His tones rang out, full, and strong, and sweet ; no one would have dreamed that he had been so strangely weak, and his wife listened in happy surprise.

The wedding took place at noon next day, in Handsworth Church. As Alexander stood with reverently bowed head by the side of his friend, such a heavenly radiance seemed to surround his tall, graceful figure, and the sweetness of his countenance was so strangely beautiful, that his wife, sitting in one of the front pews, turned with a whisper to Mr. Voke, who sat next to her, asking whether he saw it. " Yes," he whispered back, " isn't it wonderful ! " A group photograph was taken soon afterwards on the steps of the church, but the camera did not catch the strange, unearthly radiance, showing only the weakness that was hidden from visible sight.

On returning to " Tennessee " from the church, Alexander did not feel tired. It was a lovely, sunny day, and, after luncheon, he and his wife strolled round the garden together, admiring the roses, and paying a short visit to the " Den," to look through some of the hymns in which his interest never waned, and to see how the work on the new book was progressing. Then he was persuaded to return for rest to the house, which, almost for the first time since their return home, was empty of visitors. That peaceful October afternoon and evening were filled with a radiance which must have streamed through the opening gates of which both husband and wife were quite unaware, as they enjoyed sweet fellowship together, and planned for the welcome they meant to give next day to the beloved sister, Beatrice Boeke, already starting on her way from Holland for a short visit to " Tennessee." Their faithful housekeeper, Eliza Shrimpton, who had been in the Cadbury family since Mrs. Alexander's childhood, shared some of the happy hours with them, calling forth the irrepressible merriment which was always so ready to break out. The day ended, as usual, with some reading from the blessed Book they both loved, and a few words of heartfelt prayer and thanksgiving. Sweet sleep was given until about an hour after midnight, and then, through a short, sharp attack of pain, lasting but a few moments, of which he seemed scarcely to be conscious, the great, glad spirit of Charles M. Alexander passed with sudden and joyful surprise into the presence of his Master, before the unneeded help of any kind could be summoned.

> No tender yet sad farewell,
>   From his quivering lips was heard ;
> So softly he crossed the quiet stream
>   That 'twas not by a ripple stirred.
>
> He was spared the pain of parting tears,
>   He was spared all mortal strife ;
> It was scarcely dying—he only passed
>   In a moment to endless life.

> Weep not for the swift release
> From earthly pain and care ;
> Nor grieve that he reached his home and rest
> Ere he knew that he was there.
>
> But think of his sweet surprise,
> The sudden and strange delight
> He felt when he met his Saviour's smile,
> And walked with Him in white.

To her, who was left behind, had come the severest test of faith, and trust, that life could hold. Many a time, as they had sung together that beautiful chorus of his—

> I'll trust where I cannot see, Lord,
> I'll trust where I cannot see,
> No matter how dark the way may be,
> I'll trust where I cannot see !

her heart had cried out in secret—" *Not that test*, O Lord, spare me *that* test ! " But the test had been given, and with it the undying promise, ' My grace IS sufficient for thee." From bowed head, and heart, and trembling lips, came the response : " By Thy grace, I will not fail Thee—or him ! " Then the Lord did wondrously, flooding the poor, pain-stricken heart with peace that passeth understanding, as she leaned upon the unshakable promises of God. " Taken from you for a short time, in presence, not in heart," for " the Lord hath need of him." And *he* was safe for ever from any fear of that temporary loneliness from which even his brave, loving heart had shrunk. Copied from one notebook to another of his early days, were some verses that revealed how he shrank from it, even in distant anticipation— an anticipation which had faded away in the blessed hope of " His appearing."

> One of us, dear—but one—
> Will sit by a bed, with a marvellous face
> And clasp a hand
> Growing cold, as it feels for the spirit-land.
> Darling, which one ?
>
> One of us, dear—but one—
> By an open grave will drop a tear
> And homeward go,
> The anguish of an unshared grief to know ;
> Darling, which one ?

Thank God, that not for a moment was the glowing brightness of his happy nature dimmed by that sorrow, and the grace, which would have been his in like need, was given to her who must face it, alone, as a means of testimony. She did not gaze on the calm, sweet, smiling face with any sense of more than temporary farewell, and as she placed in the beloved hand the little Testament that she had carried in her pocket for years, the words rang triumphantly in her soul, " Absent from the body, at home with the Lord," and, " If the Spirit of Him that raised up Jesus from the dead dwell in you, He that raised up Christ from the dead, shall also bring to life your mortal bodies, by His Spirit that dwelleth in you." " Eye hath not seen, nor ear heard, neither hath entered into the heart of man, the things which God hath prepared for them that love Him."

So clear was the glorious revelation, through the Word of God, of the joy ahead, and even of the present joy into which Charles Alexander had already entered, so wonderful the world-wide influence of his own radiantly happy faith, that all who loved him " in Christ " seemed lifted up with him into heavenly places in Christ Jesus. Death to the body was a real fact, the grave had a temporary victory, but faith could leap on to the day when the lifeless, natural body of this believer in Christ, about to be sown in the earth in utter weakness, would be raised by the pledge of Christ's own resurrection, in glory and incorruptible beauty, and in spiritual power. Therefore, even now, in anticipation of that glorious event, faith could sing in the darkness of sorrow, " O death, where is thy sting ? O grave, where is thy victory ? Thanks be unto God Who giveth *us* the victory through our Lord Jesus Christ."

In the meantime, this was for Charles Alexander the coronation of his life of sunny trust, and his Home-going must be celebrated with joy in *his* joy, unmarred by selfish thoughts of the loneliness of those left behind. The earthly home where his voice had so often been lifted in songs of praise, and which he had filled with brightness, must have no shadows of gloom upon it—though a reverent hush must needs pervade it at the nearness of heaven. But roses everywhere must speak of that " land where the roses never fade," upon whose beauty his eyes were already gazing ; and, even though with broken tones, songs must continue to rise, and joy triumph over grief. Above all, the very suddenness of his " Home-call " must be used, through prayer, to bring souls to Christ, in fulfilment of Charles Alexander's " eager expectation and hope," that Christ should be glorified in his body, whether by life or by death.

On Saturday morning, October 16th, that precious body was laid to rest in the grave where he had placed the body of his little son nine years earlier. Before leaving " Tennessee," the friends, who had gathered there, knelt in the rose-fragrant drawing-room around the simple oak casket, which bore no other inscription than his own familiar signature, reproduced upon a plain brass plate:

Charles M. Alexander
II Timothy 2:15.

He had never left his home for a meeting, and rarely for any kind of engagement, without dropping upon his knees to ask for blessing and guidance, and now, though he himself was gone, the precious body should not be borne away without that benediction.

Owing to the fact that no funeral is allowed in Lodge Hill Cemetery on Saturday afternoons, the morning hour, at which the ceremony of burial took place, prevented many from being present, yet a company of over three hundred gathered round the flower-lined grave, that lies side by side with that of his wife's father and mother. Along the walks which his feet had trodden, the casket was borne upon a hand-

"O DEATH,
WHERE IS
THY STING?

O GRAVE,
WHERE IS
THY VICTORY?"

I Cor. 15:55

"ABSENT FROM THE BODY . . . AT HOME (R.V.) WITH THE LORD."
Oct. 15, 1920   II Cor. 5:8

"THE THINGS SEEN ARE TEMPORARY (lit. Gr.),
BUT THE THINGS NOT SEEN ARE ETERNAL."
Oct. 16, 1920   II Cor. 4:18

"IF THE SPIRIT OF HIM WHO RAISED JESUS FROM THE DEAD
DWELLETH IN YOU, HE . . . WILL ALSO . . . BRING TO LIFE
YOUR MORTAL BODIES." (Lloyd's Trans.)   Rom. 8:11

"SOWN IN WEAKNESS; RAISED
IN POWER; SOWN A NATURAL
BODY; RAISED A SPIRITUAL
BODY."   I Cor. 15:43

"MY EAGER EXPECTATION AND HOPE, THAT . . . CHRIST WILL BE GLORIFIED IN ME
EITHER BY MY LIFE, OR BY MY DEATH."   Phil. 1:20
Rev. Edward Last and Mr. W. G. Clarke waiting to enlist members in the Pocket Testament League as
soon as the graveside service closes. Many souls were won to Christ on this and succeeding days.

**AT
LODGE HILL
CEMETERY,
BIRMINGHAM,
ENGLAND**

bier, at the sides of which walked the bearers, Rev. W. Talbot Hindley ; J. Kennedy Maclean ; two nephews, Paul S. Cadbury, and William Cadbury Butler ; Leonard C. Voke, and F. S. Turney. Close behind followed Alexander's wife, and her sister from Holland, many members of the Cadbury family, and other relatives. Next, representing the Pocket Testament League, came Miss E. W. MacGill, Dr. J. Louis Fenn, and others. After these came various friends, including a deputation from the Friends' Institute at Moseley Road, where Charles Alexander had frequently attended the Friends' Sunday Morning Meeting, at which, a few days earlier, he had given an earnest message. Many members of the Young People's Service at the Midland Institute attended to help with the singing, led by Rev. Walter Young, of London. The American Consul, Mr. Wilbur T. Gracey, was also present, officially representing the American Government and the people of the United States, many thousands of whom knew and loved their fellow-countryman so well. The simple service at the graveside was conducted by Dr. Fenn, and began with the singing of a hymn much loved by Charles Alexander, " The Sands of Time are Sinking." Mr. Arnold E. Butler (brother-in-law) then read the Scriptures selected by Mrs. Alexander, as follows ; John xi. 21–26 ;. 1 Corinthians xv. 51–58 ; 1 Thessalonians iv. 13–20 ; Revelation xxii. 17, 20, 21. After prayer, led by Mr. Richard Cadbury (brother), the hymn, " Jesus, Lover of my soul," was sung, and then Mr. George Cadbury (uncle) spoke with tender earnestness, and Beatrice Boeke led in prayer. Dr. Fenn gave the closing message, emphasizing the threefold passion of Charles Alexander's life—for Christ, for the Word of God, and for souls, ending with a direct appeal for decision for Christ, and for consecration to His service. The closing hymn was sung—

> What can wash away my stain ?
> Nothing but the blood of Jesus !

In the hush that followed, Mrs. Alexander was impelled to lift her voice in a short prayer, committing the precious body into the safe keeping of Him Whom she knew and trusted, " until that day," and thanking Him for the sixteen years of heaven upon earth which had already been given to her with her beloved husband. As she prayed, both she and those about her were conscious of the upholding power of God's mighty arm, in answer to the prayers of thousands of His children in many parts of the world. As the crowd slowly dispersed, the glad strains of the " Glory Song " drew the thoughts of all upwards to a realization of the eternal glory that had begun for Charles Alexander, who now, by God's grace, was permitted to look with adoration into the face of Jesus, and hear His words of welcome : " Well done ! good and faithful servant, enter thou into the joy of thy Lord."

Meanwhile, Rev. Edward Last, and Mr. W. G. Clarke, of Southampton, had been busy, speaking to the coachmen and taxi-drivers, giving a Testament to each one who would join the Pocket Testament League. One man pulled a Testament from his pocket, saying, " Mr. Alexander signed me up himself, sir ! " When the service was over, Mr. Last, Mr. Clarke, Mr. J. Barnett Gow and others, standing by a little table loaded with Testaments, or mixing with the dispersing crowd, sought to win members for the League. A number signed the League pledge, and received the gift of a Testament, and, best of all, five of those spoken to accepted Christ as their Saviour. This was followed up in the next few days, through the kindness of earnest soul-winners, by personal work amongst those who had made the casket, dug the grave, or in any way participated in the funeral arrangements. As a result, seventeen of these, and scores of others, were led to accept Christ and to join the Pocket Testament League.

A letter from Mrs. Alexander's eldest sister, Mrs. Clarke, expressed what many experienced in those days : " It has been a great heart-stirring time. . . . This passing can only be called a triumph over death. It has lifted many into the sunshine of heaven."

Three days after the funeral, Mrs. Alexander and her sister went out to Lodge Hill, to lay some roses on the grave, at the cabled request of the dear mother and family in America. They called at the lodge to thank the head-gardener, who had once been head-gardener in Mrs. Alexander's girlhood home, for his kind thoughtfulness in all the arrangements. Straight-living, honest-hearted Scotsman as he was, Mrs. Alexander was surprised to find that he had never definitely accepted or confessed Christ as his Saviour, but in the little room of the lodge, she and her sister had the joy of hearing, first the head-gardener, and then his wife, who joined them, say that they would take Christ. After a few words of prayer, both signed the Pocket Testament League pledge, and accepted a little Testament for carrying.

On the evening of Wednesday, October 27th, a " praise and testimony service in thanksgiving for Charles M. Alexander " was held in the Central Hall. It was appropriate that such a gathering should take place in Birmingham, where, nearly eighteen years earlier, one of the most memorable of the Torrey-Alexander missions had been held, and where Charles Alexander had found his wife and had made his home. The chair was taken by Rev. T. E. Titmuss, only surviving secretary of the Bingley Hall Mission, and upon the platform, surrounding Mrs. Alexander with their love as well as their presence, were many members of the Cadbury family and their friends. The chief messages of the evening were given by Dr. J. Stuart Holden, and Rev. W. Talbot Hindley, while the choir was led by Mr. Brown-More, in whose Saturday night Song Services Alexander had become deeply interested. Only one of Alexander's own soloists was within reach, Mr. William Andrew, who came from Glasgow to sing two great messages. Two young women, who had spent the evening of September 26th at " Tennessee," also sang songs in which Alexander himself had trained them. One of these, " The land where the roses never fade," had been specially requested by cable from Alexander's mother in America. His own pianist, Leonard C. Voke, played, and also sang his new song, " Redeemed by the precious blood of Jesus." The meeting, which numbered about twelve hundred, was filled with victory and praise. Six decisions for Christ were recorded, and many Christians dedicated themselves afresh to greater zeal in the service of Christ.

CHAPTER TWENTY-EIGHT

The Beloved Singer still Leads On

WITHIN a few hours of Charles Alexander's entrance into the Glory Land, the news of his departure was being flashed around the world. Two or three days later, friends who loved him were penning lines of tender sympathy to his wife from such far distances as Australia, New Zealand, China, South Africa, and South America, as well as from countries nearer at hand. To many who had seen him recently, full of apparent strength and energy, the tidings brought such a shock of surprise as to be scarcely credible. Dr. Lynn Harold Hough, then President of the North-Western University, near Chicago, who had been a guest at "Tennessee" in the autumn of 1919, wrote to Mrs. Alexander: " I was deeply surprised to hear of the passing of Mr. Alexander. He seemed to be so full of vitality and strength, that somehow I never associated the thought of death with him. I know of no one, however, who gave me a more genuine impression of being heartily at home in both worlds, and I know how full of eager interest he would be in all the great discoveries of the new experience. There was so much for him to do here, and his capacity for friendship and companionship was so great, that his friends are deeply grieved ; and yet I know there are many people to whom heaven will be a more home-like place because he is there." Thousands upon thousands of those who had heard and seen him, especially the many who had come into personal contact with him, suffered the acute pain of bereavement, as they tried to grasp the realization that they would not hear that merry laugh or thrilling voice, or see that radiant face again under present earthly conditions. But among the hundreds of letters that began to pour in upon Mrs. Alexander, fully two-thirds shared with her the joyful trust in God's promise of resurrection, as well as of spiritual reunion, and the assurance of its nearness in the multiplying signs which herald " the blessed hope " of Christ's appearing.

Six days after the " Home-going," Mrs. McAnlis, secretary of the Pocket Testament League in New York City, arranged a private memorial service of prayer and thanksgiving for Charles M. Alexander in the Presbyterian Building on Fifth Avenue. It was attended by about three hundred friends, presided over by Dr. John McNeill, who had met Alexander first at the Moody Bible Institute in 1893, and had loved him warmly ever since. Various friends and fellow-workers, connected with the Pocket Testament League, took part in the meeting, giving grateful testimony of the inspiration gained from the Spirit-filled life of Charles

Alexander. It was a time of re-consecration, of determination to carry forward the work, whose leader had been called away. Each one present was given a small card, with a prayer-covenant upon it, to slip into their pocket Testaments. On one side of the card, beneath a smiling picture of the well-loved face, was a copy of his signature, as he had written it, in a flash of fun, below a note to Mrs. McAnlis, thanking her for a birthday cable received on October 24th, 1919 :

Pocketestamentleaguely thine

Charles M. Alexander

II Timothy 2:15

Another service of thanksgiving was held in London on November 23rd, in the large hall of the Young Men's Christian Association, in Tottenham Court Road. Here Mr. J. J. Virgo, besides being chairman, sang " The land where the roses never fade," and gave some heart-stirring incidents of his friendship and association with Charles Alexander. Rev. Samuel Chadwick, of Cliff College, and Rev. W. Talbot Hindley, also spoke, warming the hearts of the many present who were bound together by a friendship that had helped them heavenwards. Tidings came of memorial services at the Moody Bible Institute of Chicago, at Northfield, Mass., and in numberless churches in England, America, and far-away Australia Everywhere the note was one of ringing joy for a life that had been lived in the power of Christ, a note of triumph for the faith that had been kept, and the victory won, a note of earnest purpose to " follow the gleam," and carry on the work of soul-winning, to love and use the Word of God, and to sing the praises of Jesus.

New efforts were inaugurated in many places, until it seemed as though the compelling hands that had drawn forth such volumes of praise and lifted it heavenwards, and the compelling example that had drawn so many souls to Christ and thrust them forth into soul-winning, were leading still, from a higher vantage ground. The Business Men's Council of the Pocket Testament League in Philadelphia reported a special effort made to reach the street-car men of the city, which resulted in twenty-six hundred men signing up to read a daily chapter from the Bible, and to carry a Pocket Testament. More than six hundred and fifty of these men signed upon their cards, " I accept Christ." Another marvellous result was accomplished in Philadelphia through a visit of one hundred picked Christian workers to one of the great prisons, where they spent an afternoon gaining members for the League and winning souls. Further developments are in progress for establishing Business Men's Councils of the Pocket Testament League in other American cities, to carry on the work in industrial plants and other institutions. The New York Committee also laid immediate plans for the expansion of the work in the churches and religious organizations, and the Pocket Testament League for the United States was incorporated, with Dr. R. A. Torrey as president, and Mrs. J. Wilbur Chapman and Mrs. Charles M. Alexander as vice-presidents.

On January 3rd and 4th, 1921, a great Memorial Service and Bible Revival

Conference was held in the Marble Collegiate Church in New York City. Dr. Torrey crossed the continent from Los Angeles to give addresses. Dr. Burrell, of New York, and Dr. Massee, of Brooklyn, also gave addresses at the evening services, and the conference gatherings were addressed by Mr. George T. B. Davis, Dr. Elliott, Miss Grace Saxe, Rev. W. W. Rock, and others. Three of Alexander's former associates were in charge of the music, Mr. Hemminger as leader, Mr. Brown as soloist, and Mr. Barraclough at the piano.

From the many hundreds of wonderful letters filled with grateful affection that came to Mrs. Alexander, only a few sentences can be chosen for recording here —and these are given with the desire, not of eulogy, but of testimony, and of inspiration to more radiant Christian living and more zeal in soul-winning.

In Charles Alexander's life it was abundantly true that no number of new friends ever caused a slackening in the old ties of affection, as some of the letters shew. *Rev. John G. Newman, D.D.,* the minister of the Chambers-Wylie Presbyterian Church in Philadelphia, once a member of the Alexander Brass Band at Maryville, wrote : " Charlie and I were very dear friends in our schooldays. This friendship remained true, strong, and tender to the end. He used often to say to me, as we walked arm-in-arm on the old campus at Maryville College, ' John, no two boys ever came to this college who loved each other as we do.' I have loved Charlie Alexander better than any man I ever loved outside of my own family, and I want you to know that he has been a source of great blessing in my life." *Rev. W. W. Dawson, D.D.,* of Knoxville, Tennessee, wrote to Charles Alexander's mother : " Charles seemed to grow on in favour with God and men, and now I am sure he is just as much at home with God and the angels as he was with all good people here on earth. It adds a sweet sorrow to us all that he is gone—sweet, in that we are sure to meet again, and part no more for ever. Sorrow is added also in that it is more difficult to get along without him." *Rev. R. A. Bartlett,* another old school-friend wrote : " My mother was Charlie's Sunday-school teacher, and my father was his pastor, at the time he united with the church. He was my dear boyhood friend and companion. We grew up together, and knew each other intimately. His gracious smile will be missed by many thousands. His consecration to the Master was complete, and he was specially used to help Christians to the secret of the victorious life." Dear *W. S. Jacoby* wrote : " I loved Charlie from the first day I met him in the Moody Bible Institute in Chicago in 1894. I was rather backward among the students, being forty-four years old, but Charlie took hold of me and put me forward. We all loved him. He was the life, head and leader of us all. Every time Mrs. ' Coby ' and I have seen him since, it put new life and strength into us. Charlie was always trying to help some poor fellow, and thousands all over the world will miss him."

On both sides of the family he was tenderly loved. The news of his Homegoing reached his sister, *Mrs. James Shaw,* with great suddenness. Seated in a big Methodist Conference, a telegram was handed to her. " I walked down the aisle," she said, " and asked permission to speak. After commending the young ministers for their wonderful plans for God's work, I spoke of Charles's zeal for the same Master, and that now he was crowned. To-day was his coronation day ; our loss was his gain. I spoke in the light of eternity, sister, but when I had said enough, I was so full I could not go on. It is a queer grief that I am experiencing. There is a steady sadness, and sensation of a terrible loss settled over me, and yet at times I feel like shouting Hallelujah ! when I think of Charles in that new realm, singing through eternity."

Mrs. Neville Bradley wrote from China : " There have only been three men who came close to me, to influence my life. Dearest father, Charles, and my own dear husband. Charles was a great help to me, and both Neville and I loved him with a love and gratitude which went too deep for words, and perhaps even now he may know what a great blessing he has been through all the years to us both." *A young niece* wrote : " I have been so very glad to get to know Uncle Charles while you have been at home, and I shall always feel that I owe a great deal to him." *Another* said, " There are so many happy memories connected with him. I am glad that I really learned to know him during the happy days of the ' Niece party.' " Still *another niece* wrote : " You have both brought me to Jesus, to know Him as my Friend and Saviour, and I want always to work for Him. Perhaps Uncle Charlie will see that I am trying to thank him." *A nephew* wrote from his University : " I remember Uncle Charlie pointing out to me the text, ' They that be wise shall shine as the brightness of the firmament, and they that turn many to righteousness as the stars for ever and ever,' and I shall always associate it particularly with him."

Among the letters that came from relatives in America, on both sides of the family, was one from *Professor Rufus M. Jones*, of Haverford College. " I had a very deep and genuine affection for Charles. I regret that it was not possible to see him oftener, because I was never with him without having a happy time. He was a lovely spirit, and his life has been full of usefulness and helpful service."

Many beautiful testimonies came from those who had at various times been members of his evangelistic party. *William R. Andrew :* " I thought of him as always seeking his Master's glory. His life was an inspiration, and his constancy was ever before me, urging towards a better life and a higher standard." *Henry Barraclough :* " I can truthfully say that Mr. Alexander helped me on to ' higher ground,' and the four years of happy service under his leadership will remain a constant inspiration to greater endeavour in spiritual work." *Raymond J. Hemminger :* " His Home-call begins to make me homesick for heaven. He was the inspiration of my evangelistic work, and God be praised for him and his labours here." *Paul J. Gilbert :* " The thought of my friendship with Charles and the memories of his personality, so permeated with the radiant spirit of the Saviour, has been increasingly blessed to me. Quite twenty years slipping by have only served to hallow the contacts of time." *Robert Harkness :* " His influence on my life has been such as to change its course, and give me an abiding interest in the Kingdom of God. What he has done for me no one will ever fully know. I am deeply grateful to God for the happy years of association with him." *Wife of Charles Butler :* " Charlie and I have always felt that Mr. Alexander was Charlie's ' father ' in the work, and he most certainly has been his ideal all these years." *Edwin H. Bookmyer :* " The thing that impressed me most was that he was *always the same*. For all those who came in contact with him he had a cheery word, and a bright smile, no matter what hour it was, nor how tired he might be. I have never known him to lose his temper in all the days I worked with him. His serene faith in God was always the same. His habits of everyday life were just as thorough and fragrant and wholesome as his spiritual life, and made it an added pleasure to work with him. In every phase of his life he was clean. No man took better care of his employees, or was more generous to them." *Wife of E. W. Naftzger:* " I am writing at Ernest's desk. We looked upon Mr. Alexander and Dr. Chapman as fathers. Now both they and my own father are gone. I can see all three of them singing the ' Glory Song ' together in Australia, and rejoice when I realize their wonderful joy and gain now. I shall never forget Mr. Alexander's love to me when our little daughter was given to us in Australia, and words can never tell how we all loved him."

Miss Winifred Perks, secretary at " Tennessee " : " Those of us who belonged to the inner circle felt that he was one of the real saints here, and we all loved and reverenced him. I don't think any one who was ever in close contact with him could fail to be helped and encouraged, and his life literally shone. I always said yours were the happiest married lives I ever looked on at, and I think so still." *W. W. Rock:* " I shall always thank God for Mr. Alexander. You know something of what he has been to me, and all that he has done for me. Since the day that he brought me to his Saviour, with the exception perhaps of my own father, he has done more for me, than any other man, to show me that Saviour revealed in a human life. It was impossible for anyone to come in contact with him without being uplifted spiritually. It was a joy to know and love him. I think his greatest contribution to those of us—his friends—is this, he showed us how to live a radiant Christianity. He will always live in my memory as a winner of souls." *Norman Thomas:* " I shall never forget the many kindnesses he bestowed on me during the years I was with him, his thoughtfulness for my comfort at all times, and his very kind and generous appreciation of any small effort of mine. His sunny disposition, his smile, his cheeriness and his earnestness for his work, will long outshine his life in the flesh, and his memory will be a sermon to many. I feel that I have been privileged in living so close to him, and can bear testimony that his was a life of consecration and service equalled by few men. I sincerely thank God for being brought into such close touch with one so noble, so pure, and holy— a true disciple of his Master."

The peculiar reverence and chivalry with which Alexander treated all women, of every class, won for him their unbounded respect, and the deep, true affection of many a noble heart. *Mrs. Dunn*, a friend of the old days from Creston, Iowa, wrote : " He came into our lives at the time when we needed just such a friend as he was to us. It was his influence that made my three girls the fine Christian women they are to-day." *Miss Elinor Stafford Millar*, the well-known Bible-teacher, describes her first meeting with him in 1902, in Christchurch, New Zealand, where she was then working as a Wesleyan deaconess : " We had heard wonderful tidings of the work accomplished in Australia by Dr. Torrey and Charles M. Alexander, and of the unusual personality, charm, and power of your beloved. He came into our presence that first night with a radiant smile lighting his face, and immediately won our hearts. . . . He fired me with a new enthusiasm for singing, and ever since that time I have made that part the most attractive of my ministry. I loved him with a truly sisterly love, and always felt that in him I had a perfect friend."

Miss Sara Wray, of the Eighth Avenue Mission, New York City : " Just two years ago (October, 1918) you were with us at our nineteenth anniversary. It was a red-letter day to us, and we shall always think of him as we saw him that night, full of life and enthusiasm and song, so tender, and yet so strong. I wish you could have heard the dear ones in the Mission to-night, praising God one after the other, for the wonderful life and ministry of your dear husband." *Miss Phyllis Kurtz*, who nursed Mrs. Alexander in Australia, and is now a missionary in China : " Mr. Alexander's life has always been a great blessing to me, and I have often thought of things he has said. His sweet, childlike faith was beautiful." *Miss Jane Darling*, of Edinburgh : " Charles Alexander was a radiant spirit, and brought with him an atmosphere which enriched and revived all who came in contact with him." *Miss Helen J. Carlton*, of Elizabeth, New Jersey : " He was the most radiant Christian man I ever knew, and no one knows what he did for me and my experience." *Miss Emily Strong*, a former superintendent of the Women's Department at the Moody Bible Institute : " I am sure the radiant presence which has left you, will be leading some heavenly choir some day. I thank God for his abundant ministry to the world." *Mrs. Laura Barter Snow*, writer of many helpful booklets and poems : The memory of such a man as your dear husband will never die ; he has left us a legacy of song ' till He come.' Thank God we ever knew him."

Hundreds of those attending the Northfield General Conference will always remember the wonderful hours of song under Charles Alexander's leadership. *Mr. W. R. Moody* said of him : " He was perhaps the greatest leader in the sphere of Gospel singing that America has ever known, but, pre-eminent as he was in musical gifts, it is not for this that he will be chiefly remembered in the hearts of multitudes who will ever cherish his name in deepest affection. It was rather for his love of men. He had a genius for friendship, a warm generosity, a buoyancy of spirit, and a genial attitude of friendliness that quickly broke all barriers of reserve. He had a keen sense of humour, and exceptional ability as a raconteur. These same gifts found expression in his public service, and often won the heart of an audience to himself, after which he could lead them, as no one else, in songs of praise and worship.

" He had also a rare gift in being able to discover men who were not even known to themselves, and placing them in positions where they could render effective Christian service. There are scores of such men to-day, who owe the privilege of extended service to his discovery of their gifts, and his encouragement and help in their effective use. Throughout his life, the one purpose and aim, of which men soon became conscious, was his zeal in personal evangelism. He loved men, because he loved Christ, and it was this great capacity for love that was the secret of his winsomeness and personal charm."

Mrs. Ethel M. Thomas wrote : " I shall never forget those Northfield days when you were first married. I was only a girl then, but I always felt that I wanted to be a finer Christian when in the presence of Mr. Alexander." *Miss Emily B. Shaw :*

2 Paul J. Gilbert
1905

3 Charles Butler
1905-06

4 Ernest W. Naftzger
1907-13

5 Albert Brown
1913-19

6 William R. Andrew
1913-14

Raymond Hemminger
1904 and 1909

8 Leonard C. Voke
1917-20

9 Robert Harkness
1902-13

10 Henry Barraclough
1914-17

7 Theodore B. Atkinson
1919-20

11 F. S. Turney
1903-20

AT "TENNESSEE," SEPTEMBER, 1919

12 Rupert Lowe
1902-06

13 Benjamin A. Mills
1915-18

14 Edwin H. Bookmyer
1906-20

Miss Jenny v.d. Mersch
1913-20

15 William W. Rock
1909-15

16 George T. B. Davis
1904-20

17 Norman A. Thomas
1909-19

22 Mrs. B. D. McAnlis
1916-20

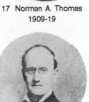

19 Allan Sutherland
1908-20

20 Miss E. W. MacGill
1914-20

21 Dr. J. Louis Fenn
1914-20

A GROUP OF CO-WORKERS

Soloists: 1, 2, 3, 4, 5, 6, 7
Pianists: 8, 9, 10

Secretaries: 11, 12, 14, 15
Photographers: 13, 17

Pocket Testament League
Associates: 16, 18, 19, 20, 21, 22

GROUP OF GUESTS PHOTOGRAPHICALLY GATHERED IN THE HALL AT "TENNESSEE" BY
NORMAN A. THOMAS AS A WELCOME HOME TO MR. AND MRS. ALEXANDER AFTER THE WAR

" I shall never forget my first summer at Northfield, and Mr. Alexander's splendid services, how much they meant to me, and what a change they made in my life." *Rev. A. T. Robertson*, D.D., of Louisville, Kentucky, whose young daughter—now in heaven—was in Alexander's choir at Northfield, wrote : " How much I loved him, and how much he helped me at Northfield ! I thank God for every memory of him. Charlotte literally adored him, and I can see her now, as she stood in the choir, and revelled in the song under your husband's magnetic leadership."

Rev. Joseph East Harrison, D.D., Professor of Bible at Mount Hermon, wrote : " I came under the charm of his fascinating personality when first I saw him in Australia sixteen years ago, and as time went on I learned to love him deeply. He was so full of the glory of the Lord, that as he led them in song men's hearts opened to the Saviour, sorrows were transformed, Heaven seemed near, and the Lord alone was exalted. I count it one of the great privileges of my life to have been permitted to call him friend. He was so entirely unspoiled by the praise which was freely lavished upon him, so ready to do a personal kindness, so absolutely the same to rich and poor, and so completely devoted to the winning of men to Christ, that it is hard to attempt to estimate his place in the Christian church without seeming to exaggerate. I thank God for his unflinching fidelity to the old Gospel, and for the beautiful consistency of his life."

Those who saw Alexander in his home-life always felt the glow of that wonderful love which had come to him and his wife as a gift direct from Heaven. *Mrs. A. P. Fitt*, D. L. Moody's only daughter, wrote, referring to the happy days at Northfield in the summer of 1918 : " What I saw at Revell Hall has never left me, and I can hardly think of any to-day whose lives seem so entirely *one* in every way. My nieces have often said, ' Their love for each other was wonderful ! ' It preached in those days a bigger sermon than either of you dreamed." *Mrs. Charles L. Carhart*, of Larchmont, New York, wrote : " I have seldom seen two people so bound together. I love to dwell on each visit made in your home. We shall cherish every remembrance of Mr. Alexander, and feel it a great privilege to have known him so intimately." The love which bound Dr. and Mrs. J. Wilbur Chapman to Alexander and his wife was deep and sacred. *Mrs. Chapman* wrote : " How could we possibly live without our faith during this time, while our blessed husbands are ahead of us in the Glory Land, and are waiting for us to come Home ? Now that Mr. Alexander and Wilbur are together again up there, does it not seem to make our love more beautiful ? My heart is too full of blessed memories to feel that God is putting upon us too heavy a burden, and every day I pray for patience and strength to do the work which falls to me."

Friends of every kind, whether the friendship was of long or of short duration, shared both the sense of present loss, and the urge of a desire to serve God more faithfully because of Charles Alexander. " I do not think I ever loved a man more," wrote *Mr. Charles H. Denison*, of Saginaw, Michigan. " What a wonderful friend ! He demanded nothing, but gave all that he had to his friends, or to any one who needed him. Just to look into his wonderful face gave one a thrill. I know of no one who had such a wonderful smile." *Mr. T. Shaw Fitchett*, of Melbourne wrote : " Your cabled words, ' my beloved Charles,' kept repeating themselves all day in my brain and heart, and I found myself saying, ' *our* beloved Charles ' again and again.   I do not think anyone in Australia loved you both so much as did my youngsters, wife and I.   To have for a friend a man in ten thousand, was something precious indeed.   This makes me realize what quiet and lasting joy must have been yours, during the happy years together.   He is only gone ahead a little way.   That is my comfort, and I know it is yours.   We'll meet, and laugh, and love again some day, as surely as the sun lifts in the east at dawn ; and what a day-break it will be in another world !   Yes, he was, and still is, ' our beloved Charles.' "   *Admiral Sir George King-Hall :* " I can never forget his singing the Gospel message, bringing multitudes to our Saviour in the Town Hall at Sydney, nor our never-to-be-forgotten re-union at Hobart, Tasmania."   *Mr. David Williamson :* " My heart has been reviewing with constant joy and thankfulness the beautiful and complete life-witness of Mr. Alexander.   Memories have been filling me with reverent joy at the thought of how much he did to bring Christ close to every one."   *Mr. Harry J. M. Thompson :* " The uplifting and invigorating influence of the days, when you and he were here in Melbourne among us, still lingers in my mind, and I have been re-inspired and made better for the Master's work by the memory of those happy days."   *R. Lawson Coad, Esq. :* " The life of Mr. Alexander was so devoted to winning souls for our Lord and Saviour, that his loss will leave a gap in the ranks of God's workers, and is a call to all of us who remain, to re-double our efforts for winning men and women to Christ."   *Mr. J. Lewis Twaddell*, treasurer of the Business Men's Council of the Pocket Testament League in Philadelphia : " Mr. Alexander radiated an influence which made every one better who felt it.   I thank the Lord that I was permitted to know him.   The great work which he started must go on."

Ministers, missionaries, and rescue mission workers in all parts of the world were helped and strengthened by Charles Alexander.   *Rev. Norman MacKenzie* wrote from Pakhoi, South China : " I value the cheer and inspiration he brought into my own life.   His works will indeed follow him.   The influence of his magnetic and kindly personality will remain in the hearts of thousands."   *Professor Charles R. Erdman*, of Princeton : " Charles Alexander was ever regarded by me as the dearest and closest of friends.   It was always a joy and inspiration to be with him, and I know of the brightness he has brought into countless lives."   *Melvin E. Trotter*, of Grand Rapids, Mich. : " The Spirit of God permeates everything connected with the life and death of dear Charlie.   I shall never forget the last day I was with him, when we planned, as we thought, so definitely, for me to visit England, and how strangely I was prevented from going.   We know why now ; the dear Lord knew before we did.   Almost every paper one picks up these days in America has something to say about Charlie, and I believe with all my heart God will let him do more in his death than in his life.   I was out this noon, and spoke at a shop meeting on the Pocket Testament League.   The whole city (Philadelphia) seems to be on tiptoe, not only to get people to carry their Bibles, but to turn souls to Jesus.   It seemed to take Charlie's death to start things going in earnest."   *Rev. Francis W. Pattison*, East Northfield, Mass. : " Opportunity was given, at our memorial service for Mr. Alexander, to speak of help received through his ministry of music. You would have been gratified and comforted by the many expressions of help which he has brought to the lives of these people. To me he was the apostle of sunshine." *Rev. M. S. Rice, D.D.*, of Detroit : " Not one here but came at once to love him, and to greatly delight at his fine, unquestioning faith in God and His Word. I wish you could have heard the testimonies of our people. We sang the songs he taught us, and as we sang ' Take it wherever you go ! ' we held up our Testaments, and renewed our pledge to the splendid work. It will never lose its influence here." *Dr. J. Ross Stevenson*, President of Princeton Theological Seminary : " At a meeting of the Synod of Ohio, where the startling news reached us, we dedicated ourselves anew, in earnest prayer, to the winning of souls. Our experience must have been shared by hundreds of others who thanked our heavenly Father for the inspiration which Charlie Alexander had brought into their lives, and who pledged themselves again to render more faithful service to the Master Whom he loved and served."

Rev. Prebendary H. W. Webb-Peploe: " His has been a short life, but few can have had more abundant influence of the highest order, or a more attractive talent of appealing to the multitude." *Rev. James Mursell:* " As minister of the City Tabernacle, Brisbane, I was privileged to enjoy much delightful fellowship with him, and learned to love him well. The miss of his radiant manhood will be hard to bear. I thank God for every remembrance of him ! " *Rev. Barclay F. Buxton*, for many years a missionary in Japan : " I have lost a dear friend, one whom I always looked up to with admiration, and endeavoured to follow. What a welcome he must have got in glory from many whom he led to Christ ! His life and geniality have inspired many in soul-winning work." *Dr. Richard Orme Flinn* of Atlanta, Georgia : " No one, amongst the many I have known, was so steadfastly radiant, and so consistent in manifesting the joy of his Lord. This was his strength. The fountain within him, in its overflow, was ever refreshing and reviving all about him." *Dr. William Carter*, of Brooklyn : " My acquaintance with Charles Alexander extended over twenty years or more of his Christian service, with an intimacy for which I have always thanked God. I always looked upon him as a young and vigorous man, carrying his youthful energy into middle life. I never saw him, under any circumstances, do anything, or heard him say anything, that was not for the welfare of men and the glory of God. He certainly adorned the doctrine and the Gospel of our Lord and Saviour Jesus Christ. He was God's man in very deed and truth." *Dr. W. H. Fitchett*, of Melbourne : " To the piety of a saint, the spiritual zeal and power of an evangelist, Charles Alexander added the soul of a musician, the loving simplicity of a child, and the practical shrewdness of an American brain. That is a very unusual combination, and it constituted a very remarkable character. Mr. Alexander's musical gifts were of a high order, and he discovered a new place and use for music in the service of religion, a place and use which it is safe to prophesy will never be forgotten or lost." *Dr. J. Stuart Holden:* " Charles Alexander simply radiated the brightness of a heart completely satisfied with Christ. The claims of the Redeemer never lost their power to charm him from engagement in every lower ideal than that of winning others to His allegiance. The outstanding virtue of his life and his example, was his ever-ready keenness to witness to the love of his Lord. He was altogether free from the gauche sort of aggressiveness which puts people off. His perfect naturalness, and transparent sincerity, disarmed opposition and criticism. Hence his success with the unlikeliest of men. A more consistently devoted man it has not been my lot to meet. All who ever came into contact with him will for ever bless the day which brought them the inspiration of his uplifting friendship." *Rev. J. H. Jowett, D.D.:* " Charles Alexander would pass into the presence of the King with all the buoyancy of a child going home. He was a brilliant spirit, and he has served the Lord with great gladness. One can only dimly realize what his emancipated spirit is doing in other fields of service in the immediate fellowship of the Lord. I am sure he will be a minister of song and inspiration, and that it will be part of his happy service to cheer the pilgrims who are still travelling along the ways of time." *Dr. I. M. Haldeman :* " I can never forget the scene when I spoke at the Fundamental Conference in Philadelphia, May 30, 1918. At the close of the sermon—the people standing—my brother, Charles Alexander, led that great multitude in such a burst of hallelujah song, with such mastery, such commanding leadership, that it seemed like one voice. . . . He was in the front rank, giving the trumpet-call of advance all along the line. But there was a place for him amid the singers on high ; he only could fill it, and the Lord said : " Come and sing." He, too, with many of us, waited for the Lord, and his voice will be among the first whose triumphant notes fall on our ears in the cloudless morning when Jesus comes."

> Friend of mine was always singing,
>   Helping folks their woes forget ;
> Sending praises upward ringing—
>   Singing yet !
>
> Singing to make burdens lighter,
>   Singing when some folks would fret ;
> Singing till the world grew brighter—
>   Singing yet !
>
> Singing songs of God and glory,
>   Singing joy to all he met;
> Singing Christ's own wondrous story—
>   Singing yet !
>
> As a skylark upward winging
>   Leaving many in his debt,
> So he left us, smiling, singing—
>   Singing yet !
>
> So, wherever I may wander,
>   Never shall I quite forget
> CHARLES McCALLON ALEXANDER,
>   Singing yet !
>
>   *W. W. Rock.*

" He that winneth souls is wise " (Prov. xi. 30).
    " They that be wise shall shine as the brightness of the firmament, and they that turn many to righteousness, as the stars for ever and ever " (Dan. xii. 3).